About Island Press

Island Press is the only nonprofit organization in the United States whose principal purpose is the publication of books on environmental issues and natural resource management. We provide solutions-oriented information to professionals, public officials, business and community leaders, and concerned citizens who are shaping responses to environmental problems.

In 2000, Island Press celebrates its sixteenth anniversary as the leading provider of timely and practical books that take a multidisciplinary approach to critical environmental concerns. Our growing list of titles reflects our commitment to bringing the best of an expanding body of literature to the environmental community throughout North America and the world.

Support for Island Press is provided by The Jenifer Altman Foundation, The Bullitt Foundation, The Mary Flagler Cary Charitable Trust, The Nathan Cummings Foundation, The Geraldine R. Dodge Foundation, The Charles Engelhard Foundation, The Ford Foundation, The Vira I. Heinz Endowment, The W. Alton Jones Foundation, The John D. and Catherine T. MacArthur Foundation, The Andrew W. Mellon Foundation, The Charles Stewart Mott Foundation, The Curtis and Edith Munson Foundation, The National Fish and Wildlife Foundation, The National Science Foundation, The New-Land Foundation, The David and Lucile Packard Foundation, The Pew Charitable Trusts, The Surdna Foundation, The Winslow Foundation, and individual donors.

Community Planning

To our respective parents, who taught us to care about communities and to make a difference in them.

Community Planning

An Introduction to the Comprehensive Plan

Eric Damian Kelly
and Barbara Becker

ISLAND PRESS
Washington, D.C. • Covelo, California

Library of Congress Cataloging-in-Publication Data
Kelly, Eric D.
   Community planning : an introduction to the comprehensive plan /
by Eric Damian Kelly and Barbara Becker.
      p.   cm.
   Includes bibliographical references and index.
   ISBN 1–55963–540–1 (pbk. : acid-free paper)
   1. City planning—United States. 2. Regional planning—United
States. 3. Land use—United States—Planning. 4. City planners—
United States. I. Becker, Barbara, 1945–   . II. Title.
HT167.K38   2000
307.1'216'0973—dc21   99–16663
                                                            CIP

Printed on recycled, acid-free paper

Manufactured in the United States of America
10 9 8

Contents

Foreword

I believe that the concept of the comprehensive plan has been central to the definition of the planning process and the planning profession and their respective development in the twentieth century. The early "planners," who were engineers, architects, landscape architects, and lawyers, created a vision of the need to plan the long-range development of cities as a public function. This concept went well beyond the definition of professional practice and the types of projects that each profession dealt with on a daily basis at the time. The planning practitioners invented the notion of comprehensiveness—emphasizing the relationships among the functional elements of the plan, the relationship of the present and the future over time, and the relationship among different geographic parts of the metropolitan area—perhaps best epitomized by the city plans prepared by Daniel Burnham for Chicago, San Francisco, and other major cities. Had they been like physicists in their propensity of labeling concepts, these early planning practitioners might have called the comprehensive plan a sort of "grand unifying theory."

Not only is the comprehensive plan a technical achievement and tool, it also was and is a tool of local democracy. The early planning efforts involved only elected officials and the civic elites. The modern plans involve citizens and neighborhoods in grassroots visioning and involvement. In the typical American community today, citizens are more likely to participate in the process of planning and of administrating related land-use controls than in any other function of local government. And legal statutory and case law developments requiring that current land-use decisions be in accordance with a comprehensive plan ensures a process in which citizens are assured of government decisions that are rational and democratic.

Over the decades there have been thousands of conference speeches and magazine and journal articles about comprehensive plans, but there have been only a few books—exactly three before this one.

In 1938 the Russell Sage Foundation published *The Master Plan* by Edward M. Bassett. Bassett was elected to Congress for one term in 1902, worked on the 1916 New York City zoning ordinance, and participated in the preparation of the model zoning and city planning enabling acts published by the Department of Commerce in 1926 and 1928. He also was the author of *Zoning*. In

The Master Plan he emphasized his conception of the seven elements of the plan: streets, parks, sites for public buildings, future land reservations, zoning districts, public utility routes, and pierhead and bulkhead lines.

T. J. Kent, Jr., wrote *The Urban General Plan* in 1964. Like Bassett, Kent presented his conception of the elements of the plan, emphasized the general nature of the plan, and especially argued that the local legislative body was the principal client of the plan. In 1990 the American Planning Association republished his book as a planning classic.

Guidelines for Preparing Urban Plans was written by Larz T. Anderson, who was both a planning practitioner and a planning teacher. This work, published by the American Planning Association in 1995, is a detailed guide for practitioners undertaking the preparation of a comprehensive plan.

Now come professors Eric Damian Kelly and Barbara Becker. Their worthy goal is to assure that students coming to the planning field have an articulate, well-reasoned, detailed exposition of the idea of the comprehensive plan. Of all the works cited above, theirs is the most comprehensive in showing how the plan ought to be prepared, with well-grounded emphasis on such topics as feasibility; the role of professionals, citizens, and elected officials; the relationship to land-use controls, housing, and economic development; and many other topics.

This book joins a small group of influential books of importance to the planning field and profession. This body of literature is a distinguished one, and this work is up there with the best. Clearly, it will be influencing the next generation of planners, who will be preparing comprehensive plans well into the next century.

Frank S. So, AICP
Executive Director
American Planning Association

Acknowledgments

One of our goals in creating this book was to provide practical examples and excerpts from plans and studies in contemporary communities. When we attended planning school (in the 1970s), we learned a lot of theory and were exposed to idealized approaches to practical issues. The reason that we have been able to provide so many specific examples from different communities is that we have had much help from some longtime friends and colleagues, as well as from some new ones. We would like especially to thank (in alphabetical order, by organization):

- with the City of Ames, Iowa—Brian O'Connell, AICP
- with the Burnham Group—C. Greg Dale, AICP; Connie Cooper, AICP; and Christie McGetrick, AICP
- with HNTB Corp.—David Wenzel, AICP
- with Duncan Associates—James B. Duncan, FAICP, Kirk Bishop; Lee Einsweiler, AICP; and Clancy Mullen, AICP
- with the City of Lawrence, Kansas—Linda Finger, AICP, and her staff
- with Muncie and Delaware County, Indiana—Marta Moody
- with the City of Norman Oklahoma—Richard Massie, AICP
- with Orange County, Florida—Bruce McClendon, AICP
- the entire planning group at Pflum, Klausmeier & Gehrum
- with the City of Pittsburgh—Eloise Hirsch, AIA, and her staff
- with the City of Pueblo—Jim Munch, AICP
- with the Pueblo Area Council of Governments—Kim Headley, AICP
- with RM Plan Group, Alfred N. Raby, AICP
- with the City of Stillwater, Oklahoma—John Wesley, AICP, and Brian Brown, AICP
- at the University of Arizona—former students Jennifer Greig and Jeff Walsh
- with the City of Wichita and Sedgwick County, Kansas—Marvin Kraut, AIA, and Dale Miller, AICP

Riad Mahayni, AICP, of Iowa State University, worked with us on the initial stages of this project and provided invaluable input to its structure and content. We missed his participation in its completion but respect his admission that he was overloaded, an admission we both tend to be reluctant to make.

Others to whom we owe particular thanks are our always helpful colleagues at the American Planning Association, including Sylvia Lewis; Frank So, FAICP; Ken East; and Jim Hecimovich. Andrew Jazewski, heir to Richard Hedman, allowed us to use the wonderful Hedman cartoons in exchange for copies of the book. Individuals who provided photographs are credited in the captions. All other photographs are by Eric Damian Kelly, FAICP.

....

Substance and Structure of the Book

This book introduces community planning as practiced in the United States, focusing on the comprehensive plan. The primary purpose of the book is to serve as a teaching text for introductory classes in planning. For undergraduate courses, the reading in the book, combined with the exercises and discussion questions, will provide a good introduction to the field. Through the use of the "further reading" suggestions, this book can become a combination primary text and syllabus for a graduate course.

Focus on Comprehensive Planning

We have chosen the comprehensive plan to introduce community planning in the United States. Sometimes known by other names, including master plan, general plan, and even local government plan, the type of plan described in this book is the predominant form of general governmental planning in the United States.

Although many government agencies make plans for their own programs or facilities, the comprehensive plan is, for most places in the United States, the only planning document that considers multiple programs and that accounts for activities on all land located within the planning area, whether that property is public or private.

One reason that comprehensive planning is so important is that it is carried out by local governments—the level of government that most directly interacts with most citizens most frequently. It is the local government—city, town, village, county, or parish—that builds and maintains roads and sidewalks, that regulates zoning and land use, that typically provides park and recreation services, that provides a police force and fire protection, and that delivers fresh

1

water and takes care of sewage. Although there are special forms of local governments and even some private utility companies that provide these services in some areas, the primary responsibility for the services and control over the providers still resides with the city, county, or other local government of general jurisdiction. Thus, local government planning is essential to provide a context in which local officials can make important decisions about these services and facilities.

Most land in this country, and in developing areas in particular, is privately owned. Although we have a strong tradition of private property rights in this country, we also have long recognized that there must be limits to the use of individual pieces of property—locating a foundry, a race track, or a slaughterhouse in a residential area, for example, would damage the quality of life of those living there. Since the 1920s, the policy of most states for most land in this country has been to delegate to individual local governments decisions about the regulation of activities on private land, largely through techniques called zoning and subdivision regulation.[1] Thus, local planning is also important to provide a context for decisions of the local government about regulating activities on private land.

These practical considerations are reinforced by state laws that encourage or require local governments to develop comprehensive plans or something similar. Although some of those laws allow local governments a choice of whether to plan or not, an increasing number of state laws require the adoption of some form of plan; laws in other states require a comprehensive plan only if the local government wants to exercise specific powers, like regulating activity on private land, charging fees to developers, or even qualifying for specific state grant funds. Even those states that do not require planning typically have laws describing the kinds of planning that local governments ought to do if they plan, and those laws, also, describe a kind of planning that is like the comprehensive planning described in this book.

Three important factors make a plan comprehensive:

- inclusion of all of the land area subject to the planning or regulatory jurisdiction of the local government preparing the plan;
- inclusion of all subject matter related to the physical development of the community; and
- a relatively long time horizon.

These factors are discussed in chapter 2.

Legal and Historical Significance

The comprehensive plan has its roots in the planning and governmental reform efforts of the 1910s and 1920s, although much of contemporary practice has evolved since the middle of the twentieth century. It is the tool that well-managed communities use to determine their needs and set the goals and objectives that direct their future development.

The Advisory Committee on Planning and Zoning of the U.S. Department of Commerce institutionalized that type of comprehensive planning in the Standard Zoning Enabling Act (1926) and the Standard City Planning Enabling Act (1928). As described in chapter 2, the zoning act required that zoning be "in accordance with a comprehensive plan," and the planning act provided the first formal definition of the type of planning discussed here.

Two subsequent federal programs provided significant funding for local planning. Both the "701" planning program, funded through the Department of Housing and Urban Development, and the "208" area-wide wastewater treatment management program, funded through the Environmental Protection Agency,[2] reinforced the commitment to the kind of comprehensive planning described here—relatively long-range planning for a defined area, with an emphasis on the physical environment.

Relationship to Other Kinds of Planning

Some planning teachers view comprehensive planning as simply one of a number of theories of planning.[3] We believe, however, that comprehensive planning is more framework than theory, providing a structure for many related types of planning. At its best, comprehensive planning incorporates many other types of planning to which the student may hear reference:

Land-Use Planning

Planning for future land uses is one of the most visible forms of community planning. We present it in chapter 6 as an essential and integral part of comprehensive planning—but not as a separate activity. Future land-use plans make sense only in the broad context provided by a comprehensive plan, which addresses related topics of roads, infrastructure, and urban boundaries.

Transportation Planning

Local transportation planning typically takes place in the context of a comprehensive plan. Transportation and circulation needs are inextricably tied to land-use patterns, and it thus makes sense to address them together. The confusing twist in transportation planning comes from the fact that many key parts of the transportation network are built by state departments of transportation, using federal money. Planning for interstate highways and other state highways and roads is often quite different, but federal law now mandates increased coordination with local land-use planning. These complex relationships are discussed in chapter 7. The details of a local transportation plan may fill a full chapter or a separate "element" of a comprehensive plan, but it is the comprehensive plan that provides a context for transportation planning.

Environmental Planning

Environmental planning takes place at many levels. Since an activist Congress began to address such issues seriously in 1970, most of the planning for air and water quality in this country has been driven by federal laws and regulations implemented under those laws by the Environmental Protection Agency. Although extremely important, those laws are beyond the scope of this book and are well addressed in other sources. Planning for environmental issues related to private land, however, remains a matter of primary local concern. Some approach this as largely an environmental issue;[5] we present it here as an integral part of land-use planning. The type of comprehensive planning described in this text starts with careful analysis of both natural and built environments and develops plans in that context.

Park and Open-Space Planning

Parks and open spaces are important land uses to be included in any good comprehensive plan. The need for parks and open spaces is in significant part a function of population and land-use patterns, which are core issues in comprehensive planning. The logical locations for parks and open space evolve easily from the kinds of analysis included in thorough comprehensive planning. Like transportation plans, detailed park and open-space plans may be contained in a specific element of the comprehensive plan—but there is little justification for planning for parks and recreation outside the context of the comprehensive plan.

Planning for Utilities and Infrastructure

Providers of electricity, telephone service, cable television, and natural gas typically follow growth patterns. The combination of a future land-use map and data about actual construction activity governs the decisions of these utility operators about their own future plans. In contrast, sewer, water, and drainage services are often provided by local governments. For reasons described in chapter 7, decisions about extensions of sewer and water service in particular may actually guide future land-use patterns. Effective planning for the efficient delivery of those services must be closely coordinated with future land-use planning and with the related subject of transportation planning; for exactly these reasons, those are logical elements of a good comprehensive planning process.

Planning for School Facilities

Many local comprehensive plans address the need for future school facilities. The history of schools in this country, however, is that most have their own governing boards, separate from other bodies within local government. Those boards typically have great autonomy on all matters, including the purchase, construction, opening, and closing of school facilities. Thus, the planning for school facilities that changes the future in most communities is that conducted

Housing is an important subject of local planning efforts.

by the school board. Some school boards work closely with the local planning commission and planning staff, resulting in coordinated planning processes. Others function quite independently, however, with the result that plans for schools may differ from or even conflict with what the comprehensive plan suggests.

Neighborhood Planning

Neighborhood planning resembles comprehensive planning in some ways, but it provides greater detail for a smaller area. Again, we believe that neighborhood planning works best in the context of a comprehensive plan. If the plan for a city or county is simply a compilation of neighborhood plans, it is likely that all of the neighborhoods will plan for single-family housing and upscale shopping facilities, while none will plan for waste disposal sites, heavy industry, lumberyards, broadcasting towers, and other items essential to modern community life. A comprehensive plan provides a context in which good neighborhood planning can occur.

Historic Preservation Planning

Where preservation planning focuses on an individual building, it is far more narrow in scope than the topics discussed in this book. Where it focuses on preservation of a downtown, a neighborhood, or a context within which one or more historic buildings exist, it is much like comprehensive planning but still with a narrow focus. Most effective preservation plans exist in the context of a comprehensive plan, with the comprehensive plan providing the land-use and other contextual items for the preservation plan.

Planning for Housing

Many communities today plan for housing to help to ensure that there will be housing opportunities for people of many different socioeconomic conditions. Housing must have a context, however. It must fit into some sort of land-use plan. Those living in housing will depend on a transportation system to provide access to work and to shopping and services. Although a good housing plan includes options for financing and other details that may go beyond a classic comprehensive plan, it is the comprehensive plan that provides the context for the provision of housing. Thus, housing is an element addressed in many comprehensive plans; detailed housing plans can then be based on the comprehensive plan.

Social Planning

Social planning is a broad term that can apply to such topics as state planning to help people move from welfare to work, local efforts to deliver specific social services, and "social equity planning," which is discussed in the next section. This book focuses largely on physical planning and thus does not address social planning in depth. It is important to understand, however, that many of the issues of concern to social planners have physical roots: quality of neighborhood services; land-use patterns in neighborhoods, particularly declining neighborhoods; access of disadvantaged people to grocery stores, libraries, and other essential services; transportation accessibility for poorer neighborhoods. Further, although the subject matter of comprehensive planning focuses heavily on the physical environment, social goals often control the plan—goals like improving the quality of life for inner-city residents, providing safe neighborhoods, encouraging development of new industry to employ local residents, and offering a range of recreational opportunities to all citizens. Although such social programs as welfare and health care programs will have operating elements that go beyond the scope of the typical comprehensive plan, good comprehensive plans address social issues and their physical ramifications.

Social Equity Planning, Advocacy Planning, and Radical Planning

Students who pursue planning studies beyond an introductory course are likely to learn about planning for social equity,[6] advocacy planning,[7] and radical planning.[8] In general, we believe that those phrases refer to political philosophies intended to change the plans and, often, many other aspects of a local community. A good comprehensive planning process is a participatory one that allows advocates and those with "radical" or other views to present them as part of the process; to the extent that the community accepts those views, they will ultimately guide the plan itself. Thus, comprehensive planning is different in its focus from advocacy planning or radical planning, but it certainly does not preclude adherents of those views from pursuing them in the context of local planning.

A good example relates to the work of Paul Davidoff,[9] whose professional career focused heavily on advocacy for increased suburban housing opportunities for people of lower income and limited choices. His primary battle was against the use of zoning to keep apartments and small homes out of the suburbs. Those are land-use issues, regularly addressed in the comprehensive planning process. Today, in part because of Davidoff's work, the state of New Jersey specifically requires that local plans include "fair share" housing elements.[10] Clearly, an effective advocate planner must influence the comprehensive planning process, and the process thus provides an important (although not exclusive) context for the activities of the advocate planner.

Some disagree with our approach to these issues, particularly as applied in specific circumstances. Norman Krumholz, when he became planning director of Cleveland in the 1970s, found a city that was shrinking, not growing— a city, in short, with no need for new land uses, new infrastructure, or the other sorts of changes normally addressed through comprehensive planning.[11] It was in that context that his approach to equity planning evolved.

The work of the social equity planners and radical planners relates closely to, and is often based on, John Rawls's *A Theory of Justice,* in which he urged, in essence, that government ought to provide the greatest services and benefits to those with the greatest need and the fewest choices.[12]

Regional Planning

A major limitation on the effectiveness of local comprehensive planning efforts is the fact that many individual communities are simply smaller parts of larger metropolitan areas or other regions. Economic, social, geographic, and other forces affecting such communities are often regional. For reasons explained in chapter 14, regional planning is weak in the United States, with some notable exceptions in Oregon, Hawaii, and a few other places. A series of individual local comprehensive plans is not a good substitute for a good regional plan, but that is what governs most regions. Changes in the approach to regional planning will come from changes to state laws and state and federal funding policies, not from simple changes in local planning practice. Chapter 14 discusses some possible and desirable policy changes to encourage more regional planning. In the meantime, most planning in the United States remains local; because this book focuses on planning as it is currently practiced in the United States, most of it addresses such local planning.

A Pragmatic Note

The primary purpose of this book is to introduce the field of community planning to people who may want to become planners. Most people who undertake that career path will spend a significant part of their respective careers helping to prepare, analyze, update, and implement comprehensive plans. There are far more jobs working with these different stages of the comprehensive planning process than there are developing radical plans, housing plans, or park plans. This book focuses on what typical planners working for local governments really do—and it emphasizes doing that well. Radical planners and others may argue that planners really ought to spend their time doing something else, but that is not our focus here.

The Role of Planners

Professional planners make planning work. Most professional planners in the United States work for local governments, because that is where most of the planning (at least the type of planning that is the subject of this book) takes place. What makes planning so interesting and challenging is that the role of planners is to help communities make their own plans. As many planners discover, and as you will learn as you work through this book, getting a whole community to agree on a plan for its future is not as simple as sitting in a quiet office and making a plan, but the excitement and satisfaction of professional planning comes from helping people collectively to define their future together.

Some planners specialize, focusing their work on transportation systems, parks, downtowns, or jobs. Many deal with all of those issues and more over the course of a year, and most will deal with a variety of planning subjects over the course of their careers. Downtown revitalization, neighborhood protection, low-income housing development, historic preservation, park building, suburban growth, highway construction, and industrial development are some of the topics that planners address in their work. This illustrates another characteristic of planning that makes the field attractive to many people—it is a field that involves a variety of work and an opportunity to learn about many different parts of a community.

Will a community have a future without planning? Of course. The future will come regardless of whether the community has a plan. Planning provides a community with the opportunity to make conscious, considered choices about what kind of future it wants to have. The resulting plan then provides a blueprint for making decisions that affect the future of the community.

Who planners are, where they work, and how they get their jobs are subjects treated in more depth in chapter 20. If you want more details on that subject, you can read that chapter now. Also, boxes at the end of most chapters in the first four parts of this book describe how planners relate to each stage of the planning and implementation process.

The Role of Individual Citizens

A comprehensive plan represents the future for a community. A community consists of a group of people who live together as part of an organized system. Most community plans are created and adopted by agencies of local government, but ultimately that government—and the plans it creates—represents and serves individual citizens.

Anyone who has ever served on a committee understands that it is sometimes difficult to get a group of people to agree even on relatively simple matters. When the issues at stake are as complicated as the future of a community, and when the affected people number in the thousands, achieving agreement or even consensus may seem like an overwhelming challenge. Achieving community consensus may be difficult, but it is also essential. Laws in every state provide for public hearings at which citizens have the opportunity to address planning issues; however, because a public hearing is a formal proceeding that usually occurs late in the planning process, most communities offer other opportunities for citizens to become involved in making plans. Those opportunities may include informal community meetings, open-ended questionnaires to help identify issues, narrowly focused surveys to determine community preferences on particular issues, workshops, charrettes, and the circulation of draft plans for comment.

Chapter 5 of this book focuses on methods of involving the larger community in the planning process, and boxes at the end of most chapters describe the opportunities for individual citizens to become involved in each stage of the planning and implementation process.

Users' Guide

Boxes

At the end of most chapters in the first four parts of the book are boxes labeled "The Role of the Professional Planner" and "The Role of the Individual Citizen." The first box summarizes the role of the professional planner in the aspect or stage of planning discussed in that chapter. The professional planner has a role to play in every stage of planning, but that role varies from data collector to information analyst to process facilitator and implementation expert, with a variety of related roles in between.

The second box contains a discussion of how citizens can participate in and influence the planning process at that stage. As you will see, some stages of the planning process are built around the participation of the individual citizen, and others are highly technical, with little opportunity for citizen participation. The ultimate role of the body politic, which represents individual citizens, is that of plan maker. As in all other parts of democracy, the individual citizen can choose how small or great a role to play in that process. In a democracy, we get the government that we deserve; if a community of citizens chooses not to plan, they will probably get—and certainly deserve—an unplanned future or a future that is planned for them by others.

Exercises and Discussion Questions

Exercises at the end of each chapter are designed to reinforce the learning in the chapter. Most of these will be most effective when assigned to small groups, creating opportunities for cooperative learning. By asking the small groups to report to the class as a whole, rather than simply to report in writing, the effective instructor can turn many of these exercises into discussion opportunities for the entire class. An individual reading this book on her or his own, however, will also find it useful to engage in at least some of these exercises.

There is at least one discussion question at the end of each chapter. The text should suggest other topics for discussion, and a number of the exercises may be adapted to use as discussion questions without the interim step of small-group work.

Further Reading and References

Materials presented in the "Further Reading" section at the end of most chapters provide more depth on some or all of the material discussed; annotations on each entry indicate the scope of the material covered there. These materials will provide good background for students interested in preparing a paper related to that chapter, for a professor preparing to lead a class in discussing unfamiliar material, or for honors or advanced students who want to (or will be required to) explore the subject in more depth than that presented in this introductory text.

In contrast, the material presented under "References" at chapter ends is generally technical material, useful for the practitioner (or group of students) trying to apply the technique but not particularly desirable as background reading material. Reference material often includes statistics, formulas, and detailed methodologies that are essential to rigorous application of the techniques but inappropriate for most class discussion in an introductory course.

On-line Resources

Because on-line resources are evolving rapidly and Web addresses are changing constantly, this book provides references to only a few key on-line resources. We will, however, maintain a chapter-by-chapter list of useful on-line resources at the Island Press Web site at www.islandpress.org. That annotated listing will provide "hot links" to reference sites, to sites providing multiple links to related sites, and to sites that provide good examples of material discussed in the chapter.

Glossary of Key Terms

We have used the following terms in very particular but consistent ways throughout the text.

Charrettes: Architects use this French term to refer to a short, intensive design exercise;

the word apparently evolved from work that French architects did on the back of small carts on the way to make presentations of their proposed plans. Planners sometimes use similar short, intensive exercises to address focused issues or small areas, and we apply the term in that way.

Citizens: We apply this term broadly to people who live or work in a community.

Community: We use this term to apply generally to the geographical planning jurisdiction, whether it is a city, county, township, or town, and the people, businesses, and institutions that are a part of it and make it a center of human activity. The typical planning jurisdiction is a city or town, but the principles and practices included in this book apply equally to counties and other local jurisdictions.

Comprehensive plan: We apply this term only to the kind of plan described in chapter 2. As we explain there, to be "comprehensive," a community plan must have at least three basic characteristics: it must be *geographically* comprehensive, including the entire jurisdiction of the local government; it must be comprehensive as to *subject matter,* addressing at least all issues affecting the physical future of the community; and it must be *long range,* typically using a planning horizon of about twenty years. We refer to other types of plans simply as plans, or by the use of some other descriptive word.

Governing body: We use this term to apply to the body that has general legislative authority in the local government—usually a city council or board of county commissioners, but, in some places, a township board, board of selectmen, board of aldermen, or board of trustees. This is the body that has the power to make and change the laws of the local government.

Local government: We use this term to apply to the formal, legally structured government of general jurisdiction (the government with zoning and other police power authority) over the planning area. In using the term, we mean the entire local governmental structure, including the mayor or other chief executive, the council or other legislative body, and all of the commissions and administrative offices that are part of it.

Planning agency: We use this term to apply to the individual or office assigned the primary responsibility for administering and/or facilitating a planning process for a community. In larger communities, that will typically be a planning department; in other situations, it may be a consultant, a planning agency with another local government, or some other local official.

Planning body: For reasons explained in chapters 1 and 2, communities sometimes use a special task force or steering committee to lead a comprehensive planning effort; we use this term to refer to the entity actually preparing the plan, whether it is the official planning commission or some other ad hoc or standing committee.

Planning commission: We use this legal term to refer to the official body within a local government identified in state law as the body with the duty and the power to prepare plans for the community and its local government. In many places, this body is called the planning and zoning commission, but it is often called simply the planning commission or planning board.

Stakeholders: We use this term to describe individuals and (usually) groups that have some real stake (economic, social, physical, or political) in the outcome of a planning process. Although all citizens of a community are stakeholders, some stakeholders may not be citizens—for example, people who work there, or who live in a nearby community and are affected by the air quality, traffic, and other impacts of planning decisions in the community.

FURTHER READING

Alexander, Ernest R. 1986. *Approaches to Planning: Introducing Current Planning Theories, Concepts and Issues.* New York: Gordon and Breach Science Publishers. An excellent, coherent treatment of planning theory.

American Planning Association, ed. 1994. *Planning and Community Equity: A Component of APA's Agenda for America's Communities Program.* Chicago: Planners' Press. A good collection of essays, many by practicing planners, all addressing practical issues in integrating social equity into traditional planning.

Faludi, Andreas, ed. 1973 (reprinted multiple times). *A Reader in Planning Theory.* Oxford, U.K.: Pergamon Press. An excellent early collection on planning theory that includes some of the classic theory articles cited here, as well as a discussion of their relationship to the comprehensive plan.

Friedmann, John. 1987. *Planning in the Public Domain: From Knowledge to Action.* Princeton, NJ: Princeton University Press. An excellent history of planning and its theoretical foundations in the United States, followed by the author's argument for radical planning.

Krumholz, Norman, and John Forester. 1990. *Making Equity Planning Work: Leadership in the Public Sector.* Philadelphia, PA: Temple University Press. An excellent case study of the application of this alternative approach to planning, with discussion of the reasons for it in the context of Cleveland in the 1970s.

Stein, Jay M. 1995. *Classic Readings in Urban Planning.* New York: McGraw-Hill. A good collection of readings, including some classic works in planning theory.

NOTES

1. Discussed in part III, esp. chapters 14 (zoning) and 15 (subdivision regulation).
2. Both are described in more detail in chapter 2.
3. See, for example, the collection of essays on planning theory edited by Andreas Faludi and the book by Ernest R. Alexander, both listed under "Further Reading."
4. For an overview, see Susan J. Buck, *Understanding Environmental Administration and Law,* Washington, D.C.: Island Press (1996).
5. See, for example, Ian McHarg, *Design with Nature, 25th Anniversary Edition,* New York: John Wiley (1992); original publication, Garden City, NY: Natural History Press for the American Museum of Natural History (1969); and Wence E. Dramstad, James D. Olson, and Richard T.T. Forman, *Landscape Ecology Principles in Landscape Architecture and Land-Use Planning,* Washington, D.C.: Island Press (1996).
6. See Norman Krumholz and John Forester, *Making Equity Planning Work;* the book describes the effort that Krumholz led to implement "equity planning" as a replacement for traditional comprehensive planning in Cleveland.

7. Paul Davidoff, an urban planning professor, developed a theory of "advocacy planning," discussed in Davidoff, "Advocacy and Pluralism in Planning," *Journal of the American Institute of Planners* 31 (November 1965); reprinted in Jay Stein, *Classic Readings in Urban Planning,* and in Faludi.

8. See, for example, John Friedmann, *Planning in the Public Domain.*

9. See note 7 above.

10. N.J.S.A. 52:27D-310 (Supp. through 1998).

11. Krumholz and Forester, chapter 3.

12. John Rawls, *A Theory of Justice,* Cambridge, MA: Harvard University Press (1971); an excerpt, setting out the basic theory, is reprinted in Stein, *Classic Readings in Urban Planning.*

Part I

The Comprehensive Planning Process

This part introduces the concept of planning and then presents the process of creating a comprehensive plan in the sequence in which communities most commonly undertake it.

Chapter 1 introduces the concept of planning, as applied in many different contexts. Comprehensive planning for a community is easiest to understand in the larger context of planning for human activity in general.

Chapter 2 describes the comprehensive plan, and places it in the context of the planning concepts explained in the first chapter, as well as the context of a community and the local government that has the responsibility for planning for that community.

The first thing that anyone needs to know when reading a map is the starting point. Chapter 3 describes techniques of "existing conditions analysis," which provides the starting point for a community planning process.

Chapter 4 explains how planners bring a sense of reality to planning, by answering the question "Where can we go?" This chapter examines alternative approaches to determining what realistic choices are available to a community.

The most important question in any plan is "Where do we want to go?" which is the subject of chapter 5. It describes goal setting and other methods of determining what results the community would like to see from the successful implementation of the plan. Much of the chapter is devoted to the topic of citizen participation in the planning process, because it is through such participation that the plan becomes a plan of and for the community as a whole.

Chapter 1

Introduction to Planning

Would you rather plan your future or just wait to see what happens? If the subject is next Friday night, waiting to see what happens may be an acceptable answer. What if, however, the subject is the rest of your life? What if the subject is the future of your community? Planning the future of an entire community may seem like an overwhelming challenge, but do you think a community ought to just wait to see what happens? Planning involves making conscious choices about the future. Those who do not plan just let the future happen.

Planning is a rational way of preparing for the future. It typically involves the gathering and analysis of data, the examination of possible future trends, the consideration of alternative scenarios, some sort of analysis of costs and benefits of those scenarios, choosing a preferred scenario, and a plan for implementation.

Every year in some community, the state transportation department improves the roads on the east side of the town, while the public works department extends new sewer and water service to the south, and the school district decides to build on the west side of town, on land that turns out to have been a bargain because it has poor road access and no sewer or water service. Communities ought not to make such mistakes in planning (or failing to plan) their own futures.

Elements of a Planning Process

Some basic elements are common to almost all forms of planning: data gathering, data analysis, policy making, implementation, and monitoring. In a simple planning process, two or even three of these elements may be undertaken simultaneously, but they are almost always distinguishable factors in the planning process.

Data Gathering

Every rational plan or decision is based on some set of information. A transportation department planning a highway gathers data on traffic demand, capacities of existing roads, budgets, road construction costs, and cost and availability of right-of-way. Planners preparing a comprehensive plan gather data on existing conditions and on population trends that will bring changes; they also gather data on the capacity of the natural and built systems of the community to absorb the effects of change.

Data Analysis

Sometimes data are self-explanatory, but usually they need some interpretation and analysis. Transportation demand, for example, is a complex topic. Planning a new road involves a great deal more than just subtracting presumed demand from the capacity of existing roadways. Raw population data tell one story about a community, but careful analysis of that data can provide a good basis for predicting future school enrollment, cemetery needs, and other trends related to the number of people in the community. In most cases, the comparison of proposed plans to the available budget is itself a critical step in the process of data analysis.

Policy Making

Data analysis sometimes limits the range of policy choices. A careful review of costs and budget may suggest that there is only one choice of where to build a road or locate a new school. Often, however, the data and their analysis provide a context for making a policy decision, which often involves choosing among alternatives. The highway planners may have to choose between a route for which construction costs would be low but that would cross a popular public park, and a route with higher construction costs but no disruption to parklands or homes. Someone must decide which choice to make. In a community comprehensive planning process, it is usually the governing body, with the advice of the planning commission, that makes such choices; usually it does so only after a public hearing or some other structured forum for receiving comments from citizens and stakeholders.

Note that the first two elements of planning—data gathering and data analysis—are essentially objective and rational. Policy making ultimately involves judgment. Sometimes analysis of the data makes the choice so obvious that the policy making is relatively rational—or "irrational" if it does not reach the obvious conclusion. In many cases, however, the policy maker will have to make difficult choices—for example, the choice between an inexpensive highway route through the middle of a park and an expensive one that goes around it.

Conceptually, the policy-making aspect of planning is the most complex, and it is thus the aspect of planning that a large part of this book addresses. Policy making for communities is particularly complex, because it is not always clear who has the power or authority to make such a policy—or those who have the apparent power or authority may not choose to exercise it.

Implementation

Meaningful plans are those that become the basis for implementing decisions.

Implementation of a plan for a new highway will typically require buying right-of-way, conducting environmental studies, designing the new road, taking bids for its construction, and then planning its construction in a way that minimizes disruption of existing traffic flow along it and related roads. Implementation of a plan for a new product involves design, legal protection (patents and trademarks), production, marketing, and distribution. Money to pay for the implementation is an element common to all plans.

Community plans are sometimes even more complex to implement. One goal in a community plan may be "to alleviate congestion on Route 38 from Broadway to High Street," for example. Highway engineers might achieve congestion relief from widening such a road, or the addition of traffic signals and turning lanes might accomplish the purpose. Other alternatives for alleviating congestion might range from closing some intersections and driveways along the road to building a parallel road to absorb some of the traffic.

To choose among such alternatives, a community needs a policy more detailed than this general goal. Thus, the basic elements of public plans often include three distinct sub-elements:

- *Goals.* Goals are the general aims of the community, such as alleviating traffic congestion on a designated road.
- *Objectives.* Objectives are more specific sub-elements of goals, usually providing measurable, mid-range strategies. Thus, the objective for alleviating the traffic along a designated road might be to build a parallel road at a specified location.
- *Policies.* Policies are operational actions, usually with the purpose of relatively short-term implementation. Policies for the objective of building a new road might include: (1) making the new road the highest-priority item in the capital budget; (2) assessing an impact fee (see chapter 13) to developers desiring access to either road, with the revenues to be added to a fund to help pay for the road; (3) deferring approval of new development along the existing road until construction on the new road has begun.

Another way to think of this list is this:

- *goals,* including general aims with some details;
- *strategies,* including additional details of the objectives and specific methods for making them occur; and
- *actions,* focusing on the fiscal or physical implementation of the plan.

Sometimes the goals, objectives, and policies are all included in a local comprehensive plan (discussed in depth in chapter 2). More typically, however, objectives are established through some sort of mid-range implementation planning process. Often, establishment of the specific objectives to implement a goal requires additional study. A capital improvements program is one sort of mid-range implementation plan often used by local governments, but there are others. Policies and objectives may evolve from the same stage of the planning process, but policies are often specific tools that are approved by a separate agency. Thus, the public works department of the local government, perhaps with the advice of the planning commission, may develop the objective of building the parallel road, while the implementing policies require the approval of budgets and the adoption of ordinances by the governing body.

The terms *goals, objectives,* and *policies* are not used with complete consistency in the field of comprehensive planning. Thus, a plan may use the term *policies* to refer to what are called *goals* here. In general, however, when the terms are used together, they are used in the hierarchy described here—with goals setting the long-range, general aims of the community; objectives establishing more specific, mid-range strategies to meet the goal; and policies requiring specific implementation actions, actions that are usually relatively immediate.

Monitoring

The best plans include a feedback loop that provides monitoring of the plan. Transportation departments check traffic counts, speed, and flow before and after construction of the new road to determine whether it improves the situation. Environmental enforcement officers measure the effluent from sewage treatment plants to ensure that the plant is accomplishing its purpose. Community planners observe and map changes in land use, comparing them to the plan.

One aspect of monitoring is as a part of implementation. Zoning enforcement officers (see chapter 10) check new buildings to ensure that they conform with zoning, for example, which is one of the implementation tools for planning; zoning officers have a variety of methods for stopping construction on a building that is inconsistent with the plan. Another aspect of monitoring goes beyond implementation, however, and provides the foundation for updating a plan—and preparing its replacement. Communities base their plans on projections of future population growth and other changes. If the population grows more slowly, or more quickly, than planners anticipated, that difference in rate will affect the plan. Community planners monitor such changes and suggest plan updates and amendments based on them.

Community Planning in Concept

Planning for a community is very different from planning for many other organizations, because the first step in planning for a community must be to identify a collective set of goals or a common vision. Many organizations that plan already know what their goals are. Some of the leaders in effective planning are business and military organizations. Their goals are firm and clear. A business must make a profit. It may have objectives of offering excellent customer service and providing a healthy and happy working environment, but the ultimate goal must be a profit. A business that does not make a profit eventually exhausts its capital and ceases to exist, at which point concepts like "customers" and "employees" become irrelevant.

Similarly, the clear goal of a military organization is to take ground or hold ground. In peacetime, society may forget that—but military planners never do. Further, in most cases, the specific ground that the military organization must try to seize or defend is an objective determined outside that organization and given to it as an assignment.

There are many other examples. The local United Way plans its annual campaign knowing that its goal is to raise money for social services and other charities in the community. The school district knows that its goal is to provide an education to children and youth of specified ages, in accordance with standards set out in state law.

Thus, the task in the kind of planning used by businesses, military organizations, and others with defined goals is to determine how best to meet those goals. A good community planning process, in contrast, must begin with a process to determine the goals.

Alternative Approaches

There are several different approaches to community-wide planning. Planners have used all of these approaches as the basis of comprehensive plans in different communities at different times. Each has strengths and weaknesses. The choice of approach (or approaches) will depend on local needs and preferences; that choice will in significant part define the process that is used and will influence the respective roles of professional planners and interested citizens, as well as the role of the planning body. Here are the basic approaches:

- *Goal-Driven.* This is the classic approach to planning. It establishes long-range goals for the community, and those goals guide the rest of the planning process. Establishing long-range goals is often a complex process, however, sometimes requiring sophisticated management. Public participation in this process is very important but sometimes complicated; ultimately, the task of framing the goals must fall to a smaller group, such as the planning body or the governing body. (Note that *trends analysis* and *issue identification,* both discussed below, are often used as inputs into a goal-driven process.)

- *Trends-Driven.* A trends-driven approach to planning simply projects current population and land-use trends into the future and uses those as the basis for planning. This is a relatively technical and not particularly participatory approach. Because trends are so likely to change, it is not the ideal approach to form the core of a community planning process. It can provide a useful point of reference, however, for other planning approaches.

- *Opportunity-Driven.* In an opportunity-driven planning process, a community assesses its future based on opportunities and constraints rather than on simple projections of trends. Often, citizen participation efforts in local planning involve identification of opportunities and strengths. Professional planners often identify objective opportunities, such as underused transportation facilities, large and vacant industrial buildings, and availability of cheap energy sources.

- *Issue-Driven.* In an issue-driven planning process, a community identifies the critical issues facing it and focuses its planning efforts on those issues. This is a simple and practical approach to planning that can be broadly participatory. It is typically very results oriented. Issue-driven planning can take one of two forms. Sometimes it poses challenging questions like, "What type of industry can replace our historic dependence on the auto industry?" In other cases it may be the obverse of the opportunity-driven approach, with the "questions" really representing problems, such as, "How do we eliminate the traffic congestion that discourages new industry from coming here?"

- *Vision-Driven.* Although the term *visioning* is now sometimes used loosely to refer to a goal-setting process, the term *vision* is more accurately used to apply to an overarching goal that controls the entire process. True visions generally arise from within a community through strong leadership (which is often informal leadership). A plan to fulfill a vision can be one of the most exciting kinds of plans to develop. It is difficult to use a vision-driven planning process to extract a vision where one does not exist, however.

Most local plans are developed using some combination of approaches. Sometimes separating the approaches, as above, oversimplifies matters. On the other hand, simplification makes them easier to explain and understand. In preparing a plan, communities should blend one or more approaches to best meet their unique local needs. Trend-driven planning works best as an input to other types of planning approaches, illustrating what will happen without a plan for managing a change in trends. All of the other approaches represent valid approaches to planning, each useful in its own way.

Systems Thinking and Planning

Systems analysis provides a rigorous framework for making some planning decisions. It is easily adaptable to computerized analysis and testing of alternatives, making it an appealing tool to those who want quantifiable, defensible decisions.

Equally important to planning, however, is the notion of systems thinking. Systems theory starts with three basic concepts:

1. Everything is a system.
2. Every system is a part of one or more larger systems (and thus, by corollary, every system is made up of other systems).
3. Most systems are open systems that exchange energy with their environments (which are larger systems).

A student is a system, made up of many biological systems. That student is a part of several larger systems, perhaps including a class in which this book is used as a text. That class is a part of a larger system, probably an academic department. That department, in turn, is part of a school or college that is part of a university, which itself is part of a state.

Understanding the relationships among systems involved in a planning study is often critical to the success of that planning effort and its implementation. Understanding systems can be particularly important when facing difficult problems, because a problem that is not solvable at one system level may be easily solvable at a higher system level. Consider parking as an example. Today many communities require that new development include adequate "off-street" parking to serve the buildings and land uses in the development; that usually implies creating parking opportunities on the same lot. In that context, each lot is a system. Trying to address parking needs on individual building lots in a downtown area, however, may interfere with other goals of creating a dense and pedestrian-friendly environment. At the system level of the individual lot, there is no good solution to that. If planners consider an entire block, or even the whole downtown, however, it becomes practicable to think about solving the parking problem off the individual lot but within the larger system; for example, First Street might be pedestrian oriented, with buildings filling every lot, while Second Street would be lined with parking lots behind the First Street buildings. A problem that has no good solution at one system level may have one or more easy solutions at another system level. Thus, it is often useful in planning to define the systems involved and to consider solving a difficult problem by moving to a different system level.

Planning Traditions in the United States

Planning has been an essential element in building this country and remains an important and pervasive activity. Businesses plan their operations and marketing campaigns. Television networks plan their seasons. Armies plan battles, campaigns, and entire wars. Some engineers plan highways, while others plan sewer systems. College students plan their programs of study. Professionals plan their days, often using computer systems to track multiple appointments and other commitments.

Planning is a fundamental activity, essential to any sort of complex or long-range endeavor. It is much older than our nation, but it has played an important role in our nation's evolution. The Constitution that guides us some two hundred years after it was drafted was a plan for a nation—a plan developed when the proposed Articles of Confederation proved unacceptable. The creation of the District of Columbia resulted from a plan to create a national capital outside the boundaries of any state. Even today the capital reflects the remarkable planning of a Frenchman, Pierre L'Enfant, which was updated more than one hundred years later by the MacMillan Commission (a congressional body)[1] and again in the 1990s by the appointed National Capital Planning Commission.[2]

An early example of physical planning that helped to shape the nation is provided by the Erie Canal, the famous waterway that effectively connected the Great Lakes to the Atlantic Ocean, although the canal itself ran only from Buffalo on Lake Erie to Albany on the Hudson River, which in turn flows out to the Atlantic around Manhattan Island. Major cities grew up along this

---

Homestead Act of 1862:

An Act of the Thirty-Seventh Congress, Session II, Chapter 75, 1862

Be it enacted by the Senate and House of Representatives of the United States of America in Congress assembled, That any person who is the head of a family, or who has arrived at the age of twenty-one years, and is a citizen of the United States, or who shall have filed this declaration of intention to become such, as required by the naturalization laws of the United States, and who has never borne arms against the United States Government or given aid and comfort to its enemies, shall, from and after the first of January, eighteen hundred and sixty-three, be entitled to enter one quarter section or a less quantity of unappropriated public lands, upon which said person may have filed a pre-emption claim, or which may, at the time the application is made, be subject to pre-emption at one dollar and twenty-five cents, or less, per acre; or eighty acres or less of such unappropriated lands, at two dollars and fifty cents per acre, to be located in a body, in conformity to the legal subdivisions of the public lands, and after the same shall have been surveyed.

The preamble to the Homestead Act of 1862, one of the two major pieces of Congress's grand plan to open the West.

important route of commerce, and thus later planners for railroads and then for highways placed their major infrastructure along this route. Even today, a map of the major cities in New York State looks like an inverted letter *L*, reflecting the route of the Erie Canal through the middle of the state, connecting on the east to the Hudson, which forms the leg of the *L*.

The combination of two grand plans opened up the West, as the United States acquired more western territory through purchase and conquest. One plan promoted settlement through the "homestead" program, under which a family or individual could acquire a quarter section (160 acres) of land in the new territories simply by claiming it, living there, and beginning to improve it or use it productively. Much of the private property in the western United States today traces its history to original grants from the United States of America to homesteaders.[3]

A related plan for the new territories was a development plan, and that was the plan for railroads. Under that program, beginning after the Civil War, the U.S. government granted millions of acres of land in the new West to the railroads. As an incentive, the government granted to the railroads not only the right-of-way necessary to build the railroad lines, but also designated parcels of land along the right-of-way whose development into new settlements would profit the railroads. Many midwestern farm communities were laid out by railroad surveyors on just such land in the last half of the nineteenth century, and those early survey grids still form the heart of many communities today.[4]

The national coordinate survey system represented a different sort of planning, one that was essential to the homesteading and railroad land grants. Determined to avoid the chaos that often resulted from Colonial land titles, which might describe a parcel of land as running, for example, "along the Newtown Road to a large rock, thence west to the creek, thence north approximately 220 feet along the meander of the creek to a large oak tree." There were often disputes over which rock and even which road, while trees disappeared and streams changed their courses, with or without human help. Thus, engineers working with the new national government developed the national coordinate survey system to describe lands in the new western territories. This system, first used in the Ohio Territory in the 1780s, created a grid based on lines of longitude and latitude. Major lines in the grid were at six-mile and one-mile intervals, creating townships that were six miles by six miles and sections that were one mile square, containing 640 acres; there were, of course, thirty-six sections in a township. Townships, ranges, and sections were numbered in accord with a uniform system.[5] The acre became the standard measure of land in the United States; it represents 40 percent of the size of a hectare, which had been the common measure before creation of this system.

The same system of describing land defines real property in most of the United States today. The exceptions are the original colonies, Texas, and parts

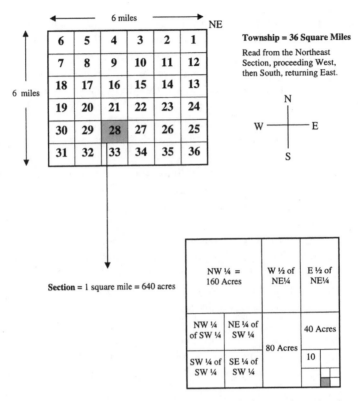

The elements of the national plane coordinate system include range lines (north and south) and township lines (east and west) that define "townships," which are broken into "sections," which can in turn be divided into geometric parts. This illustration shows a typical township, with the standard numbering of sections within it and the typical method of describing parts of sections. Illustration by Jeff Walsh.

of the Southwest that trace their titles to original Spanish and Mexican land grants. Homesteads were based on quarter sections, or squares that contained 160 acres of land and measured one-half mile on a side. The railroad land grants were always based on full sections. In many of the western states, specific sections in every township were retained for the state as "school lands," and those remain sources of support for public education in many states today.

Later examples of national planning in the United States include the national park system, which is the result of the vision of a few people a century ago,[6] and the interstate highway system.[7] The interstate system became a reality under President Dwight Eisenhower, who as General Eisenhower had led the United States in much of World War II. He believed that an efficient road system for the movement of troops, equipment, and supplies was essential to the future defense of the nation. Today, the principal purpose of it has become one of serving commerce and convenience, and many trips on the system are intra-urban, not interstate. The important point, however, is that this system developed from a national plan. It can trace its planning roots to such landmarks as the National Road, the first major interstate highway, most of which became part of U.S. 40, and the Lincoln Highway (now mostly known as U.S. 30), which was the first coast-to-coast road.

Although our society remains very different from those in which even the economies are centrally planned, a great deal of planning is essential to the operation of the nation. Without planning, there would be chaos. There would be roads without bridges, bridges without roads, railroad stations in the middle of the prairie and cities without railroads, schools without students and students in other communities without schools. Although no system is perfect, planning is more notable for its success in helping the United States achieve remarkable growth and prosperity than for its occasional failures.

Planning in a Contemporary Democracy

One of the great challenges of planning in a democratic society is to balance the complex, differing, and often competing interests of many different constituent groups. In many ways, the simplest form of government for planning is that of the benevolent despot. The despot presumably holds all the power necessary to make decisions and to implement plans; yet because he (and despots have historically been male) is benevolent, he presumably cares about those who will be affected by the plans and thus will act in consideration of their interests. The first modern planning laws that affected the United States were the Laws of the Indies, urban planning guidelines published by rulers of Spain, most notably King Philip II.[8] Those design guidelines resulted in the creation of the plazas and defining central areas of San Antonio, Texas; Santa Fe, New Mexico; and St. Augustine, Florida. As the reigning monarch, the king did not have to consult anyone before publishing those plans—although it is likely that he consulted the seventeenth century equivalent of today's professional planners.

Planning in a democracy is considerably more complicated. It is difficult for large groups to make collective decisions on complex topics, yet the very notion of democracy is that major decisions about the future ought to be collective ones. Anyone who has ever served on a committee of ten or more, trying to plan an event, certainly has experienced the difficulty of making decisions. Imagine trying to convene a meeting of tens of thousands of interested people in a community to develop a common vision. Although it is possible to ascertain the collective will through referendum on a simple question ("Shall the city borrow fifty million dollars to build a new stadium for the Black Sox professional baseball team?"), determining the collective will on a large number of questions with a range of intersecting answers is an overwhelming task.

Government in the United States is not a pure democracy, however—it is largely a representative democracy. Citizens depend on elected representatives to make policy decisions. Although there are a few communities still use the town meeting to make such decisions, in most communities, comprehensive planning is carried out by some sort of representative group. Such a system is much more workable than an effort to call all of the citizens of a community together to make a plan, but this delegation creates other problems.

Democracy itself is troublesome to some planners, because it is "political." People vote for candidates for city council or the county commission because the candidates espouse popular positions—like cutting taxes or encouraging economic development. Few citizens vote for candidates for public office thinking, "This person will make a good planner." Further, a representative democracy is often reactive and short sighted. Many decisions are made in response to the short-term concerns of those who happen to attend a hearing on the matter, not with the sort of long-term perspective one expects for a comprehensive plan. Finally, elected officials are necessarily concerned with balancing the current year's budget and may have difficulty thinking much further than that, even when they want to.

Thus, beginning more than a century ago, professionals working in the planning field suggested that local community planning ought to be disconnected from politics. The result of that suggestion was the creation within local government of the appointed planning commission, a body that is charged with the duty and responsibility of preparing comprehensive plans in most communities in the United States today. The system is more complex than that, however. Planning commission members are volunteers, most of whom have other professional and personal commitments. Planning commissions in larger communities thus typically depend on professional planning staffs to assist them. Although there are a few communities where the planning direc-

Richard Hedman on democracy in planning. Copyright by Richard Hedman. Used with permission.

tor actually is an employee of the planning commission, in most communities the staff is part of the executive branch of government and reports to a city manager, mayor, county commissioner, or county administrator. The work program of the planning staff is often determined within that executive branch, leaving little opportunity for the appointed commission to guide the work of the staff that is supposed to assist it.

The politics of comprehensive planning are the subject of the next chapter, but it is important to recognize here that in undertaking community planning in a democracy we have removed that process two steps from the purest form of democracy—first assigning it to elected representatives and then delegating it to an appointed body.

That removal of planning from the people creates conceptual problems in the process of comprehensive planning, because the comprehensive plan for a community presumably represents the collective will of the people. Many people who are willing to delegate the complexities of local government budgeting to elected officials and even to allow an appointed body to act on such apparently obscure matters as "subdivision review" may object to a comprehensive community plan in which they have not been involved. The next chapter discusses alternative models of assigning the final policy-making function, ranging from delegation to the planning commission to use of a special task force or creation of a joint working group involving elected officials, as well as others who may be appointed. Under all of those models, however, finding practical, effective, meaningful ways to involve individual citizens is an important challenge.

Maps as Planning Tools

A map is a communication tool. When someone wants to get from one city to another by highway, it is certainly possible to get driving directions that consist entirely of words—either spoken or written. Many people, however, prefer to look at a map, because it gives the user a visual image of the relationship between the two places and the routes that connect the two.

Similarly, maps are extremely useful visual representations in planning (see color plates 1–4 for examples). Local plans frequently include maps of:

- existing land use
- transportation routes
- parks and open space
- utility lines
- municipal boundaries
- future land-use and transportation plans

This short section describes some basic characteristics of maps and some principles that are important to understand when working with maps. Although some of the material will be familiar to those who have studied geography, this section also presents some unique aspects of maps in a comprehensive planning context.

Units of Measure, Orientation, and Scale

It is important for planners to understand some basic units of measure as they deal with maps. Some derive from the national grid coordinate system, described and illustrated earlier in this chapter. Units of measure with which planners—and planning students—must be familiar include those described in table 1.1. Note that land surveys are based on a flat earth. No one really thinks that the earth is flat, but creating a logical survey grid requires that everyone start from something flat. Thus, a mile measured along a hilly road may be something less than a mile when recomputed for survey purposes. Surveyors traditionally use transits to measure the slope of the land from one point to another; by applying principles of geometry to the measure of the distance between those two points and the angle of the slope, it is possible to calculate what the distance between the two points would be if the earth between them were flat. It is that distance that will be shown on surveys and most maps, not the actual distance along the roads. Highway maps are created using the same principle, but the numeric representation of distance on the maps (as opposed to that measured using the scale of the map) is typically the driving distance along the road, not the surveyed distance.

Maps used in planning and other important studies are always drawn to a *scale*. The scale indicates the relationship of a unit of measure on the map to a unit of measure on the ground. Highway and other consumer-oriented maps contain a drawn scale, usually illustrating the distance on the map that represents a mile, half mile, or other common distance on the ground. In referring to maps, however, it is useful to describe scale in words and numbers. Scale for maps used in planning is described in one of two ways: a "one-inch-equals" scale, which simply states what ground distance is represented by one inch on the map, or a "ratio" scale, such as 1:24,000, which indicates that one unit of anything on the map equals 24,000 of the same unit on the ground. As a quick test of your understanding, convert a 1:24,000 scale to a one-inch-equals scale.

Table 1.1. Planning Units of Measure

Unit	Equals
Acre	43,560 square feet
Section	640 acres
Quarter section	160 acres
Mile	5,280 feet
Square mile	640 acres

A scale of 1:24,000 allows the presentation of a relatively large area on a designated sheet of paper; to show such a large land area on any sheet of paper, however, results in the elimination of a lot of detail. A scale of 1:2,000, for example, allows the presentation of much more detail but reduces the amount of land area that can be shown on the same sheet of paper.

Most maps have north at the top. Many maps have a "north arrow" or "north orientation arrow" to show where north is on the map. Where a city street grid has many streets that run almost—but not quite—north and south, map makers may align the streets with the edge of the map and use the north arrow to show the deviation of the map from having "true north" at the top. That kind of minor deviation in orientation will not affect most users, because they are interested only in the general direction of north and not in the exact orientation to the magnetic north pole. Because people expect to find north at the top of a map, however, it is confusing to present a map with north at one of the sides or at the bottom—even with a north arrow to show the orientation.

Currency, Accuracy, and Relationship to "Known Points"

One important issue to examine in using a map is how current it is. The copyright or publication date provides one piece of information; the user can be certain that all of the information on the map is at least as old as that date. As a practical matter, however, there is a lag time between the gathering of data for a map and the publication of that map; that lag time is often measured in years. Thus, a planner must examine a map carefully to learn when the data was gathered (or updated), as well as when the map was made.

Even if the map is reasonably current, it may not be possible to find details such as a particular building on it, for two reasons: One is that the scale of the map may not allow for such detail; the other is that the map may be accurate only to within a half mile or so. Such an accuracy is more than adequate to find a city but is grossly inadequate to find an individual building. The people who prepare state highway maps would typically not even note the location of individual buildings, because that is not relevant to the purpose of the map. In contrast, a city street map, which contains much more detail, should enable the user to find the piece of land on which an individual building sits, which usually serves the purpose of finding a building in an urban area. A city street map should be accurate within forty or fifty feet or maybe a little better.

Someone drawing a map to show a friend how to find her house may not be very worried about accuracy and may simply want to show the major roads and where the turns are. A map like that may serve a limited purpose very well, without much accuracy. Note that some maps of that sort are *schematic* and really have no scale at all. Such a map might show only that, to go from point A to point B, it is necessary to go some distance and then to turn left and watch for point B along the way. Such a map may not even be drawn to scale. Obviously, the accuracy of such a map is very low.

There are really two levels of accuracy that are important in examining a map, however. One is the accuracy within the map, which depends on how closely the relationships shown on the map approximate the same relationships on the ground. The other level of accuracy is the relationship of points on the map to "known points" on the ground. As a result of the national coordinate survey system, the U.S. government has established known survey points throughout much of the country. Applying principles of geometry, if one can identify two known points, those can be used to describe very accurately the location of any other point. The best maps are "tied down" or clearly related to two or more known points on the ground, usually points shown on the national coordinate survey system; those points, which are identifiable on the ground, are clearly shown on the map. That kind of accuracy makes it possible to locate any point shown on the map with great accuracy on the ground.

As you learned in geometry, using principles of triangulation it is possible to use two known points to provide an accurate description to any other point on the same plane. Maps of this accuracy usually contain multiple points on the map that are clearly tied down to identifiable points on the ground, providing the basis for using geometry to either: (1) add new buildings or other features to the map with considerable accuracy, by locating them in relation to mapped points that are known on the ground; or (2) find improvements on the ground that can be located on the map (such as an underground utility line).

Why is this important? It is important because the most accurate, detailed maps in each community may not all fit together. Usually the most accurate maps available for individual parts of a community are *subdivision plats,* discussed in chapter 11. A subdivision plat usually represents a city block or several city blocks. If the maps of one subdivision started from one point, however, and the maps of other subdivisions started from other points, they may not fit together. Sometimes the differences are only a few inches, but sometimes they are significant.

Existing Maps Useful for Planning

Many types of government and other agencies create maps of communities, counties and, regions. Some of those are particularly useful for planning purposes:

- *USGS Quadrangle Maps.* The U.S. Geological Survey is the successor to the agency that created the national coordinate survey system. Its *quadrangle* maps are the most common, tangible representation of that system today. They are available for the entire nation. The maps most often used by planners are the 7 1/2-*minute* series quadrangle maps, which are 1:24,000-scale

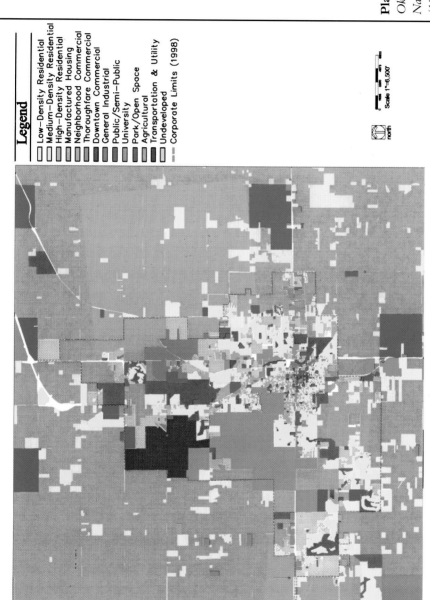

Legend

- Low-Density Residential
- Medium-Density Residential
- High-Density Residential
- Manufactured Housing
- Neighborhood Commercial
- Thoroughfare Commercial
- Downtown Commercial
- General Industrial
- Public/Semi-Public
- University
- Park/Open Space
- Agricultural
- Transportation & Utility
- Undeveloped
- Corporate Limits (1998)

Scale 1"=6,500'

north

Plate 1. *Existing land use, Stillwater, Oklahoma. Source: RM Plan Group, Nashville, for the City of Stillwater (1998).*

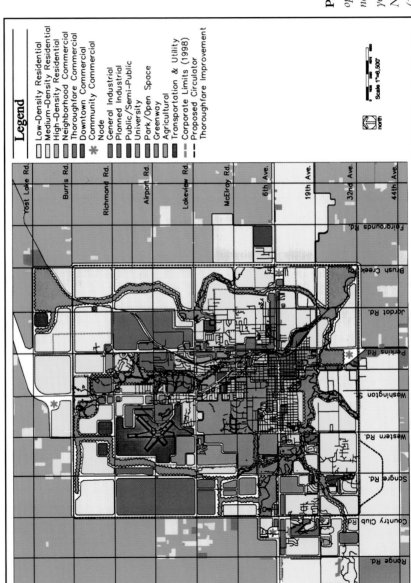

Plate 2. *Future land use, intermediate option, Stillwater, Oklahoma (proposed; no action on this proposal by city as yet).* Source: *RM Plan Group, Nashville, for the City of Stillwater (1998).*

Legend

- Low-Density Residential
- Medium-Density Residential
- High-Density Residential
- Neighborhood Commercial
- Thoroughfare Commercial
- Downtown Commercial
- Community Commercial
- ✳ Node
- General Industrial
- Planned Industrial
- Public/Semi-Public
- University
- Park/Open Space
- Greenway
- Agricultural
- Transportation & Utility
- ‑‑‑ Corporate Limits (1998)
- ‑‑ Proposed Circulator
- ‑‑ Thoroughfare Improvement

Scale 1"=6,500'

north

Plate 3. *Potential development map based on environmental considerations, Bardstown–Nelson County, Kentucky. Source: Pflum, Klausmeier & Gehrum, Cincinnati, for the city and county (1998).*

PDA Boundary

City Boundary

Agriculture PDA
Residential PDA
Industrial PDA
Commercial PDA

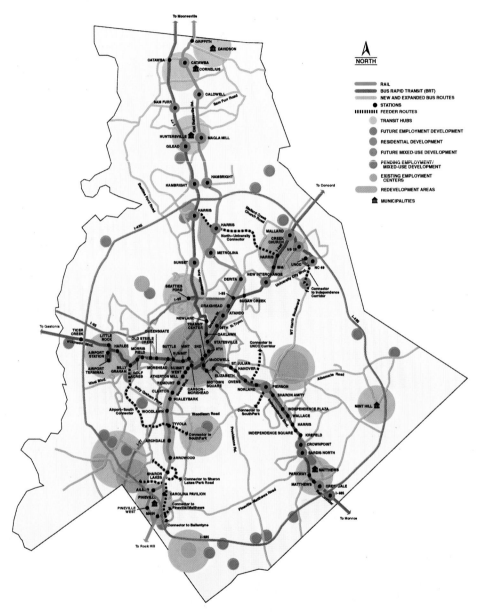

Plate 4. *2025 Transit land-use plan, Charlotte–Mecklenburg County, North Carolina.*
Source: *LDR International for the city and county (1998).*

maps (the scale differs for Alaska and Puerto Rico). Each of these quadrangle maps covers some fifty to seventy square miles. They use *contour lines* to illustrate the slope of land and show patterns of vegetation and development, roads, rivers and streams, and, in rural areas, individual buildings and other landmarks. Keys on these maps show the location of known survey point markers on the ground, useful for tying down more detailed survey maps. Because they are used by hikers and bicyclists, as well as by surveyors and farmers, copies of these maps for local areas are often available at bike and outdoor shops, as well as at blueprint and survey supply stores and some bookstores. They are also available from USGS.[9]

- *Orthophoto Quadrangle Maps.* Orthophoto quadrangle maps, also available from USGS, are high-altitude photographs coordinated with the quadrangle mapping system. Someone familiar with the maps can infer additional information about vegetation from such maps, and it is often possible to identify physical features not shown on the basic quadrangle maps. These are not as commonly available locally as are the quadrangle maps, but some of the same outlets may have them. Otherwise, they can be ordered from the USGS.[10]

- *Soil Survey.* According to the Natural Resources Conservation Service (NRCS), which conducts soil surveys in this country:

  A soil survey describes the characteristics of the soils in a given area, classifies the soils according to a standard system of classification, plots the boundaries of the soils on a map, and makes predictions about the behavior of soils.

  The different uses of the soils and how the response of management affects them are considered. The information collected in a soil survey helps in the development of land-use plans and evaluates and predicts the effects of land use on the environment.[11]

  Soil surveys provide valuable raw and interpretive data about the character of soils and, in many cases, their underlying geology. They are remarkably accurate, often considered to be accurate to within two hundred feet. Soil surveys are published as loosely bound volumes, with maps and text, usually for a county. The local office of the NRCS or a county extension agent should have a copy of the local soil survey. For information on other sources of soil surveys, contact the NRCS.[12]

- *TIGER (topography integrated geographic encoding and referencing) Maps.* Beginning in 1990, the Bureau of the Census began to make census data available in the form of maps, which also show major political boundaries, as well as streets and roads, to provide context for the data. These maps are available for free on many CD-ROMS that contain census data or from the census Web site.[13] The TIGER Web site even includes the option to customize the maps to show particular areas and details needed by the user. Note that these maps are generated electronically and are not readily available in hard copy. The accuracy of the TIGER maps varies; they are generated from other maps and are no more accurate than those maps. For example, in the city where one of the authors lives, a state highway that appears on the map to end actually becomes a local road, a change that is not apparent in any way on the map.

- *Floodplain Maps.* As part of the national flood insurance program, the Federal Emergency Management Agency (FEMA) publishes generalized floodplain maps for most areas. Local and state agencies may have more detailed or more accurate floodplain maps in many areas. The purpose of the FEMA maps, called FIRM (for Flood Insurance Risk Management) maps, is to identify property that is either in or so close to a floodplain that it should have flood insurance. The local planning or public works office should have a copy of the FIRM map for the area, but the maps are also available from FEMA.[14]

- *State Maps.* Many states have state geologists or geographers or other state offices that create specialized maps for that state. Each state's Web site or a public information office in the state capitol should provide information on what maps are available and how to obtain them.

- *Street and Highway Maps.* Street and highway maps can be very useful for local planning purposes. They provide an easy frame of reference for local plans because most citizens can easily find their homes, places of employment, and other sites of interest on them. Planners must be careful in considering the use of those maps, however; some are created by private companies and are copyrighted.

- *Utility Maps.* Sewer and water systems may not be glamorous, but they are important to planners. The availability of those services significantly influences the patterns of development (see chapters 12 and 13). The local public works department or other providers of essential utility services should have maps of such systems. In planning for an area larger than one community, it is important to determine what agencies besides the central community may provide such services within a region and then to obtain maps of their service areas.

- *Political Maps.* Planners must have accurate information on the political boundaries of the entities for which they plan. Most local governments have good maps showing their boundaries. Note that, because of *annexation,* a concept discussed in both chapter 12 and chapter 18, a city's boundaries may change from time to time. The TIGER maps and many state maps show political boundaries, but they are often not completely current in those maps.

- *Zoning Maps.* Planners should always refer to the current zoning map for the community. That type of map is described in more depth in chapter 10.

Assembling Information on a Base Map

All of the maps listed above contain information that is useful for planning purposes. All of that information is most useful if it can be combined into a single map or a single set of maps. That is often a challenging task, because the maps are prepared at different scales with different levels of accuracy.

The starting point for the task of assembling data on a single map or series of maps is the selection of a *base map*. The base map must be a map that has a number of known points that are readily identifiable on other maps (providing a context for the transfer of data) and that contains data at the same scale and level of accuracy for the entire jurisdiction. When launching a new planning project, a community sometimes discovers that it has separate maps for parts of the community and no accurate base map for the entire community. Under those circumstances, a community may decide to pay for the creation of a base map. There are private firms that can create such a map within a few months using very accurate aerial photography. When such a firm is conducting an aerial survey of the community, some observant citizens will find large "X" figures with a dot in the center painted at (or near) key intersections or staked with cloth in fields. Ground surveyors place those markers to provide ground references for the aerial photographs.

When working on a generalized plan (or a student project), it is often sufficient to use a noncopyrighted street and highway map as the base map for a study. Note, however, that the accuracy and currency of the base map will affect the usefulness of all of the data mapped as part of the study.

The Role of Geographic Information Systems

Later chapters describe some of the ways that planners use data, including mapped data. It is often useful to ask questions like "How much land do we have that is within a half mile of an existing sewer line and that is not in a floodplain?" and "Do we have any land with access to both a railroad line and an interstate highway?"

Landscape architects have long used "overlay" maps to help answer such questions. Instead of creating maps on solid sheets of paper, they make maps on clear layers of acetate. They might show soils on one map, slopes on another, roads and utilities on another, floodplains on another, and existing land use on still another. By laying these acetate sheets on top of one another in a variety of combinations, they can conduct a visual analysis of the characteristics of different parts of the community.

Geographic information systems (GIS) have automated that process. A geographic information system creates the same kinds of maps described above as separate map files and then electronically creates the same kinds of layers described above. Although the traditional acetate maps required that users make hand measurements of things like distance to sewer lines (unless someone had created a separate map layer for that), but a sophisticated GIS system can actually conduct those measurements.

Some GIS systems amount to little more than stored layers of maps. The best modern systems, however, link the maps to database systems. Thus, the user can "click" on a spot on an on-screen map to find nonmapped information like ownership and taxation information, as well as to see the many available layers of mapped data.

One of the greatest challenges in creating a GIS system for a community is to establish an accurate base map. Many communities that believed that they had reasonably accurate maps discovered, when staff members entered those maps into a computer, that there were many errors, ranging from inches to feet. Resolving that problem may be as simple as having a skilled GIS professional "rubbersheet" the maps together, making minor adjustments in each map until all the boundaries fit together, or as complex as resurveying and remapping much of the community. Communities whose GIS system was acquired by the tax department to keep track of parcels may discover that such a system is not accurate or sophisticated enough to be used for planning.

Mapping Land Use

The most visible part of most community plans is a map showing current land-use patterns and plans for future land use. Current land use is rarely mapped, so planners often have to make such maps in the first stages of a planning study. To plan for future land use, it is essential to know what the current patterns of land use are. See color plate 1 for an example. Typically, planners present existing land use as a map, with supporting tables summarizing the data. The maps often include major transportation routes. See color plate 4 for an example of an integrated transportation and land-use plan.

The basic categories included on a land-use map are: industrial, commercial, residential, and agricultural. Other uses commonly designated on such maps are: vacant, park and recreation, and institutional. Many communities identify two or more categories of residential land use, broken down by density. Some identify separate categories of commercial uses, although that is less common.

Based largely on an earlier edition of the Kaiser, Godschalk, and Chapin book *Urban Land Use Planning,* cited at the end of chapter 3,[15] the color scheme shown in table 1.2 is widely accepted in the planning profession (see color plates 1 and 2). Early GIS systems, which largely used black-and-white data storage and printers, substituted various schemes of cross-hatching for these color codes (the method illustrated in the current edition of Godschalk et al.); the color codes are very useful for display maps for large meetings, however, and seem likely to continue. Color plate 1 shows an example of an existing land-use map.

For more details on creating an existing land-use map, see chapter 3.

Table 1.2. Color Coding for Land-Use Maps

Use	Color
Low-density residential	Yellow
Medium-density residential	Light orange
High-density residential	Orange
Commercial	Red
Industrial	Purple or gray
Open space	Green
Agriculture	Brown (not used consistently)

Conclusion

Understanding the context in which community planning in the United States occurs—that of democratically elected local governments—is essential to understanding the planning process described in the chapters that follow. The next chapter describes the comprehensive plan.

The Role of the Professional Planner

As the discussion under "Planning in a Contemporary Democracy" in this chapter suggests, it is important to remember at all stages that good community plans are the products of the community, not its planners. However, professional planners do play essential roles in the planning effort, which include:

- gathering background data
- analyzing and interpreting that data
- communicating that data to the planning body and the public
- organizing and often facilitating meetings of the planning body
- organizing and often facilitating meetings and other means of obtaining participation from interested citizens
- compiling, organizing, and analyzing comments from meetings
- projecting current trends and developing alternative scenarios, to help the planning body understand the implications of different decisions
- turning the policy decisions of the planning body into a plan document
- making the plan document accessible and meaningful to the larger public
- managing the process of final public hearings, final amendments, and adoption

- preparing and publishing the final plan
- educating public officials and the public at large about the plan
- monitoring the plan and its implementation

Most of the words, maps, tables, charts, and illustrations in the final plan will be those of the professional planners involved, but the plan, its policies, and its objectives should reflect the will of the community, as represented by the planning body.

Some planners would prefer to be left alone in their offices to develop plans for the future of the community. That would be a far simpler process than the one described in this book—but it would also ultimately be unsuccessful. Because the success of a plan depends heavily on the elected officials of a community and the citizens who elect them, good planning processes involve those groups in the development of the plan. What has made this field exciting and challenging to us and to the many professionals with whom we have worked is the very challenge of facilitating a democratic process that leads to a consensus in support of a new and truly comprehensive plan for the future of a community.

The Role of the Individual Citizen

A community plan ought to represent the will of the community, which is made up of its citizens. Thus, the fundamental role of the citizen in the process is that of planner. Though the professional planner plays a major role in making the process work, citizens, or the bodies representing them, should make community plans.

In most parts of the United States, planning is carried out by a planning commission or other special body appointed to represent the citizens of the community in the planning process. It is easier for a smaller, representative body to give form to a plan than for a town meeting of some sort to do so. There is an old adage that a camel is a horse put together by a committee. Community plans, prepared through a participatory, democratic process, are often unwieldy. The professional planners involved should help guide the commission in taking some of the extra humps off the camel, but a plan resulting from such a process is unlikely to look like a thoroughbred, certainly not one that is ready to win the Kentucky Derby. Few communities are in a race, however. The goal is to move forward—deliberately, decisively, knowingly—to *define* the future rather than simply to let it happen.

Sometimes the role of interested citizens must begin before the planning process itself—sometimes it is the initiative of individual citizens that leads a community to make the decision to prepare a new plan. Nearly half of the planning projects in which we have been involved began because of substantial grassroots support from one or more interested groups in a community. Thus, a citizen who believes that her or his community ought to create a new plan can often play an important role in making that happen.

EXERCISES

1. Identify two or three different kinds of plans that you have made for yourself or your family during the last year. Where these long-range or short-range plans? What data was involved in making the plans? Were the policy decisions difficult to make, or did the data make it obvious which choice made sense?

2. Identify at least one group planning effort in which you have been involved, in an organization, a class, or a dorm. Who made the policy decision for that group? Did you vote? How did the group decide who would make the policy decision? What approach to planning did it use?

3. Identify all of the systems of which you are a part. For at least one of those systems, try to identify all of the systems of which it is a part. Try to draw a schematic diagram showing how the systems relate to one another. How is energy exchanged between each system and its environment?

4. If you wanted to show your whole community on a map that would fit on one page of the local newspaper, what scale would you use? Can you find a map at about that scale? Is that a realistic scale to show details about land use and other factors in your community?

5. Gather as many maps as you can find about your community. Compare their currency, scale, apparent accuracy, and other information. How easy would it be to combine the information from all of those maps onto one?

DISCUSSION QUESTION

Should the policy-making body for community plans be an elected body or an appointed one, removed from politics? Why?

FURTHER READING

Ackoff, Russell. 1968. *A Concept of Corporate Planning*. New York: Wiley-Interscience. An examination of planning in a corporate context by one of the founders of operations research and a leader in systems analysis.

————. 1978. *The Art of Problem Solving: Accompanied by Ackoff's Fables.* New York: John Wiley. A systems approach to problem solving, presented in a lively and user-friendly format.

Braybrooke, David, and Charles E. Lindblom. 1970. *A Strategy of Decision: Policy Evaluation as a Social Process.* New York: The Free Press. A classic work on how public decisions are made.

Churchman, G. West. 1968. *The Systems Approach.* New York: Delacorte Press. Probably THE classic work on systems thinking.

Forester, John. 1989. *Planning in the Face of Power.* Berkeley: University of California Press. A readable but scholarly treatment of planning in the context of politics.

Kelly, Eric Damian. 1986. "Planning vs. Democracy." *Land Use Law & Zoning Digest* 38, no. 7 (July). A brief essay on one approach to achieving a balance between planning and democracy.

Makower, Joel, ed. 1990. *The Map Catalog,* 2nd edition. New York: Vintage Books. A very detailed description of many types of available maps. It is far more than a catalog, with good descriptions of the different types of maps and their appropriate uses.

Scott, Mel. 1971. *American City Planning,* paperback edition. Los Angeles: University of California Press. An extremely thorough treatment of planning history, providing a useful context for those not familiar with the evolution of the concepts discussed in this book.

NOTES

1. Discussed in Mel Scott, *American City Planning.* Los Angeles, CA: University of California Press (1971), 50–56.
2. See *Extending the Legacy: Planning the Nation's Capital for the 21st Century,* Washington: National Capital Planning Commission (not dated, but transmittal letter shows date of 1997).
3. See the Homestead Act of 1862, an act of the Thirty-Seventh Congress, Session II, Chapter 75.
4. For a description of this process, see Daniel J. Elazar, *Cities of the Prairie: the Metropolitan Frontier and American Politics,* Lanham, MD: University Press of America (1976).
5. For a historical account of the evolution of this survey system, see Elazar, pp. 115–122.
6. See Ethan Carr, *Wilderness by Design: Landscape Architecture and the National Park Service,* Lincoln, NE: University of Nebraska Press (1998).
7. See Henry Moon, *The Interstate Highway System,* Washington, D.C.: Association of American Geographers (1994).
8. For a good discussion of these laws, see John Reps, *Town Planning in Frontier America,* Columbia: University of Missouri Press (paperback edition, 1980; originally published by Princeton University Press, 1965 and 1969).
9. See http://mapping.usgs.gov/ or contact USGS by mail at 508 National Center, Reston, VA 20192, for catalogs and other information.
10. Ibid.
11. From the *Soil Survey Manual,* Ecological Sciences Division, Natural Resources

Conservation Service, as quoted at http://www.nhq.nrcs.usda.gov/BCS/soil/survey. html.

12. See http://www.nhq.nrcs.usda.gov/BCS/soil/survey.html or write NRCS, P.O. Box 2890, Washington, DC 20013.

13. See http://tiger.census.gov/cgi-bin/mapbrowse.

14. See http://www.fema.gov/MSC/hardcopy.htm or Federal Emergency Management Agency, Map Service Center, P.O. Box 1038, Jessup, MD 20794.

15. Chapin, F. Stuart, Jr., and Edward J. Kaiser, *Urban Land Use Planning,* 3rd edition, Champaign: University of Illinois Press (1979).

Chapter 2

....

Introduction to the Comprehensive Plan

The comprehensive plan is a tangible representation of what a community wants to be in the future. It may consist of a short report or of multiple volumes. Some plans illustrate the future primarily with maps and pictures, while others describe it in text. (The form of the plan is addressed in more depth in chapter 8.) This chapter discusses the substance of a comprehensive plan, and chapters 3 and 4 describe the kinds of data gathering and analysis that provide the background and context for an effective plan.

Before we discuss the details of how to develop a comprehensive plan, however, it will be helpful to understand what a comprehensive plan is. A good contractor can build a house from plans without ever seeing a picture of what the finished house is supposed to look like, but the job is easier and more satisfying if the contractor and the key workers have seen a picture and know what it is they are trying to build. In this chapter you will get a sense of what a comprehensive plan is—or should be.

Some communities may use the term *master plan* or *general plan* to refer to the document that this book calls a comprehensive plan. The name does not matter, but the contents do. Three important factors, first presented in the introduction, make a plan comprehensive:

- *Geographical coverage.* A comprehensive plan should include all of the land area subject to the planning or regulatory jurisdiction of the local government preparing the plan.
- *Subject matter.* A comprehensive plan should include all subject matter related to the physical development of the community: land use, transportation, water and wastewater, drainage, parks and open space, school sites, other public and institutional activities, floodplains, and wetlands. In addition, the

comprehensive plan should include at least the physical aspects of plans related to economic development and other programs. A comprehensive plan may be broader and may actually include some programmatic plans (such as economic development or recreation), but it must include at least all of the physical plans for the community's future.

- *Time horizon.* A comprehensive plan must consider a relatively long time horizon. Professional planners in the United States generally use a time horizon of about twenty years for comprehensive planning; time horizons longer than that tend to exceed our abilities to predict and control the future, and time horizons shorter than that are too short to encourage comprehensive thinking. Over a time horizon that long, the community will have the opportunity to change some of the variables that affect its future— things like the location and capacity of roadways and other infrastructure.

The 1992 General Plan for Las Vegas, Nevada, included the following definition and statement of purpose:

> *It is generalized:* It provides general guidance and direction for City growth and development. More specific guidance is given with the implementation tools of the General Plan, which include (primarily) the City's Zoning Regulations and Subdivision Regulations, and the Capital Improvements Plan for financing of public improvements.
>
> *It is comprehensive:* In addition to the primary components of Land Use, Community Facilities and Circulation, the General Plan addresses all of the components which affect the physical, economic and social concerns of the City and its residents. The elements include: Infrastructure (sewer, water supply, flood control, and solid waste); Public Finance; Economic Development; Housing; Urban Design; Environmental Quality and Natural Resource Conservation; and Historic Preservation.
>
> *It is long range:* It plans not only for the pressing concerns of today, but considers the ultimate needs of the community, with projections for "buildout" scenarios of its population, based on recommended future land uses.
>
> The General Plan is intended to function as a policy document that will guide growth and development within the City.[1]

Comprehensive Plan Defined: Examples

In a classic work, T.J. Kent defined the "general plan" (using the language of the law of California, where he had much of his career) as a document of local government that: "sets forth its major policies concerning desirable future physical development; the published general plan document must include a single, unified general physical design for the community, and it must attempt to clarify the relationships between physical-development policies and social and economic goals."[2]

The Standard City Planning Enabling Act, which provided the model for most state planning laws, set out this purpose for the master plan:

> The plan shall be made with the general purpose of guiding and accomplishing a coordinated, adjusted, and harmonious development of the municipality and its environs which will, in accordance with present and future needs, best promote health, safety, morals, order, convenience, prosperity, and general welfare, as well as efficiency and economy in the process of development; including, among other things, adequate provision for traffic, the promotion of safety from fire and other dangers, adequate provision for light and air, the promotion of the healthful and convenient distribution of population, the promotion of good civic design and arrangement, wise and efficient expenditures of public funds, and the adequate provision of public utilities and other public requirements.[3]

The South Carolina planning law, originally based on the standard acts but significantly revised nearly seventy years after publication of those acts, suggests, more simply, that the plan should be considered the expression of recommendations regarding "the wise and efficient use of public funds, the future growth, development, and redevelopment of its area of jurisdiction, and consideration of the fiscal impact on property owners."[4] In short, the comprehensive plan, like any good plan, provides a context for important future decisions.

Among the kinds of decisions that a comprehensive plan helps to guide are:

- *Requests to change zoning* of a particular parcel of land; the comprehensive plan provides the community with a context of proposed future land uses as well as information about the availability of future services to support proposed land uses.
- *Decisions about expansion of major infrastructure,* such as sewer or water plants or major roadways; the comprehensive plan provides a realistic assessment of the probable need for such expansion.
- *Decisions about location of new infrastructure,* such as individual sewer and water lines or new fire stations or parks; by indicating the probable and/or desirable future directions for growth in the community, the plan shows where infrastructure is most likely to be useful.
- *Decisions about annexation of additional territory;* for those communities that can expand their boundaries under applicable state law, only the comprehensive plan provides the broad context that allows them to make rational decisions about whether, when, and where to undertake such expansions.

- *Decisions about major public investments,* such as stadiums, conventions centers, and other facilities; the comprehensive plan shows where similar facilities are or will be located and where such essential supporting facilities as access roads and parking are available.

The development and use of comprehensive plans is not limited to cities and towns. Counties, some regional entities, and a limited number of state agencies use comprehensive plans as basic tools of decision making. In the last decade, a number of states have turned to these plans as a foundation for growth management techniques. Recognizing the need for coordinated efforts in growth management, Florida, Oregon, and Washington have legislatively mandated the creation and even the implementation of comprehensive plans by all local governments.

Historic Evolution of the Comprehensive Plan

Comprehensive planning has roots in the City Beautiful movement, dating in large part to the Columbian Exposition in Chicago in 1892, as well as in the governmental reform movement of the early twentieth century. A 1912 summary reported the planning efforts of twenty-eight cities, ranging from the predictable ones such as New York City and Los Angeles to such diverse communities as Waterloo, Iowa; Bangor, Maine; Reading, Pennsylvania; and Oklahoma City.[5] Not surprisingly, during a period when the City Beautiful movement was extremely influential and when landscape architects like Warren Manning, Charles Mulford Robinson, and Frederick Law Olmsted were among the most active planning consultants, a major focus of these early planning efforts was on parks, green spaces, and public buildings and places.

As early as 1911, Frederick Law Olmsted, Jr., began to espouse the concept of comprehensive planning. In an address to the National Conference on City Planning that year, Olmsted outlined the scope of comprehensive planning, which dealt with guiding physical growth and development.[6] Comprehensive planning received its most serious attention in the work of a commission appointed by Secretary of Commerce Herbert Hoover in 1921. Initially, it was called the Advisory Commission on Zoning; later, recognizing an expanded scope, it became the Advisory Committee on City Planning and Zoning. Leading the commission was lawyer Edward Bassett, who had led the team that drafted the nation's first comprehensive zoning ordinance, for New York City, which adopted the ordinance in 1926. Although the initial focus of this advisory committee was on preparing a model zoning act, to respond to a rapidly growing interest in that tool, the commission later expanded its efforts to include planning as well. The results of the commission's work, the Standard Zoning Enabling Act of 1926, and the Standard City Planning Enabling Act of 1928, were published by the Department of Commerce as model laws for use by the states.

Ultimately, every state adopted some form of the Standard Zoning Enabling Act, and most adopted at least some of the elements of the planning act. Although some states have updated their laws, all such laws have their roots in these two model acts. Updates and amendments to the laws have focused on making planning more effective, not on redefining its nature. Two distinct but limited trends characterize many of these later planning acts: (1) provisions making planning mandatory for some or all local governments; and (2) language requiring that local governments consider their plans as more than general, advisory documents

The Standard City Planning Enabling Act first defined a master plan and created the concept of planning by an appointed planning commission. The act required that a plan include recommendations for:

> the general location, character, and extent of streets, viaducts, sub-
> ways, bridges, waterways, water fronts, boulevards, parkways, play-
> grounds, squares, parks, aviation fields, and other public ways,
> grounds and open spaces, the general location of public buildings
> and other public property, and the general location and extent of
> public utilities and terminals, whether publicly or privately owned
> or operated, for water, light, sanitation, transportation, communica-
> tion, power, and other purposes; also the removal, relocation, widen-
> ing, narrowing, vacating, abandonment, change of use or extension
> of any of the foregoing ways, grounds, open spaces, buildings, prop-
> erty, utilities, or terminals; as well as a zoning plan for the control of
> the height, area, bulk, location, and use of buildings and premises.[7]

Although this early model law provided communities with the legal authority to plan, planning was not nearly as widely implemented as zoning in the early days. Publication of this model law was followed only a year later by the stock market crash and the beginning of the Great Depression. By the time the economy began serious recovery from the depression, the country was preparing for World War II and all planning efforts were focused on the need for military men and supplies. Construction of training camps, air bases, and war production factories was driven by the strategic needs of the military, not by any sort of local planning.

It was only after World War II that the nation experienced the kind of private growth and development that precipitated the need and demand for comprehensive planning for communities. As the federal-aid highway program of the 1950s and the federal participation in mortgage guarantees (begun in 1948) facilitated the spread of growth to the new suburbs, there was a significant increase in the interest in planning. A number of schools started planning programs to supply professionals for an increasing number of local planning agencies. Then, in the Housing Act of 1954, Congress included a subsidy for local planning, generally known as the 701 program, referring to the section of the law that contained it. Through that program, which reached the height of its funding in the 1970s, the Federal Housing Administration and, later, the Department of Housing and Urban Development, provided funding for thousands of local governments to develop comprehensive, or master, plans. Many local governments used consultants to prepare those initial plans, but others hired staff—and many of those then found local funding to keep the planning staff after the federal funding ran out.

The "208" program for regional planning for sewage treatment extended the federal subsidy to planning for several years. Funded by the Environmental Protection Agency (EPA) under section 208 of the Federal Water Pollution Control Act Amendments of 1972, the program provided many regional agencies with an opportunity to develop an environmental database for planning and to develop regional plans for wastewater treatment.

By the 1980s, federal subsidies to comprehensive planning were largely a thing of the past, although some planning agencies have obtained funding from federal programs for particular projects. Nevertheless, the programs had had an impact, significantly increasing the number of plans, planners, and planning agencies in the nation. Planning had become an accepted, and an expected, activity for most local governments with a population of 20,000 or more or with a significant trend of growth or change.

Elements of a Comprehensive Plan

Planners talk about "elements" of a plan. Typically, the term *element* refers to a part of the plan that deals with a discrete subject, such as transportation or parks and open spaces. Less frequently, a plan element may deal with a specific geographical part of the community, such as the downtown. In many plans, elements are simply chapters of a larger report, which is collectively called the comprehensive plan. In some communities, however, elements are published as separate reports; some of those may be so large that they seem like separate plans. Many communities refer to the transportation element of the local plan as the circulation element.

The examples below illustrate the kinds of elements that communities typically include in plans. Some state laws are very specific about elements a plan must contain; others leave the local government with great discretion about the contents of the plan. A community preparing a plan must address all of the elements required by its state law. It is useful, however, to see some examples of the topics that plans typically cover.

The South Carolina planning law, which was updated in 1996, requires the following basic parts to a comprehensive plan:

- an inventory of existing conditions;
- a statement of needs and goals; and
- implementation strategies with time frames.[8]

It is important always to remember the focus on "community." Here, students at McClelland School in Pueblo, Colorado, are shown with the "box city" that they built to help them better understand planning for their own community. Photo by C. Gregory Dale, AICP.

Comprehensive plans have long included inventories of existing conditions, and a "statement of needs and goals" is implicit in the very concept of planning. Only in the 1990s, however, did local plans begin to include implementation elements, a concept discussed in part III of this book.

The South Carolina law requires that the plan address at least the following subject-matter elements:

- a *population* element that considers historic trends and projections, household numbers and sizes, educational levels, and income characteristics;
- an *economic development* element that considers labor force and labor force characteristics, employment by place of work and residence, and analysis of the economic base;
- a *natural resources* element that considers coastal resources, slope characteristics, prime agricultural and forest land, plant and animal habitats, parks and recreation areas, scenic views and sites, wetlands, and soil types;
- a *cultural resources* element that considers historic buildings and structures; commercial districts; residential districts; unique, natural, or scenic resources, archaeological and other cultural resources;
- a *community facilities* element that considers the transportation network; water supply, treatment, and distribution; sewage system and wastewater

treatment; solid waste collection and disposal; fire protection; emergency medical services; general government facilities; education facilities; and libraries and other cultural facilities;

- a *housing* element that considers location, types, age, and condition of housing; owner and renter occupancy; and affordability of housing; and
- a *land-use* element that considers existing and future land use by categories, including residential, commercial, industrial, agricultural, forestry, mining, public and quasipublic, recreation, parks, open space, and vacant or undeveloped.[9]

A 1997 plan adopted by Norman, Oklahoma, included the following background sections, which provided the basis for the rest of the plan:

- identification of *planning issues;*
- map and summary of *existing land uses;*
- analysis of *development capacity* (based in large part on community facilities); and
- projection of *future land demand.*

The plan also included these future-oriented sections:

- *goals and policies* on managed growth, infrastructure-supported growth, economic stability and enhancement, nonurban growth, and greenbelt development;
- a mapped *land-use and transportation plan;*
- *special planning areas* (policies for mapped areas);
- *growth areas* (map and policies); and
- *transportation policies* on highways, urban streets, rural roads.[10]

A more complex plan, prepared for the booming city of Las Vegas, Nevada, in 1992, and nearly three inches thick, contained the following general section headings: Introduction, Land Use, Community Facilities, Infrastructure, Circulation, Public Finance, Economic Development, Housing, Urban Design, Environmental Quality, and Historic Preservation.

Every community must comply with the minimum requirements of its state law in developing a plan. Those requirements, however, are fairly general and typically leave communities with great latitude in determining the elements that will make up a plan. Note that it is common and perfectly acceptable practice to develop plan elements as separate reports, even at separate times; as long as they are coordinated and consistent, those multiple separate elements can still form a truly "comprehensive" plan.

The actual content of a plan will vary considerably from one community to another. Florida, Oregon, and California have longer lists of "required" planning elements than many other states. In states without long lists of state requirements, the depth of the plan may vary with the size of the community, the availability of a budget for a detailed plan, and the inclinations of the planning body and the planning agency that supports its efforts.

Role of the Planning Commission

The planning commission is the body charged with both the power and the legal duty to prepare the comprehensive plan in most states, as described in chapter 1. This section describes that body.

Why Planning Commissions Exist

Planning and zoning in this country evolved from a number of roots, including the government reform movement of the early twentieth century. From that movement, which was led in significant part by engineers, came a number of efforts to make government more professional and less political. One of the most significant results of that is the civil service system, a merit-based system of hiring and retaining public employees that replaced the old patronage system of hiring public employees in the federal government, most state agencies, and most local governments. That reform directly affects planning, because many local government planners have the job security of civil service laws, protecting them from discharge by political whim or vendetta.

The entire system of planning and zoning, with its planned and rational structure for land-use decisions, is representative of the values of the government reform movement. The most tangible remaining evidence of the influence of the government reformers in the system, however, is the existence of the planning commission. All of our zoning laws today and most of our planning laws trace their history to the Standard Zoning Enabling Act and the Standard City Planning Enabling Act. One of the fundamental concepts included in the system was that of removing planning from politics. Thus, rather than placing planning responsibility with the city council, county commissions, or other local legislative body, those model acts created the predecessor of today's planning, or planning and zoning, commission. Under those laws, and under most state laws today, the primary responsibility for planning was assigned to the planning commission. Although many states today require or at least allow for approval of a plan by the governing body, under early versions of the laws, as widely adopted, the planning commission simply "certified" a plan to the governing body.

There is a good deal of logic in assigning the planning function to an appointed body that is not involved in the day-to-day functions of government. Legislative bodies are often bogged down with the minutiae of parking ordinances, local budgets, negotiations of labor agreements, and the other complexities of local government. Thus, it is often difficult for the elected members of a legislative body to devote the time for reflection and study that

Richard Hedman on public meetings. Copyright by Richard Hedman. Used with permission.

is critical to the development of a good plan. Further, as the drafters of those early laws perceived, elected officials are often so focused on the immediate issues facing them that it is difficult for them to focus on a long-term view of the sort that is essential for a truly comprehensive plan. In those respects, the original model is useful.

As the boxes at the end of the chapters in this book suggest, however, much of the work of developing a plan falls to the professional planners in the agency that supports the planning commission. In most communities, those planners, whether staff or consultant, effectively report to the executive branch of the government—for it is the executive branch that controls their consulting contracts or salaries, that determines their annual budgets, that helps to set their work programs, and that supervises and evaluates their work. Thus, the planning commission has the legal authority and duty to develop a plan, but the professionals who do most of the work report to someone else. In many local governments, there is good cooperation among elected officials, executive and professional staff, and the appointed planning commission. In those communities, the system can work reasonably well, but the appointed commission also seems less necessary in such a context. In most communities, there will be consensus on many goals. Where the issue of control of the work of the planning staff becomes important is on contentious issues—like the routing of a new road. On such issues, the scope and nature of technical studies may steer the policy decision in a particular direction.

Thus, despite the best efforts of the government reformers, planning remains political with a small *p*. At its best, it transcends politics and builds consensus across political coalitions. At its worst, it can become so embroiled in local political issues that it loses its credibility and effectiveness.

Current Challenges

The biggest conceptual problem with the idea of delegating the planning function to an appointed body arises at the stage of implementation. Part 3 of this book examines the implementation of plans—making plans work.

As you will see in the chapters of part 3, the governing body makes many of the critical decisions that determine whether a plan becomes reality. It is the governing body that decides what new roads to build, what new parks to fund, and what changes to make to the zoning map. Where the original model of the apolitical planning commission fails is in the expectation that political officials will follow an apolitical plan in making political decisions. One of the fundamental requirements of a comprehensive plan is that residents, landowners, and others who will be affected by a plan must play a role in developing that plan. Clearly, the same principle applies to elected officials, whose official roles should be guided by the plan. To expect a governing body to abide by an apolitical plan that it has not helped to develop is no more realistic than to expect a college junior to attend a series of 8 A.M. classes that her parents picked for her without her participation. It is unlikely to happen.

The model of the appointed planning commission fails in another respect in many communities today. Many planning commissions have become so overwhelmed with decisions about proposed zoning map amendments, subdivisions, and site plans that they have become essentially permit-review bodies that lack the time for study and reflection—for real planning. Further, in rapidly changing communities, where both business people and residents are interested in the development process, these bodies often become subject to nearly as much political pressure as elected officials.

Creating a Practical Process

A critical element in the success of a planning effort is its leadership: the planning body. That can be the governing body, the planning commission, the two working together, or a steering committee or task force appointed specifically to undertake the process. Although sometimes a professional staff leads a planning effort, plans are more likely to attract broad community support if they are led by interested citizens, whether elected or appointed. Thus, the starting point in most planning efforts must be identification of the entity that will conduct the planning process.

In many communities, the planning commission will be the logical body to take primary responsibility regarding the policy issues involved in the planning process. That is typically what state law requires, and that is typically the expectation both of planning commission members and of the community that they serve. Where the planning commission lacks the time or the interest to play that role, it is common today to create a steering committee or task force to manage a comprehensive planning process. One advantage of using a

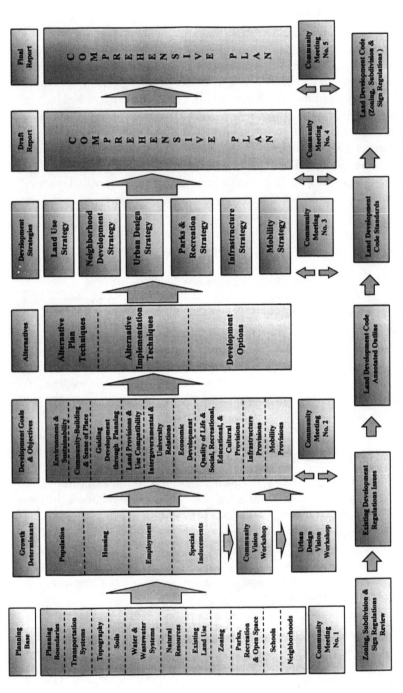

This comprehensive planning process chart shows a process that begins with collection of data on existing conditions, followed by an opportunities and constraints analysis (growth determinants), which then feeds through a community determination of goals and objectives. From those steps, planners lay out alternatives and work with the community to develop plan alternatives and then the elements of the final plan. Source: RM Plan Group, Nashville (1998).

steering committee is that it can be made larger than the planning commission (the size of which is usually restricted under state law to five, seven, or nine members) and thus can be more representative of the larger community. A task force or steering committee of limited duration, with a specific focus, will sometimes attract community leaders who may be unwilling to make the time commitment to serve on the planning commission.

In some small communities, the governing body may have both the time and the interest to play a leading role in the development of a plan. Most governing bodies in larger communities or in rapidly growing ones are too busy to tackle such a project, but there are communities where the governing body wants to lead the planning process.

The body selected as the planning body for a particular community must then address the other issues raised here. If that body is not the governing body, then it must determine how to involve the governing body in the process, long before the plan is in final form. Similarly, if the planning commission will not lead the planning process, then the steering committee or task force must decide how to involve the planning commission. Typically, it is a good idea to have one or two representatives of the governing body and the planning commission on the planning body, but it is also important to hold periodic meetings with those other bodies to inform them of and involve them in the development of the plan.

The planning body then must arrange for the performance of the technical, professional, and administrative work that will support the planning effort. That work ranges from gathering basic data about the population, the economy, and the environment of the community, to making projections for the future and developing alternative future scenarios. Further, there is a good deal of administrative work involved in supporting any complex process—sending out meeting notices; taking minutes; following up requests for information; answering correspondence and phone calls; and preparing the final plan reports, maps; and related materials.

In many communities, a professional planning staff undertakes all of those tasks. The staff that supports the process need not necessarily be in the planning office, although staff members should have a planning background. In some communities, planners working at the chamber of commerce, a community development agency, or even a local utility support the planning process.

Where the planning staff is small or its time is severely constrained, it often makes sense to hire a consultant to handle the technical and/or administrative work on a plan. Although consultants may seem expensive, it is often cheaper to hire a consultant for a year or two than to add a full-time planner and an extra support person to the staff for the long term; thus, many communities choose the consultant option.

The importance of the governing body to this entire undertaking will immediately become apparent—the staff or consultant to support the techni-

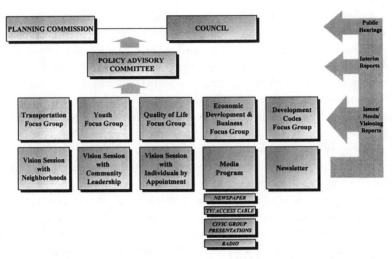

This citizen participation process chart shows the use of focus groups, goal-setting (vision) sessions with selected stakeholder groups, key person interviews, and a broad public input process (including media), all filtered through a "policy advisory committee," which serves as the planning body. Source: *Christie McGetrick, The Burnham Group, Little Rock (1998).*

cal effort will cost money, and, in most cases, that money will come, directly or indirectly, from the governing body. Even where an existing planning staff will support the planning effort, that staff either will require additional help or will have to set aside other duties while it undertakes the planning process; both have fiscal implications for the local government—exactly the sort of issues that governing bodies address.

Then the planning body must determine how it will involve citizens in the process (see box at the end of the chapter). The traditional model of planning involved the preparation of a plan by the planning body, with help from professional staff or consultants, and presentation of that plan to interested persons at a public hearing. That is still the model included in most state laws.

The difficulty with that model is that it brings citizens into the process very late. A planning body may have spent as much as 80 percent of its planning schedule and budget by the time it has a draft ready for public hearing. If citizens at that point identify new issues or suggest entirely different concepts or approaches, it may be too late to include those ideas in the plan. Public hearings typically result only in fine tuning around the edges. Further, it may be difficult for citizens to comment effectively on a comprehensive and holistic document. Although the state laws mentioned above only require formal hearings at the end, common planning practice is to include citizens earlier in the process, where they can influence the creation of the plan.

Thus, today most planning efforts involve citizens very early in the process.

Although the mechanics are discussed in more depth in chapters 3 and 4, it is important to understand the alternative conceptual approaches by which that may be accomplished. The approaches to planning described in chapter 1 have very different effects on citizen participation.

The *issue identification* approach (discussed in more depth in chapter 4) involves citizens in defining much of the scope of the planning effort. As suggested in the previous chapter, a true *vision* usually comes from a leader or leadership group, and the only real role of citizens is in validating and helping to define it. Goal setting is an approach that is more open to citizen participation; some goal-setting processes involve citizens at every stage, but some simply involve the planning body, with reaction from citizens at a public hearing. Plans built around *trends* in population, employment, land use, and housing are often highly technical and may not involve much opportunity for citizen participation; when the trend projections are used as the basis for goal setting, citizens can still participate in the other process. When *opportunities and constraints* define the plan, the work may be heavily technical, also without a lot of opportunity for citizen participation; again, if the opportunities and constraints analysis is used as a basis for goal setting, citizens can participate effectively in the goal setting.

The decision about how and when citizens will be involved in the process is a critical one and that can influence the entire rest of the process. Chapter 5 addresses in more detail the logistics of citizen involvement, but it is important to understand that the choice of a planning method has a significant effect on the role of citizens in it.

The other major issue that must be considered at the beginning of the process is the role of the governing body. A number of states now require or encourage governing body action on a proposed plan, but there is nothing in any state law that prevents a governing body from ratifying, accepting, or otherwise taking formal action on a plan. Clearly, a plan formally approved in some way by the governing body will have greater stature before that governing body and before the rest of the community than one that is not so approved. Thus, this is a critical step, and it is one that should be contemplated from the beginning—so that as governing body members attend work sessions with the planning body to discuss the plan, they know that they will ultimately be asked to vote on it.

Updating the Plan

Completing a community plan for the next twenty years does not mean that planning is finished for two decades. Comprehensive plans require regular review and revision for two reasons: first, new circumstances may dictate changes in the plan; second, the community's goals may change. Changes in technology have radically affected many local plans, and the values of many communities have changed. Further, as the nation has moved from an industrial economy to a heavily service-based economy, many fundamental assumptions about land use and transportation planning have changed; commuting patterns are much more complex than they once were, because working patterns are more complex. Finally, some things just do not work out as planned—a policy proposed and implemented in good faith may have failed or had unintended consequences; for example, a city may try to limit its growth and discover that the result is sprawling growth in rural areas, creating worse traffic problems and higher costs for providing infrastructure.

Although the comprehensive plan is long term, it should be formally reviewed annually and updated at least every five years. The updating process should include a comparison of current data to goals and projections in the plan, as well as a review of the substance of goals, objectives, and policies. In a rapidly growing community, the twenty-year plan may require a major revision or even a replacement planning program after about ten years. Other communities may be able to rely on a twenty-year plan for fifteen years or more, but all should begin a new planning process before reaching the time horizon specified in the original.

Why update a twenty-year plan in five years and replace it in ten or fifteen? It is a twenty-year plan in concept, not in reality. The reason for looking twenty years out is that decisions made today about building new streets and sewers and allowing rezonings for new homes and shopping centers will affect the physical future of the community for at least twenty years, typically even more. Thus, in making those decisions, it is critical to think about what the community will be like ten or twenty years in the future. By 2015, a 2020 plan conceived in 2000 will be short-sighted, even if it was an innovative and forward-looking plan when it was adopted.

Conclusion

Through comprehensive planning, a community can choose and design its own future. The future will come, and local officials will make decisions about it whether or not they plan. Only through planning, however, can a community collectively make rational choices for a sustainable future. The following chapters describe the elements and processes that make up a successful comprehensive plan.

The Role of the Professional Planner

The professional planner provides all of the technical and professional work that support a good comprehensive planning process. The particular tasks typically include the following:

Professional Tasks

- gathering data on existing conditions (chapter 3)
- mapping appropriate data on existing conditions (chapter 3)
- developing projections for the future, based on existing trends or other scenarios (chapter 4);
- designing, administering, and analyzing surveys to gather citizen input regarding strengths, weaknesses, and issues of the community (chapter 5)
- developing possible responses to analyses of strengths and weaknesses, opportunities and constraints (chapter 4)
- developing analyses of issues identified through surveys or other parts of the planning process (chapter 4)
- preparing maps, reports, and other final plan documents (chapter 8)

Administrative Tasks

- organizing meetings
- sending out officials meeting notices and otherwise publicizing meetings
- keeping minutes and other records of meetings
- coordinating the work of consultants
- managing the planning budget
- managing reports and data and making them accessible to the planning body and to interested citizens
- educating the planning body and the community at large about the importance of issues that might otherwise be overlooked—issues like the importance of the natural environment or the need for more housing opportunities for people of limited means (Though this may resemble "advocacy planning," it can also stop short of advocacy and simply provide education.)

Planners are essential participants in the planning process, but they do not make the plans. Good planners help communities make their own plans—and the best plan is one that citizens identify with their own community and its leaders, not with the planners who prepared it.

The Role of the Individual Citizen

The role of citizens in the comprehensive planning process varies widely, although the best plans are typically those that include the most citizen participation, from the beginning to the end of the process.

At least, citizens are entitled to comment on the plan at a formal public hearing before the planning commission adopts it—that is the law in every state.

At best, citizens should help the planning body to:

1. identify important issues on which the planning process will function (chapter 4);
2. identify strengths and weaknesses of the community (chapter 4);
3. develop a vision or goals for the community (chapter 3);
4. comment on alternative plan scenarios and various aspects of the plan as it evolves (part III); and
5. comment formally at a public hearing before the planning commission adopts the plan.

A citizen who is interested in the status of comprehensive planning in the community should contact the planning office within the local government. If there is not an obvious listing for such an office in the telephone directory, a call to the office of the mayor, city manager, or other chief executive of local government is a good place to start.

EXERCISES

1. Does your community have a comprehensive plan? When was it adopted? When was it last reviewed? When was it last updated?
2. If your community has a plan that is five or more years old, with a "future land-use" map in it, take that map and drive, walk, bike, or bus through newer parts of the community—how closely has new development followed that map?
3. Make a table of contents for a new plan for your community; use the laws and examples quoted in this chapter as starting points, but make it to fit your community.
4. Make a list of agencies that you would contact for data to be used in an existing conditions analysis. Even if you do not actually gather the data, at least identify the actual name of the agencies (not just "schools," but the name of the school district, for example) and give a phone number for each. Is any of the data that you would need available in the university library? The public library?

DISCUSSION QUESTION

What body is best suited to prepare a comprehensive plan for your community—the governing body, the planning commission, or some other group? Why? You may not be able to answer this question now, but you should be able to answer it by the time you finish the book. You will need to read the local newspaper regularly, watching for planning-related stories, and you will need to attend at least one meeting of the governing body and one meeting of the planning commission to help you answer it.

FURTHER READING

Hammack, David C. 1988. "Comprehensive Planning before the Comprehensive Plan: A New Look at the Nineteenth Century American City," in *Two Centuries of American Planning,* Daniel Schaffer, ed. Baltimore: Johns Hopkins University Press. An interesting description of the evolution of planning as a government activity in cities in the United States.

Hollander, Elizabeth L., Leslie S. Pollock, Jeffry D. Reckinger, and Frank Beal. 1988. "General Development Plans," in *The Practice of Local Government Planning,* 2nd edition, Frank S. So and Judith Getzels, eds. Washington, DC: International City Management Association. The only chapter on broad-based planning in the 1988 edition of this standard reference work; a new edition is under development as this book goes to press. Hollander and her colleagues describe a much narrower sort of planning than the comprehensive approach discussed in this book.

Kelly, Eric Damian. 1993. *Selecting and Retaining a Planning Consultant: RFQs, RFPs, Contracts and Project Management.* Planning Advisory Service Report No. 443. Chicago: American Planning Association. A technical report that discusses the role of consultants in the development of a comprehensive plan.

Kent, T.J., Jr. 1990. *The Urban General Plan.* Chicago: Planners Press. A classic work on comprehensive planning for cities; excellent reference work.

Reps, John. 1980. *Town Planning in Frontier America.* Columbia: University of Missouri Press. Originally published by Princeton University Press, 1965 and 1969. An excellent historical work on the planning of particular communities in the United States in its earliest decades.

Scott, Mel. 1971. *American City Planning.* Los Angeles: University of California Press. An extremely thorough treatment of planning history, providing a useful context for those not familiar with the evolution of the concepts discussed in this book.

NOTES

1. City of Las Vegas, *General Plan,* adopted by City Council, April 1, 1992.
2. Kent, T.J., Jr., *The Urban General Plan,* Chicago: Planners Press (1990), quotation from p. 189; originally published in 1964.
3. Standard City Planning Enabling Act, §6, Department of Commerce, 1928.
4. South Carolina Code §6-29-510(E).
5. Kimball, Thedora, "A Brief Survey of Recent City Planning Reports in the United States," *Landscape Architecture* 2:111–126 (1912).
6. *Proceedings of the Third National Conference on City Planning,* Philadelphia, May 15–17, 1911.
7. Standard City Planning Enabling Act, ß6, Department of Commerce, 1928.
8. S.C.Code §6-29-510(C).
9. S.C.Code §6-29-510(D).
10. "Norman 2020: Land Use and Transportation Plan," approved by the Norman City Council by Resolution R-9697-57, February 25, 1997.

Chapter 3

Where Are We?
Analysis of Existing Conditions
in the Community

When looking at a map or directory at a mall or an airport, the first thing that most people try to find is the little circle that says, "You are here." Identifying the location of the card store, the food court, or the restroom on the map is useful only in relation to one's current spot in the building; only by knowing both an origin and a destination can one use the map to get from one to the other.

Planning for a community is similar in some ways to finding one's way on a map—even if you know where you want to go, it is important to know where you are before you can determine how to get there. Most communities want more jobs, more recreational opportunities, more diversity of shopping, and more activity downtown. Those may be entirely reasonable goals for a planning process, but there are two reasons it is important to know how many jobs, what recreational opportunities, what shopping diversity, and what downtown activity exist now. First, it is essential to have a benchmark—so that the community will know when it actually has more jobs or more recreational opportunities. Second, it is important to evaluate the community's current situation in comparison to the past, in comparison to accepted standards, or in comparison to similar communities. A community that wants more recreational opportunities may discover, from study, that it has more golf courses per capita than any other community in the state but is short on tennis courts and softball fields. A community that wants more jobs may discover that its unemployment is largely among untrained workers—a finding that would suggest that a job training program might be more important than an economic development program. Alternatively, a community that wants more jobs may discover that its sewage treatment plant is nearly full—a potential problem for economic developers.

Thus, a thorough assessment of existing conditions is an important early step in any major planning process. The gathering and analysis of information and data provide the basis for strategies and policy recommendations that are a part of the comprehensive plan. The use of accurate and timely data is essential in planning. Some communities constantly track the planning data they need—monitoring infrastructure capacities, population changes, housing trends, employment statistics, and other baseline data. Further, some data change more than others. Patterns of land uses in stable neighborhoods may change little between planning efforts; basic geology and soil types typically do not change (except in the case of certain natural disasters). In contrast, traffic conditions and housing patterns on the fringes of growing communities change significantly over time. As a community begins a comprehensive planning process, it may find that some of the essential information about "where we are" already exists. At a minimum, the comprehensive planning process should involve the assembly of that data into a consistent format, using the same base dates, compatible mapping scales, and other techniques to ensure that the "existing conditions" analysis consists of useful information, not just a collection of data.

It is through analyzing and creating projections based on the best possible data and information that planners are able to do comprehensive planning that includes the physical, economic, and social elements that create the community. The use of accurate and timely data is essential to projecting the status of the planning area into the future and providing the basis for strategies and policy recommendations to achieve the different goals set forth in a comprehensive plan.

Data are available from a variety of federal, state, and local sources, from government agencies, universities, research centers, and chambers of commerce and from a variety of data providers, including an increasing number on the Internet. Today the challenge is not finding data but making them useful. Here are the basic steps in gathering data for an existing conditions analysis:

1. Identify the subjects for which data is needed.
2. Assemble all existing reports and studies that include such data within the agency.
3. Check with libraries, universities, and appropriate federal, state, and local agencies for other pertinent data.
4. Review, cross-check, and validate the data.
5. Identify missing data.
6. Develop methodologies for gathering missing data and implement them.
7. Analyze the data and turn them into information in the form of one or more reports, with appropriate maps, charts, tables, and other tools that make the information easily accessible to the planning body, other decision makers, and interested citizens.

What existing conditions ought to be included in the analysis? Some, discussed in the next section, are basic. Others are a matter of choice. Here is the list from the Wichita/Sedgwick County, Kansas, 1993 comprehensive plan, entitled "Preparing for Change":

- population/employment
- physical factors
- land use and growth
- transportation
- water
- sewer
- stormwater
- solid waste
- law enforcement
- fire protection facilities
- emergency medical services
- park and open space
- libraries
- public schools
- historic preservation
- community appearance
- housing and neighborhoods

Any good comprehensive plan will include population, employment, land use, housing, transportation and circulation, parks and recreation, and fire protection and emergency medical facilities. Most will also include community appearance and neighborhoods, and historic preservation elements are increasingly common today. Law enforcement and libraries are often service oriented, operating from existing, central facilities; for that reason, some communities do not include those elements in physically oriented comprehensive plans. Although school facilities should be a key element in any logical local plan, school districts and corporations in many communities act very independently in making decisions about the timing and location of providing school facilities, and they are thus often omitted from the planning process, frequently by their own choice. Even when the schools are not involved in the planning process, however, it is useful to include school facilities in the existing conditions analysis.

Practical Aspects of Existing Conditions Analysis

Analyzing existing conditions is one of the most technical areas of planning. Most academic planning programs have at least two "planning methods" courses focused on it. Although it is not practical or necessary at this stage to provide a rigorous introduction to the assembly and analysis of those data, it is important to introduce some of the basic concepts and provide resources for further study.

Population

One of the first questions anyone asks about a community is "How big is it?" usually meaning "How many people live there?" That is also one of the first questions that planners ask about a community. Fortunately, the U.S. Census, conducted once every ten years, provides a wealth of answers. Long published in multivolume sets and now available on the World Wide Web and on CD-ROM, the census provides more data than most planners need.[1] Some basic census information that is useful to any planning effort includes:

- total population for the community
- total population for the region or, where pertinent, the county
- age of the population (broken down into at least four groups—children up to age eighteen, young adults, the middle-aged, and those sixty-five and over)
- employment patterns of the population
- trends in all of the above, usually for at least the last thirty years (determined algebraically or with graphs from individual census counts)

Community planning rarely starts with a blank slate. It starts with an existing community, and existing conditions analysis provides an objective view of that community. This is downtown Bloomington, Indiana. Photo by Michele Chiuini.

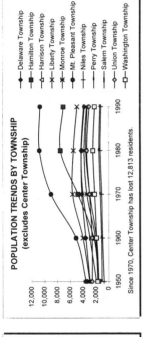

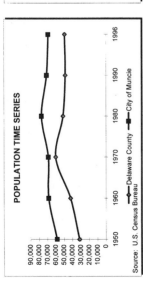

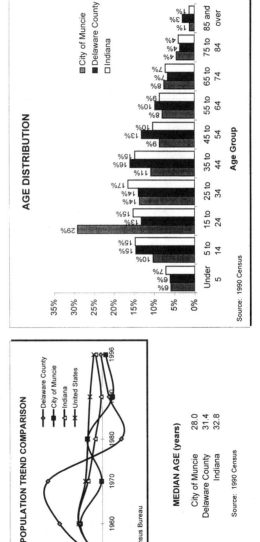

Population trends from the Muncie–Delaware County Comprehensive Plan. These charts show population trends, breaking them out for individual townships within the county and also showing comparisons to state and national trends. Note that although the population actually shrank between 1970 and 1990, the number of households increased by nearly 20 percent over that time because average household size also shrank. Source: HNTB Corp., Indianapolis (1998).

Rapidly growing communities sometimes go to the expense of having a special census taken, but that is too costly for most communities. The official census data are used to determine the growth in population and to profile the population over a long period of time. Official census data are also used as the basis for a number of federal and state grant and funding programs.

One of the fundamental pieces of information to be learned from the population analysis is the long-term trend in population. Growth is a fundamental concern for communities. One way of measuring this is to determine absolute growth or decline, which is calculated by comparing the number of residents in one census to the number of residents in the previous census. Population changes are also often calculated as percentages rather than absolute numbers.

One reason that the census is so widely used is the range of information on the population that it provides. The population is broken down into subgroups by such categories as ethnicity and gender. This information, combined with the age data, makes it possible for communities to analyze the population in terms of such concerns as the aging of the population or even the aging of the population between different census tracts in the community. The census can also illustrate trends in migration and residential mobility, racial and ethnic makeup of the population, and local levels of income and employment, by population group.

While the census is a tremendous source of information, there are some drawbacks in the use of census data. The census may undercount the population because a percentage of the population is not English-speaking or is illiterate and therefore fails to respond to census questions. Factors contributing to a falling response rate to the census include the increase in junk mail that has led people to throw away some mail without opening it; and the growing number of people who don't wish to have contact with or cooperate with the government.[2] While undercounting poses some real problems, particularly in communities where federal grant money is based on population counts, the census does have the advantage of having been conducted over many decades, so that changes in population, employment, housing conditions, and incomes of an area can be traced over time.

One of the most important factors to consider for local government planning is the anticipated future size and composition of the population. Although some communities simply project current growth rates as a basis for predicting future population, there are more accurate methods. Planners can examine the number of people in each age group and their likelihood of living and staying in the community for the next ten or twenty years, as one method of projecting future population; because this method projects the future population of each *cohort* (or age group) of the population, it is often referred to as the cohort method or something similar.

Life insurance companies have developed excellent statistical databases that allow reasonably accurate projection of how many people out of a given group will survive for ten or twenty years. The less predictable variables in population projections are those related to *in-migration* and *out-migration*—or how many people will move into or out of the community over the planning period. That often depends on economic factors that are difficult to project.

Another challenge in projecting population relates to births and family sizes. Birth rates in the United States dropped significantly from 1970 to 1990. That, and later marriage dates, led to shrinking family sizes. Population projections based on 1970 birth rates would likely overstate 1980 and 1990 population figures; in some cases, however, they understated housing needs, because the smaller family size meant that it took more housing units to hold the same number of people.

Housing

Housing is such a critical part of community life that most local governments have housing plans, although most of the housing is provided by the private sector. In addition to population data, the census provides detailed housing information, ranging from unit types to the number of units that are vacant or lack indoor plumbing. Other demographic data commonly utilized from the census include the average household size, the sex and ethnicity of heads of households, and information on the housing stock such as occupant ownership versus rentals, value of housing, and the number of rooms per unit.

Table 3.1. Historical Population Trends for Indiana, Delaware County, and Selected Townships

	Center Township			Mt. Pleasant Township		
	1970	1980	1990	1970	1980	1990
Population	87,469	80,012	74,656	9,008	10,812	10,711
Dwelling Units	31,287	33,475	34,669	2,778	3,969	4,285
Households	29,651	31,255	31,634	2,705	3,807	4,088
Persons per Household	2.95	2.56	2.36	3.33	2.84	2.62

	Delaware County			Indiana		
	1970	1980	1990	1970	1980	1990
Population	129,219	128,587	119,700	5,193,669	5,490,224	5,544,159
Dwelling Units	43,950	51,248	52,341	1,730,099	2,065,115	2,246,046
Households	41,954	48,160	48,462	1,609,494	1,927,050	2,246,046
Persons per Household	3.08	2.67	2.47	3.23	2.85	2.68

Source: U.S. Department of Commerce, Bureau of the Census. Compiled by HNTB Corp. (Indianapolis).

Field surveys provide an important means of assessing housing conditions in a community. In a housing field survey, a planner travels through a neighborhood recording conditions such as peeling paint, broken steps and windows, and sagging porches on a house-by-house basis. With those data, a community can identify residential units needing assistance and entire neighborhoods requiring further study or special help. Field surveys take time and personnel, and the comprehensive planning process is a good opportunity for communities to make an investment in establishing those baseline data on housing and neighborhood conditions. In the future, less rigorous spot checks could be used to identify areas of the community that would need intensive field surveying.

In some communities, the housing stock is reasonably diverse, relatively affordable, and in excellent shape. Other communities have shortages of certain housing types. Only by analyzing the housing data from the census (or other sources) is it possible to determine the adequacy of a community's current housing situation. If there are deficiencies in the housing stock, it will be

Table 3.2. Housing Tenure and Units in Structures for Ames, Iowa, 1980–1990

HOUSING TENURE			
Tenure	*1980*	*1990*	
Number owner occupied	6,571	6,885	
Percentage owner occupied	44.4	42.9	
Number renter occupied	7,444	8,728	
Percentage renter occupied	50.3	54.3	
Number vacant	792	445	
Percentage vacant	5.3	2.8	
Total units	14,807	16,058	

HOUSING UNITS IN STRUCTURES				
	1980		*1990*	
Type	*Units*	*Percentage of Total*	*Units*	*Percentage of Total*
1 unit detached	6,218	46.5	6,800	42.3
1 unit attached	951	7.1	1.018	6.3
2–4 units	1,674	12.5	2,733	17.0
5–1,451	10.8	1,543	9.6	
10+ units	2,496	18.6	3.152	19.6
Mobile home	605	4.5	658	4.1
Other	0	0	154	1.0
Total	13,395	100.0	16,058	100.0

Source: U.S. Census, 1980 and 1990. Compiled by RM Plan Group (Nashville).

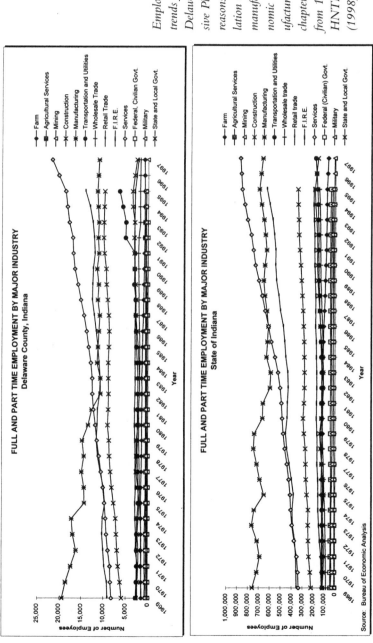

Employment and economic trends from the Muncie–Delaware County Comprehensive Plan. These charts show the reasons behind the loss of population in this old glass and auto manufacturing community; economic base employment in manufacturing (a topic discussed in chapter 11) declined steadily from 1970 to 1995. Source: HNTB Corp., Indianapolis (1998).

important to address those in the plan, whether through direct programs of delivery (such as construction of units by a housing authority) or through regulatory reforms and incentives to encourage the private sector to fill the needs.

Note that housing data are also directly relevant to land-use data and land-use planning. If the community needs more housing of a particular type, it will be essential to ensure that land is available for such housing in a new plan and in its implementation tools.

Economy

Understanding the local economy is essential in forecasting future employment and business opportunities. A number of sources are available to analyze the different aspects of the economy. The census can serve as a general source of information for such community attributes as per capita income. The census collects data on wages and salaries, self-employment, and public assistance. The U.S. Bureau of the Census also defines such categories as poverty threshold and income distributions. These categories and measures are important in figuring the proportion of households that fall below and above certain income levels when comparing a region to state or national norms.

The local or metropolitan chamber of commerce or economic development agency is typically the best source of current local economic data. If there is a business school at a local or regional university, it may also track economic and employment data. Information available from those agencies that is not available from the census often includes actual current employment at major operations, trends in orders and backlogs, and investment in buildings and capital equipment. All of those are useful indicators of likely future economic trends.

Other sources of important information are the offices in state governments that deal with economic development, such as the departments of economic security and state comptroller's offices, and the U.S. Bureau of Economic Affairs. These entities publish monthly, quarterly, and yearly data on employment and wages for different sectors of the economy. The federal and state governments use the international standards of industrial classification of all economic activities (SIC codes). There are eleven major SIC codes, which are then broken down into major groups that provide more specific classifications of business activity. The third level gets even more specific; tax information is always coded to that most specific category. However, the data used in planning rarely go beyond the second level of classification. That information is extremely helpful in understanding a diverse assortment of economic information, from the largest types of existing employment and future opportunities to the mean wages earned in each sector.

There are multiple purposes for such economic data. Economic development and diversification are often key goals of a comprehensive planning effort, and such data are critical in the implementation of such goals. Further, the local or regional economy will drive most of the employment trends for the community, and those employment trends will drive the demand for housing, recreation, transportation, and private commercial development. Thus, those are essential baseline data.

Land Use

The most visible part of most community plans is a map showing current land-use patterns and plans for future land use. To plan for future land use, it is essential to know what the current patterns of land use are. Typically, planners present existing land use as a map, with supporting tables summarizing the data. The maps often include major transportation routes.

The basic categories included on a land-use map, as described in chapter 2, are: industrial, commercial, residential, and agricultural (see table 1.2). Other uses commonly designated on such maps are: vacant, park and recreation, and institutional. Note that *land use,* as the term is used in planning, refers to human-oriented land uses; assessment of the natural character of the land is addressed in the next section.

Many communities identify two or more categories of residential land use, broken down by density. Some identify separate categories of commercial uses, although that is less common. One mistake that some communities make is in mapping public parks, vacant land, and agricultural land all in the same "open space" category; land-use maps ought to distinguish publicly owned open space that will remain open over the long run from privately owned land that happens to be in agriculture or open-space use when the map is made.

At this point, it may be useful to look back at the standard color scheme widely used for representing land uses on plans; it is contained in table 1.2. Color plate 1 shows an example of an existing land-use map.

The traditional method of mapping existing land use involves deploying squads of people, armed with base maps and pens or markers; while one person drives, others in the vehicle make notes of the apparent land uses of every piece of property observed. Obviously, that is a relatively time-consuming and expensive process. Today, there are a number of alternatives. Most property tax assessors now have computerized databases that include at least a generalized use category for every parcel of property; increasingly, assessor's offices are linking those files to geographic information systems, creating the potential to print maps showing existing land uses. Although maps generated from the assessor's files may not always show as much detail as planners might like, they can at least provide a starting point, changing the fieldwork from full data gathering to limited data checking. In those communities using integrated GIS systems, planners may have direct access to very current land-use data.

For a community undertaking a plan with a limited budget and without a GIS system, there are alternatives. A very general land-use survey can be

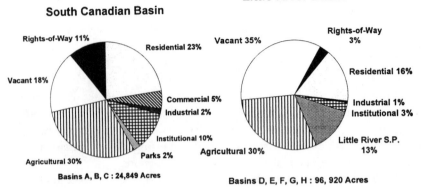

This simple pie chart shows how land was used in Norman, Oklahoma, when the 1996 plan was prepared; note the large proportion of vacant land because of the city's aggressive annexation policies. Source: City of Norman and The Burnham Group, Cincinnati, Little Rock, and Birmingham (1996).

derived from up-to-date aerial photographs and, to a limited extent, from satellite images, now available for the entire United States.[3] For planning purposes, the land that is of most interest is the land that is susceptible to change. The land most susceptible to change usually includes land in potential redevelopment areas, vacant land surrounded by development, and vacant land on the fringe of an urbanized area. Thus, another option for a community is simply to label large developed areas "urbanized" and then map land uses in detail in those areas most susceptible to change.

Once specific land uses are identified, further analysis includes determining the proportion of land dedicated to different uses and the density of those uses. In residential areas, density is described in terms of dwelling units per gross acre of developed land; in industrial areas, density is in terms of employees per gross acre of developed land.

Natural Environment

Information on the natural environment is generally shown on a series of maps. Twenty years ago, most such maps were prepared as a series of cross-hatched or colored overlays, allowing visual analysis through physical combinations of the maps. Today, environmental data are most useful when entered into a geographic information system, allowing the electronic combination of various maps.

Basic environmental information useful for planning usually includes descriptions of at least the following: soil types, or soil suitability groups; slope; vegetation; floodplains and wetlands; and significant geologic formations or features, where known. Additional information sometimes mapped includes information on particular plant species, wildlife habitat, and additional data related to waterways and bodies of water.

There are two primary sources of environmental information used in planning: the U.S. Geological Survey (USGS), for its maps, which are readily available through map dealers, local hiking and biking shops, and a variety of other sources; and the Natural Resources Conservation Service, formerly the Soil Conservation Service, which has, through careful fieldwork, prepared detailed soils maps of much of the country. Most states have water resource departments that have information about and maps of both above- and below-ground water sources. Other useful sources of environmental data include environmental impact studies for local projects and local floodplain maps. The U.S. Army Corps of Engineers also creates maps that define various floodplains for many areas along major rivers. Note that, because of the length of time

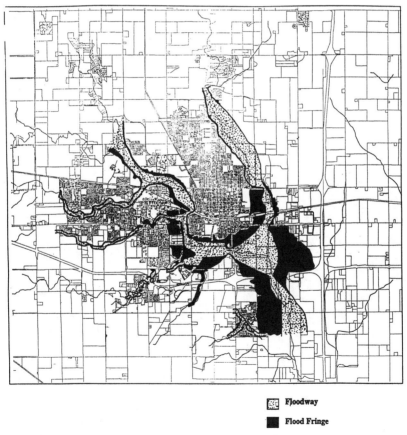

Floodway

Flood Fringe

The Ames, Iowa, floodplain. Source: *City of Ames and RM Plan Group, Nashville (1996).*

required to prepare such maps and the constant changes in floodplains caused by urbanization (and the resulting increases in runoff), these maps may not be as accurate when distributed as they would have been in the month or year when the data were collected.

Biological information, including information about endangered species, can be obtained from the National Biological Survey, the U.S. Fish and Wildlife Service, and state universities. Climate and meteorological data can also be obtained from state universities, as well as the National Weather Service. Environmental hazards vary according to local conditions. Some areas are well-known earthquake zones, while others must try and identify more specific hazards such as the potential for sinkholes in a karst topography.

Sophisticated environmental planning efforts may involve environmental engineers, biologists, hydrologists, and other experts. Effective major planning efforts have at least one team member who has some background in environmental planning.

Note that many environmental inventories include agricultural lands as an important category. The best agricultural land (determined from the soil survey) is not always the land currently being used in agriculture (as determined from the land-use study), in part because land suitable for agriculture is also

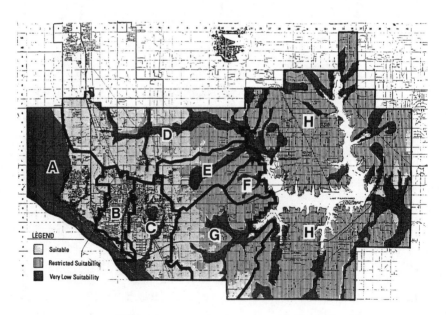

Combined urban suitability classifications for Norman, Oklahoma. The letters A through H designate drainage basins, a topic discussed in more depth in chapter 12. Source: City of Norman and the Burnham Group, Cincinnati, Little Rock, and Birmingham (1996).

well suited for urban development. Some environmental inventories also identify important mineral resources (which in some states are protected from
urbanization by state law) and archaeological sites.

Landscape architect Ian McHarg has advocated that most planning efforts
begin with obtaining such environmental information, by conducting an
"opportunities and constraints analysis," based primarily on environmental
data (discussed in more depth in the next chapter).[4] Just from basic information available from the USGS maps and from the soil survey, it is possible to
identify lands particularly suitable for agriculture; lands suitable for (or constrained from) urbanization; lands suitable for (or constrained from) septic
tanks; lands subject to landslide or geologic hazard; lands subject to flooding;
wetlands; wooded areas; low places; ridgelines; and important or unusual topographic or geographic features. Although most communities do not use this
approach as the central one in a comprehensive planning effort, it is important
to have this information and to consider it along with other information.

Resources and Sustainability

Closely related to the issues of the natural environment are those of resource
use and sustainability. Plans for communities in the United States often seem
to assume the availability of almost limitless resources. Most urban areas in the
United States today are heavily dependent on fossil fuels, which are the source
of gasoline, which powers the most frequently used form of transportation in
those communities. There is a limit to the availability of fossil fuels, a limit that
may not be adequately reflected in the relatively cheap price of gasoline in the
last years of the twentieth century. An oil embargo by the Middle Eastern
countries from which we receive much of our supply could create a practical
shortage of this important resource long before there is a real one.

In short, the communities that have evolved in the 1990s are largely not
sustainable over the long run, because at some point there will not be enough
cheap fuel to move people around them. But transportation is not the only
area in which today's development practices lack sustainability. Here are other
examples:

• *Land.* Mark Twain recognized more than a century ago that land is a scarce
  resource. It has become more so. Yet today's metropolitan areas are sprawling, consuming land at an increasing rate. Part of the problem is that densities of new developments are in many cases lower—sometimes significantly
  so—than densities of older developments. Thus, not only are communities
  taking new land to serve new needs, but they are taking more land than they
  once would have taken to serve those needs. Further, in many communities,
  vacant lands in the core are being abandoned, leading to an even greater
  waste of land. Some of the land being lost to development is valuable agricultural land, and all of it has some value as part of the larger natural sys-

tems. Even those who argue for the primacy of humans and a corollary right for humans to use the resources they need must begin to recognize that today's development patterns involve the consumption of land far in excess of reasonable needs. The United States is different from many western nations in that it does not consider the scarcity of land in public policy decisions about how private land ought to be used.

- *Water.* Urban development in the United States is not necessarily consumptive of water. Many communities treat and return to the source nearly as much water as they take from it. Urban development is often disruptive to the hydrologic cycle on which the water sources depend, however. Many communities in the country depend on wells for their water supplies. Those wells tap into underground aquifers. Those underground aquifers depend on rain and melting snow that soaks through the soil to recharge their water supplies. As humans pave the earth and the water runs off directly to nearby streams and rivers, many underground aquifers are depleted. There are methods of managing runoff that restore some of that recharge cycle to aquifers. Other concerns in water management, however, include the quality of runoff. Although wastewater is carefully treated and often returned to a river in such a condition that the river is both swimmable and fishable below the discharge, stormwater runoff contains motor oil and other automobile residue from streets, lawn chemicals, and pet droppings. In some states, this seems not to be a problem, because water is usually plentiful; even in those states, however, water can become short in a particular place at a particular time. And in states such as New Mexico, Utah, Nevada, and Arizona, the water issue is critical.[5]

- *Wetlands.* Besides representing rich sources of biodiversity, wetlands also represent nature's best flood management tools. In wet weather, they act like giant sponges, soaking up large amounts of water. During dry periods, they gradually release that water, which then flows downstream. Because flooding is almost always a temporary problem resulting from a major storm, such temporary storage of water is all that is necessary to alleviate most or all of the potential damage from flooding. In 1992 the Midwest suffered from devastating floods, which resulted in significant part from decades of efforts to drain the wetlands of the upper Midwest; ironically, the federal government, which ultimately paid much of the bill for the flood damage, probably caused the floods with the approval of the "Swamp Lands Act," which provided both policy and fiscal support for those draining programs. Far from being swamps just waiting to be filled, wetlands represent valuable economic as well as ecological resources to a community.[6]

- *Buildings.* Most building projects in most communities today involve new buildings. In some cases, the new buildings meet new needs. In others, they replace existing buildings—sometimes physically replacing buildings that are torn down and sometimes simply leading to the abandonment of buildings

elsewhere. In other countries, it is common to add on to and remodel buildings extensively, often over many generations and several centuries. That
represents a different set of values.

- *Building materials.* A public building in Indiana may include wood from Oregon forests and marble from Italy, as well as plumbing and electrical fixtures
from manufacturers around the world. Yet Indiana remains a leading steel-
producing state, and steel can easily replace wood in many applications;
there are natural and human-made products available in the state that can
be used as alternatives to marble in floor and wall finishes. In building design
little or no consideration is given to the true cost of obtaining and trans-
porting the materials used in the building.

- *Space conditioning and lighting.* People lived in this country for the first 175
years without air conditioning. The earliest known city builders in the
United States, the cliff dwellers of the Southwest, created buildings that
gained much of their heat from the sun and used the earth as insulation.
Although citizens of the United States have depended heavily on fuels for
heating, they depended on natural convection for cooling through the first
half of the twentieth century and on the sun for many lighting needs
through the early part of the twentieth century. Today, many public and private buildings have rooms without any natural light and other rooms with
windows that provide light but not air. Although some of the electricity that
provides cooling and lighting (and a limited portion of heating) comes from
nondepleting hydroelectric sources, much of it also depends on dwindling
fossil fuels. Again, this is not a sustainable pattern.

- *Industrial inputs and outputs.* Early smelters in this country were located near
the mines they served. Steel plants located near sources of iron ore and the
coal used in coke making, an essential part of the early steel-making process.
The location of natural resource inputs into industry has always influenced
the location of industry. In contrast, the source of manufactured inputs into
industrial processes is often not a factor in determining industrial locations.
Taking advantage of special provisions of the North American Free Trade
Agreement, many companies moved part of their production facilities to
Mexico in the 1990s, leaving other parts in the United States. Delivery of
essential parts for manufacturing processes by aircraft became common in
the 1990s. Industry in one community heated water as a byproduct of its
need to cool equipment, while industry in another community used boil-
ers to heat water for space heating and manufacturing processes. Waste recy-
clers sold old paper to buyers around the world, while paper manufacturers
in the United States continued to make much of their paper from new trees.
These processes are remarkably dependent on transportation, which is heavily dependent on fossil fuels. Such systems are not sustainable over the long
run and may break down in the event of a major transportation strike; they
will become economically impracticable as fuel prices inevitably rise. Chat-

tanooga, Tennessee, broke out of this pattern with an economic development strategy focused on seeking industry that would use both products and
byproducts of the region in production processes.[7]

- *Wildlife habitat and biodiversity.* Planning in the United States is largely
human centered, with little concern for the impacts on other species. There
is a growing view, however, that humans have a higher moral obligation to
other species.[8] There is also growing evidence that preserving biodiversity is
in our own self-interest.[9] For a community that places value on habitat and
biodiversity, there are a variety of methods for protecting them.[10]

It is important to include in an existing conditions analysis an assessment
of the sustainability of the community. That must start with a realistic assessment of the ecologically valuable features of the community. Does the community depend on wells? If so, how is the aquifer recharged? Is recharge continuing at a reasonable rate, or is development causing a reduction in the rate?
Are there wetlands in or near the community? How do they function, hydro-
logically and physically? Are parts of the local environment particularly fragile? Are there unusual natural hazards, such as geologically unstable areas or
areas subject to wildfire? Ian McHarg's *Design with Nature,* cited repeatedly in
this text, remains the basic guide to this kind of analysis. Color plate 3 shows
a similar analysis performed for Bardstown and Nelson County, Kentucky.

The other part of a sustainability analysis is a sort of performance audit
of the community's current level of sustainability. To what extent is the community dependent on resources that are dwindling or that come from distant and uncertain sources? To what extent are its basic local functions,
including manufacturing, dependent on transportation? Are development
and building patterns increasing dependence on energy for local transportation, lighting, and space heating? Are development patterns destroying critical natural resources, including wetlands, habitat, and other areas of significant environmental value?

Circulation

Planners typically talk about "circulation" rather than transportation, because
circulation (getting around) is the goal of the citizens they serve, whereas transportation is just a method of achieving that goal. A good circulation plan
includes more than streets and roads—it includes means of pedestrian and bicycle circulation and, in many communities, some form of mass transportation.

Although good circulation plans involve more than roads, the starting
point for an existing conditions analysis of circulation is a map of streets, roads,
and highways in the community. The analysis ought to include more than a
map, however. It should indicate the capacity of major roads and the current
traffic load and/or level of service on those roads. Other background infor-

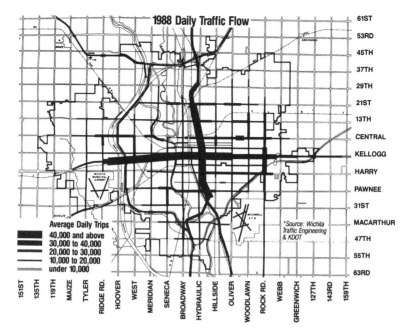

This map shows the daily traffic flow on major roads in Wichita, Kansas. Source: *Metropolitan Planning Department, Wichita (1993).*

mation necessary for the existing and proposed land-use sections of the comprehensive plan regards the transportation system.

The state transportation department should have good maps and data on use and levels of service of major roads to and through the community. In many communities, the local streets or public works department will have additional data on local streets and roads. Communities in or near most major metropolitan areas will find that the metropolitan planning organization (MPO)—a planning organization created locally to coordinate planning for federal- and state-funded transportation projects—has good data on the capacities and demands of the existing road network. MPOs and some other agencies may also have projections of future demand. Where such data are not available or are out of date, the professional planning staff can work with local transportation planners to determine the capacity of existing roads, and transportation technicians can use counters to determine current loads on key sections of those roads.

Transportation influences land-use patterns, and, in turn, land use affects demands on the transportation system. A map showing the road system and any proposed additions, extensions, or enhancements must be shown and discussed. Some of that information can be gathered from the county and state departments of transportation for projections and plans for the roads they control. Decisions concerning roads built and maintained by the community and other forms of transportation are dependent on forecasts of land use, demand, population growth, and economic activity. Forecasting transportation needs involves estimating the number of trips that will be generated by new residential, commercial, and industrial activity, the route of those trips, and the means (mode) of that travel. Standards for the types of road are set based on the projected levels of service and on the functional categories of road: expressway, arterial, collector, and local. Transportation planners use trip generation models to determine the types of roads that will be needed in the future.

Transportation planners use a number of sophisticated models to make travel demand projections, that is, to determine the number of vehicles likely to travel over a section of road or through an intersection during a particular time interval in the future. Common forms of projections are for "average daily trips," which is exactly what the name suggests, and "peak-hour trips," the number of trips that occur at a specified rush-hour period. It is important that these models use the best possible data on existing travel modes and patterns and projections of future land use. Transportation planning includes more than planning for the automobile. Mass transit is a major part of transportation planning, along with other alternatives such as bicycling and walking, which must be accommodated in the planning process.

Transportation and circulation are always important elements in comprehensive plans; many summary maps from comprehensive plan studies show plans for land use and transportation, leaving everything else to other maps or to a report format. Because major transportation improvements create new development opportunities (through either new access or increased convenience of access), they directly influence land-use patterns. The corollary, however, is that land-use patterns largely determine transportation demand (e.g., if everyone lives in the suburbs and works downtown, there will be large amounts of traffic going toward center city in the morning and leaving it in the evening). Thus, understanding the current transportation and circulation system is essential to understanding the base from which the new community plan will start.

Other Infrastructure: Community Facilities and Services

Although invisible to most citizens and less exciting to planners than some of the other topics in this book, the sewer and water systems that serve a community significantly influence its potential for and patterns of growth. The location of fire stations, schools, libraries, and other facilities can also be important factors in developing a new plan. Thus, it is important to include in the existing conditions analysis an inventory and map of existing facilities.

Some communities also map the availability of electricity, natural gas, and telephone; because under the laws of most states, providers of such services must (and generally do) serve all who request it (sometimes subject to cost-sharing arrangements for initial hookups), it is not unreasonable for most communities to assume that those services will be available as and where needed. It is always wise to consult with the providers of such services to determine whether they have plans or policies that differ from this general practice, but it will be rare to find significant deviations. Cable television is also important to many consumers, and operators continue to expand and improve systems rapidly; good service is thus available in most developed and developing areas.

The public works department or other sewer and water provider should be able to provide good information on those systems. With each,

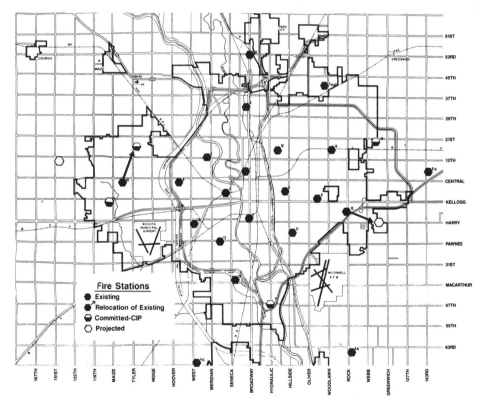

It is useful to map existing public facilities on a map with a common scale, as Wichita, Kansas, did with fire stations in its 1993 plan. Source: *Metropolitan Area Planning Department, Wichita (1993).*

it is important to understand not only where the lines are, but what the service area is and what the capacity is. System capacity is typically determined by capacity of the treatment plant. Although lines can often be extended over the short run at reasonable cost, plant expansions usually require major capital investments and a good deal of planning time for design and regulatory approvals. Service areas for water systems are usually defined by elevation, everything below a certain elevation falling in the service area. Most water systems are gravity driven, and the break in the service area is defined by the highest elevation to which the existing gravity system can deliver adequate water pressure to fight fires. Sewer service areas are also determined by gravity; all areas from which sewage can flow by gravity to the treatment plant are generally within the reasonable service area of a particular plant. Although developers and even local governments sometimes supplement a water or sewer system with extra pumps to serve a development that would otherwise be outside the service area, those systems are expensive to maintain and most operators thus plan for a system that is gravity-driven.

Line capacity can also be a problem with sewer and water systems. Sewage feeds from individual collector lines into trunk sewer lines that go to the plant; if the trunk line is overloaded, it will not make sense to extend the collector lines farther from it. Similarly, water pressure to any given area is limited by the size of the supply lines, as well as by gravity, and—as anyone who has tried to take a shower in the morning in a house with several teenagers probably knows—there is a limit to how much water is available from a pipe of a given size. Long dead-end lines in water systems also create pressure problems, and most long-range planning for water systems requires looping such lines into others, to maintain balance in the system. Well-managed sewer and water providers have both maps and data addressing such issues; some planning departments track such information internally, because of its significance for planning.

Fire service areas are defined by response times from fire stations. In communities that provide emergency medical services from fire stations, the response time is usually measured in terms of the rapidity necessary to save a stroke or heart attack victim. Where the only consideration is firefighting, a response time of six to eight minutes is often acceptable. Although response time is partly a function of distance, it is also affected by road patterns and traffic. Being across the river from a fire station is of little benefit if there is no bridge nearby. Many slowly growing communities have had to build new fire stations only because the patterns of growth have distorted response times—not because absolute population growth demands additional investment. In short, the location of fire station and emergency medical response facilities is closely linked to the patterns of growth and thus to long-range land-use planning.

Fire stations such as this one in Lawrence, Kansas, are among the many public facilities that should be included in an existing conditions analysis.

Police stations, libraries, and government offices relate differently to the planning process. Although it is important to plan for needed future facilities to serve all of those purposes, the location of such facilities is rarely growth limiting or growth determining. As a practical matter, a community could responsibly address such needs simply by ensuring that it acquires a site of five acres or so for development of "future public buildings" in each major growth area—it could decide later where it needs the facilities. Some communities acquire park sites large enough to meet recreational and open-space needs and still provide some land for development for public buildings.

It is not essential that a planner be a technical expert on all of these subjects—presumably, an administrator from each of these units will serve as a planning liaison to the rest of local government and will provide the maps and data to make these sorts of determinations. It is important, however, that the planner understand these concepts well enough to receive and evaluate the information critically, to ask good questions about it, and to understand its implications for planning.

Schools

Planning for the location of schools is a challenge. In principle, it is no different from planning for any other major public facility. In practice, it is radically different.

In most communities, schools respond to their own elected school boards,

Schools such as this one in Muncie, Indiana, should always be considered in comprehensive planning efforts. It is important to coordinate planning for schools with the school board and administration responsible for operating them.

which hire their own professional administrators and assign staff professionals (usually teachers) to engage in a form of planning. Many school officials feel a responsibility to serve the school needs of the community, wherever and whenever they might occur, and they do not always see the value in trying to plan where and when growth might take place and how that might relate to demand for schools.

The land-use approach to planning for schools has also changed. In the 1950s and 1960s, many educators and public planners believed that the ideal neighborhood was a one-mile circle, with a park and a school in the middle. With densities of about three dwelling units per acre (fairly typical of development in that period) and with 2.3 children per household (also fairly typical), and allowing some land for commercial and other uses, the result was an elementary school population of about three hundred students within a half-mile walk of the school. Today, new elementary schools often include facilities like swimming pools and full gyms, increasing their cost to the point that administrators may want a base population of seven hundred or more elementary students in a school. Further, there are now fewer children per household in newer neighborhoods than the old planning model suggested, and some of the older neighborhoods are populated largely by grandparents, who have no children living at home. The result is empty school buildings in some areas and growth in areas without school buildings and without adequate population density to support a walking-distance elementary school. Most districts have at least some busing, even to elementary schools, today. Once children are in a bus, the exact distance to school is not as critical as it once was, but most communities still try to keep some semblance of "neighborhood" schools, rather than busing students back and forth across town.

Is it important to include schools in the planning process? Yes, but, as previously stated, it may be a challenge. At the stage of the existing conditions analysis, planners should include an inventory of school facilities. The importance of education to the community requires no further explanation. The two kinds of circumstances that lead to major citizen concern about growth and planning are significant increases in traffic and overcrowded schools. Regardless of how it is finally used, planners need information about the location and capacity of schools in the community, as well as about planned schools and available school sites.

Parks and Recreation Facilities

Many communities have separate plans for parks and recreation facilities, but at some point those plans must be integrated with the long-range land-use plans. Many such facilities are neighborhood oriented and must be integrated into neighborhood plans. Those that serve the whole community (such as soccer and softball complexes) must be located where there is convenient access.

Where residents are basically satisfied with current park and recreation facilities, it is important to know what the current levels of service are. How many acres of park does the community have for every thousand people? How many tennis courts, swimming pools, and soccer fields does it have for every thousand people? If those ratios are adequate, they ought to become standards that guide the community in expanding its facilities as it grows. If people are dissatisfied, or the facilities are overcrowded, it is important to compare service levels to those in other communities to provide a context for evaluating possible expansion.

An inventory of park and recreation facilities must be mapped, but the map must be supported by data. The map may show tennis courts at a particular location, but it is important that a legend or a report indicate how many tennis courts exist at each location and how many serve the entire population. This topic is treated in much more depth in chapter 15.

In communities that have separate boards responsible for park and recreation planning, the resulting plans often include operational plans for recreation programs as well as physical plans for parks and playfields. In using such plans to inform a comprehensive planning effort, planners should recognize the difference between the two—the operational program for recreation is like a school curriculum and is largely beyond the scope of the planning effort for the community, except that, in the final analysis, the facilities must serve the programming needs.

Other Inventories

If a planning body wants to include historic preservation, archaeological resources, or tourist facilities in its plan, the professional staff should prepare an inventory of existing facilities and sites as part of the existing conditions analysis. The lists at the beginning of this chapter suggest what some of the other topics of such inventories might be.

Conclusion

The final task of the planner in determining "where we are" is to bring all of this material together, placing schools, parks, roads, and residential areas all on the same maps—or at least on similar maps—so that the planning body and interested citizens can see how they relate to one another. It is also important in bringing this data together to ensure that they are consistent. If the traffic data show terrible congestion on a segment of road where the surrounding land uses are all labeled "vacant," the planner needs to figure out why there is a traffic problem there—or if there is an error in one map. If the census data show 1,122 people under the age of eighteen in the community and there are only 336 students in the public schools, the planner needs to find out where the rest of the children are—or which data are correct.

When the planners have brought all of these data together and made them meaningful, they will provide the basis for answering the question "Where can we go?" See chapter 4.

The Role of the Professional Planner

The existing conditions analysis is almost entirely technical. Thus, the professional planner plays the most important role of anyone in this stage of the planning effort. The effective planner will do several things at this stage:

1. gather data (the obvious task);
2. turn the data into information (by making it meaningful);
3. communicate the information in meaningful form to the planning body and interested citizens (by going a step beyond the previous step—using maps, illustrations, graphics, tables, and charts to make the information user friendly); and
4. identify other agencies and bodies interested in the planning process (any agency that gathers data useful for the existing conditions analysis should be a candidate for some sort of inclusion in the planning process).

The Role of the Individual Citizen

The work at this stage is primarily technical and is thus largely the responsibility of the professional planner. It is difficult to involve individual citizens in the data gathering, although communities have used volunteers (usually in organized groups like Scout troops or service clubs) to help with traffic counts or existing land-use surveys.

Sometimes at this stage, however, a community may wish to begin a process of "issue identification" (discussed in depth in chapter 5) or other means of involving citizens in defining the scope of the plan. The most direct means of getting citizen input is to hold public meetings where everyone can voice opinions and concerns on specific issues. The often used example of democracy at its best is the town hall meeting. For small communities, that type of public participation is possible. Larger communities often use a series of public meetings based on neighborhoods, precincts, or other widely recognized subsections of the community; others may hold meetings in the region around the city, in the areas likely to be most affected by future growth. Planners can then interpret the citizen input collected at those meetings to form goals and objectives for the community. Still another approach is to use a formal survey; popular means of reaching large numbers of people are through newspaper ads or supplements or through inserts in utility bills. More and more communities are using Web sites, with simple response forms contained at the site. Although this is an important modern means of communication, it is important to remember that not all citizens have access to computers—and that those who do have access to computers are representative of only part of the socioeconomic community.

Although much of the substantive work on the plan at this stage is technical, it is important to involve citizens in the process early, regardless of the method selected.

EXERCISES

1. Working as a group, gather some basic data on your community. Assign someone to get a soil survey, someone to get USGS maps, and someone to get a map of utility systems and service areas; if you have more people, assign more of the topics discussed in this chapter. Examine the data that you have gathered. What do they tell you about your community, even without taking the further steps necessary to analyze the data?

2. Obtain basic data on your community from the last three available cen-

suses. What are the population trends? How do those compare to the trends of your county or metropolitan region? To those of the state? Is the population getting older or younger? Why? From what you know about the community, can you explain those trends?

3. Obtain copies of the most recent comprehensive plans prepared for your community. Compare the information in those to some of the descriptive data that you have obtained. Do those plans provide a realistic starting point for an existing conditions analysis?

4. Look at the growth patterns of your community and study any recent building projects of the local school board or district. Are they complementary, or at least compatible? If not, why not?

DISCUSSION EXERCISES

1. Invite your local planner to come to class and give a talk on existing conditions in the community. After the speaker leaves, discuss what she or he has presented in the context of what you have read here. Does your community (at least as represented by that professional) have a good understanding of where it is now?

2. See exercise 3 above, which would also make a good full-class exercise.

FURTHER READING

Dandekar, Hemalata C., ed. 1988. *The Planner's Use of Information.* Chicago: Planners Press. An excellent treatment of virtually every aspect of the role of the professional planner in carrying out the tasks discussed in this chapter; although it predates the World Wide Web, supplementing it with Jeer, below, will make it a work of continuing use.

Jeer, Sanjay. 1997. *Online Resources for Planners.* Planning Advisory Service Report No. 474/475. Chicago: Planners Press. A broad and useful work, although the subject matter is changing rapidly.

Kaiser, Edward J., David R. Godschalk, and F. Stuart Chapin, Jr. 1995. *Urban Land Use Planning,* 4th edition. Urbana: University of Illinois Press. The latest edition of a classic work on land-use planning, a definitive work on analysis of and planning for land use.

Kelly, Eric Damian. 1993. *Planning, Growth and Public Facilities: A Primer for Public Officials.* Planning Advisory Service Report 447. Chicago: American Planning Association. A practical treatment of the relationships between infrastructure and growth, and the related use of information in planning.

Reid, David. 1995. *Sustainable Development: An Introductory Guide.* London: Earthscan. A good introduction, covering both ecology and economics.

So, Frank S., and Judith Getzels, eds. 1988. *The Practice of Local Government Planning,* 2nd edition. Washington, DC: International City Management Association. Essentially the fourth edition of a standard reference work, but the titles on the first three are different. Several chapters are included on technical aspects of opportunities and constraints analysis. A new edition is due out in 2000 and should contain similar material, updated.

REFERENCES

Bureau of the Census. Multiple census reports. A great variety of useful material, including helpful user's guides. See also http://www.census.gov.

Institute of Transportation Engineers. 1997. *Trip Generation Manual,* 7th edition. Washington, DC: Institute of Transportation Engineers. A standard reference work, regularly updated; predicts the number of trips likely to be generated from specified land uses, used in conjunction with highway capacity information to determine how much capacity remains.

Insurance Services' Office. 1992. *The Fire Suppression Rating Schedule.* New York: ISO Commercial Risk Services. Good reference on levels of service for fire protection.

Mertes, James D., and James R. Hall. 1996. *Park, Recreation, Open Space and Greenway Guidelines.* Alexandria, VA: National Recreation and Park Association. A standard reference on this topic; although the organization once published "standards" on these topics, it now provides "guidelines" to help a community determine its own needs.

Myers, Dowell. 1992. *Analysis with Local Census Data.* Boston: Academic Press. A very practical user's guide, written by a planner.

Transportation Research Board. 1985. *Highway Capacity Manual.* Washington, DC: Transportation Research Board, National Research Council. The standard reference on this topic.

NOTES

1. The Web address is http://www.census.gov. For easy access to the data from a map, start at http://www.census.gov/datamap/www/index.html.
2. DeMaio, T., "Refusals: Who, Where and Why?" *Public Opinion Quarterly* 44: 223–233 (Summer 1980).
3. A good set of satellite images is available to interested users at http://terraserver.microsoft.com.
4. Ian L. McHarg, *Design with Nature,* New York: John Wiley (1992).
5. For a contemporary discussion of this issue, see Charles Wilkinson, *Crossing the Next Meridian: Land, Water and the Future of the West,* Washington, DC: Island Press (1992).
6. See David Salvesen, *Wetlands: Mitigating and Regulating Development Impacts,* Washington, DC: Urban Land Institute (1990), which discusses both the value of wetlands and methods for protecting them in the development process.
7. See Mary L. McLean and Kenneth P. Voytek, *Understanding Your Economy,* Chicago: American Planning Association (1992); and Nigel J. Roome, *Sustainability Strategies for Industry,* Washington, DC: Island Press (1998). The McLean and Voytek work takes a planner's approach to creating logical clusters of industry locally; the Roome book considers issues of sustainability from the perspective of industry.

8. See Stephen R. Kellert, *The Value of Life: Biological Diversity and Human Society,* Washington, DC: Island Press (1996); and Thomas Berry, *The Dream of the Earth,* San Francisco: Sierra Club Books (1988).

9. See, for example, Yvonne Baskin, *The Work of Nature,* Washington, DC: Island Press (1997).

10. Among recent titles that address this are: Sheila Peck, *Planning for Biodiversity,* Washington, DC: Island Press (1998); Christopher J. Duerksen, *Habitat Protection Planning,* Planning Advisory Service Reports No. 470-71, Chicago: American Planning Association (1997); and Timothy Beatley, *Habitat Conservation Planning,* Austin: University of Texas Press (1994).

Chapter 4

....

Where Can We Go?
Projecting Possible Futures
for the Community

Answers to the question "Where can we go?" will sometimes produce a more limited range of options than answers to the question in the next chapter, "Where do we want to go?" and will sometimes produce a broader range of options. This chapter discusses two related issues: 1) how to answer the question "Where can we go?" and 2) at what point in the process the answers to this question ought to be shared with those addressing "where do we want to go?"

"Where can we go?" is in a sense a question of feasibility, but feasibility is sometimes in the eye of the beholder. Russell Ackoff in *The Art of Problem Solving*[1] and Thomas Kuhn in *The Structure of Scientific Revolutions*[2] describe methods for redefining problems (or, in Kuhnian terms, "shifting paradigms"), something that often changes the professional's perception about what is feasible. Ackoff's *An Approach to Corporate Planning*[3] and G. West Churchman's *The Systems Approach*[4] describe problem solving in systems terms; a brief discussion in chapter 1 (this volume) suggests that it is sometimes possible to change what is feasible by viewing it from a different system level. For example, the driver of an automobile who is puzzled about how to get over a tree limb in the road without damaging his car can move to a higher system level—outside the limited system of the car—and simply get out and move the branch.

It is important to distinguish *possibility* from *practicability*. Many discussions of feasibility have a strong undertone of economic feasibility, something inherent in the concept of practicability. Although it is rarely useful to consider truly impossible alternatives, it is often useful to keep impracticable ones under discussion, at least through the initial rounds of analysis. If a community in the Nevada desert is planning its future, it is probably not useful to consider the alternative of becoming a beach resort (impossible because there is no beach), but it may be useful at least to contemplate the possibility of becoming the home of the nation's next major theme park (something that is possible though unlikely, because of market and accessibility considerations). The discussion of building a theme park may not result in luring Disney or Six Flags to town, but it may suggest some alternative, recreation-oriented scenarios (taking advantage of an often favorable climate) that are feasible.

Techniques for Determining What Is Feasible

There are three related techniques often used in answering the question "Where can we go?" in a planning context. All are methods of identifying opportunities that are possible or feasible and eliminating from consideration directions or activities that are not feasible. The three techniques are: opportunities and constraints analysis; strength and weakness analysis; and issue identification.

Opportunities and Constraints Analysis

The classic method of determining "where we can go" is to conduct an analysis of *opportunities and constraints* affecting the community. Opportunities and constraints include topics in a number of categories:

- *Geographic.* A community in the Colorado mountains may have the potential to become a ski resort, an opportunity not shared by a community on the plains of Georgia. A community located along major transportation routes has opportunities that others do not. A suburb of a large city has opportunities that a freestanding community of similar size does not have. Geographic opportunities and constraints are generally fixed, or long term—that is, they are unlikely to change during the time included in the planning horizon. Thus, they essentially become defining parameters for the planning problem.
- *Environmental.* Environmental opportunities and constraints are closely related to and usually defined by geographic ones. The character of the land defines (or ought to define) the type of development that can take place. The capacity of the water and air to handle additional pollutant discharges is an important determinant of the types of development that are acceptable today. Several large cities have significant unresolved air pollution problems, often related to automobiles, and are thus limited by federal and state laws in their ability to accept additional auto-dependent development. Those laws primarily affect major metropolitan areas, where planners are well aware of both their application and their implications.

- *Natural resources.* Also closely related to geography, but often varying greatly within a geographic region, are natural resources. Communities with easy access to natural gas offer different opportunities than do those with easy access to coal. An area with a raw material that is key to industrial processes clearly has an advantage in attracting industry dependent on that material. Although natural resources in the broad sense are usually an opportunity and not a constraint, the desire to protect certain natural resources (such as prime agricultural land) from development and to ensure future availability of those resources may be considered a limitation on certain types or locations of development. In such a case, the natural resources, combined with some public policy choices, become a sort of self-imposed restraint affecting certain planning choices.

- *Infrastructure.* Also related to geographic opportunities and constraints, but easier to control, are infrastructure facilities and capacities. Typically included in the analysis of infrastructure are roads and bridges; sewage collection and treatment systems; stormwater collection systems; water supply, treatment, and distribution systems; and such generalized facilities as fire and police stations. A community with a surplus of treated water may be able to attract a brewery or soft-drink bottler, whereas a community with a water shortage cannot realistically consider that objective over the short run. Local sewage treatment capacity also affects the ability of a community to absorb additional growth, and the type of treatment available will affect what types of industry can move into the community. Communities have long based their economic development strategies on access to railroads or interstate highways, recognizing their importance to heavy industry. Today, some commerce moves by aircraft and some by electronic means, making access to airports and to major fiber-optic routes important aspects of infrastructure. Note that over the middle to long term, it is possible to use fiscal opportunities (discussed below) to address and change infrastructure constraints.

- *Private land and Facilities.* During the 1990s, the economy in the United States became so strong that most modern factories were operating at full capacity, and many manufacturers sought expansion space. In that context, empty factories, which had traditionally symbolized lost jobs and a sagging economy, became a resource for economic development, much sought after by expanding companies. Although residential development can take place in a variety of contexts, major manufacturing plants and regional shopping malls require relatively large tracts of land with good access; a community with a shortage of such land may have difficulty in attracting industrial and commercial development. Often the availability of good shopping, health care, and cultural facilities in a community significantly influence the decisions of both individual families and companies to relocate there. Thus, communities with good private support services should list those as an opportunity, and others may need to consider the lack of those services to be a constraint.

- *Fiscal resources.* The taxing and borrowing capacities of agencies of local governments often represent invisible but important opportunities and constraints. A community that can, under its state law, borrow significant additional money through bonds and increase tax revenues by raising rates clearly has opportunities for expansion that a community reaching its tax-rate or borrowing limits does not. Whether those fiscal resources are used as direct incentives to attract particular types of new growth or for the general expansion of infrastructure to support growth, the availability of those resources—or the limits on them—is a critical factor in any analysis of community opportunities and constraints. In some cases, the general unit of local government (city, town, or county) may be in solid fiscal health, but the local school district may lack the borrowing or taxing ability to expand its facilities to absorb significant additional growth.

- *Economy.* Distinct from the local government's fiscal condition, but equally important to the community's future, is the economic base of the community. What brings money into the community? manufacturing? agriculture? tourism? The economic character of a community does not usually change quickly. A community with a large base of skilled machine operators will be far less successful in attracting a software company than will a university town. Thus, the existing economic character of the community must be considered both an opportunity and a constraint. A number of old manufacturing communities have managed to change their economic strategies and economic bases, but others have failed. This should be treated as a medium-term opportunity and constraint. Many local planning efforts include particular examination of two elements of the local economy:

  1. *Labor force.* A key element of the economy is the available labor force. A community with a surplus of skilled workers (sometimes resulting from a plant closure) has obvious opportunities to attract a new industry needing such skills. In contrast, a community with overly specialized or undereducated workers may have difficulty in attracting new industry. In today's rapidly changing job market, job training and retraining programs are often key elements of local social and economic development programs.

  2. *Industrial input–output.* Another subset of the economy is the local industrial input and output stream. A community with several machine shops that can make custom parts and tools has an obvious advantage in attracting manufacturers and others that use technical equipment, and a community with an industry that generates a usable by-product

may be able to attract another industry to use that by-product as an input; but a community far from auto parts manufacturers may have difficulty in attracting an auto assembly plant, which depends on those manufacturers for input.

- *Housing.* Both the availability and the cost of housing are factors that can create opportunities or severe constraints. Communities with high housing costs and/or low availability have trouble attracting both new residents and industry that will need new residents as workers.
- *Local policies toward growth and change.* Sometimes called the regulatory climate, local policies toward growth and change create significant opportunities and constraints. In general, antigrowth communities are likely to grow less than similarly situated progrowth communities. These polices are only

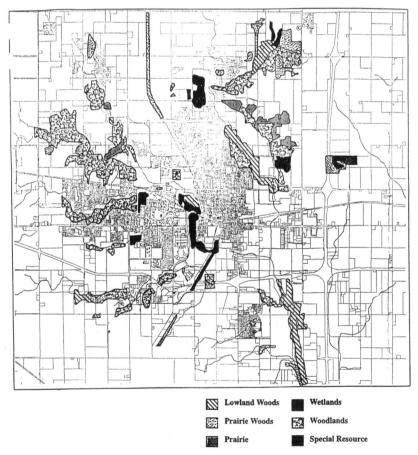

	Lowland Woods		Wetlands
	Prairie Woods		Woodlands
	Prairie		Special Resource

This map from Ames, Iowa, shows major environmental constraints to development.
Source: *RM Plan Group, Nashville (1998).*

one part of the larger system and are not independently meaningful—a progrowth attitude is unlikely to create growth in a community with over-loaded infrastructure, and an antigrowth attitude alone will not keep people from flocking to a popular beach community. These policies are extremely important at the margins, however, and can have a significant impact over the long run.

The emphasis in the list above is on community-wide opportunities and constraints. Some opportunities and constraints are localized, however. Schools in one part of the community may have excess capacity, while others are over-crowded. Many environmental constraints affect only specific areas of the community.

The analysis of opportunities and constraints can (and should) be objec-tive professional work. Land-based opportunities and constraints can actually be mapped, and others can be inventoried. The existence and capacity of sewer and water plants, highways, and airports are documentable facts. Sources of data include:

- USGS and soil survey maps for geographic and environmental data, includ-ing some natural resource data
- project-related environmental impact statements for other environmental data.
- state department of natural resources (or agency with similar responsibili-ties) for additional natural resources data
- public works department reports and maps for infrastructure capacity and location data (Because not all local governments track capacity and utiliza-tion data, it may be necessary to develop some of these data from raw num-bers on plant and line capacity and current usage base.)
- state department of transportation for maps and capacity data on state and federal highways
- chamber of commerce and local Realtors for data on available private land and facilities
- chamber of commerce and university research centers for models of and information on the local economy
- state department of labor for data on workforce, employment, and wages and trends in all three
- local government finance offices for budget, tax, and bonding authority (This "capacity" information is sometimes not included in published ver-sions of the data and may require inquiries of the chief financial officer.)
- chamber of commerce "targeted industry" or other studies for industrial input-output data (This may require field survey work with major indus-tries, also.)
- census reports for housing, population, and labor force data.

- interviews with business people and residents regarding regulatory climate and local policies (The perception of the policies is at least as important as the substance of the policies, and it is thus difficult to make an objective review of this factor in the system.)

Note that almost all of the necessary information is likely to exist somewhere on a map, in a report, or in a database. The gathering of data is, nevertheless, a critical and often time-consuming step in the planning process. It is important, because bringing all of these data together, so that they provide a total picture of the community, turns them into information—something far more useful than the individual items of data contained in separate reports in separate government files. This task is time consuming, because finding all of the data is not as easy as this simple checklist might suggest, and because it is important to make it all comparable—placing all mapped data on the same base map, at the same scale; adjusting all statistical data to the same base year(s); and reconciling all data to ensure that they are consistent and not contradictory. Color plate 3 shows a mapped version of such information for a county in Kentucky; it is labeled, appropriately, "potential development map based on environmental considerations."

Computers obviously provide a powerful tool for conducting this work. Much of the data can be managed in spreadsheet programs. The better geographic information system programs include links to databases or spreadsheets, thus connecting mapped information to tabular data. With the best systems, it is possible to ask the computer program to identify such things as "all parcels of more than one hundred acres, with industrial zoning, along an existing sewer line, within one-quarter mile of a railroad track."

Some of the factors discussed here are independently important—sewer service availability, natural resource opportunities, and a strong local fiscal situation are useful for any community—but others are meaningful only in comparative studies. When considering the availability of labor and its relative education and wage expectations, for example, it is important to compare those data to similar data from other communities against which the base community competes in economic development. Housing cost data are meaningful only in comparison to regional, state, and national trends. Thus, another key part of this task is the development of comparative data.

The analysis of opportunities and constraints can be published as a separate report or as a chapter in the comprehensive plan. See chapter 8 for a discussion.

Strength and Weakness Analysis

Another way of approaching issues similar to those identified through an opportunities and constraints study is through an analysis of strengths and weaknesses, sometimes given an acronym like SWAP, for "Strength and Weakness Analysis Program." Although philosophically related to an analysis of opportunities and constraints, the methodology for strength and weakness analysis is quite different. Strengths and weaknesses are at least as much a matter of perception as a matter of fact.

Clearly, when a technical study shows that the sewage treatment plant is almost at capacity, that fact must be reported as both a constraint and a weakness, regardless of whether it is perceived as a weakness by local residents. The inventory of weaknesses, however, may also include items such as "bad traffic," "inadequate parks," and "poorly maintained schools" when an objective comparison of the community to others of similar size and age in the same part of the country would suggest that in fact traffic is a relatively minor problem (perhaps amounting to what one planning faculty member in a small city has called a "rush minute") and the parks and schools are surprisingly good.

A *strength and weakness analysis* typically involves a combination of professional analysis of objective factors and the use of a variety of citizen participation techniques to determine public perceptions (see discussion in chapter 5). One very good way to develop a useful strength and weakness analysis is to use an open-ended input technique for a first round of data gathering and then some sort of review process to give it more structure. In such a process, the planning agency will use public meetings, mailed surveys, telephone surveys, or other techniques to ask people to "list three strengths and two weaknesses" of the community, or something similar. The planning professionals then tabulate all of the results and take them to the planning body or an advisory committee to group, rank, and validate the list. The final step usually involves some sort of validation of the list of strengths and weaknesses by a larger public group, often in an informal public meeting but sometimes through publication and distribution for comment. (See table 4.1.)

Like the analysis of opportunities and constraints, the analysis of strengths and weaknesses can be published as a separate report or as a chapter of the larger plan; because it is usually relatively short, it typically makes sense to include it as part of some larger report.

Issue Identification

A third way to approach the "Where can we go?" question is through an *issue identification* process. The purpose of such an approach is to provide focus for the planning effort. It can take a form similar to that of the strength and weakness analysis, asking participants to identify critical issues in the community.

The list of weaknesses developed in a strength and weakness analysis can actually be considered a starting point for a list of issues under an issue identification approach.

The strength and weakness analysis should produce a comprehensive list of strengths and weaknesses. In contrast, the issue identification approach produces a list of important issues without attempting to be comprehensive. Thus,

Table 4.1. Summary of Citizen Participation in Identifying Strengths and Weaknesses, Opportunities and Constraints in Muncie and Delaware County, Indiana

	Strengths	Weaknesses	Opportunities	Constraints
Yorktown (27 participants signed in)	Volunteer force Nice people White River Central location Taxes Ball Memorial Hospital	Nonprofessional government Poor streets, parks upkeep Poor infrastructure Poor political perception Loss of manufacturing jobs Taxes Lack of city pride	Ball State growth River development Tax break incentives	Loss of jobs, businesses Taxes Newspaper negativity Downtown deterioration
Delta (12 participation signed in)	Ball State Cultural offerings Workers and facilities Good geographic location Cost of living Medical services Regional retail provider	Uncontrolled growth Aesthetics Deteriorated neighbor-hoods Lack of planning High property taxes Apathy Cost of living in com-parison to income	Ball State Areas of history Youth employment Increased youth social standards	Taxes Types of jobs Laborers underrepresented Loss of productive farmland Threats from nonagriculture uses Youth leaving the community Lack of implementation
Central (58 participants signed in)	Ball State University Ball Memorial Hospital Civic theater/arts Horizon Center White River	Taxes Newspaper negativity Local government Alternate transportation	Downtown Parks Sports center Empty manufacturing space Town cooperation	Drugs Crime Loss of jobs Urban sprawl High property taxes Lack of planning commitment

(continues)

Table 4.1. Continued

	Strengths	Weaknesses	Opportunities	Constraints
South Side (41 participants signed in)	Ball State University Ball Memorial Hospital White River Convention center Prairie Creek Cardinal Greenway Nice people Volunteers	Loss of manufacturing Politically divided Political corruption Infrastructure	Ball State Ivy Tech Vacant structures City parks programming Adult/community education Downtown development	Lack of jobs Apathy Lack of regulation enforcement Loss of business Local government Insufficient planning
Email	Proximity to Indianapolis Ball State Ball Memorial Hospital Low cost of living People trying to make changes	Apathy Downtown deterioration Lack of communication across neighborhoods Commuter airport facility (lack of?) Public transportation No country-wide library Local government City-county beautification Race relations Youth activities	Better connections to Ball State, Ball Memorial, county Downtown development Extending SR67 to connect to S. Madison Expressway from CBD to 169 Landscaping for new businesses Linkage between Ft. Wayne and Indy	Apathy Closed community Loss of youth Cardinal Greenway Downtown deterioration Government waste of money Community school system

Source: HNTB Corp., Indianapolis (1998).

if a community has a good but not exceptional road system, that will turn up as a strength in a strength and weakness analysis but probably will not show up in an issue identification study because there does not appear to be any issue requiring resolution. A strength and weakness analysis may show both "rural character" and "agricultural base" as strengths of a community, while an issue identification approach in the same community may include "effect of growing sprawl on the agricultural base."

With an issue identification process, it is important to use an advisory committee, planning commission, or some other group to rank and, if necessary, narrow the range of issues to a manageable one. Often, a tabulation of responses will be self-limiting, with a dozen or fewer issues clearly rising to the top and others receiving only scattered mentions. If the process results in an unwieldy number of issues, it is important to narrow the list to twelve or fifteen that can be thoughtfully addressed in a planning process.

Feasibility and the Comprehensive Planning Process

The planning body and planning agency must make choices about how to use answers to the "Where can we go?" question in the planning process. Those include a choice of techniques and a choice of the timing of those techniques. Injecting the notion of feasibility into the process too strongly of too early can have a constraining effect on the process, limiting the consideration of alternatives. On the other hand, bringing feasibility into the process too lightly or too late may result in the expenditure of time and effort on futile plans to accomplish the impossible.

One of the authors of this book accompanied a group of planning consultants to a meeting with a committee representing a major institution in the community for which the consultants were developing a plan. At the meeting, the consultants provided a summary of their strengths and weaknesses analysis to the committee, which had been charged by its institution with developing an institutional plan to help the larger community. After hearing the report, the chair of that committee commented, "I have never been so depressed about this community in my life." Fortunately, the committee was far enough into its own planning process that members decided to continue, despite a strengths and weaknesses analysis that highlighted some serious weaknesses. That kind of response, however, can stifle discussion or even stymie an entire planning process. Thus, it is important to develop an appropriate strategy for injecting this sort of reality check into a planning process that ought to be open and optimistic.

Choosing a Technique

The analysis of opportunities and constraints provides a useful planning basis for almost any comprehensive plan. Such an analysis also provides data that are useful to those developing more focused plans, plans focused on issues such as economic development or downtown revitalization. If conducted rigorously, it can be relatively expensive, and it is always somewhat time consuming. Thus, those with serious budget or time limitations may want to use a scaled-down version of this technique or one of the related techniques. If the opportunities and constraints analysis is based largely on technical studies (assessing the local economy, infrastructure, demographic trends), it is important that there be a parallel process of public participation, to involve citizens and stakeholders in the process from the beginning.

A strengths and weaknesses analysis is usually heavily participatory. It is often used as a way to initiate a planning process in a small community. Because it is participatory, it often provides a good vehicle for public education—documenting some things that people probably know but do not actively consider. It is often used in smaller communities that cannot afford (or believe they cannot afford) a full opportunities and constraints analysis. Although a strength and weakness analysis can be open ended in the list-building phase, there must be a rational and relatively rigorous method for winnowing the list to a publishable number of strengths and weaknesses that truly represent the views of the community.

The issue identification technique is primarily useful at the beginning of the process. It is very effective for obtaining community input early in the planning process and should be therefore used only where the planning body is willing to take seriously major issues that arise from this process. If the planning body already knows what issues it wants to address, using this technique may simply waste time and result in frustration for participants.

Choosing one of these techniques, or some other, to provide a feasibility perspective to the planning process is in part a function of the available budget, but it is also in part a function of the character of the community and the personality of the planning body.

When to Use the Technique

Clearly opportunities and constraints analysis, strengths and weaknesses analysis, and issues identification are all processes that produce useful information, information that will form a significant foundation for a final plan. The risk with all of these techniques, however, is that the feasibility information may unnecessarily limit the scope of discussion. All of these techniques have roots in the scientific method, which is sometimes criticized as "reductionist."[5] Examining the parts does not necessarily produce an accurate view of the whole, and feasibility analyses necessarily focus on parts.

A successful plan usually comes from a vision or a set of goals. Although at some point the vision or goals must be tempered by what is feasible, introducing the notion of feasibility too early in the process, as mentioned previously, may limit creative thinking. Disneyland, the transcontinental railroad,

Richard Hedman on tough decisions. Deciding when to bring the concept of feasibility into the goal-setting process is a difficult decision. Copyright by Richard Hedman. Used with permission.

electricity, and powered human flight did not meet normal concepts of feasibility when they were proposed. They were dreams as much as plans and the result of commitment to goals as much as to understanding of the scientific method. Communities like Vail, Seaside, and Las Vegas would not exist—at least not in their present form—if those who developed them had been limited in their thinking by traditional feasibility studies. No rational planner viewing an opportunities and constraints analysis of the Bay Area would propose building a city where San Francisco is today (the combination of steep slopes and unstable subsurface geology would color it black on most opportunity and constraint maps that use white to suggest optimal development sites), but it is a great city—and in many ways a very successful one.

Of the techniques described here to determine "where we can go?," issue identification carries with it the fewest risks for constraining the planning process because it does not place parameters around the future. Both opportunities and constraints and strengths and weaknesses analyses tend to create boundaries that limit the planning solutions considered. The risk with issue identification, however, is that it may limit the planning process itself—with the planning body and interested citizens focusing exclusively on the identified issues and not considering other possibilities.

The strength and weakness analysis can be a discouraging or a highly motivating piece in the planning process. If the planning body focuses on building from the strengths and eliminating the weaknesses, it can be an effective planning tool—and can very effectively drive a goal-setting process. If the planning body focuses on the message of the weaknesses, however, it may become so discouraged that it accomplishes little.

The opportunities and constraints analysis is almost always limiting. It is largely applied scientific method, and it carries with it all the hazards of projecting existing trends (a topic discussed in more detail in the next chapter). Russell Ackoff, cited at the beginning of this chapter for his work in systems analysis, has referred to trendline projections as "something that we know will not happen but that, nevertheless, provides a useful frame of reference." In a sense, that is the best way to view an opportunities and constraints analysis—the constraints are not necessarily all real, and the opportunities may not be, either, but any vision or goal that is inconsistent with the analysis will certainly require some additional study and some extra planning effort.

An effective way to integrate this practical but possibly limiting knowledge into the process is to begin efforts at goal setting or developing a vision before any of this sort of analysis is available to the planning body or the public. The processes can begin simultaneously—the professional staff can begin the opportunities and constraints analysis at the same time the planning body begins discussing its vision or goals for the future. Similarly, surveys or other participatory methods used for issue identification or strength and weakness analysis can begin simultaneously with a goal-setting or visioning process.

Then, with a preliminary set of goals and a draft of the feasibility analysis resulting from the examination of issues, opportunities and constraints, or strengths and weaknesses, the planning body, with the assistance of planning professionals, can compare the two. It can discuss whether the goals are consistent with the technical analysis. If not, that group can consider what would be required to reconcile the two—sometimes the expenditure of money can make what seems impractical entirely feasible, and sometimes it is possible to redefine weaknesses or constraints—or goals—to bring the two into alignment. Perhaps that community in Nevada cannot be either a beach resort or the site of the next Disney attraction, but it may be able to build a small lake with the best water park in the state—and attract lots of tourists from the hot summer desert.

If the constraints analysis shows that the local labor force is trained only to make parts for 1970s vintage cars, the community may need to shift its emphasis temporarily from economic development to job training, thus redefining a constraint and creating a new paradigm for economic development.

Conclusion

The existing conditions analysis described in chapter 3, is only a first step. Knowing where we are as a community lays the groundwork for determining where we can go. This chapter presents three alternative (but overlapping) methods of determining where a community can go—opportunities and constraints analysis, strength and weakness analysis, and issue identification. Those are invaluable techniques in planning, and it is essential to use at least one of them—or some closely related technique—in any comprehensive planning process. It is important, however, to use the results of such analysis carefully, to avoid limiting unnecessarily the answers to "Where do we want to go?" Reconciling a feasible future with a desirable or exciting future is one of the greatest challenges that faces any planning body.

The Role of the Professional Planner

The role of the professional planner will vary with the choice of techniques. With some techniques, the planner conducts much of the analysis; in others, the planner facilitates the process, obtaining much of the information from other people. With all of the techniques discussed in this chapter, the professional planner must take the resulting information and make it meaningful.

Opportunities and constraints analysis consists largely of technical, professional work. Thus, the professional planner has the primary responsibility for this work, usually with limited participation from the planning body and from individual citizens.

Assessing strengths and weaknesses requires participation, but it should be structured participation. The role of the professional planner in strengths and weaknesses analysis is to facilitate the process, validate it, and interpret it. This process should include significant participation by the planning body and by interested citizens.

Issue identification is a citizen-driven process, but it requires a professional to make it work. In this technique, the professional planner becomes primarily a process facilitator.

It is the professional planner who then has the responsibility to make this work meaningful, reviewing it in the context of the existing conditions analysis discussed in chapter 3. If the wastewater treatment plant is nearing capacity and that is a constraint on desired growth, the planner must investigate—to find out if there are plans to expand the plant and if funding is available to accomplish that. If people perceive traffic congestion to be a major issue in the community but the existing conditions analysis does not reflect major traffic problems, the planner needs to look behind the data to see whether there are real problems that the objective study missed or simply problems of perception. Sometimes the strengths and weaknesses, opportunities and constraints, and issues analyses lead to obvious conclusions. "Build a new sewer plant" is a straight forward response to limitations on sewage treatment capacity, for example. In other cases, however, planners must examine alternative responses to strengths and opportunities or to weaknesses and constraints.

Usually, the planner will produce a report or memo, outlining the results of this work for the planning body. Although much of this work is technical, it is always a good idea for the professional planner to ask representative members of the planning body to review a draft of the data collected and of the analysis. Sometimes even the best technical work includes a mistake or two. Sometimes an initial draft does not clearly express what the professional intended, or includes words or phrases that have particular local connotations that may attach unintended meanings to the work. It is always better to learn about such problems before publishing a report. In the final analysis, the professional planner should decide whether to revise her own technical work, but it is certainly wise to understand the scope of any possible problems of interpretation well before a public meeting.

One of the most important things for the professional planner to remember in undertaking any of this work, however, is that planning is ultimately a policy-making not a technical process. Thus, no matter what the technical analysis coming from this stage of work may seem to show, it is the planning body, the legislative body, and the public to which it is accountable, that will finally determine the community policies that the plan will represent.

The Role of the Individual Citizen

Much of the work in determining what is feasible is technical in nature and does not directly involve the individual citizen. There are four important roles for interested citizens in this process, however:

1. participate thoughtfully in any assessment of strengths and weaknesses;
2. participate thoughtfully in any issue identification process;
3. carefully review reports on opportunities and constraints or strengths and witnesses and seek corrections of obvious errors; and
4. ask hard questions to help determine whether the professionals have been too conservative or too liberal in assessing what is feasible and what is not.

EXERCISES

1. Working separately or in a small group, make a list of four or five issues facing the community in which you live or study; then compile the lists (combining similar items that simply use different terminology). How many issues are there? Conducting this exercise with a large group will usually yield only eight to twelve dominant issues.
2. Working in a small group, assess the strengths and weaknesses of the community in which you live.

3. Design a process for involving a representative group of people from the community in a process to assess strengths and weaknesses.

DISCUSSION QUESTION

Using the results of exercise 2, choose two or three weaknesses that might reasonably be considered constraints on the future of your community. Can you think of ways to redefine the problems hidden in those weaknesses so as to mitigate or eliminate them—or even to turn them into strengths? Of what system are those problems a part? Who or what controls that system? Can you think of ways to make that locally controllable—or at least subject to local influence?

FURTHER READING

Braybrooke, David, and Charles E. Lindblom. 1970. *A Strategy of Decision: Policy Evaluation as a Social Process.* New York: The Free Press. A classic work on how public decisions are made.

Kaiser, Edward J., David R. Godschalk, and F. Stuart Chapin, Jr. 1995. *Urban Land Use Planning,* 4th edition. Urbana: University of Illinois Press. The latest edition of a classic work on land-use planning. Discusses analysis of land needs and development of a land-use plan.

Kelly, Eric Damian. 1993. *Planning, Growth and Public Facilities: A Primer for Public Officials.* Planning Advisory Service Report 447. Chicago: American Planning Association. Discusses the ways in which public facilities provide both opportunities for and constraints on growth and development patterns.

McHarg, Ian. 1992. *Design with Nature, 25th Anniversary Edition.* New York: John Wiley. Original publication 1969, Garden City, NY: Natural History Press for the American Museum of Natural History. A landmark work that used the techniques of landscape architecture at a regional scale to define opportunities and constraints based on the character of the land and the natural environment.

So, Frank S., and Judith Getzels, eds. 1988. *The Practice of Local Government Planning,* 2nd edition. Washington, DC: International City Management Association. Essentially the fourth edition of a standard reference work, but the titles on the first three are different. Several chapters are included on technical aspects of opportunities and constraints analysis. A new edition is due out in 2000 and should contain similar material, updated.

Thompson, George F., and Frederick R. Steiner, eds. 1997. *Ecological Design and Planning.* New York: John Wiley. A more recent contribution that addresses many of the same issues as the earlier McHarg work.

Wackernagel, Mark, and William Rees. 1996. *Our Ecological Footprint.* New York: New Society Publishers. A useful handbook for planners and a good educational guide to concepts of sustainability.

NOTES

1. Russell Ackoff, *The Art of Problem Solving: Accompanied by Ackoff's Fables,* New York: John Wiley (1978).
2. Thomas Kuhn, *The Structure of Scientific Revolutions,* 2nd edition, enlarged, Chicago: University of Chicago Press (1970).
3. Russell Ackoff *A Concept of Corporate Planning,* New York: Wiley-Interscience (1968).
4. G. West Churchman, *The Systems Approach,* New York: Delacorte Press (1968).
5. See Ackoff, Kuhn, and Churchman, notes 1–4.

Chapter 5

....

Where Do We Want To Go?
Involving Citizens in Making a Plan

All of the data gathering, analysis, and citizen participation are useful only if they help a community answer the question "Where do we want to go?"

The best plans are those that represent the collective will of the community. It is important at this stage of planning to remember that the goal of the planning process is consensus support for a plan, not unanimity of opinion on every subject addressed. In most communities, a planning commission or a steering committee will have the primary responsibility for developing the consensus planning document; ideally, the governing body would be so closely connected to the process that it would quickly ratify the action of the planning body.

Chapter 1 discussed the concept of planning in a democracy from a conceptual perspective. Dealing with that from a practical perspective is the focus of this chapter—leading a community through a participatory process that arrives at consensus support for a plan. The planning commission will play some role in that undertaking in almost every community, because it is the planning commission that, under state law, has both the duty and the responsibility to prepare a plan for the community. When a community decides to use a steering committee or task force as the planning body that carries out the process, the recommended plan must then go to the planning commission for formal action. Even in those states that make a plan effective only after the governing body has approved, accepted, or otherwise formally acted on it, the planning commission must act first.

This chapter addresses the relationship of the planning body, whether a planning commission or special committee or task force, to the larger body politic. In that sense, this entire chapter might appear in the box labeled "The Role of the Individual Citizen." But the professional planner, also, plays an important role here—often a pivotal role in the success of the process.

Richard Hedman on public meetings. Copyright by Richard Hedman. Used with permission.

Methods of Achieving Citizen Participation

Different methods of citizen participation are used to accomplish different things. During the 1970s, there was an emphasis in some agencies on achieving contact with the maximum possible number of citizens in any planning process—that method, which placed great emphasis on using sign-up sheets at meeting after meeting, has been referred to as "the body count method" of citizen participation. Today, most planners place greater emphasis on representative and meaningful citizen participation and less on the number of citizens participating. *Representative* and *meaningful* mean different things, however.

"Representative" citizen participation suggests a process that includes citizens who represent a broad perspective of views and values in the community—young people and old, rich and poor, retired and working, rural and urban, white-collar and blue-collar (and on the dole), west-siders and east-siders, college graduates and high school dropouts, white people and people of color, native-born and permanent residents who are recent immigrants. Some communities create a steering committee or planning body for a new plan primarily to achieve greater representation. Often people who serve on a planning commission represent a relatively narrow part of the community, and in most places that body is limited to five, seven, or nine members. With a steering committee of even twelve or fifteen members, the community can assemble a more diverse and representative group of citizens. Further, people will serve on a short-term task force, even for a year or two, who do not have the time or the desire to commit to long-term public service on a planning commission.

In seeking representative citizen participation, planners and other facilitators typically seek participation from specific groups of stakeholders. Stakeholder groups with an interest in comprehensive planning typically include neighborhood organizations, the chamber of commerce, environmental groups, agricultural groups (in rural areas), business owners, university leaders, social activists, educators, and other groups with common interests.

"Meaningful" citizen participation, on the other hand, suggests that citizens will actually influence the plan through their participation. Under the "body count" approach, some agencies went to public hearings with a finished plan and counted the participation process as a great success if a lot of people showed up—even if they all protested aspects of the plan that the agency had no intention of changing. Meaningful participation suggests early participation, allowing citizens to be part of a plan as it evolves.

The role of citizens in the process varies significantly, however, with the approach to planning. The next section reviews the approaches introduced in chapter 1 and discusses how citizens participate in each.

Approaches to Planning and Citizen Participation

Chapter 1 introduced six different approaches to planning: trends-driven; opportunity-driven; issue-driven; goal-driven; vision-driven; and a blended approach, combining several of those elements. Each implies a different type of planning process and a different type of participation in the determination of where the community wants to go. This section describes the different opportunities that these alternative approaches offer for citizen participation.

Trends-Driven Approach

A trends-driven approach to planning extrapolates current trends into the future and uses those projected trends as the basis for planning. This approach is based on the assumption that the population will continue to grow at its current rate and that, if employment is holding steady, it will continue to do so. Projecting trends is largely technical work that must be accomplished by professional planners. There is little role for citizens in such an approach—but there is little role for anyone to make choices, because the very selection of this approach suggests that the community has decided not to make choices—but just to accept what the future brings.

Projecting trends can be a very useful part of a larger planning exercise, providing frames of reference to show what might happen if the community does not plan. The only safe statement about any trendline, however, is that it will change. Trend projection ought to be used as a context for other planning efforts, not as a primary tool for selecting a future for a community.

Opportunity-Driven Approach

In an opportunity-driven planning process, a community assesses its future based on opportunities and constraints, rather than on simple projections of trends. Typically conducted as a fairly technical exercise, opportunity-driven planning is also not a particularly participatory process. For example, technical analysis may indicate that the community has an ideal combination of skilled workers and proximity to natural resources for manufacturing wood trusses and other building products; that opportunity then influences the community's economic development efforts (contacting building product manufacturers), its land-use plans (designating appropriate sites for this relatively heavy industry), and its transportation plans (ensuring that it has good truck access to its industrial sites). This technique is best used in areas where natural and human-made opportunities and constraints are the driving issues.

One critical step in such a process, however, is soliciting citizen comments on the opportunities and constraints, and citizens thus help to define the parameters for the plan. If local citizens are hostile to the logging industry, the planning body may want to go to the next step. That step involves choices. A community may identify multiple inconsistent or diverging opportunities and must use some sort of process to make choices among them. A community that discovers that one of its greatest constraints is a lack of industrial land or poor workforce skills may decide to mitigate such a constraint with a public-private partnership to build an industrial park or with a new job training program. Finally, as the example at the beginning of this paragraph suggests, some communities may consciously choose not to pursue an obvious opportunity.

Thus, citizen participation in an opportunity-driven process is usually highly structured and may not be particularly visible in the final plan—but it can play a significant role in defining that final plan. An opportunities and constraints analysis can be used in a blended approach with a goal-driven planning process. In that case, it is the goal-setting process that defines the roles of citizens, with the definition of opportunities and constraints simply providing a context.

Issue-Driven Approach

In an issue-driven planning process, a community identifies the critical issues facing it and focuses its planning efforts on those issues. This is a simple and practical approach to planning, in which citizens drive the process, because it is the citizens of the community who must identify the issues.

Communities use a variety of techniques to identify issues, ranging from public meetings to workshops to focus groups to surveys conducted by phone or by mail. This process is one that involves citizen participation very early in the process—and that participation defines the rest of the planning process. Although preparing proposed plans to address and resolve the issues usually falls to the planning body, the work of the planning body is defined by the initial efforts of citizens in identifying the issues.

Goal-Driven Approach

The goal-driven approach is the classic approach to planning. It establishes long-range goals for the community, and those goals guide the rest of the planning process. In principle, this is probably the simplest planning approach to understand. In practice, it is the most complicated process to manage.

It is complicated because it involves asking an entire community to agree on goals for the future. Achieving consensus in an issue-driven planning process is easier, because the identification of the issues defines the questions and limits the answers. For example, if one of the issues facing the community is an unacceptable level of traffic on a particular road, it should not be particularly difficult to use cost-benefit analyses and other techniques to help a group reach agreement on some proposed solution to that problem. In contrast, asking a large group to reach collective agreement on some specific goals and priorities among them, poses an open-ended question. Some may suggest a goal of improving traffic flow in the community, while others suggest that the real goal ought to be to get more people to walk or ride bikes, and yet another group insists that traffic is an irrelevant and trivial issue and what the community really needs to focus its efforts on is reducing crime and increasing job opportunities.

Starting with a clean sheet of paper and asking a large group of people to agree on a set of goals regarding the future of the community is a daunting task. Thus, any goal-setting process involves a great deal of management—and the nature of that management will define the level of citizen participation. Sometimes a goal-setting process starts with an issue identification or an opportunities and constraints analysis to provide context. Such a preliminary step narrows the range of discussion and creates a greater likelihood of consensus. This is one of many combinations of approaches that logically fall under the blended approach, discussed below. In other goal-driven processes, the planning body may prepare an initial set of draft goals for discussion at public meetings. Such discussions, however, typically focus on what has been proposed rather than on what may have been omitted—arguing over the wording of the goals regarding traffic and crime and missing entirely the fact that there is no goal whatsoever regarding the quality of life, for example.

Some communities assign discussions of various topics to different task forces, allowing each to develop its own goals. That increases the opportunities for participation by individuals (because there are more task forces and committees, needing more individual members), but it also increases the risk of confusion from the development of conflicting or diverging goals. (The issue of trying to reconcile different goals developed by different subgroups working under the planning body is discussed in more depth in chapter 8.)

If well managed, the goal-driven approach to planning includes citizen participation at every stage of the process and at appropriate stages weaves into it information developed from other techniques, including opportunities and constraints analysis, strength and weakness analysis, and trend projections. The goal-driven approach is the one most likely to result in a consensus plan.

Vision-Driven Approach

A true vision is an overarching goal that controls the entire planning process. True visions generally arise from within a community through strong leadership (which is often informal). A plan to fulfill a vision can be one of the most exciting kinds of plans to develop, but it is often one of the least participatory.

Veteran ski troopers from World War II had a vision of making Aspen a ski resort. Walt Disney had a vision of creating his own "land" near Anaheim and, later, his own "world" near Orlando. A handful of people, some with colorful backgrounds, had a vision of making Las Vegas a gaming capital. James Rouse had a vision of an entirely new town in Howard County, Maryland, and he built Columbia. It was visionary leadership that attracted the Baltimore Colts and, many years later, the headquarters of the National Collegiate Athletic Association, to Indianapolis. Yellowstone Park, Hoover Dam (and Lake Powell behind it), and Colonial Williamsburg are spectacular examples of implemented visions. These examples represent powerful visions but typically not participatory ones.

The only real role of citizens in a truly vision-driven approach is to ratify (or reject) the vision. Far more visions are thwarted than realized, and often it is public participation that does the thwarting. Citizen participation can help to reshape or redefine a vision, but a vision that is strong enough (or has strong enough leadership) to change a community is often strong enough to repel most attempts to modify it. On the other hand, if the vision is that of an external force rather than of community leaders, it may not succeed; a later Disney proposal to build a history-oriented theme park in Virginia turned out to be *only* a Disney vision—with significant support from some state and county officials but without the kind of community support that could make it a reality.

Some communities, and a number of consultants, use the term *visioning* loosely to apply to a goal-setting process. There is nothing wrong with that use of the term, but it is not the meaning intended here. Other communities use the term to refer to a goal-setting process uninformed by any of the data gathering and analysis suggested in this text as essential to a planning process. That approach is sometimes attractive because it is relatively simple and inexpensive, but suggesting that a community set goals without information is a little like asking an eight year old who has no concept of budget to plan a family vacation. When a community uses a participatory process to define a series of things that it hopes to achieve in the future, it is using a goal-driven approach.

The term *vision* here refers only to that single, focused, overarching idea that defines the rest of a plan. Because a true vision usually begins with a leader or small group of leaders, both citizen participation and technical analysis (Does the community have the necessary strengths and opportunities to make it work? Are there significant constraints or weaknesses that may impede its realization?) come later in the process. The vision drives the plan, and everything revolves around and reacts to that. A truly vision-driven plan is relatively rare, but it can be very powerful.

Blended Approach

Most local plans involve some combination of planning approaches, and the dominant approach typically defines the role of citizens. Thus, if an approach is primarily goal-driven but is informed by an analysis of strengths and weaknesses from the opportunity-driven approach, it is the goal-driven process that will define the form and level of citizen participation.

Techniques for Citizen Participation

There are many different approaches to citizen participation in community planning. This section describes the ones used most frequently.

One of the major issues in citizen participation is the reality of people's lives. Citizen participation methods are useful only if people participate. Today's families are busy. With many one-parent households, with two working parents in many other households, with senior citizens often back in the labor force, and with a wide variety of recreational opportunities available in communities, it is often difficult for citizens to find time to participate in civic life. Recognizing the value of citizen participation, some local governments have turned to marketing and public relations to gain citizen involvement in the process.

The approach most often used by planners combines marketing techniques such as advertisements in newspapers and spots in broadcast media, the latter usually produced as public service announcements, to educate citizens about the process. Direct mailings of surveys, flyers, and brochures are employed to solicit citizen views when public opinion on specific elements and issues of the plan is needed. Newspaper supplements and display boards moved among shopping malls and other public locations offer good ways to expose more complex ideas to citizens—both to educate them and to engage them in the process with the intent of encouraging a response. Local governments increasingly use Web sites and other electronic means to encourage participation. Some planning processes use dedicated electronic kiosks at key community locations to provide information to residents and to encourage feedback.

Public Hearings

Required by most state laws before planning commissions and governing bodies can vote on plans and ordinances, public hearings represent the most formal and most traditional kind of citizen participation. As the official body with planning responsibility, the planning commission holds the public hearing on a new plan in most communities. A public hearing usually involves the presentation of a specific proposal by its proponents or sponsors, followed by comments from interested citizens and groups.

State laws typically require certain forms of notice for a public hearing and may define other aspects of the process. Most state laws require at least that the subject of the public hearing be announced by publication and by posting on an agenda at the seat of local government (typically city hall or the county courthouse). Planners facilitating a comprehensive planning process will usually seek news stories on a public hearing and may make direct mailings about it to interested groups. Notice is a critical element of the hearing process. To be effective, notice either should provide enough information about a proposal to allow citizens seeing the notice to begin to form an opinion ("The city proposes to vacate Fourth Street between Main and Grand") or should identify a way that interested citizens can obtain such information ("Copies of the plan are available in the planning office, at all branches of the public library, and on the city's Web site").

Of necessity, public hearings occur late in the process—typically right before adoption. At a public hearing discussing a proposal to change the fines for overtime parking from five dollars to seven dollars, it is quite possible for citizens to participate in a meaningful dialogue with the governing body considering the ordinance. At a public hearing on a complex plan—whether 23 pages or 223 pages—that has evolved from a year-long effort by the planning body, it is much more difficult for citizens to participate meaningfully. Although the hearing provides a good forum for people who want to object to a particular proposed policy or even seek correction of an apparent factual error, it is not an effective means for people to raise new questions or suggest alternative policy approaches. At that stage in the planning process, both the planning body and the project budget are likely to be nearing exhaustion. Major opposition to a proposed plan at that stage is as likely to result in defeat and abandonment of the plan as to result in significant change in the plan.

In short, public hearings are an essential but often not an effective means of citizen participation in the comprehensive planning process.

Other Public Meetings

Most comprehensive planning processes involve other open, public meetings at which citizens can voice their concerns and views. Such meetings are sometimes held early in the process to help identify issues or concerns and usually begin with little more than an introductory statement about the process.

Other meetings may occur somewhat later in the process, after professional planners have developed trend projections, opportunities and constraints analyses, and other background data. At such meetings, planners usually share the background data and analysis prepared to date to provide citizens with a context in which to talk about issues and goals. Such meetings serve a dual purpose: educating citizens about the state of the community and its opportunities and constraints, and seeking comments from them early enough in the process to define its shape and form. The earlier citizens are involved in the planning, the better educated they will be about the process and the greater the likelihood that they will help to make it a success. One outcome of citizen participation is the creation of a sense of community, and that is most likely to come from a process of public meetings.

Some planning processes use community-wide meetings, while others focus on neighborhood meetings. The advantage of neighborhood meetings is that they almost always reach more people, but there are two major disadvantages of this approach. One disadvantage is the obvious one: the cost of the time and effort to handle multiple meetings. The other disadvantage is more subtle. Neighborhood meetings are likely to attract groups of people with similar backgrounds and similar interests. Thus, everyone at the north-side neighborhood meeting may agree that the most important issue facing the community is the need for a new northeast bypass around their area; if they hear only their own voices, people may leave that meeting believing that indeed that is the number-one priority for the entire community. People at the south-side meeting may have other priorities, like a new park. It may be possible to accommodate all of the priorities in the final plan, but the burden on the planning body increases with the use of multiple meetings. If all interested citizens attend the same meeting, they can hear from each other that there are different priorities for different people and different parts of town; if they attend separate meetings, the planning body or the professional planners must carry the messages of citizens from one meeting to another.

Public meetings conducted at key stages of the process are one of the most important and most effective forms of citizen participation. A public meeting with a truly open agenda—at which the planning body really wants to listen—is almost always a satisfying event. The real challenge is to synthesize the information and comments from it and make them meaningful to the process.

Stakeholder Group Meetings

It is often useful at the beginning of a planning process to meet with known stakeholder groups—neighborhood associations, environmental organizations, chambers of commerce, home builders, bankers, economic development groups, leagues of taxpayers and interested citizens, and other known interest groups.

These meetings are particularly useful for issue identification. The goals and political positions of the groups may seem fairly obvious, but it is important to understand what issues are of concern to each. There may be surprises at these meetings. The chamber of commerce may actively seek more restrictive sign controls and the economic development group may urge the adoption of better landscaping requirements to create a more pleasing aesthetic appearance for the community. Stakeholder groups can also provide significant assistance in the assessment of strengths and weaknesses, and opportunities and constraints.

Perhaps even more important, meetings with stakeholder groups begin to build a constituency to support the planning process. Organizations are much more likely to support the planning process if they believe that they will play an important role in it—and there is nothing that delivers that message better than a private meeting with leaders of the effort early in the process. This can also be an invaluable opportunity to establish communications with key interest groups, encouraging informal as well as formal input into the planning process.

The involvement of stakeholder groups must be structured to provide actual and perceived balance. Stakeholder groups included in the process ought to include a broad cross-section of interests in the community. Even at that, stakeholder meetings do not replace public meetings. Not all interested citizens are part of organized stakeholder groups, and not all members of organizations believe in everything that the leaders of the organization say. Thus, public meetings remain an essential element of public participation.

Key-Person Interviews

Some planning processes use interviews with key people as a method of issue identification and constituency building early in the planning process. Often the key people interviewed are leaders of stakeholder groups, but they may also be independent community leaders and public officials who would not be included in meetings with stakeholder groups.

The benefits and risks of key-person interviews are similar to the benefits and risks of stakeholder group meetings, but key-person interviews may be even less representative. Such interviews ought never to be viewed as the basis of a consensus or representative view, but they can provide an excellent format for the identification of issues, the establishment of communications, and the creation of a constituency for a plan.

Focus Groups

The focus group is a concept borrowed from marketing. It typically involves a group intended to be reasonably representative of the community, to which the planning agency—or other process facilitator—poses one or more questions on which it would like to assess the larger community's probable views.

The focus group provides a useful technique for issue identification and even for the development of drafts of goals and policy statements. It can be a particularly useful tool when the planning body is small and not broadly representative of the community.

Some meeting facilitators create random focus groups as breakout groups from larger public meetings. In a community in Oklahoma, one of the authors of this book helped to facilitate a kick off meeting for the planning process, attended by 150 leaders, broadly representative of the community. After providing an overview of the planning process, the professional planners asked those in attendance to break up into ten separate groups and asked that each group develop a list of the three or four most important issues facing the community. All of the groups then reported to the larger meeting with their lists. In theory, there might have been thirty or more issues (three or four issues per group multiplied by ten groups); actually, eight issues clearly formed the top of the list when the responses of all groups were compiled. Such a process provided a relatively quick and effective way to define the major issues facing the community. The planners later supplemented that information with key-person interviews, stakeholder group meetings, and informal group meetings, as well as survey techniques—but the issues identified at that first meeting remained at the top of the list.

Surveys

Public meetings are useful but not necessarily representative. If the primary goal is issue identification or analysis of strengths and weaknesses, the process of public meetings can work well—people with strong feelings about issues and community characteristics are likely to attend meetings and ensure that their voices are heard. Politicians who talk about a "silent majority," however, speak accurately—most people in most communities do not attend public meetings or speak on public issues. Some of those people simply have no views or no strong views on the issues; others may have strong views but lack the time or the will to appear in public to state them.

Sometimes community leaders want a more representative sense of the views of citizens. The best way to get representative views is through surveys. Survey techniques vary significantly and produce different sorts of results. Professionally managed, random surveys of the sort used by national opinion-polling firms can produce results that are reasonably representative of the community as a whole. They use a variety of "sampling" methods to provide some assurance that the participants in the survey are representative of the larger

	More Funding	Same Funding	Less Funding	No Opinion
Maintaining or improving utility services (sewer/water)	39.1	52.5	2.0	1.7
Improving storm drainage system	36.7	50.7	7.0	2.9
Improving highways and streets	46.9	45.2	4.4	0.6
Improving the bus system	16.9	49.6	24.2	5.2
Improving airport services	16.0	52.5	24.2	3.8
Creating new jobs/increasing the economic base	48.4	35.6	10.8	1.5
Revitalizing downtown Wichita as a regional employment center	44.3	27.7	23.3	2.3
Revitalizing downtown Wichita and the river corridor as a cultural & recreational center	43.7	23.9	27.1	2.0
Preserving historic buildings	23.3	48.7	23.3	1.7
Improving housing in older neighborhoods	37.0	42.9	15.5	1.5
Improving physical image and appearance	33.8	48.7	11.1	2.0
Improving code enforcement activities (housing maintenance, unsightly or dangerous property, etc.)	48.4	40.2	7.6	0.9
Improving police services	49.3	44.6	3.2	1.2
Improving fire services	38.8	53.1	4.1	1.7
Improving emergency medical services	28.0	63.3	4.7	2.0
Improving the library system	18.7	61.8	15.2	1.5
Improving the park/recreation system	22.2	60.6	12.6	1.5
Maintaining environmental quality (pollution: air, water, etc.)	42.9	49.3	4.1	0.3
Improving social services (public health, elderly/public housing, etc.)	27.1	51.9	15.5	2.0

Other: Citizen Participation; leash law/stray animal enforcement; maintain AFB; control property tax; NE police station; corresponding police/fire service area; less corporate subsidies; county recreation areas; sidewalks; school/education services; Kellogg freeway; tourism; new industrial base; gov'n't salaries; building code education; quality of life; improve environment quality; revitalize downtown; people living near downtown; alternate sources for landfills; get rid of drug dealers; keep criminals in jail; early retirement; joint use of schools; water plan/supply; leave river alone.

This chart shows a summary of the results of a survey on major planning issues used as part of the planning process in Wichita and Sedgwick County, Kansas. Respondents were asked their opinion, based on their experience and knowledge, regarding future funding for the various considerations relative to current spending. Source: *Based on Metropolitan Area Planning Department (1993).*

	Very Important	Moderately Important	Not Important	No Opinion
Protection of prime agricultural land	42.9	31.2	19.2	2.9
Preservation of floodplains for public use	29.7	48.4	11.1	5.2
Use of incentives to encourage rehabilitation and infill development in older areas	46.4	39.7	7.9	2.0
Use of policies to strengthen the downtown area as the major concentration of office employment for the region	44.3	31.2	18.4	2.0
Improve zoning ordinances to ensure more compatible land uses	50.1	34.1	6.7	3.5

One good way to find out what is important to people is to ask them what projects ought to be funded by the local government. Here, respondents in Wichita and Sedgwick County, Kansas, were asked to rate various land-use issues by level of importance. Source: *Metropolitan Area Planning Department (1993).*

group. Such scientifically controlled studies are quite different from open surveys, in which anyone can participate, because individual respondents decide on their own whether to participate.

Planners are more likely to use the open survey, however, both because it is often cheaper and easier to administer and because it involves more people. Common examples of such surveys are those published in the newspaper with a mail-back or fax-back form, those conducted on-line at a Web site, and those stuffed in utility bills. In theory, surveys stuffed in utility bills to every household in a community ought to produce results broadly representative of the community—in fact, people who are better educated and more affluent are far more likely to respond to those surveys than others, and retired people are more likely to respond than young families in which all of the adults work.[1]

Random, controlled surveys are usually conducted by telephone. Even that builds in a certain amount of bias (pollsters falsely reported that Thomas Dewey had been elected president in 1948, based on carefully controlled random telephone surveys—later analysis showed that the flaw in their sampling technique was that Republicans were more likely to have telephones than Democrats).[2] But telephone surveying offers the most cost-effective means of conducting a controlled sampling technique. A sample size as small as two hundred in a properly managed study can give a good indication of community views, and a sample of five hundred should give a very representative indication of community views, with a high confidence rate.[3] National opinion polls are typically based on sample sizes in the range of one thousand people.[4]

Some communities use surveys to elicit citizen views on very particular subjects. Anton Nelessen has trademarked a concept called a Visual Preference Survey™, which he uses to determine exactly what the name suggests.[5] The Burnham Group's Chris McGetrick, of Little Rock, Arkansas, has developed a similar technique, which she calls a "community choice survey." Both techniques involve taking a survey based on pictures. Because the technique uses a large number of colored pictures, this survey works best when taken in structured meetings, administered by someone familiar with the technique. The facilitator shows slides, pairs of slides, or groups of slides and asks participants to make choices among them and to rate their desirability.

Surveys, like public meetings, can provide a valuable means of determining public views and concerns. At the end of the process, however, the job of preparing the plan falls back to the planning body. Whether the survey is scientific or not, representative or not, the planning body must weigh it against facts, analysis, trends, and its own knowledge of the local situation in developing a proposed plan.

Simulations and Scenario Development

Communities sometimes use the presentation of alternative scenarios of the future to encourage citizen participation. When such scenarios show very different futures, they can encourage a lively discussion and engage citizens who may have difficulty comprehending community planning in the abstract. With the growing sophistication of computer technology, planners have been able to use computer modeling and photographic imaging techniques to help citizens visualize the possible results of planning and development goals. Computer images can be created by adding, deleting, and reorganizing elements of a picture. These imaging techniques can be used at many scales. At a small scale, planners may propose a bike lane on a major street, buffering the new lane from automobile traffic with trees and shrubs. Using the graphic capabilities of modern computers, a skilled operator can easily show residents what the new street would look like, complete with cars and bikes on it. At a larger scale, planners can drop a new skyscraper into a downtown, a new regional mall along a highway, or a new automobile plant into a rural area.

Computer imaging is accessible, comprehensible, and often dramatic. Simulations can help citizens to express educated views about alternative scenarios and can help those who do not think abstractly to understand how the future might look. It is a very effective means of encouraging intelligent participation in making choices about alternative futures.

A simulation technique used long before computer simulations became so easy is gaming. It remains a popular tool today because it can be highly interactive. The *Sim City*™ computer simulation of decision making in a city is a good example. In some forms of planning-related gaming, participants are given a scaled map of the community with schematic models of buildings and allowed to rearrange and rebuild the community to meet whatever goals they define. Most computer simulations are presented to interested citizens for reaction, but gaming techniques directly involve citizens in making decisions and developing the scenarios. They can have great value when they accurately represent the choices available to the community. When participants begin moving existing buildings around downtown, something that is unlikely to happen in a real community, the exercise becomes less useful.

Charrettes

The charrette is a concept adopted from architecture, where it refers to a short but intensive collaborative effort to develop a detailed and finished plan for a specific project. It comes from a French word for the small carts on which architects sometimes finished their drawings on the way to a project site or presentation. Today it sometimes refers to a planning tool used to address a very specific issue or a plan for a small area of the community—a neighborhood park, a downtown plaza, or an entranceway.

Communities sometimes sponsor a series of charrettes that last only two or three days each to engage residents and others interested in an area in working with professionals to develop a design solution. The best charrettes require a good deal of preparation by professionals, who typically prepare a "design brief" that defines the project and sets out the parameters for the solution.

Residents of Kosciusko County, Indiana, participate in a planning charrette conducted by students and faculty of Ball State University. Photo by James Segedy, AICP.

Charrettes produce a solution in a short period of time. They can be used to address a specific, narrowly defined element of a comprehensive plan or to provide greater detail for a concept identified in an adopted plan. One of the authors of this book was involved with a charrette process used to achieve consensus on a new auto and pedestrian circulation plan for a downtown area, a need that was discovered in the context of designing a comprehensive land-use and circulation plan for the entire community. The downtown needed a more detailed plan because of the desire of many residents to change the traffic patterns on several streets and to improve parking. Charrettes can be a particularly effective technique for involving citizens in decisions about physical design, such as developing a plan for a new plaza or a community center. Because citizens can participate in the design exercise directly with the designers (rather than simply reacting to designs prepared outside their presence), they can both understand and influence the design process.

Conclusion

Effective community plans are plans that are "of the community" and "for the community," if not entirely "by the community." It is through citizen participation that a body charged with the responsibility for developing a plan can ensure that the plan truly is for the community. It is also through citizen participation that the planning body and planning agency involve the community in the process, so that those in the community who care can participate sufficiently that they believe that the plan is truly representative of the community and its collective will.

The Role of the Professional Planner

Although the focus of citizen participation is on the citizens who participate, it is the process managers—often professional planners—on whom the process depends for success. The professional planners or other organizers must arrange and attend meetings, publicize meeting times and places, provide background information and data, and assist with such details as recording the meetings.

In some communities, the planning body itself will conduct most public meetings, and its members may even handle focus group meetings and interviews with stakeholder groups. Many planning bodies, however, handle only the major public meetings themselves and expect professional planners to conduct neighborhood meetings, focus group meetings, and interviews with key people and stakeholder groups. In such a community, the planner must be facilitator, synthesizer, and reporter—bringing back to the planning body an organized and accurate summary of the parts of the process attended only by the planner.

Planners with mediation skills can be particularly effective in this process. Disagreements will arise in a process of public participation, and a good mediator can help people come together. Often conflicts arise from differences in values. Helping participants to understand those values can depersonalize and defuse conflicts. Sometimes what appear to be conflicts are simply differences, and an effective planner-mediator can identify an approach that responds to the varied goals of participants, sacrificing none of them but perhaps redefining some.

Perhaps the most difficult task for a planner—particularly a beginning planner—at this stage of the process is to recognize that the plan evolving is the community's plan, not the planner's plan. There will be times when a planner will just know the perfect way to approach a problem with which a group is struggling, and other times when a planner may be absolutely certain that the consensus reached by the group is wrong as a matter of policy. Although it is certainly acceptable for a planner to provide suggestions at appropriate points in the process, he or she must guide the process without dictating its results. One of the wonders of democracy is that a democratic group will accept more easily and with more conviction the answer developed by the group through an hour of discussion than the one presented by the professional in a minute—even if the two are the same answer.

The Role of the Individual Citizen

The role of the interested citizen is twofold: to ensure that the process of developing a new plan in the community is appropriately participatory, and to engage responsibly in that process.

This chapter provides a guide for the types of participation that people ought to see offered in local planning processes. If someone sees her or his community developing a plan without some of the types of citizen participation described in this chapter, it is important to ask why. Media reporters, particularly those who work for newspapers, may be interested in the subject.

It is critical that interested citizens actually take advantage of the opportunities to participate. Take time to return the survey. Attend at least one of the public meetings, even if there is housework to do or a favorite TV show on that evening. Read about the plan in the newspaper. Obtain copies of drafts. Submit comments if the process is open to that. Involve friends, neighbors, and colleagues.

Finally, attend the public hearing. Anyone who supports the plan should be there to be sure that it is adopted. Anyone who opposes any major part of it should be there to make one last attempt to seek an amendment or revision. Although it is important to participate in the planning process as early as possible, and usually long before the public hearing, it is also important to attend the public hearing.

EXERCISES

1. Find a copy of the computer game *Sim City*,[6] and play it with a group. Test some alternative scenarios for the future of the "simulated city."
2. Attend a public hearing of your local planning commission. How much citizen participation is there? How useful is it? How effective is it? Do you think that the citizens participating are truly representative of the community? Do the members of the planning commission seem to understand that?
3. If possible, attend an informal public meeting discussing a planning issue. Compare it to the public hearing. Which one do you think is the more effective vehicle for addressing a complex issue?
4. Make a list of stakeholder groups in your community. If you interviewed all of the groups on your list, do you think it would give you a good cross-section of the views of the community?

DISCUSSION QUESTION

Is there a collective vision for the future of your community? If not, could you help your community to develop some goals?

FURTHER READING

Gil, Efraim and Enid Lucchesi. 1988. "Citizen Participation in Planning," in, Frank S. So and Judith Getzels, eds. *The Practice of Local Government Planning,* 2nd edition. Washington, DC: International City Management Association. An important discussion of the role of citizens in developing a plan.

McClendon, Bruce W., and Ray Quay. 1988. *Mastering Change: Winning Strategies for Effective City Planning.* Chicago: Planners Press. A leading work on the role of professional planners in facilitating the planning process and managing the planning function of local government.

Miller, Thomas I., and Michelle A. Miller. 1991. *Citizen Surveys: How to Do Them, How to Use Them, What They Mean.* Washington, DC: International City Management Association. A very practical guide, designed for use by local governments.

Nelessen, Anton C. 1994. *Visions for a New American Dream.* Chicago: Planners Press. Describes his Visual Preference Survey™ technique.

Rodgers, Joseph Lee, Jr. 1977. *Citizen Committees: A Guide to Their Use in Local Government.* Cambridge, MA: Ballinger Publishing. A classic work by a planning educator who taught some of the leading planners in the United States, including Bruce McClendon (see entry above).

Smith, Herbert H. 1979. *The Citizen's Guide to Planning.* Chicago: Planners Press. Planning from the citizen's perspective. A classic, reprinted many times.

Solnit, Albert. 1987. *The Job of the Planning Commissioner,* 3rd edition. Chicago: Planners Press. A classic that will not soon be outdated; it provides a somewhat different perspective on these issues, considering them from the perspective of the citizen planner.

van Houten, Therese, and Harry P. Hatry. 1987. *How to Conduct a Citizen Survey.* Planning Advisory Service Report No. 404. Chicago: American Planning Association. A practical and useful guide to a variety of participatory techniques; out of print but available in many libraries and planning departments.

REFERENCES

Asher, Herbert. 1995. *Polling and the Public: What Every Citizen Should Know.* Washington, DC: CQ Press. A discussion of the benefits and hazards of public opinion polling.

Gallup, George. 1944. *A Guide to Public Opinion Polls.* Princeton, NJ: Princeton University Press. A defining classic in the field; interesting discussion of sample sizes.

Moore, C. Nicholas. 1995. *Participation Tools for Better Land-Use Planning.* Washington, DC: Center for Livable Communities. Describes in more detail several of the techniques discussed briefly here.

Walsh, Mary L. 1997. *Building City Involvement.* Washington, DC: International City Management Association. A practical guide for local government in general.

NOTES

1. See Herbert Asher, *Polling and the Public: What Every Citizen Should Know.* Washington, DC: CQ Press (1995).

2. The pollster's own earlier discussion of the accuracy of his technique is interesting in this context. See George Gallup, *A Guide to Public Opinion Polls,* Princeton: Princeton University Press (1944).

3. See, for example, Celinda C. Lake, with Pat Callbeck Harper, Public Opinion Polling: A Handbook for Public Interest and Citizen Advocacy Groups, Washington, DC: Island Press (1987); Norman M. Bradburn and Seymour Sudman, *Polls and Surveys: Understanding What They Tell Us,* San Francisco: Jossey-Bass (1988); and Thomas I. Miller and Michelle A. Miller, *Citizen Surveys: How to Do Them, How to Use Them, What They Mean,* Washington: International City Management Association (1991)

4. Bradburn and Sudman, p. 125.

5. Described by its creator in Anton Clarence Nelessen, *Visions for a New American Dream,* Chicago: Planners Press (1994).

6. Published by Maxis. Contact at 800-245-4525, 2121 North California Blvd., Suite 600, Walnut Creek, CA 94596, or at http://www.maxis.com. Available in many stores that carry software and at some libraries.

Part II

The Tangible Plan

Planning is a process. To be effective, the process must lead to a tangible result. The tangible result of the community planning process is the comprehensive plan document. This part of the book describes the essential elements of a good comprehensive plan and the form that such a plan might take.

Chapter 6 discusses what is often the most visible part of a comprehensive plan, the plan for future land use. Because it is the part of a plan that most affects private property owners and other individuals, it is the part that is often the most controversial.

Chapter 7 discusses the related topic of planning for public facilities to serve the community. Construction and expansion of such facilities represent the largest capital investments made by local governments; they also represent the most powerful tools that the local government has to implement the comprehensive plan. Public facilities that affect or depend on comprehensive planning efforts and implementation include roads and highways, sewer and water lines, park and recreation facilities, and a variety of public lands and buildings ranging from trails to schools to fire stations.

Finally, chapter 8 examines how to bring the whole plan together into a cohesive document or set of documents that will be useful to guide decisions for the community. It examines the practical and political issues involved in preparing the final plan and guiding it through the adoption and implementation process.

Chapter 6

....

How Do We Plan for Future Land Use?

Future land use is a central concern of comprehensive planning. One of the most troublesome issues in planning in the United States, however, is that local governments do not own most of the land for which they develop plans.

Planning for roads, utilities, schools, and other essential public services depends in part on effective planning for future land use. Residents, businesses, and managers of industry depend heavily on zoning (see chapter 10) to create predictability in uses around the property where they live and work. Zoning a developed area can be a fairly straightforward process if the planning body simply zones the area to match the current use. To zone outlying and developed areas for future use, however, requires a good future land-use plan.

This chapter discusses some of the special issues involved in the creation of a future land-use plan for a community. In a broad sense, this entire book is about the future land-use plan, which is the central element in a comprehensive plan; this chapter, however, focuses on those issues that make the future land-use planning process particularly challenging.

Creating the Future Land-Use Map

The future land-use map is very different from the maps described in the first few chapters of this book. Those are all maps of how things are now. The maps summarizing and analyzing existing conditions are like photographs, in that they represent physical conditions at a particular point in time. Preparing those maps is largely technical work, involving professional judgment but no public policy.

Designating lands for future uses, however, requires major public policy decisions—decisions that directly affect private land. The future land-use map designates some neighborhoods for preservation and others for redevelopment; it identifies historic districts that may be heavily regulated and leaves others districts alone; it shows patterns of urban development that will encourage some farmers to sell their land for development while seemingly similar lands remain rural; it identifies where industry will go and where people will shop. If implemented, it will make some land more valuable than it is today, and it may make some less valuable. The plan will make some residents happy by designating desirable land uses around them, but it will make others unhappy, because the high-impact and less desirable uses have to go somewhere.

The principles described here build on those discussed throughout the first part of the book. The strengths and weaknesses analysis as well as the opportunities and constraints analysis should contribute to the creation of a viable future land-use plan.

Basic Principles

Some basic principles govern the development of a future land-use plan. They are discussed in the following pages.

- *Existing uses.* One of the main reasons that people engage in planning for a community is to protect what they value about it. Remember that one of the primary reasons that zoning was developed was to protect neighborhoods from unwanted change. Similarly, planning today places an emphasis on protecting the desirable and stable parts of the community. That results in a presumption that the future use of land already in active use will be the same as the present use. Not all communities apply that principle to agriculture, which is sometimes considered "undeveloped," but some do. Clearly, this principle does not apply to a blighted area or other area obviously in need of revitalization, nor does it apply to old uses that are incompatible with the surrounding neighborhoods. Despite these exceptions, in most comprehensive plans, 90 percent or more of developed areas of the community will show the same future land use as the current one.
- *Use compatibility.* Land-use planning evolved simultaneously with its implementation tool, zoning, which is based on the principle of separating land uses into compatible districts. Today, the most basic principles of compatibility separate industrial uses from residential ones, for the protection of each of those categories of use, and generally also separate residential uses from intense commercial uses. Early plans treated apartments and mobile homes as incompatible with other residential uses, and residents of many communities today support such an approach. Larger communities typically recognize that commercial uses like lumberyards and auto dealers generate such heavy automobile traffic that they are incompatible with pedestrian-friendly uses like dry goods and other retail stores.

Some of the neighborhoods seeking protection by means of early zoning ordinances included healthy mixes of residential and commercial uses—they simply sought protection from industrial uses. At some point, many communities extended the principle of separation of uses to separate commercial uses from residential uses, thus eliminating plans for future neighborhood business districts and even eliminating the second-floor apartments above downtown retail stores—residential units that served an important part of the housing market.

The Federal Housing Administration published a "land-use intensity" system that created a matrix of intensities, recognizing that a big apartment complex and an office building resemble each other more in their impacts on the community than the office building would resemble commercial uses with which it might otherwise be classified or than the apartment building would resemble other residential uses.[1] John Rahenkamp has used "impact zoning"[2] and Lane Kendig "performance zoning"[3] to address the same principle—that a simple use chart is not sophisticated enough to provide the basis for a good plan, that impacts are the real issue.

Note that the focus on land-use compatibility planning is really on *incompatibility* planning. A realistic approach to compatibility planning would suggest that residential neighborhoods need commercial areas and that downtown areas benefit from having people live there. Nevertheless, the concept of land-use incompatibility is often a driving force in creating a plan. There is also a "political" element to it in some established areas, where residents and business owners may oppose anything different from what is already there.

- *Land demand.* A starting point in land-use planning is often land-demand projection, typically focusing on developed land needs. Professional planners project future population and then determine how much land will be necessary to house that population, using current density patterns or some other model that makes sense in the context of the plan. That part of land-needs analysis is relatively straightforward. Some planners project industrial land needs based on an economic development plan, but others attempt to compute the industrial land that would be necessary to employ the number of working people likely to live there in the future; obviously, the latter is not a useful calculation in a suburb, and it is one with some unrealistic built-in assumptions. Commercial land needs are usually projected as a function of population—assuming that commercial land will grow in direct proportion to population or residential land. This technique has been used in planning for more than sixty years.

Housing plans (discussed in chapter 18) may dictate some of the land needs used as the basis of future land-use plans. Housing considerations are particularly important in communities with a shortage of affordable hous-

Table 6.1. Household Forecast by Structure Type and New Land-Use Acreage Forecast for City of Norman, Oklahoma, 1995–2020

A. HOUSEHOLD FORECAST TYPE, 1995–2020

Type of Structure	1995	2000	2005	2010	2015	2020
Single-family detached	22,788	24,452	26,070	27,635	29,094	30,331
Duplex	1,212	1,321	1,427	1,529	1,624	1,705
Triplex/quadriplex	2,240	2,441	2,637	2,825	3,002	3,151
Townhouses	1,330	1,449	1,565	1,677	1,781	1,870
Multi-family	7,528	8,202	8,859	9,493	10,085	10,586
Total	35,098	37,865	40,558	43,159	45,586	47,643

B. NEW LAND-USE ACREAGE FORECAST, 1995–2020

	1995–2000	2001–2005	2006–2010	2011–2015	2016–2020	Total
Private sector						
Office uses	24	20	18	16	11	89
Retail uses	136	116	106	93	74	525
Industrial/ warehousing	64	53	47	39	30	233
Public sector						
Parks	126	47	47	48	47	315
Residential						
Single-family detached	517	502	486	453	384	2,342
Duplex	21	21	20	19	16	97
Triplex/quadriplex	36	35	34	32	27	164
Townhouses	19	18	18	16	14	85
Multifamily	49	48	46	43	36	222
Total	992	860	822	759	639	4,072

Notes: A. Single-family breakdowns for five-year intervals derived as a linear interpolation of single-family growth to the increase in total units. Multiple unit breakdowns calculated at the same proportion as 1995 for each type to all units in multiple unit structure. B. All figures are in acres.
Sources: The Burnham Group for the City of Norman (1995).

ing; it is essential that future land-use plans include land appropriate for targeted categories of affordable housing, such as apartments and townhouses.

Table 6.1A and 6.1B show forecasts of households and land use that will be needed in the year 2020, as projected from current use (in 1995).

- *Environmental opportunities and constraints.* Some communities based the future plans for undeveloped parts of the community almost entirely on an analysis of environmental or land-based opportunities and constraints, a technique discussed in chapter 4. This technique can help a community decide which areas are most appropriate for future development, which ought to be protected for agriculture, and which ought to be protected because they are environmentally sensitive. This approach is always used in combination with other approaches, because the natural opportunities and constraints analysis provides information that is most useful for undeveloped lands. For infill and redevelopment in developed areas of the community, it is more appropriate to use other future-use planning techniques.
- *Transportation influences.* Transportation significantly influences land-use patterns, a topic discussed in more depth in chapter 7. For example, industry has special land needs, typically focused on major transportation routes. Similarly, major retailers want to locate along busy roads, and the community wants them there—not on smaller roads, where they may create unreasonable levels of traffic and interfere with residential traffic. Most communities prefer to see apartments and office buildings also located at least along collector roads and, in some cases, arterial ones. Major institutional uses—certainly including colleges and universities, hospitals, and major sports facilities—also belong next to major transportation routes.

  Another aspect of transportation influences in future land-use planning is the compatibility of particular land uses with types of roads. Few people would want to own a nice single-family home along a busy highway or major commercial street. Thus, one of the first decisions that a community often makes in developing a land-use plan is to place nonresidential uses along major roadways. Obviously, most of the impact of the road affects the first half block or block along the road; as a result, communities often designate a one-block (half block on each side) or two-block strip along a major roadway as "commercial," resulting in a pattern of development that most people appropriately call "strip commercial."

  Intersections along interstate highways or even major state highways are often designated in a "highway-oriented commercial" category, typically suggesting the construction of motels, fast-food restaurants, and convenience stores with gas stations.
- *Trip generation.* Another transportation-related approach to future-use planning focuses on trip generation, recognizing the major impact that one land use has on adjacent uses. A law office is a lower-impact neighbor than a bank or a medical office, because the law office will typically have less traffic. A lumber yard is a higher-impact neighbor than an electronics store, because the lumberyard will have more truck traffic. Trip generation models of planning for land use generally place major trip generators along col-

lector and minor arterial streets, or on a major arterial with access from a connecting minor arterial or collector street. The alternative of providing a major trip generator direct access to a major arterial road will interfere with the functioning of the street for its principle purpose, which is moving a high volume of traffic moderate distances at a steady pace. Trip generation models offer a good basis for distinguishing neighborhood-oriented business uses from regional ones, for distinguishing heavier industry from light assembly plants.

- *Development capacity analysis.* Some communities base future-use designations in significant part on the capacity of the area for development, typically using roads, sewer, water and other infrastructure elements as determinants of development capacity. Over the short run, that approach makes a great deal of sense. Over the long run, it makes less sense, because capacities will change. An existing road may become congested, and the state may then build a new highway, opening a different part of the community to development; similarly, utility and public works departments constantly extend sewer and water service, creating new capacity in new areas. Where the development-capacity analysis is based on long-term factors, such as the boundaries of drainage basins (see discussion under "Planning for Sewer and Water Systems" in chapter 7), the long-range plan may make sense. If transportation and infrastructure planning is so thoroughly integrated with the comprehensive planning process that the future timing and location of road and line extensions are reasonably predictable, then this method may also work well. Where providers of these services may, for a variety of reasons, deviate in any way from the comprehensive plan, however, this method may yield a plan that is both logical and meaningless, an unfortunate combination.
- *Downtown plan.* Goals, or a larger vision, for the future of downtown often determine the future uses assigned to downtown. A community that wants to bring retailing back to the downtown will certainly include that as part of the mix of downtown uses. An increasing number of communities today recognize that revitalizing the downtown will require bringing people back for reasons other than shopping, and many of them now include residential and entertainment uses in the downtown. A downtown is one area in which most communities today recognize the desirability of some mixture of uses.
- *Neighborhood plans.* Communities that base their plans on principles of neighborhood planning often reach very different conclusions about neighborhood land-use patterns than those concerned only with the apparent incompatibility of certain uses. Planners and residents alike typically recognize that neighborhoods benefit from the availability of limited commercial services—laundries, hair salons, convenience stores (perhaps without gasoline sales), and some professional offices. Communities recognizing these principles include limited commercial uses in residential neighborhoods.

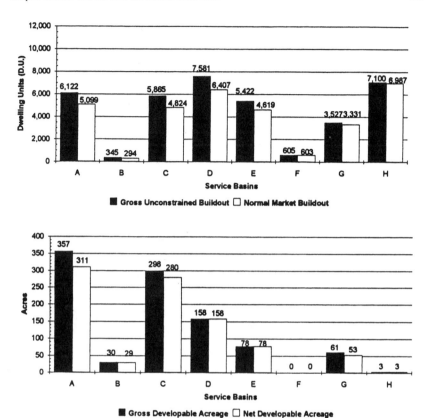

These bar graphs show the development capacity of Norman, Oklahoma. The Norman planning study also included an assessment of current development capacity, to provide a benchmark to which to compare projected land demand. Source: *The Burnham Group for the City of Norman (1995).*

They also typically avoid creating a commercial strip along a major road that passes through a residential area, preferring to allow commercial uses only at selected major intersections and to encourage a mixture of apartments, office buildings, and uses of similar intensity along the rest of the road.

• *Redevelopment plans.* A major exception to the practice of using existing land use as the basis for designating future land use arises in areas slated for redevelopment. Although large-scale urban renewal is no longer practiced (see chapter 17), many communities target certain areas for active redevelopment, often in a different pattern of land uses than the one that exists. The future land-use plan should recognize the potential for redevelopment and lay out desired future uses for redevelopment areas. Note that this is a significant exception to the rule stated above that most future land-use plans protect existing active uses and address primarily the potential for change on vacant land.

- *Agricultural preservation.* Good agricultural land is also easily developable. Thus, in growing communities where agriculture is an important part of the economic base, or an important part of the culture, agricultural land preservation is often a priority. Protecting the agricultural land becomes a major principle of land-use planning in such communities—ensuring that activities in agricultural areas are compatible with agriculture. In general, no development besides agriculture and related support services is compatible with agriculture. The encroachment of ex-urban residential subdivisions into agricultural areas brings with it a number of factors characteristic of family households (including wayward children and pets) and a risk of nuisance suits that limits the freedom of farmers to spray fertilizer, run heavy equipment all night, and otherwise carry out the capital-intensive business of modern agriculture.

  Protecting agricultural areas is not as simple as it once was, however. Some pork and poultry producers now operate on a massive scale, more like an industry than a traditional family farm. Family farmers and even some large-scale row-crop farmers are no more eager to live next to a large hog confinement or cattle feedlot than are suburban residents. A number of states have adopted "right-to-farm" laws that protect farmers and often limit the application of zoning laws to agriculture; in some cases, these laws are broad enough to exempt even large, industrial-scale feeding operations from local planning and zoning efforts.

- *Historic preservation.* In communities where historic preservation is a priority, that affects land-use plans. Clearly, future uses in historic areas must be generally compatible with the character of those areas and the types of buildings that conform to the historic design of the neighborhood.

- *Resort areas.* Resort communities must use land-use planning to protect their resources. If the principal resource of the community is a lakefront or ski mountain, it is important to plan uses of adjacent lands for tourist-oriented and other land uses that are compatible with the resort activities. Although that may seem like an obvious statement, a number of potential resort communities have lost opportunities because other uses have consumed the best land for development into commercial uses. Even tourist-oriented uses like strips of fast-food restaurants and T-shirt shops can threaten the ambience that attracts people to the area around a national park or natural resource area.

- *Areas not likely to develop.* In communities where agriculture is not a significant part of the economic base, planning for the future of land that is not likely to develop during the planning horizon is a particular challenge. Establishing a "no development" land-use category is likely to be politically unpopular with affected landowners (even if the intent of the category is simply to reinforce the obvious) and creates a potential legal liability for the community for interfering with possible "property rights" incident to development of the property. Designating such land for agriculture is a good alternative in some areas but not in others. Some communities have used "holding zone" designations on such property, not defining the future use; but that approach can also create legal and political problems. Designating such land for large-lot residential use is a popular alternative (recognizing that development on small lots is not practicable in areas without sewer and water service), but where it leads to actual development of the large lots, it is an approach that wastes land.

- *Institutional development.* Where a university or other major institution is part of the community and its economic base, it is important to consider the compatibility of land uses around the institutional use. Hospitals in particular often find themselves surrounded by incompatible land uses and are faced with the unattractive alternatives of acquiring and tearing down adjacent buildings or moving some or all of their operations to another location. Although future land-use planning cannot entirely prevent such situations, it is important to address institutional land needs in the long-range land-use plan; the best way to accomplish that is with a cooperative planning effort that includes planners for the institution.

- *Areas around airports.* Many communities with airports do not own enough land around the airport; areas of private land suffer from noise impacts and even from the risk of air crashes on the land or into buildings that extend too high into operating air space. Over the long term, the airport should own the land affected by its operations. Over the short term, the local government with jurisdiction around the airport must plan for reasonably compatible land uses.

- *Floodplains and hazard areas.* Some locations are so dangerous to human life or property that they ought not to be developed. Floodways (main flood channels, in the center of a floodplain) are prime examples, and some communities have geological hazard areas, areas undermined by the removal of minerals, and other areas that create risks to people who live or work there. Although complex legal issues are involved in the regulation of development in such areas, it is important that the land-use plan recognize the risks of such development.

Mapping Uses

The first section of chapter 8 discusses alternative approaches to creating the future land-use map, whether to use very specific boundaries between different types of uses or to use "blobs" to represent the general locations of future uses. The conventions of representing future uses on a map are the same as the conventions of mapping existing uses, shown in table 1.2.

Preparing the actual future land-use map is one of the more challenging parts of creating a comprehensive plan. Although professional planners will initially make recommendations for the shape of the map, the planning body guides the plan in two ways. First, the choice of planning approaches (or combinations of approaches) listed above itself significantly affects the plan—a future land-use plan based on land needs may look very different from one based on the natural character of the land. Although sometimes the choices of methods and factors are made by the professional planners without much consultation with the planning body, in most cases the planning body will play an important role in determining the methodology for developing the map.

Few committees actually draw maps, so it will be professional planners who present a first draft of the map to the planning body. That body, however, almost always makes changes in the proposal, often in response to comments of interested citizens and stakeholder groups. Some parts of a future land-use plan will be easy and obvious—there is likely to be quick consensus on the classifications of certain areas. For areas in transition and along important boundaries in the map, the final decisions typically involve a good deal of discretion by the planning body (color plate 2 shows a future land-use map).

Conclusion

The future land-use map will be one of the most visible parts of an adopted plan. It is likely to be shown in a large, colored format in the room where the planning commission meets. The commission and the governing body should refer to it frequently in making decisions on project approvals. Rational land buyers will rely on it in choosing development sites, and careful home shoppers will do the same. It is far more than a map. It is a guide to the future. Although at first glance, it may look like a collection of colored geometrical shapes that a planner might have put together sitting alone at a drafting table, the reality is that it takes all of the steps described in chapters 2 through 6 to create a workable land-use map—and the best ones benefit from many of the additional studies discussed in chapters 16 through 19.

The Role of the Professional Planner

The professional planner is the process facilitator, the information gatherer, the map maker and the technical expert in the preparation of the future land-use plan. Although the final plan should reflect the will of the planning body, it is the professional planner who makes this process work at every stage. Future land-use planning is the focus of much of planning education, and it is probably the central activity of most long-range planning departments.

The Role of the Individual Citizen

The future land-use plan is a critical public-policy element of the comprehensive plan. Thus, citizens should be involved in every stage of developing this document.

Citizen involvement is sometimes limited by the fact that this appears in many ways to be a highly technical process. The planning body may decide to work with professional planners in creating a relatively complete future land-use map before showing it to a broader public. A better process involves interested citizens in discussing what methods should be used to draw the map and what priorities should influence it—for example, if agricultural preservation, historic preservation, and downtown revitalization are important goals coming out of other parts of the comprehensive planning, those principles should govern the preparation of the map.

Because the future land-use element is such a central piece of the plan, it should be an element that truly represents the will of the community. Accomplishing that requires significant citizen participation in its preparation.

EXERCISES

Save your work from these exercises, even if it is only in the form of rough notes. You will be asked to refer to this work at the end of chapter 9.

1. If you have previously obtained a copy of your community's future land-use plan, evaluate it now. How good is it? Does it follow the suggestions of this chapter? Do those suggestions make sense in your community?

2. Drive around the developing areas of your community. Are the evolving land-use patterns there compatible? Would you want to live in the houses in those new areas? Why or why not? Are your reasons ones that the planners may have (or should have) considered?

3. Using the criteria suggested in this chapter and whatever data you have gathered for exercises in earlier chapters, try to identify the best sites in or near your community for the following: a major new industry that will require more than one hundred trucks per day coming in and out; a new regional shopping mall; a new hospital; a new neighborhood of affordable housing; and a small industry that would like a site of about four acres (about one city block in many communities) "in town."

4. Invite a member of the planning commission to come to your class and talk about how your community's current "future land-use map" was

developed and how it is used by the commission in its decision-making processes.

DISCUSSION EXERCISE

Choose different people in the class to represent the following positions and then discuss the strengths and weaknesses of the process of mapping future land uses: (1) residents of a small development of about twenty houses located about one thousand feet from a site designated as "future landfill"; (2) residents of a neighborhood shown on the map as "future redevelopment"; (3) owner of a property on the edge of town shown on the map as "permanent agricultural area"; (4) owner of a property on a different edge of town shown on the map as "future mall site." Other members of the class should participate in the discussion as advocates of the plan.

FURTHER READING

Kaiser, Edward J., David R. Godschalk, and F. Stuart Chapin, Jr. 1995. *Urban Land Use Planning,* 4th edition. Urbana: University of Illinois Press. The latest edition of a classic work on land-use planning, with many good examples of plans.

Kent, T.J., Jr. 1990. *The Urban General Plan.* Chicago: Planners Press. A classic work on comprehensive planning for cities, including good examples of plans that remain relevant today.

NOTES

1. U.S. Department of Housing and Urban Development, *Land Use Intensity,* Washington, DC: HUD (1971 reprint).
2. Described in American Society of Planning Officials, Rahenkamp, Sachs, Wells & Associates and David Stoloff, *Innovative Zoning: A Local Official's Guidebook,* Washington, DC: Department of Housing and Urban Development, 1977.
3. Lane Kendig, Susan Connor, Cranston Byrd, and Judy Heyman, *Performance Zoning,* Chicago: American Planning Association (1980).

Chapter 7

How Do We Plan for
Public Facilities?

Public facilities define a community. Roads and highways link it to the outside world and define its internal circulation. Parks, schools, and recreation areas become gathering places and activity centers. The patterns of roads and sewer and water lines define the patterns of growth and the locations of major centers of private activity, ranging from shopping malls to housing developments. These public facilities are important to the planning process in several ways:

- While some provide essential services (delivery of water, fire protection), others establish the quality of life in the community (parks, recreation facilities).
- The local governments that make the plans also provide many of the public facilities. Thus, the plans for public facilities are plans that the local government can implement by direct action.
- New houses, shopping areas and industrial areas need public facilities to serve them. There must, therefore, be a close relationship between the future land-use plan and the plans for public facilities.
- Public facilities typically represent large investments of local taxpayer dollars. Plans help to ensure the efficiency and the utility of those expenditures.
- Some public facilities—most notably roads and sewer and water lines—are also instruments of change. The location of roads and infrastructure shapes the future development patterns of the community. Builders and developers actively seek land with good access and the availability of public facilities. Thus, if a community builds new roads and sewer and water lines to the west, for example, whatever growth occurs is likely to favor the west side of town.

This chapter addresses two interrelated issues: planning for infrastructure and integrating infrastructure into comprehensive planning as a tool of implementation as well as a subject of the plan.

Overview of the Issues

One of the challenges in planning for roads and some other public facilities is the involvement of multiple agencies. Large roads that have significant growth-shaping effects are typically state and federal highways, planned and built by state transportation or highway departments. Many sewer and water systems are operated by special districts or even, in some cases, by private utility companies. Even those operated by local governments typically fall under a utility or public works department that focuses primarily on engineering, operating, and fiscal concerns; unfortunately, the location of a major new sewer line that is most efficient from engineering, operating and cost perspectives may not be the location that makes the most sense in relation to future land-use plans.

Most agencies that build and manage infrastructure provide service in response to demand. Community planners look at a proposed highway and ask whether building the road in that location will encourage the sort of growth patterns suggested by the comprehensive plan. Transportation planners often have little interest in that issue, focusing instead on projected transportation demand. Similarly, most providers of sewer and water service understand their primary mission to be providing service where it is wanted, within some fiscal constraints. A sewer department may extend a major line through a wetland that the community does not want developed, for example, because that is the cheapest route to use in connecting the line to a proposed new development.

Planning for roads and infrastructure, while often carried out separately from other planning, should be consistent with the comprehensive plan. If planners and planning commissions made the major decisions about where and when to build roads and infrastructure, that might happen more easily. With multiple decision makers involved, it often does not happen.

The most significant example of public facilities planning in operation involves the construction of highways. Federal and state highways provide major arterials for commuting communities while linking communities across the United States. In the past these roadways were often built with no regard for local comprehensive plans and often in direct conflict with local land-use plans. In 1991, the federal government recognized the role of highways in influencing the location of growth with the Intermodal Surface Transportation Efficiency Act, referred to as ISTEA ("ice tea"). In that act, the federal government required for the first time that, in building new federally funded highways, state and federal planners give due regard to local land-use plans.[1] Both ISTEA and its successor, TEA-21 (Transportation Efficiency Act for the 21st Century),[2] require that state and federal officials consider local land-use plans in their highway planning and that they consider the land-use impacts of their decisions. These policies represent a significant departure from many highway planning practices, which focused on building new roads in a relatively straight line between two points, regardless of what might be in the way; neighborhoods, prime agricultural land, and community plans sometimes suffered from the old policies.[3]

Roads are only one part of the larger system of infrastructure. While most residents do not spend much time thinking about sewer and water lines, developers do. Water pollution laws adopted since 1972 prohibit development in areas with inadequate wastewater, more commonly called sewage, treatment. Thus, the availability of sewage treatment is often a critical factor in selecting development sites. Developers usually try to connect to an existing system rather than take the financial risks involved in building their own.

Often communities extend sewer and water lines into remote areas for good reasons but without considering the costs involved. Typical examples include extensions of service to an industrial park around the local airport or to a remote subdivision where the original utility systems have failed. Those new lines, however, which are almost always designed with extra capacity, often serve as growth attractors, leading developers who want to build in the region to locate along their path—particularly if that path is reinforced with a good road system. If that path is a logical place for growth, the result can be good. If, however, that path represents a long tail or other weird geographical distortion of an otherwise symmetrical community, the result can be poor. One Texas community that had very little growth nevertheless had to invest in two new fire stations in the 1980s because the location of a major new sewer line had distorted the growth patterns of the community. In that particular community, the sewer line led to the airport industrial park, and some of the new residential development along the sewer line was so close to the airport that it represented a potential hazard to residents.

Thus, it is important to integrate planning for roads and infrastructure into planning for the larger community—and to develop strategies for influencing the location of those facilities that will clearly influence the location of future growth. Plans for those facilities must also consider the financial and engineering implications of future building plans.

Federal, State, and Regional Involvement

The federal government has played a significant role in building roads and infrastructure in the United States. The largest public works program ever undertaken began in 1956 with the Federal-Aid Highway Act.[4] That act provided the means of paying for construction of the Interstate Highway System with the Highway Trust Fund. The major highways built in that period linked communities across the United States and made comprehensive planning on a regional scale mandatory. The Federal-Aid Highway Act of 1962 required a formal comprehensive planning process for roadways.

Major improvements to sewer and water lines were financed during the

1930s through the national Works Project Administration (WPA) and Civilian Conservation Corps (CCC). As communities grew after World War II, these projects were funded through bonds and other financing mechanisms, often aided by federal and state grants. Even today, regional, state, and federal entities often assist in funding for major infrastructure projects. All funding entities require capital improvement plans before assistance is given.

Standards for public roads and infrastructure are set at the federal, state, and local levels—from federal standards for roadway construction to local building codes. Adequate public facilities are the basis for protecting the health, safety, and welfare of citizens so a major function of planners reviewing subdivisions and site plans is ensuring appropriate sewer and water and road systems.

When rapid growth occurs, communities often face flooding, serious traffic problems, and overburdened sewer and water systems. Since the 1970s many communities have looked to more cost-effective means of providing public facilities through regional approaches. Since water and sewage treatment plants are very expensive, combining the resources of a county and one or more communities can enable them to build cost-effective facilities large enough to handle present and anticipated needs.

Planning for Roads and Other Infrastructure

Planning for roads and infrastructure involves estimating the demand for facilities and then considering different ways of meeting that demand and the estimating costs of those alternatives. Although there are traditional planning implications to all of those decisions, the most immediate considerations in building facilities involve costs and engineering. Not surprisingly, engineers, with the assistance of fiscal officers, do most of the planning for infrastructure. Roads, like sewer and water lines, are laid to last a long time and are expensive; planning therefore includes capital improvement plans so that financing, capacity, maintenance costs, and other issues can be carefully considered before investments are made.

Infrastructure planning, like all planning, deals with the future as well as the present. An important question for planners to ask at the beginning of any planning process involving infrastructure is whether the infrastructure provider has good figures on current system capacity and demand; if not, gathering that data becomes one of the first tasks in the planning process. Engineers can easily measure current use levels of facilities. Some utilities constantly monitor their usage by sector; all monitor demand on the central treatment facilities. Tracking demand on roadways requires field measurements, often handled with mechanical measuring devices connected to rubber hoses that stretch across the road—every time a heavy object travels over the device, it trips a switch that counts one-half of a vehicle; when both axles of an auto have traveled over it, the result is the addition of one vehicle to the demand measurement.

Gathering data on current system capacity and demand is conceptually straightforward, although it can be expensive and time consuming if the community or service provider does not already have the data on hand.

The task of estimating future demand is conceptually a good deal more complex. It begins with projections of future population and economic activity, projections often developed by community planners as part of a comprehensive planning process. The baseline projections for the future are those involving population. They give a general sense of the total demand likely to exist in the community at particular times in the future. Those projections may provide adequate data for planning for central sewage and water treatment facilities.

To plan for the location and sizes of future roads and utility lines, however, it is necessary to know more than total future population—it is essential to have some idea of where that population might work and live. The projections addressing the location and timing of growth are those that forecast future land use and economic activity. Chapter 9 explains some of the complexity injected into those projections by the operation of the local land market, and chapters 11 and 12 discuss ways in which the community can attempt to guide that market to make the timing and location of future facilities demand somewhat more predictable. Those techniques, however, simply make demand projections more accurate; they do not affect the use of the methods described below.

Most infrastructure planners rely heavily on the future land-use map developed in the comprehensive planning process (see chapter 6) as the starting point for projecting the location and level of future demand on infrastructure systems. Engineers and other infrastructure planners then estimate future demands through models. Those models use existing land use and roads and infrastructure as part of the equation to predict the future. Most of those models are based on past history and simply extrapolate into the future current trends in travel, utility usage, and other lifestyle issues, adjusted for the comprehensive plan's projections of changes in population, household size, and other demographic factors.

Although demand projection for infrastructure looks like a science, with elaborate models, extensive data, and many technical terms, there is a great deal of art in it. Some of the problem areas that significantly affect the results are:

- *Changes in household size.* Average household size shrunk by nearly 20 percent from 1970 to 1990; thus, even communities that were extremely accurate in projecting future population were often wrong in projecting the number of households—and the resulting number of automobile trips and use of utility services.

- *Changes in living patterns.* There are far more automobile trips per household today than twenty-five years ago. Thus, many road systems are overcrowded, even though every other aspect of the planning for them was accurate.
- *Timing of development.* Future land-use plans show what will happen and where—but typically do not show when. Most future land-use plans show potential development for decades' worth of growth. Transportation planners, however, want to know what will happen when—for example, will the east side develop before the west side? For reasons discussed in chapter 9, typical future land-use plans really cannot answer that question.
- *Effects of infrastructure.* Infrastructure planners typically take the position that they simply satisfy demand. In fact, there is a great deal of evidence that major roads actually "generate" trips—the convenience of the new roads encourage people to make trips they never made before. Further, the combination of new investments in roads and sewer and water lines in an area may attract more development than land-use planners anticipated.
- *Unforeseen changes.* The opening of a major new factory or shopping center, for example, or the closure of an old one, can dramatically change infrastructure demand patterns in a community.

Because infrastructure planners are aware of those and other risks to the accuracy of their projections, they often respond by "oversizing" facilities—building facilities that are larger than the projections suggest might be necessary. Where demand actually exceeds projections, the investment in oversizing proves to be a wise one. The net result over an entire community, however, is a vast investment in badly underutilized infrastructure—usually at the expense of taxpayers.

Some public officials do not worry about oversizing, assuming that eventually the full capacity will be needed. In some cases, that is a reasonable expectation. Roads, however, require constant maintenance, and a local government may spend as much in maintenance of a road over ten years as it spent to build it; thus, building a road ten years too early increases maintenance costs. Even sewer and water lines have a reasonable life expectancy of only forty or fifty years. Many communities have enough unused capacity in sewer and water lines to serve one hundred or more years of growth at present rates—meaning that some of that capacity will not be used during the reasonable life expectancy of the facility.

Because of the way the land and development markets work in the United States, it is impossible to make the system entirely predictable. It is useful, however, for a community to attempt to manage the timing and location of growth, which is the topic of chapter 12. Although the growth management tools described in that chapter are used by only a limited number of communities today, they are important tools that every community ought to consider for the implementation of their comprehensive plans.

Planning for the Movement of People and Goods

Most of the emphasis of transportation planning in the United States is on roads and highways. That is also the major emphasis of this section, but it is important to remember that roads are only part of the transportation system in most communities; some major cities have subway and other fixed-rail transit systems, many have bus systems, and most rely at least to some extent on pedestrian and bicycle travel to meet the needs of residents. Thus, transportation plans ought to be *intermodal*—dealing with multiple modes of transportation as part of an integrated system.

With the growing reliance on the automobile, suburban development, increasing reliance on air travel, and the development of major highway systems by the federal government, transportation planning has become one of the most complex and technology-based forms of planning. It incorporates engineering, land-use planning, economics, environmental and cultural impact studies, and computer models dealing with the complex logistics involved in the constant flow of goods and people in the United States. Where some planning can be isolated to a single community, transportation planning also has to take into account entire regions often containing a number of jurisdictions.

The key to transportation planning involves projecting travel movement. Since that involves a large range of variables such as road systems, alternate modes of transportation, multiple destinations, and other land forms and land uses, transportation planning relies on computer models. Regions are typically broken down into zones that are further analyzed according to population, households, incomes, number of automobiles, economic activities, and so forth. Each one of those variables can be further broken down into more defined variables. For example, in commercial areas, data may include number of employees, floor space per employee, and type of economic activity according to level of traffic it might generate, such as retail store versus warehouse. Those data are then put into models that can project patterns of circulation.

A number of models are used to determine how well the present system is working, as well as to estimate future travel and how changes in the system will affect future travel behavior. Four basic models (described below) with major variations are created independently and make it possible for transportation planners to determine future supply and demand. The output of one model is often used as part of the input for the next model, but there is no standard sequencing of the models. Before these models are used in predicting future travel demands and supply, they are first calibrated to fit the community or region by using existing data. While no models are perfect, these do enable transportation planners to identify future demands.

The most basic model deals with *trip generation*. To estimate how many trips are generated from a residential area, such variables as household income, number of people and vehicles per household, and population density are used to estimate the average number of trips made per household per day. While the example used here is residential, trip generation models estimate the number of trips generated by many different types of land use. A standard handbook provides trip generation rates for individual land uses.[5] Most models assume that every trip is "generated" by one of the trip ends—the residence, office building, or other land use where the trip begins or ends. Better models recognize that some uses only "attract" trips in progress—people typically make such stop-off trips for things like gas for the car. On the other hand, supermarkets and grocery stores typically generate trips.

Another model deals with the destinations of trips made. *Trip distribution* models estimate where in the community or region the generated trips will go. For example, a large shopping mall will generate trips from throughout a region, but a small commercial strip with businesses offering services such as shoe repair and a barber shop will generate fewer trips from a much smaller local radius. Trip distribution models use such variables as floor space in a commercial or industrial enterprise, total employment in a business, numbers of housing units, and household incomes. Usually, distance is taken as a straight-line distance from the center of one zone to the center of another.[6]

Yet more sophisticated models estimate *modal splits*—the form of transportation that is used in the generated trips. The choices in transportation mode range from automobile, bus, and rapid transit to bicycle. Basic models assume that each trip will be made in the same mode of transportation, but more sophisticated models can even account for a combination of modes. For example, some commuters drive their cars to park-and-ride lots, where they transfer to a bus to a central location, where they might even change to rapid transit before arriving at their destination. Much of this model is determined by the estimated length of travel time and the costs involved. Many people do not use buses because they stop frequently, making the trip take a long time. Others choose to take a bus rather than rapid transit because the bus fare is cheaper. While many variables are used in this model, knowing distances and income distribution is important.

A fourth model is the *trip assignment* model. This model assigns trips for each mode of transportation to actual or projected routes. This type of model is used to predict what routes travelers will use in going from a designated point of origin to a particular destination. If certain routes are determined to be major routes from one point to another, transportation planners typically choose among a number of options, which can range from widening roadways for greater capacity to creating alternative routes or modes of transportation for the same trip. The trip assignment model helps the planner to evaluate the relative costs and benefits of those choices.

The purpose of these models is to predict demand for particular modes of transportation and particular routes of those modes. Transportation planners use other models to analyze the costs of alternative solutions to the projected demand, weighing the respective costs and benefits.

Sophisticated transportation planning models focus on "peak hours," the morning and evening commuting hours when roads are most likely to be congested. "Average daily traffic" figures (which are often readily available) combine the empty hours on the road with the busy ones and thus fail to give an accurate picture of the road at its busiest times.

Planning for highway capacity, particularly at peak hours, involves certain levels of judgment. Highway engineers have established a generally accepted system of classifying "levels of service," ranging from level A (typically a residential road with almost no traffic on it) to level F (which is so congested that humorists in the field refer to it as "parking lot"). Table 7.1 provides abbreviated descriptions of those six levels of service.

Table 7.1. Road and Highway Levels of Service

Level of Service	Characteristics
A	Free-flow; individual users virtually unaffected by presence of others; free choice of speed and maneuver; level of comfort excellent.
B	Stable flow, but presence of other users noticeable; slight decline in freedom to maneuver. Level of comfort and convenience less than in A
C	Stable flow, but individual users significantly affected by interactions with others; selection of speed affected by presence of others; freedom to maneuver requires substantial vigilance; comfort and convenience declines noticeably.
D	High-density but stable flow; speed and freedom to maneuver are severely restricted, and driver and pedestrian experience generally poor level of comfort; small increases in traffic cause operational problems.
E	Operating conditions at or near capacity level; all speeds reduced to low but relatively uniform value; freedom to maneuver is extremely difficult; comfort and convenience levels are extremely poor; operations unstable, because small increases or minor perturbations cause breakdowns.
F	Forced or breakdown flow; traffic approaching a point that exceeds the amount that can traverse the point; queues form; operations characterized by stop-and-go waves, extremely unstable.

Source: Institute of Transportation Engineers, *Highway Capacity Manual.* Washington, DC: Institute of Transportation Engineers, 1985.

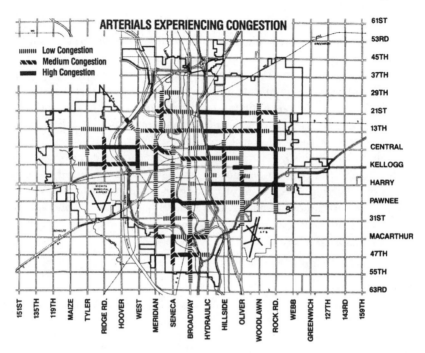

This map identifies those major arterials that did not (on the date of the map) meet current level-of-service policies in the Wichita, Kansas, area. This is one important analytical tool in planning for road improvements. Source: *Metropolitan Area Planning Department (1993).*

It is not practical or even desirable to build major roads in a city or metropolitan area large enough to maintain level A or even level B at peak hour. Where judgment enters the planning process is in deciding whether to have a goal of achieving level C (a which people would have to stop occasionally for stoplights at rush hour) or to accept level D (more frequent stops, longer waits, and more difficult driving conditions) or even brief periods at level E. Of course, all drivers would prefer level C, but most taxpayers would probably agree that it is not worth increasing the cost of a road by 50 percent just to avoid having service drop to level D for thirty or forty-five minutes each day. Some communities have only a "rush minute," rather than a rush hour. Allowing a lower level of service at that time may actually encourage drivers to modify their own behavior—leaving for work a little earlier or going home a little later—to help mitigate rush-hour congestion. Also, there is considerable evidence that the expansion of roadways does not necessarily diminish congestion. Studies have shown that new roadways or improved strips bring more drivers, so that capacity is quickly filled.[7]

One attractive alternative to the automobile is fixed-rail public transit, which ranges from "heavy-rail" solutions of traditional railroads, subways, and elevated trains, to "light-rail" solutions involving trolleys or similar vehicles. Fixed-rail is fast and efficient and generally helps to conserve air quality. New York, Philadelphia, and Boston grew up with a network of "railroad suburbs" that evolved around stations on major railroad lines. That long history of rail dependence has helped those communities to continue to integrate fixed-rail systems effectively into transportation networks. One advantage they have over later cities is that there are major activity centers, with shopping, multi-family housing, and employment opportunities, surrounding the train and transit stations. The easy access from train to destination makes commuting by train practicable. San Francisco, Washington, and Atlanta have successfully retrofitted the metro areas with heavy-rail systems like those in New York. Portland, Oregon, and some other communities now use light-rail systems (which many consumers refer to as trolleys). Los Angeles is beginning the implementation of plans to retrofit that city, famous for its freeways, with a fixed-rail transit system.

The sprawling patterns of single-family suburban development in other cities, however, make it very difficult for a fixed-rail system to succeed. Cities in which the patterns of growth have been influenced heavily by the automobile lack the concentrated nodes of activity that make rail transit work. In such communities, people who want to use mass transit are likely to need an automobile to get to the transit station from their homes and then some other form of transportation to get from the station at the other end to their real destinations. Residents of such communities are heavily dependent on the automobile.

Transit systems are typically locally subsidized, and cities that have low density find it almost impossible to maintain a system at a reasonable rate with enough routes to function adequately. Automobile travel is also subsidized, but most of that subsidy comes through the federal government and is somewhat invisible to the consumer; further, it receives political support from the large highway-building industry. Thus, it is rare for planners in the United States to make a true-cost comparison between fixed-rail and highways to serve the same community.

Instead, communities have tried to address how to make existing transportation systems operate more efficiently. Special lanes have been created on freeways to encourage carpooling, thus reducing the number of cars on the road and reducing congestion. Some transit systems have different rates for peak and off-peak fares. The growing number of "park-and-ride" facilities shows progress in linking the automobile to transit systems more efficiently. A major part of transportation planning will continue to involve finding ways to more efficiently use existing road and transit systems while adjusting to changes in demand due to changing demographics and employment trends. There is also growing interest in *transportation demand management,* sometimes called TDM.[8] Techniques of TDM include a variety of efforts designed to reduce total transportation demand or to shift it away from peak hours. Some of these include:

- promoting "flex-time" work schedules with employers;
- increasing the cost of all-day parking in congested areas; and
- using "congestion pricing," in which a road system operator charges or increases tolls during peak hours, to encourage people to drive at other times.[9]

Although there is no record of anyone trying it, systems expert Russell Ackoff long ago suggested a different form of congestion pricing in which autos entering congested areas would be equipped with prepaid metering devices that would deduct a charge from the prepaid balance each time the driver touched the brake pedal. The logic of such a system is that there is far more need to use brakes in congested areas and times than in uncongested ones, so this fee would provide a financial incentive to drivers to avoid congestion.[10]

A concept closely related to TDM is *transportation system management,* which uses operational controls to increase the effective capacity of a section of road.[11] Techniques include limiting access to a road, using metering on ramps to provide an even flow of traffic entering the road, improving intersection control (an intersection protected by stop signs will handle more traffic than an unprotected one; an intersection with traffic lights will handle more traffic than one with stop signs).

One of the current debates in planning for local streets and roads is whether to use a grid system or a hierarchical street system that places residences along loops, cul-de-sacs, and other streets designed to carry only local traffic. To understand the debate, it is important to understand that transportation planners refer to several different classifications of streets, each with its own purpose. Table 7.2 shows a basic classification system.

Because the issue of whether to follow a grid arises most frequently in relation to the design of new subdivisions, the argument is discussed in more detail in chapter 11, on subdivision regulations. Some readers may want to skip forward to that material to consider that issue in the context of community-wide transportation planning. Although individual developers can propose subdivisions that are not part of a grid, the local government can ultimately require that new subdivisions conform to the community's master street plan, whether for a grid, modified grid, or street hierarchy. Thus, the final policy decision is the local government's, and that decision should be based on the plan.

There is a growing school of thought that one solution to the transportation problem in some major metropolitan areas is to quit building roads. If faced with growing congestion, drivers may seek other forms of transportation

Table 7.2. Classification of Streets and Roads

Type	Function
Cul-de-sac	Land access and local traffic movement, open at one end with turn-around at other.
Local	Land access and local traffic movement.
Collector	Land access and traffic movement between local and arterial streets.
Secondary (minor arterials)	Limited land access and area traffic movement.
Major (major arterials)	Limited land access and city traffic movement.
Expressways	No land access and metropolitan and city traffic movement.
Freeways	No land access and regional and metropolitan traffic movement.

or travel at other times.[12] This approach is entirely consistent with the notion that building roads attracts traffic, discussed above. A new study from the United Kingdom now provides additional support for this approach, finding that, when a road is closed, some traffic goes elsewhere, but some seems to disappear entirely.[13] This is not a common approach to transportation planning and not one that is well accepted among transportation planners. Thus, a new planner may not encounter this approach in transportation planning efforts. It is important to consider, however. Good planning involves the consideration of all reasonable alternatives, and sometimes doing nothing (and spending nothing) is the best alternative.

There are some good handbooks out that provide suggestions for such approaches to transportation planning. In *Transportation & Land Use Innovations: When You Can't Pave Your Way out of Congestion,* Reid Ewing focuses on "mobility" and notes that contemporary transportation planning must include consideration of pedestrian and bicycle transportation, as well as automobiles and traditional mass transit.[14] A key element to his and other approaches to this issue is the integration of land-use planning and transportation planning, considering the transportation demands of alternative land-use patterns and weighing the monetary and other costs of those demands in choosing among land-use patterns. Stated more simply, if everyone lives closer together, trips are shorter; if more people live closer to shopping and work opportunities, there should be fewer and shorter trips. That guide also notes the importance of creating nodes of activity that can provide the critical mass of trip ends necessary to support buses or other mass transportation.

In *At Road's End: Transportation and Land Use Choices for Communities,*

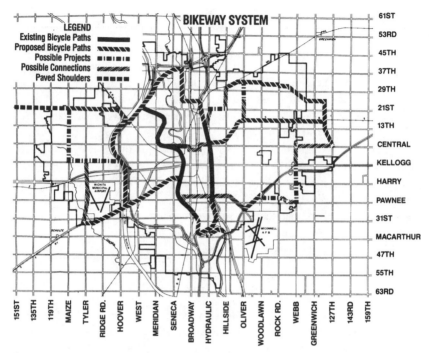

This map shows Wichita's plans to include bikeways as part of its transportation system.
Source: *Metropolitan Area Planning Commission (1993).*

Daniel Carlson, with two co-authors, emphasizes the importance of integrated transportation and land-use planning, increasing the range of choices available for addressing transportation issues.[15] The book provides a number of good examples of cases where such approaches have been successful, sometimes as a result of mediation springing from litigation. Color plate 4 shows an integrated transit and land-use plan for Charlotte and Mecklenburg County, North Carolina.

These holistic approaches to planning for transportation needs are entirely consistent with the integrated, comprehensive planning approach advocated in this text. They are quite different, however, from traditional transportation planning, which placed a heavy emphasis on ensuring that people who wanted to go from one place to another could do so easily, in an individual automobile driven in a relatively straight line. Planning for transportation, like planning for other types of infrastructure, historically has focused on satisfying consumer demand, without fully considering the social and environment costs of doing that. Because most of the cost of building the facilities is paid with revenues from gasoline taxes, those facilities are viewed as "user-funded," and there has thus been surprisingly little concern about the public costs of new highways. At one level, the traditional system seems user-friendly, because it focuses on satisfying individual consumers. At another level, however, the decisions to build highways to satisfy perceived demand have led to massive sprawl, which has led to the need for more roads, in an endless cycle.

Planning for Sewer and Water Systems

Although sewer and water systems involve complex engineering, the basic principle behind them is a simple one—gravity. Sewage generally flows through pipes downhill to a sewage treatment plant. Most water providers pump water uphill into tanks (often on towers) or reservoirs, and water then flows downhill through a system of pipes to reach individual users. These systems work best when operating within a single drainage basin—a geographical area whose outer boundaries consist of ridgelines that define the highest points in the area, so that all the rain that falls inside those ridgelines drains into the same creek, stream, or river.

For those reasons, a sewage treatment plant is generally located downstream from a community, and that plant can (up to its capacity) serve any land above it in the same drainage basin. As anyone who takes showers knows, water pressure is a critical issue in water service. Because pressure is a direct function of the difference in elevation between the water tank or reservoir and the point served (locations farther below the tank get better pressure than ones at higher elevations), there is a particular elevation within every water service system that defines the maximum elevation to which the system can provide acceptable pressure. What determines the minimum acceptable pressure is the

Water service providers pump water uphill to tanks like these (or tanks located on towers in flat areas); gravity flow from the tank provides the pressure to deliver water to users.

water pressure needed for fire protection. Pressure adequate to put out fires generally also provides excellent service for domestic use when no fire hoses are connected to the system. The minimum acceptable pressure can be used by engineers to determine the maximum acceptable elevation at which service can be offered, because pressure will decrease as a function of the increase in elevation of the location to be served.

The planning implications of these basic principles are very significant. A planner, possibly with some help from an engineer or a landscape architect, can draw a line around the top of the drainage basin served by a current sewer system and another line at the maximum elevation that can be served by the corresponding water system. The geographic area falling inside those lines is the area that ought to have the highest priority for growth—expansion beyond either of those lines will require new sewer or water plants or other expensive engineering solutions, such as additional pumps in the system. Here, again, is an ideal use of geographic information systems. Where the GIS system contains information on slopes and topography, the system can generate maps showing the respective service areas for sewer and water and can easily create a separate map showing where they overlap.

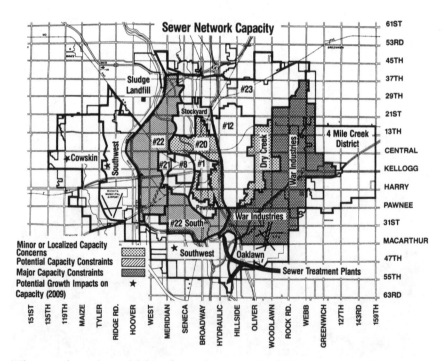

This map shows the availability of sewer capacity in the different drainage and service basins in Wichita. Source: *Metropolitan Area Planning Commission (1993).*

This is really a form of opportunities and constraints analysis, described in chapter 4, and thus represents a key element in comprehensive planning that ought to precede planning for infrastructure. Just as transportation planning ought to take place in a way that is fully integrated with comprehensive planning, so should planning for sewer and water systems.

There are peak issues in planning for sewer and water systems, also, but they are different from transportation peak issues. With sewer and water systems, planning focuses on a peak day. Peak days are typically the same for both systems, although peaking is less a problem with sewer systems than with water. Peak days for water use are days that involve car washing and lawn watering. Although most water used in homes and businesses goes back into the sewer system, water from those outdoor uses does not.

In determining the availability and the capacity of system supply, there are two sets of issues. The basic capacity issue with both sewer and water systems involves calculating the capacity of the treatment plant. That is an engineering calculation that can be converted to "gallons per day," making it easy to compare projected demand to available supply. It is also important, however, to consider the location and the capacity of lines. Some land within the appropriate drainage basin for a sewage plant with lots of extra capacity may be located so far from the existing network of lines that it would be difficult to obtain service in the foreseeable future. Some areas may have lines that are already at their service capacity, meaning that additional service to those areas would require laying either larger lines or additional lines.

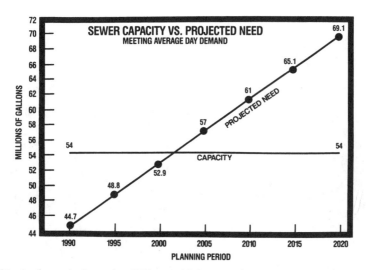

This simple graph shows that Wichita is likely to need a new sewage treatment plan by about 2001. The "capacity" line is flat because the capacity of existing plants is fixed. Source: *Metropolitan Area Planning Commission (1993).*

Sewer and water planning is not glamorous, but it is important. The availability of sewer and water service plays a significant role in shaping growth within a region. Thus, the decisions that planners of that infrastructure make are likely to have a major influence on the future land-use patterns in the region—a topic of primary interest to community planners.

Planning for Parks and Open Space

Communities once commonly planned for small parks in every new neighborhood. However, park directors and local government finance directors discovered that such scattered sites are expensive to maintain, particularly for departments that use heavy equipment for most maintenance. Further, small parks often lack swimming pools, playing fields, and other amenities that people want. For both of those reasons, most communities today have shifted their emphasis to regional parks, serving large sections of the community. Many communities and regions today have specialized parks, locating large numbers of soccer fields in one, for example, and swimming and picnic facilities in another.

One of the results of this shift in emphasis is that community leaders sometimes forget that the expansion of the community into new areas means that the community will need more parks, or at least more parkland. Thus, it

Parks and playgrounds are important to neighborhoods. Photo by Jennifer Greig.

is essential that a growing community have a long-term plan for parks and recreation facilities and that it engage in a continuous process of property acquisition for those facilities.

Parks and open space serve a number of public purposes. Most people associate parks with active recreation, and that is certainly a major purpose of them. Open space also helps the city to breathe, playing an important ecological role, particularly in densely developed areas. Well-maintained parks often provide a point of beauty in the community, something that helps to define neighborhoods or whole sections of the community. Developers as well as interested citizens recognize the value of parks and green spaces in a community.[16]

Today, there is an increasing interest in open-space linkages that provide visual and environmental connections among parts of a community. Often called greenways, these linkages provide routes for bike and pedestrian trails as well as essential connections among habitat areas, allowing wildlife to thrive even in urban areas. Communities with complete systems of greenways find them heavily used, often for passive recreation—walking and biking and just enjoying the environment. The topic of preserving open space for purposes other than park use is discussed in chapter 15.

Parks and open space serve the community best if they exist in most parts of the community. Because the open-space needs of a community may amount to as much as 5, 6, or even 8 percent of its developed area, the only way to ensure that land will be available for that purpose is to acquire or preserve it as the areas around it develop.

Local park and recreation departments often conduct their own planning efforts. Those plans often get into details of recreation activities such as numbers of softball fields needed and other matters that go beyond the typical level of comprehensive planning. It is essential, however, that plans for land acquisition for such purposes be integrated with the comprehensive planning process.

Planning for Schools, Fire Stations, and Other Facilities

Schools, fire stations, and other local facilities like libraries are important to the future of the community. Typically, those facilities do not play as direct a role in shaping the community as do the linear public facilities—roads and sewer and water lines. Schools are an exception in metropolitan areas where the choice of housing location may include the choice of a school district. In general, however, most agencies that plan for such facilities react to growth patterns and provide the facilities as needed. Sometimes the only expectation that those planners have from the comprehensive planning process is the identification and reservation of future sites for facilities.

Fire departments locate fire stations based on "response times," which is a measure of the length of time from an emergency call until the first equipment arrives at the scene. Although a response time of eight minutes or even more may be acceptable for fire protection, many fire departments also provide emergency medical response. Emergency medical providers like to have the first unit on the scene within about three minutes of the call, which gives them time to revive a heart attack or stroke victim without serious brain damage. Obviously, this complicates the planning process for fire facilities, because the implication of the shorter response time is a greater number of facilities. More and more communities today have a small number of major fire stations and a larger number of stations with one or two relatively small pieces of fire equipment, plus an emergency medical vehicle.

Fire station and emergency medical station sites rarely require more than an acre of land, often less. Thus, finding sites for them is not usually difficult. Some developers consider those facilities an enhancement to new development and willingly provide free sites. Although it is possible to build and equip

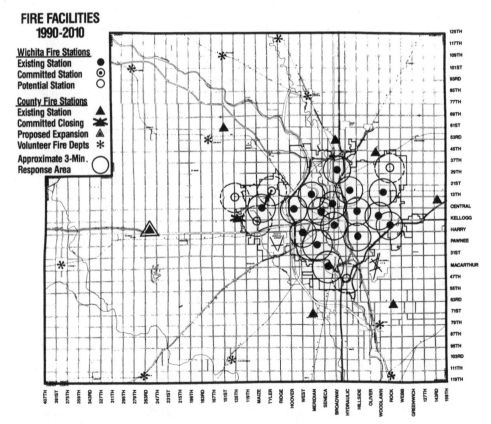

This plan shows existing and proposed fire stations in Wichita, Kansas, for 1990–2010, along with the approximate three-minute response area for each. Source: *Metropolitan Area Planning Commission (1993).*

a new fire station for a fixed cost of a million dollars or a little more, the real expense comes in staffing it. A fire station is most useful (and the computed response times accurate) only if there are firefighters and/or emergency medical technicians (EMT) stationed there at all times. Even with minimal staffing of two drivers, two firefighters, and an EMT (a staffing level that assumes that most calls will be supplemented with personnel and/or vehicles from other stations), it requires twenty or more full-time employees to cover all shifts, allowing for minimal vacation and sick leave. Assuming a low cost of $25,000 per person per year for salary and benefits, the personnel costs alone would amount to more than $500,000 per year. Maintenance, utilities, and other costs add to that. Thus, adding a fire station to a community's system involves a major fiscal commitment by the local government.

The critical aspect of comprehensive planning in relation to the provision of fire and emergency medical facilities is a consideration of the patterns of growth and how that affects the number of facilities needed and the related number of staff to support them. A compact community, built essentially in a circle with a good internal road system, might get by with four fire stations, while a community with exactly the same population in a sprawling and less regular development pattern might require five or even six. The difference can amount to a significant cost burden for the sprawling community.

School districts, or school corporations (as the providers of public schools are called in some states), often do their own planning. A few employ community planners, who typically work closely with the local comprehensive planning office, but many have people trained as teachers or facility managers in charge of planning. Although often well qualified to facilitate the work of architects in providing appropriate buildings and other facilities, these people often lack the background to plan well for future school sites. Most school districts take the position that they respond to the needs of the community, following the patterns of growth. All too often, however, they select poor sites, away from the growth patterns and, even worse, away from good road access

School administrators sometimes use temporary or "portable" classrooms to respond to overcrowding. Such units are often a symptom of a larger problem.

and utilities. Many local governments and their utility departments spend money every year making a new school work by extending infrastructure to it—when, with some planning, the school might have located where infrastructure already existed.

Finding sites for schools is more challenging than finding sites for fire stations, because schools require more land. School administrators today typically want elementary school sites of six or eight acres or more and secondary school sites of fifteen or twenty or more acres—depending on the extent of proposed on-site athletic fields. Without planning, it is hard to find such large parcels of land—at least at a reasonable price—in developing (or developed) areas, and it is thus crucial that school planners and comprehensive planners work together to identify logical future school sites and to plan for and acquire them while they are still available at a tolerable cost.

Over the long term, the growth of a community influences the need for libraries, public offices, and even jails. Such facilities typically serve an entire community, or a large part of it, and it is thus not critical that there be locations for such facilities in growing areas. A community experiencing major growth may want to reserve one or more sites for new branch "civic centers," leaving open a range of possibilities for use—including possible branch libraries and offices or even relocation of the main facilities.

Someone will plan for future fire stations, schools, and other facilities, even if they are not considered in the comprehensive plan. The result will be better, however, if the planning for those facilities is coordinated with the comprehensive planning process. For community planners and planning commissions to plan for those facilities without consultation of the providers is rarely an effective technique; the providers employ their own experts and expect to participate in the process. Communities will achieve the best results when all of those planning their futures work together.

Planning for Telecommunications Infrastructure

In the "information age," some of the most important highways are electronic ones. Omaha, Nebraska, is home to a number of travel reservation centers and credit card "back office" operations, because it is situated at an early crossroads for major fiber-optic cable lines. Within a community, access to fiber-optics, high-quality wire lines, and basic telephone services is extremely important to many businesses.

The Telecommunication Act of 1996 changed the way cities and states deal with the provision of telecommunications. Prior to the passage of that federal legislation, the placement of communication lines was primarily handled by utility companies, with some supervision from local governments, since regulations were set at the state and federal levels. Local governments could force major transmission towers to the outskirts of cities and prohibit dishes and antennas in neighborhoods. The Telecommunication Act of 1996 mandates that both state and local governments act as regulators, providers, and facilitators as the federal government moves to ensure that all companies within the industry can compete in what were once monopolies.

A major challenge in many communities relates to towers that hold antennae to serve cellular phones and digital "personal communication systems." Unlike radio and television broadcast antennae that often serve several communities from one location, these towers serve only small areas, or "cells," within a community; the corollary of that situation is that each provider requires multiple antenna locations to serve a single community. In the 1980s, there were typically one or two providers of such services in a community, offering service only in limited, central areas. Today, as many as four or five separate providers compete in a market. Each typically wants its own towers. All are working to expand their coverage into lower-density and rural areas, thus requiring more towers.

While local governments can control the siting, construction, and modification of cellular and other wireless facilities as well as charge rents, taxes, or fees for the use of public rights-of-way, those governments are not completely free to regulate the actual placement and size of the towers and facilities; thus, planners may be able to prevent the erection of a cellular tower at a particular location, but, where such facilities are permitted (and the federal law requires that there be many such locations), planners cannot keep them out of front yards or unreasonably control their size. Thus planners are directly involved

The number of telecommunications towers grew rapidly in the 1990s because of increased demand for cellular phones and other wireless communications devices. Courtesy of Pflum, Klausmeier & Gehrum, Cincinnati.

with these important facilities through land-use planning and regulations. Planning allows communities to determine the role of city government as the regulator, service provider, and facilitator to the industry. Some communities are amending comprehensive plans to include goals and objectives for telecommunications, while others are creating freestanding policy documents until the existing comprehensive plan is revised or redone.

Sunnyvale, California, created a major planning document, separate from the comprehensive plan, to address telecommunications. It is a freestanding policy document with goals, policies (objectives), and action statements (implementation strategies). Below are the major goals:

- Retain control of public property within the confines of state and federal legislation to regulate telecommunications services provided to Sunnyvale citizens.
- Promote universal access to telecommunications services for all Sunnyvale citizens.
- Use telecommunications to maintain and enhance information resources and services provided to Sunnyvale citizens.
- Promote use of telecommunications technology, where appropriate and within the scope of available resources, to enhance the economic vitality of Sunnyvale.
- Facilitate the creation of an advanced telecommunications network infrastructure, within given resources, for Sunnyvale citizens, businesses, and industries.

Where telecommunications facilities are not included as part of infrastructure planning, many communities are simply responding to permit requests without achieving such goals as universal service within the community. All plans that include telecommunications should address how that entity will deal with being a regulator, provider, and facilitator.

States have reacted to these changes by leaving the regulatory issues of competition, universal services, and limiting free speech to the Public Utility Commissions. Most have also created some other department or commission to oversee how public demand is being met, often having to ensure that smaller communities receive basic services. Today there are a larger proportion of states planning telecommunications infrastructure than local communities, where planning is the most necessary.

Conclusion

The most expensive investments of most local governments are found on and in the ground, in the form of roads and other infrastructure. While facilities do not create growth, they do guide growth and thus shape communities. The large investment of resources requires careful planning to link land-use with transportation and infrastructure.

Community planners, and the planning commissions they serve, often hope and even expect that officials planning public facilities will simply follow the comprehensive plan. In fact, those officials may look to the future land-use plan to determine needs such as the size of lines, the locations of pumping stations, and the capabilities of new plant facilities. Unfortunately, comprehensive plans are often ignored in the day-to-day decisions that ultimately determine where facilities will be built.

Facilities planning is often reactive rather than proactive in directing development. It sounds simple to extend lines and roads according to the comprehensive land-use plan. As chapter 2 of this book indicates, however, comprehensive plans project the future well beyond what is likely to occur in the next decade, and most communities cannot afford the luxury of extending services where they will not be used soon. Just labeling an area as suitable for a particular future use (which is the real implication of future land-use designations on most comprehensive plans) does not mean that it is immediately developable as planned. As a practical matter, the road, sewer, and water planners who want to know what the development patterns will be will themselves help to decide that. Thus, the only cost-effective and practical way to plan for infrastructure is to integrate the immediate planning process with comprehensive planning—involving the infrastructure experts in developing the comprehensive plan and allowing the factors that they use for planning to influence the comprehensive plan, as well as anticipating that the comprehensive plan will influence the construction of their facilities.

The Role of the Professional (Community) Planner

Agencies that build roads, sewer and water lines, and even schools and fire stations often consult community planners far too little. Most such agencies have staff members who function as planners, and others use consultants who play that role. Many of those staff members and consultants are engineers or subject-matter professionals in fields such as education and recreation; many lack a general background in planning as well as a real understanding of the broader land-use and other planning issues faced by the community. Although some infrastructure and facility planners look to the comprehensive planning process as a basis for projecting the quantity and location of future facility demand, few depend on the comprehensive plan to tell them what to build where and when.

Community planners are most likely to play a role in planning for such facilities if they ensure the involvement of the experts who work with those facilities—and the policy boards that they serve—in the comprehensive planning process. With an integrated planning process, the resulting plan can serve the needs of those important providers of community services, as well as the needs of the planning commission, making it far more likely that the providers will follow the plan.

The Role of the Individual Citizen

The role of the individual citizen in planning for future infrastructure is often small. Although transportation and school planners sometimes hold public hearings to discuss their specific proposals, they are much less likely than a planning commission to seek active involvement of individual citizens in the development of the plan. Citizens are more likely to have some opportunity for involvement in planning for schools and parks, but even those processes are typically less than comprehensive and often controlled by "experts."

Thus, individual citizens, like professional planners, ought to seek the integration of planning for these facilities into the comprehensive planning process—which almost always includes a significant degree of meaningful citizen participation.

EXERCISES

1. Visit some of the areas of your community that have developed most recently. Why did those areas develop? Was there a major road that helped to attract growth? Try to find out when major sewer and water lines were built to those areas.

2. Find out if your community has a plan for parks and open space. Is it part of the comprehensive plan? Is it coordinated with the comprehensive plan?

3. Using topographic maps for the area, draw a line around the top of the drainage basin in which your community is located. Find out what the maximum service elevation for water is and draw another line around the drainage basin at that level. Does most of the community fall within those two boundaries? What is the trend of growth? Does the community seem likely to grow beyond one of those lines in some direction? Why? Is it because of a major road or other growth attractor?

4. When was the last school built in your community? How does that relate to the growth patterns of the community? Was it a logical location for a school at the time it was built? Has it turned out to be a logical location for a new school? Are there new areas of the community without schools?

DISCUSSION QUESTIONS

Does your community seem to have a good system of parks and open space, including sections in developing areas? Are there greenway connections? Are there locations where such connections might be appropriate? How might the community improve the open-space system?

FURTHER READING

Branch, Melville C. 1985. *Comprehensive City Planning: Introduction and Explanation.* Chicago: Planners Press. A broad-based planning text with a general description of transportation planning and capital improvement budgeting.

Carlson, Daniel, with Lisa Wormser and Cy Ulberg. 1995. *At Road's End: Transportation and Land Use Choices for Communities.* Washington, DC: Island Press, Surface Transportation Policy Project. An excellent examination of new approaches to transportation planning, with examples and a discussion of the practical implications of ISTEA.

Chen, Donald D.T. 1998. "If You Build It, They Will Come . . ." *Progress* 8, no. 1 (March). An interesting study that relates infrastructure to growth and development.

Ewing, Reid. 1997. *Transportation & Land Use Innovations: When You Can't Pave Your Way out of Congestion.* Chicago: American Planning Association. A handbook prepared to help Florida address its growing congestion problems but useful elsewhere.

Kelly, Eric Damian. 1993. *Planning, Growth, and Public Facilities: A Primer for Local Officials.* Planning Advisory Service Report No. 447. Chicago: American Planning Association. An introduction to the relationship between planning and public facilities.

Patterson, William T. 1979. *Land Use Planning Techniques of Implementation.* Dallas, TX: Van Nostrand Reinhold. Basic study of land use techniques, some now dated, but draws on relationship between land-use and transportation.

Robinson, Susan G., John E. Petersen, Thomas Muller, and Isaac F. Megbolugbe. 1990. *Building Together: Investing in Community Infrastructure.* Washington, DC: National Association of Counties and National Association of Home Builders. A good reference work for understanding the relationship between infrastructure planning and capital improvement budgets.

Rosenbloom, Sandra. 1988. "Transportation Planning," in *The Practice of Local Government Planning,* 2nd edition, Frank S. So and Judith Getzels, eds. Washington, DC: International City Management Association. This chapter goes into detail on the basics of transportation planning. It is an excellent resource but it is now in revision and should be an even more appropriate reference.

Wachs, Martin. 1985. "Ethical Dilemmas in Forecasting for Public Policy," in *Ethics in Planning*, Martin Wachs, ed. New Brunswick, NJ: [Rutgers University] Center for Urban Policy Research. Excellent for bringing forth issues in transportation.

REFERENCES

Institute of Transportation Engineers. 1997. *Trip Generation Manual*, 7th edition. Washington, DC: Institute of Transportation Engineers. A standard reference, regularly updated; predicts the number of trips likely to be generated from specified land uses, used in conjunction with highway capacity information to determine how much capacity remains.

Insurance Services' Office. 1992. *The Fire Suppression Rating Schedule*. New York: ISO Commercial Risk Services. Good reference on levels of service for fire protection.

Mertes, James D., and James R. Hall. 1996. *Park, Recreation, Open Space and Greenway Guidelines*. Alexandria, VA: National Recreation and Park Association and American Academy for Park and Recreation Administration. A standard reference on this topic; although most communities do not reach these somewhat idealized standards, they at least provide a useful benchmark. This updated version recognizes the importance of greenways and other passive open spaces, as well as traditional park and recreation areas.

Transportation Research Board. 1985. *Highway Capacity Manual*. Washington, DC: Transportation Research Board, National Research Council. The standard reference on this topic.

Urban Land Institute. 1975. *Residential Storm Water Management: Objectives, Principles & Design Considerations*. Washington, DC: Urban Land Institute, American Society of Civil Engineers, and National Association of Home Builders. An excellent handbook that considers alternative approaches to stormwater management; definitely not outdated.

NOTES

1. P. L. 102-240, 105 Stat. 1914.
2. P. L. 105-178. There is an excellent discussion of the practical aspects of making this new kind of planning work in "Implementing the Intermodal Surface Transportation Efficiency Act," part 2, of Daniel Carlson, with Lisa Wormser and Cy Ulberg, *At Road's End: Transportation and Land Use Choices for Communities*, Washington, DC: Island Press, Surface Transportation Policy Project (1995).
3. See, for example, William H. Whyte, Jr., *Urban Sprawl in the Exploding Metropolis*, Anchor Books, New York: Doubleday (1958), 114–39, 126–27; and Lewis Mumford, *The Highway and the City*, New York: Harcourt, Brace & World (1963).
4. Federal-Aid Highway Act of 1956, 70 Stat. 374.
5. *Trip Generation Handbook*, 7th edition, Washington, DC: Institute of Transportation Engineers (1997).
6. For further information on trip distribution models, see John D. Edwards, Jr., ed., *Transportation Planning Handbook*, Washington, DC: Institute of Transportation Engineers (1992).
7. For a policy essay, documented with references to many studies, see Anthony

Downs, *Stuck in Traffic: Coping with Peak Hour Traffic Congestion,* Washington, DC: Brookings Institution; Cambridge, MA:Lincoln Institute for Land Policy (1992).

8. See, for example, Erik Ferguson, *Transportation Demand Management,* Planning Advisory Service Report No. 477, Chicago: American Planning Association (1998).

9. For a good discussion, see Carlson, note 2.

10. Described in Russell Ackoff, *The Art of Problem Solving: Accompanied by Ackoff's Fables,* New York: John Wiley (1978).

11. Some techniques are described in Reid Ewing, *Transportation & Land Use Innovations: When You Can't Pave Your Way out of Congestion,* Chicago: American Planning Association (1997).

12. See Downs, note 7.

13. Sally Cairns, Carmen Hass-Klau, and Phil Goodwin, *Traffic Impact of Highway Capacity Reductions: Assessment of the Evidence,* London: Landor Publishing (1998).

14. Ewing, note 11.

15. Carlson, note 2.

16. The Urban Land Institute, an organization largely representing major developers, has recently published a major book advocating the value of open space. Alexander Garvin, Gayle Berens, and Christopher Leinberger, *Urban Parks and Open Space,* Washington, DC: Urban Land Institute in cooperation with the Trust for Public Land (1997).

Chapter 8

....

Putting It All Together

This chapter addresses the completion of the comprehensive planning process: preparation and adoption of the plan. This is a critical step in the planning process and one typically greeted with a sense of joy and relief by those involved in bringing the plan from the idea stage through the steps described in the previous chapters.

Adoption of the plan is in many ways only the beginning. A plan has meaning only if it is implemented. (Part III of this book deals with implementation tools and strategies.) Note that in some communities, adoption occurs before all of the planning in part IV is complete. All of the steps in part I and the basic analysis of future land use (chapter 6) and at least the transportation-circulation elements of public facilities plans (chapter 7) are essential to the adoption of the plan. Some communities may include elements such as neighborhood plans, downtown plans, park plans, and housing plans in the completed comprehensive plan, but others may first adopt the basic plan and then complete those other elements in the context of an overarching plan for land use and circulation.

The Adoption Process

The ultimate goal of the planning process is implementation, but a major intermediate objective is formal adoption of the plan. In virtually every community in every state, the planning commission must at some point adopt the plan for it to take effect. For reasons discussed in chapter 2, it is politically and practically useful to ask that the local governing body also formally vote on the plan, an action required by law in some states. The official actions by those two bodies, however, are only a small part of the adoption process.

Laws in every state require a public hearing on a plan before its adoption. Although that is an important legal and ceremonial forum for citizen participation, it is in many ways inadequate, for reasons discussed in chapter 5. Even where the planning body has kept the plan simple and accessible, perhaps included in a map and a few pages of text, the concepts represented by the plan will remain complex and interrelated. The public hearing is a good forum for people to raise major objections to a plan, its methodology, or its contents. If the planning body has followed the participatory approach suggested in chapter 5 and has paid attention to the citizen comments, there typically will not be major objections at the final hearing—most should have been incorporated into the plan or at least addressed. A major objection to an element of the plan by an influential group may, if raised at a public hearing, snowball into major opposition to the entire plan, which is one reason that many planning bodies try to address most major issues before the final public hearing.

With the best of plans, however, interested parties will raise a number of more focused issues, identifying omissions and inconsistencies and bringing up smaller questions that may not have arisen earlier in the process. Such questions may include such things as the exact location of a proposed major roadway (even if everyone agrees that the roadway is needed, there may be disagreement on the route), the precise (or even general) boundaries for the intense-use area surrounding a busy intersection, the mix of uses appropriate to encourage revitalization of downtown, and the area to be designated for future industrial use. It is difficult for individuals—particularly citizens without a professional planning background—to comment meaningfully on such details at a public hearing, and it is often even more difficult for the planning body to assimilate and use such comments.

Thus, politically astute planning bodies distribute draft copies of the complete plan—and sometimes, even parts of the plan earlier—for public comment. By this late stage of the planning process, the planning body ought to know what interest groups are likely to devote the time necessary to provide useful comments, and it is common practice to provide courtesy copies to those groups, as well as making copies available to the general public in public libraries, schools, and other locations. In some communities, planners or members of the planning body hold discussion workshops to discuss the plan with people in particular parts of the city or with designated interest groups.

Among the interest groups that must be included in this informal review process are all agencies and bodies that can significantly influence the success of its implementation. At a minimum, that typically includes:

• the governing body
• the planning commission, if it is not the body developing the plan
• the school board

- any board controlling a sewer or water provider, if separate from the governing body of the community
- the district highway or transportation engineer
- the parks board
- planning commissions of other local governments significantly affected by the plan
- where applicable, a regional planning commission or the equivalent

Often the planning body membership includes representatives of some or all of these groups. At this stage, however, it is important to take the plan back to the other constituent groups as bodies and not to rely solely on the views of representatives of those groups. Often there are policy disagreements within a group, and the introduction of a tangible plan may raise questions and issues that the other bodies have never discussed.

Those other bodies are in one sense just like other interest groups who participate in the process—land developers, neighborhood organizations, the chamber of commerce, and other established and ad hoc groups. There is a critical difference, however. All of the groups listed above have the authority to take regulatory action and/or to make capital expenditures that can help to implement the purposes of the plan—or thwart them. Thus, they are critical players in the success of the plan.

In most cases, it will not be possible for the planning body to accommodate every view in the final plan. The goal of the process is to obtain consensus support for adoption—and the very concept of consensus recognizes that people may disagree on some items but support the total document despite those minor concerns or disagreements. Often a complex bill passes Congress with the votes of many people who disagree with parts of it but support other parts of it and recognize that the totality is the best available package that will include the provisions that they do support. The adoption process for a plan is similar.

By summarizing, analyzing, and discussing comments from an informal (but structured) process like this, the planning body can address the major remaining issues affecting the plan before submitting a revised draft of it for formal consideration at a public hearing.

The Final Plan

One of the great challenges in planning is presenting the issues, policies, and other concepts that result from the planning process in an accessible format that is useful to decision makers and the larger community. Making the plan user friendly will enhance its prospects for adoption and will significantly increase the likelihood that it will actually be used by local officials as they make decisions about the future of the community.

Should the Plan Be a Map?

The most traditional representation of a plan for the future of a community is a map. During the 1970s and 1980s, there was a significant movement toward the use of unmapped policy plans. Today the best practice involves the combination of a map and a set of policy statements. There are advantages and disadvantages to including a map in the plan, however, and it is important to understand both.

Chapters 2 and 3 discuss the use of maps to represent and analyze existing conditions. Mapping existing conditions is always useful and rarely controversial. If the work is accurate, the maps represent reality and simply reinforce what people already know. In contrast, a plan for the future represents a combination of goals and policies that become a guide. Mapping those goals and policies may make them appear both more real and more rigid than they are. A map works well for established neighborhoods and other developed areas—it provides a tangible, graphic representation of the desired pattern of development, which is usually the existing pattern of development, sometimes with minor modifications. The map similarly works well in dealing with agricultural and other areas that are unlikely to feel development pressure during the planning period. The map is a much less effective tool in areas that are likely to develop between the date of the plan and the planning horizon. Consider the kinds of judgments that professional planners and the planning body must make in developing a map for future land use in an undeveloped area within the projected growth area of the community:

1. You are helping to develop a plan for a community of forty thousand. The major retailers in the old downtown have closed, due largely to competition from retailers in two larger communities, each about twenty miles away. Everyone agrees that this community would benefit from having a regional shopping mall. There is also a general consensus that, for such a mall to be viable, it must be located within one mile of the edge of town along a major east-west state highway; sewer and water service are available for at least a mile in each direction. Do you recommend putting the mall east of town or west? North or south of the highway? How do you decide? Someone has suggested just projecting future commercial uses for five hundred feet on either side of the highway for one mile on each side of town, noting that a number of other communities have used that approach. Is that a good solution?

2. As you study possible locations for a shopping mall, you realize that there are two intersections between the state highway and major county roads on both sides of town—one at Road C about three-quarters of a mile east of the current town, and the other at Road G about one-half mile west of the town. You expect both to be surrounded by residential uses, but traffic on the roads is heavy, making them unattractive as residential addresses. Although the roads can absorb more traffic, they are major

roads, and it is unlikely that people will want to live in houses facing on them. Assuming that you recommend one of those intersections as the logical location for the regional mall, what do you recommend for the other? Other commercial? Offices? Apartments? Industrial? How do you decide?

3. A realistic projection suggests that the town is likely to grow by about sixteen thousand people, or somewhat fewer than ten thousand house-holds over the twenty-two-year period, based on current census data regarding family sizes. At current development densities, that number of units, together with supporting commercial services, would require no more than three thousand acres of land, or about five square miles. Sewer and water lines currently extend a mile or a little more to the east, south, and west of the city, and the utility department plans to extend lines at least a half mile farther in each direction; the three-quarter circle that would include all of the served by the expanded system includes about twenty square miles of undeveloped land. Assuming that the planning body has made a policy decision to reserve a three thousand-acre area for industrial development, how much of the rest would you show as "residential" on the future land-use plan?

4. As the professional planner leading the planning effort, you and the planning body are convinced that neighborhood commercial services, within walking distance of most new homes, are essential to the quality of life of future neighborhoods. Where will you show the neighborhood commercial centers on the map for neighborhoods that will be developed in the future—neighborhoods for which the location of the streets is still an unknown?

Planning bodies and the professional planners who advise them must make judgments like those constantly. It is probably obvious that there are no "right" answers to any of those questions. The mall could go on either side of town and on either side of the road, and one side effect of mapping it in a particular location may be to make the landowner think that she or he has a particularly valuable piece of property and to ask such a high price for it that potential mall developers will look elsewhere—perhaps on the other side of the road or the other side of town, or perhaps in a nearby community. Land at either of the intersections is probably suitable for any relatively intense use setback from the roads—it could be commercial, office, industrial, medium- or high-density residential, or even an institutional use like a hospital or high school football stadium. Determining in advance which of these uses would be most appropriate in which quadrant of which intersection is difficult at best and, at worst, a virtual guessing game.

Designating too little land for future residential use may constrain the market and create artificial increases in the selling prices of land available for residential uses, thus unnecessarily increasing the future cost of housing. On the other hand, it is certainly unnecessary and often irresponsible to plan for three or four times as much land for development as is actually needed—particularly if one of the implications of that plan is that the utilities department will use tax revenues and user fees to expand service to the entire area, even though serving half of it might be adequate.

In short, it is very difficult to prepare a future land-use map that is a reasonable enough projection of the future that it is useful without also upsetting some landowners and residents. Neighbors may be upset because the plan shows commercial uses on vacant land where their children now play, and landowners may be upset because the plan suggests that their property be used for less-intensive (and thus less valuable) purposes than they had hoped. That is why some communities have adopted plans without maps—the map may create more controversy than it is worth.

A mapped representation of the plan, however, is extremely useful in many ways. It provides a simple, visual representation of the future of the community to landowners, developers, and interested citizens. It creates a sense of predictability. It provides guidance to those planning roads and utilities, allowing them to plan the extension of infrastructure to projected growth areas. It also provides guidance to those who may want to invest in agricultural operations, allowing them to choose land outside the growth areas and away from development pressures and potential conflicts with new neighbors.

One way to create a useful map that raises fewer questions than it answers is to make the map flexible. Future land-use maps sometimes look like zoning maps, showing exact boundaries for every different use area and relating those boundaries precisely to property lines. A map need not be that specific. Many communities use a "bubble" or "blob" map to show future land uses, particularly in developing areas; such a map indicates the general location of future uses without setting out the precise boundaries of the area. Further, a particular bub-

Richard Hedman on the problems of creating a future land-use map. Copyright by Richard Hedman. Used with permission.

ble need not indicate a specific use. The bubble for a future residential neighborhood may be linked to a legend or even a brief policy statement indicating that the bubble represents, for example: "low-density residential uses with included neighborhood commercial services located along collector streets in centers not exceeding 20,000 square feet of commercial space at one location." The bubbles around the two major intersections outside the community used in the above problems might simply denote: "activity centers, including higher-density residential uses, offices, regional and highway-oriented commercial, and institutional uses." Color plate 4 shows an integrated transportation and land-use plan using bubble format to identify major activity centers.

Of course, some planners argue that bubble maps are simply collections of blobs and not accurate enough to provide a basis for planning, and those same people typically argue that a mapping category that refers only to a range of uses, rather than to a narrowly defined class of uses, also fails to provide predictability. The debate is one that the profession is unlikely to resolve in the near future, because, as with so many questions in planning, there is no right answer. If choosing between a less specific map that has a reasonable chance of being both accepted and right, and a more specific map that will clearly be proven wrong over five or ten years, the authors would choose the less specific map as the better planning tool.

Regardless of the type of map chosen by a community, it is important to link the map to policies included in the plan. Several years ago in a community in Nevada, there were a number of disputes over whether hotel-casinos ought to be allowed on sites labeled on the future land-use plan as "tourist commercial." Unfortunately, the plan did not define tourist-commercial and gave no indication whatsoever as to the circumstances in which it ought to be allowed. It would have been much more useful to have a map that simply included those sites in more general intensive-commercial areas with an attached policy that said, "hotel-casinos will be allowed in this area on sites of at least X acres, where the proposed casino building will be located at least Y feet from any land zoned for residences or used for religious or educational purposes, and where the proposed site plan includes a landscaped buffer of at least Z feet between the development on the site (including parking) and any adjacent land zoned for residences." Tying policies to the mapped plan is common practice today and makes the map much more meaningful.

The Best Format for an Adopted Plan

The comprehensive plan has one overarching purpose: to serve as a guide to the future for decision makers in a community. That purpose ought to determine its format. Consider the following real-life examples:

1. a planner in a midsize city in Iowa presenting a proposed new plan containing more than 180 different policies under fourteen general head-

ings, all in a report that consisted of 165 pages of text, single-spaced, without illustrations, tables, or charts;

2. a city manager in Colorado picking up, apparently for the first time, the two thick volumes of the adopted local plan, slamming them down on the table and then turning to a group of young leaders in the community and saying, "Nobody will ever read a plan that thick—twenty-three pages is long enough for a plan";

3. a planner in a Colorado county proudly displaying a 17-by-22-inch copy of an adopted plan, saying, "This will never turn into a dusty planning report sitting up on the shelf, because no one can get it onto a shelf";

4. an award-winning plan in North Carolina that sold for twenty-five dollars a copy.

The city manager in #2 certainly should have read the longer plan, but it is entirely unreasonable to expect volunteer planning commission members of the governing body, who receive lots of other reading material, to read and comprehend hundreds of pages of material for a plan. Although some public officials may read a plan of 165 pages, how much of it will they remember? The goal of the process is to have them use the plan in making decisions—that means that they need to be able either to read it and remember it, or to refer to is easily at meetings. Although the large-format plan had lots of maps and illustrations and was one that people might remember after reading it, the 180-policy plan was not.

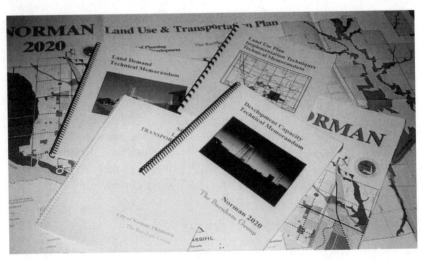

The 1996 "2020" plan for Norman, Oklahoma, included several individual reports, as well as a summary report (about twenty-seven pages with two fold-out maps) and a poster plan, printed in thousands of copies for mass distribution. Source: *City of Norman (1996).*

Neither the large-format plan nor the two-volume plan is the type of document that officials are likely to carry to meetings with them regularly. Although the 180-policy plan was only a little more than an inch thick and was fairly portable, it was far from accessible—even if a planning commission member had the plan at a meeting, finding all of the policies applicable to a particular case would take a significant investment in time.

The twenty-five-dollar plan raises a different set of issues. In that particular community, planning commission and governing body members received free copies of the plan, but the cost of the plan, as well as the inconvenience of going to the planning office to pick it up and pay for it, made it far less accessible to much of the rest of the community—and, in fact, many members appointed to a technical advisory group to help implement the plan had not seen copies of it before being appointed to the group.

The presentation and format of a final plan ought to be user friendly, accessible, and short. If the plan is short, people are more likely to read it and remember it; and, if they do not remember, they can easily read it again. If it is user friendly and accessible, people can find the information they need quickly and easily, even if the do not remember it in detail—that is useful to decision makers at public meetings, to residents interested in the future of their neighborhoods, and to investors considering the purchase of real estate in the community.

Such a plan can take a variety of formats. Here are some common examples:

- a report containing primarily the planning policies and related implementation strategies, supported by separate maps;
- a report containing a summary of the background studies used in developing the plan, together with the adopted planning policies and related implementation strategies, supported by separate maps;
- a "poster plan," typically containing the future land-use and transportation plans and related polices on one side and other policies (and sometimes more detailed maps) on the other (see the Orange County, Florida, example in the accompanying figure); and
- a poster or tabloid designed as a newspaper supplement.

These are some good approaches to developing a relatively brief, user-friendly, and accessible plan, and there are many others.

Electronic media are evolving rapidly, and at this time, electronic publication is an excellent supplemental choice but does not appear to offer the accessibility necessary for a primary publication. Today, some plans are being published on CD-ROM and on the World Wide Web,[1] as well as in hard copy—to date, we are aware of no plans that have been published exclusively in electronic format. There are several reasons for that. First, despite the rapid spread of Internet access, not all of the population has access to the Internet,

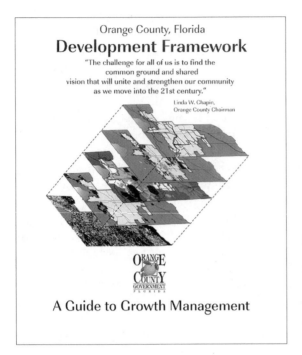

This is the cover of the poster-format plan for Orange County, Florida. Source: *Orange County Department of Planning and Development, Bruce McClendon, director (1998).*

and many of those who do have access use it primarily for electronic mail and not for obtaining complex information. There are also significant socioeconomic differences among those who use electronic communication and those who do not, and any shift to a plan that is entirely electronic would reduce access by those of limited means.

Further, although electronic communications offer wonderful accessibility for "hot-linked" cross-references and searches for all instances of a word or phrase through a large document, typically entry into an electronic document takes longer than opening a book, and, in many situations, it is difficult to obtain electronic access quietly during a meeting. Thus, for people who just want to browse and for officials who want to make their own spot checks of plan policies during a public meeting, the paper format still offers significant advantages. Nevertheless, the electronic world is evolving rapidly. Thus, users of this book a year or two after its initial publication may find that there are new options in electronic publication that address many of the issues raised here and that may, at some point, replace partly or entirely the traditional publication of a comprehensive plan.

What Does the Official Plan Include?

Obviously, it is necessary to limit content to make a plan short, accessible, and user friendly. What should such a plan include? What happens too all of those background studies, described in chapters 2, 3, and 4? What happens to records of the policy discussions, the subject of chapter 5?

In the 1970s, when federal funding paid for many local planning efforts—and that funding came with a long list of requirements—adopted plans were often several inches thick and included all of the background studies prepared as part of the planning effort, ranging from a history of the community to detailed descriptions of the existing sewer and water systems. Such background information is extremely useful and perhaps essential to an effective

Goal 1.
Managed Growth

Ensure that growth in Norman is affirmatively and responsibly managed based on available public services and suitability of the land for development.

Policies:

	Regulatory Techniques							Public Facilities Financing Techniques						Miscellaneous Implementation Techniques			
	Minimum Zoning Density Standards	Industrial-Initiated Zoning	Developing Area Industrial Overlay	Country Residential Preservation	Transitional Urban Reserve Residential Zoning	Cluster Zoning	Overlay Zoning	Wastewater Plant Investment Fees	Water and Sewer Utility Payback Fees	Street Improvement Recoupment Program	Improvement Districts	Adequate Public Facilities Program	Capacity Allocation Program	University Comprehensive Planning and Development Agreements	CBD Enhancement Programs	Proposed Outer Loop Study and Interim Controls	Greenway Program
1. Adopt a land use plan and establish a growth management system that will proactively accommodate the projected year 2020 population of 117,000 people.	■			■	■							■	■				
2. Use infrastructure as a tool to guide development into locations where the land is most cost effectively serviced by urban level services.	■	■	■					■	■	■	■	■					
3. Balance development on the east and west sides of the urbanized area of Norman.	■		■	■				■	■	■	■	■	■	■	■	■	
4. Adopt regulations that protect or restrict development in floodplains, aquifer-recharge areas, erosion-prone soils, Lake Thunderbird and the Garber-Wellington aquifer.	■			■		■	■									■	
5. Promote development that is more pedestrian-oriented with its design and mix of land uses.	■						■								■	■	■

The Norman, Oklahoma, plan includes an implementation strategies report. This section of a larger chart identifies techniques to be used to implement policies under one of the goals of the plan. Source: *City of Norman and the Burnham Group, Cincinnati, Little Rock, and Birmingham (1996).*

planning effort. It is not necessary, however, to include it in the adopted plan. Any of the plan formats described in the previous section can (and should) be supported by multiple volumes of background studies and analyses. Those that wish to do so can even ask the planning commission and the governing body to "adopt" the background studies, although that is hardly necessary.

A final plan containing all of that material is likely to consist of several volumes, although some of the volumes may be relatively short. One way of organizing the material in such a plan is to allow the organization to reflect the planning process:

1. background (including community history)
2. existing conditions analysis
3. issues and goals developed from citizen participation
4. alternative scenarios and policies
5. final plan and policies
6. implementation strategies

Another approach to presenting the plan is a functional approach, with separate reports focusing on separate systems within the community or separate segments of the community. Such a plan might include the following elements:

- land use
- transportation and circulation
- utilities and infrastructure
- parks and recreation
- natural systems
- demographics
- economic systems
- summary of policies (with supporting maps)

With this approach, each functional piece of the plan contains its own section on existing conditions, its own analysis, its own set of policies, and, ideally, recommendations for implementation. It is important practically and politically to provide a summary report for such a multivolume plan, because it is that summary report (and map) to which people will most frequently refer.

Is the Final Plan Internally Consistent?

Some communities divide the task of developing a plan among committees or task forces, with each usually focusing on a particular functional area of the community. Typical topics assigned to such task forces include:

- natural environment
- affordable housing
- economic development

- transportation, circulation, and infrastructure
- downtown
- parks and recreation

The city in Iowa that wound up with more than 180 policies used such task forces as described here. Each task force recommended eight to twelve policies, a number that seemed reasonable when isolated but, when added to those of the other committees, became unwieldy and thus probably unreasonable.

The most serious risk in the functional approach, however, is not that of length but that of inconsistency. Suppose in such a process that the natural environment task force recommended a policy that said, "Preserve agricultural land," and the economic development task force suggested a policy that said, "Encourage a more diverse economic base." Both are entirely reasonable policies likely to be included in the adopted plan without much discussion. Suppose then that a major manufacturing company proposes a new plant that will employ 850 people and will be located along the railroad tracks on land now in agricultural use. Would such a plan help local officials resolve those differing interests? The final plan must set priorities among policies or otherwise provide a basis for resolving such major inconsistencies.

Consider another possible scenario. Suppose that the affordable housing task force recommended a policy that said, "The community should pay the costs of infrastructure for new areas, to limit development costs and to reduce the burdens on new housing," and that the transportation and infrastructure task force recommended one that said, "Make new growth pay for all necessary infrastructure, to ensure adequate capacity in the system and to limit the burden on current taxpayers." Again, both are reasonable policies likely, if considered separately, to be adopted by the planning body. What is the message, however? Should the community charge developers for the costs of extending infrastructure to new areas or not?

Any planning body that uses task forces or committees to prepare recommendations on particular functional areas, and, in fact, any community that breaks the planning process into functional segments, must at some point review all of the recommended policies in depth, eliminating inconsistencies (such as the policies regarding who should pay for infrastructure) and setting relative priorities among differing policies (such as the ones in the example about the manufacturing plant on the farmland) that are not inconsistent on their face but may come into conflict in a case like the one given in the example.

Typically, when one planning body develops all of the major policies included in a plan, the issue of internal consistency will resolve itself—members of the planning body are likely to recognize internal inconsistencies and policy divergences as they arise in the policy-development process.

Where there are multiple contributors to the policy-development process, however, or where the policies are developed in functional groups, it is essential to include in the process a method for addressing these conflicts and divergences.

Conclusion: Adoption, Publication, and Distribution

A public hearing almost always results in at least some changes to a comprehensive plan. The final step in the adoption process is the publication of the plan, reflecting all of those last-minute changes, correcting any remaining errors, and showing the date of adoption. That final version of the plan should be widely distributed. If the primary form of publication involves slick pages and lots of color—or other characteristics that make it expensive to reproduce—the planning body should arrange for less costly reproduction that can be made widely available. Any local government with an electronic Web site should publish the plan on the Web. In many small or midsize communities, a local newspaper will publish a poster or tabloid version of the plan and include it in the paper at little or no cost to the local government. Once such a plan is set up to run on newspaper presses, it is inexpensive to run an extra several thousand copies for additional distribution.

The key to the success of an adopted comprehensive plan is implementation. One of the keys to implementation is public knowledge about and support of the plan—and those are best achieved with wide distribution.

The Role of the Professional Planner

This is the stage at which every professional planner begins to appreciate all of those required courses in professional writing, graphic communication, and public presentation. The primary role of the professional planner at this stage is that of synthesizer and communicator. Although in most cases, the professional planner will continue to play a role in organizing and facilitating meetings, communication is particularly important at this stage.

Typically, the professional planner will have primary responsibility for preparing the public drafts of the comprehensive plan. In many cases, the professional planner will have the primary responsibility for conducting meetings with neighborhood and other interest groups. In other cases, the role of the professional will be to prepare scripts and visual aids to be used by members of the planning body in handling such meetings.

Communication is a two-way activity. The professional planner will typically have the largest responsibility for recording, summarizing, and assimilating the comments from a variety of people and groups in a number of different meetings before adoption of the plan. The final challenge to the professional planner is to share all of that information with the planning body, to discern the will of that body in response to the comments, and incorporate that will into a final document. Finally, the planner typically plays a major role in publication and distribution of the document, followed by public education based on the adopted plan.

The Role of the Individual Citizen

At this point, the role of the individual citizen is largely reactive—responding to proposed policies and to a complete plan.

The most effective citizen at this stage will be one who takes time to read every draft of the plan (or at least those sections of interest to the individual or the group he or she represents) and to submit careful, reasoned comments on each draft—preferably in writing—both to the professional staff and to the planning body. This is the time for politics, not polemics. The plan is beginning to take shape, and, in most cases, that general shape will survive the adoption process, even if details change. The real opportunity here is typically not to "defeat" the plan or to change it radically but to achieve adjustments in policies or other parts of the plan. Citizens who oppose a plan at this stage are often ignored. Those who say things like, "I support most aspects of the plan, but I have two specific areas of concern—first, if you will turn to paragraph 1.C on page 3 . . . " can have an enormous impact.

At the public hearing, active citizens must balance concerns about particular parts of the plan with some perspective on the value of having a plan. Opposition to a major section of a plan at the public hearing can lead to rejection of the entire plan. All too often that is the end of the planning process, leaving the community with no plan. If a plan does not represent the will of the community, it ought not to be adopted. When a plan generally represents the will of the community but includes one section that is objectionable to a significant part of the community, the issue is much more difficult to resolve. At that point, democracy becomes more important than planning in resolving the issue.

EXERCISES

1. In one of the exercises in a previous chapter, you should have obtained a copy of the most recent comprehensive plan for your community. Look at its format. Is it an effective format, based on the criteria set out in this chapter? Do you agree with those criteria in the context of considering that plan? Can you think of changes that would make the plan more effective and useful?

2. Is the plan for your community internally consistent? Are you sure? Compare the provisions on infrastructure financing (and/or taxes) with the provisions on housing costs; compare the provisions on economic development with provisions on the natural environment.

3. Check in the library or with colleagues and obtain copies of several different plans from different communities. Which one is most accessible and user friendly? Why?

4. To explore the concept of consensus, work with a group of seven or eight people. Each of you should choose the plan format that you like best (preferably based on exercise 3 in this chapter) and prepare a draft table of contents or outline for a plan for your own community (based generally on the contents of the actual plan for your community—but not necessarily on its format). After each of you has prepared an outline and a proposed format, meet as a group and decide on a single format and outline acceptable to all of you. Try to accomplish that in one meeting.

5. Look at the electronic versions of some plans. Web addresses for some current ones will be available at this book's on-line Web site.[2] How do those plans compare in user friendliness and accessibility to the paper copies of plans that you have reviewed—do you think your grandmother would agree?

6. Go back to exercise 2 in chapter 2. If you found the land uses at some locations in developing areas to be inconsistent with the future land-use map, are those uses consistent with relevant *policies* in the plan?

DISCUSSION QUESTION

Should a comprehensive plan include a future land-use map? Should the use classifications have hard edges that are easily identified on the ground, or should it use a "bubble" format? If you owned land near one of the borders between two different future-use categories, would you respond differently to this question? What if you were a developer looking for a site for an office building?

REFERENCES

Kaiser, Edward J., David R. Godschalk, and F. Stuart Chapin, Jr. 1995. *Urban Land Use Planning,* 4th edition. Urbana: University of Illinois Press. The latest edition of a classic work on land-use planning, with many good examples of plans.

Kent, T.J., Jr. 1990. *The Urban General Plan.* Chicago: Planners Press. A classic work on comprehensive planning for cities, including good examples of plans that remain relevant today.

McClendon, Bruce W., and Ray Quay. 1988. *Mastering Change: Winning Strategies for Effective City Planning.* Chicago: Planners Press. A leading work on the role of professional planners in facilitating the planning process and managing the planning function of local government—including good material on presenting plans to the public.

NOTES

1. For an example, see http://www.mdccomplan.com and other sites linked from the book's cross-reference Website, identified in the introduction.
2. http://www.cyburbia.org contains links to many local (and other) planning sites.

Part III
....

Making Plans Work

Planning is only the beginning of the process. Planning commissions, governing bodies, professional planners, and interested citizens alike want to see plans become a reality. The part of the book discusses techniques for implementing plans.

This part begins with an examination of the land development industry and related real estate market (chapter 9), the driving forces behind many of the local changes for which planners plan.

The next two chapters address the regulation of land use through zoning (chapter 10) and the management of land development through subdivision regulation and exactions (chapter 11). Chapter 12 discusses contemporary techniques of growth management, a set of tools used in combination with zoning and subdivision controls to address the timing and location of growth.

The next chapter, chapter 13, covers a different type of implementation tool—direct investment by the local government, rather than regulatory control of the actions of private owners and developers—used to deal with the construction of new roads, sewer and water lines, and other public facilities.

Chapter 14 deals with the complex question of regional planning. While this book focuses largely on planning by local governments, many local governments are parts of larger metropolitan areas, in which dozens or even hundreds of local governments may make their own plans without the context of a regional plan to guide such major decisions as the location of new highways.

Finally, chapter 15 discusses the growing importance of open space and some of the techniques used to provide it. Although communities have long had public parks, modern communities benefit from many different kinds of open space, often controlled by multiple public and private owners, using a broad array of forms of ownership and control.

It is through this combination of techniques that communities make plans work. These are the tools that actually change the shape of a community.

Chapter 9

....

Decisions That Change the Land

Local governments use zoning (chapter 10) to limit the types of use that are allowed in developing areas. They use subdivision regulations (chapter 11) to ensure the quality of new development. Some use conscious management of the location of new roads and sewer and water systems (chapters 12 and 13) to encourage development in some areas and, indirectly, to discourage it in others.

What local governments generally cannot do is make development happen. In the 1960s and 1970s, many midwestern agricultural communities colored vast areas on their future land-use plans purple (for industrial use) and considered that an important element in their economic development strategies. Not surprisingly, most of that land remained in agriculture. Simply coloring it purple on a map did not change its basic character, nor did that create a demand for industrial land in those locations.

How Development Occurs

Most development in this country occurs because a private developer invests money to change the land. That developer, often with advice from professionals in marketing, engineering, and finance, will select sites that seem most likely to facilitate a successful and profitable development. A major developer may already own property near the community and may attempt to develop that land before buying more, regardless of the priorities of the community. Land that seems to the community to be desirable for development may not be for sale. Variations in the pricing of land on the market may lead developers to make different decisions than the community might hope regarding the siting of new development And some communities at some periods in history are

IS IT POSSIBLE THE PRIVATE
MARKET KNOWS SOMETHING WE DON'T ?

*Richard Hedman on the private market and
planning. Copyright by Richard Hedman.
Used with permission.*

simply not attractive to any developers for anything; such communities can make all the plans in the world, but if no one decides to invest in new development there, the community will remain just as it is, possibly deteriorating along the way.

For nearly half a century, a certain West Texas community was shaped like a pie with a piece cut out of it equal to about one-quarter of the pie. The community had logical plans for filling in that quarter of the pie, but new development actually created a long tail off one side of the pie (in the direction of the sewage treatment plant). The missing quarter was owned by one family that was perfectly happy continuing to operate its ranch, adjoined on two sides by city, and it simply had no intention of selling the property. Many redevelopment projects have been thwarted because a particular landowner would not sell a key parcel, even at a fair price.

Simply planning for a use does not ensure that the use will occur at that location. Communities that are serious about planning will typically try to keep other uses from occurring at that location, waiting for the right use, but sometimes they wait until the next planning cycle and, finding the land still vacant, change the plan. In planning for residential expansion, it is not necessarily a problem if some of the land remains undeveloped—presumably the housing market will provide most of what people need, and if there is less housing than planned, that may mean that there are fewer people than the community expected. Where a community plans for industry or a major shopping center, and even invests in infrastructure to encourage the development of such uses, a lack of development may leave real gaps in the community, such as inadequate employment centers or no shopping mall.

Why does planning not work better? The answer is simple. The plan is a consensus plan, representing the will of the community as a whole, but the actual decisions about changes in land use are made by many different indi-

viduals and businesses, concerned with many factors in addition to (or sometimes in spite of) the community's plan. One obvious factor is the availability
of land for sale. There were undoubtedly developers in the Texas community
who would cheerfully have developed within the missing quarter of the pie,
but the land was not for sale. Thus, they looked elsewhere. The planning commission and governing body in the community were unlikely to (and did not)
deny development approvals in other locations, because everyone wanted the
community to grow, and it was obvious that it could not grow in the most
logical direction (filling in the missing quadrant) as long as the land was not
for sale.

Another factor is the availability of infrastructure. Where the extension of
public services is closely connected to the comprehensive plan (chapter 13),
such extension will encourage development in the desired locations. There are
communities, however, where decisions about extending service are made
without much regard for the comprehensive plan. In the 1980s, a city in the
Southwest designated a major area as "environmentally sensitive," in which
development should be discouraged. Within weeks, the local utilities department extended sewer and water service into the middle of that area. When
asked why he had allowed the extension of those services, which were bound
to (and did) induce development pressure in the area, the utilities director
responded that it was his obligation to extend service anywhere within the
county that he could do so profitably—and the situation in question met that
criterion.

*Regardless of community plans, changes in the land usually occur only when an owner
decides to sell and a private developer invests money in the improvements necessary to
create a new development.*

Rational developers are much more interested in the availability of services than in the characterization of a site on the plan. Extending services costs money. Developing in a way that is inconsistent with a plan happens so often that many developers expect it. Further, most are smart enough to acquire only an option to purchase land until they find out if the local government will approve a change in the plan and the related zoning to allow the proposed project; with an option, the developer who is unsuccessful in persuading the local government to change its mind can walk away from his or her down payment (or option fee) and go look for another piece of land.

How Planning Can Distort the Market

Sometimes planning actually distorts the land market. Consider a community of thirty thousand people that wants its own regional shopping center. Suppose that, as part of a comprehensive planning effort, it designates a site a half mile west of town on a major highway for a future regional shopping center. The landowner may be delighted to learn that she or he now owns a prime piece of commercial property and may decide that land that yesterday was worth $2,000 per acre for agriculture is now worth $20,000 per acre for commercial development. Suppose that a site selection representative for a major shopping center developer comes to town and begins to look at sites; she discovers that she can acquire one hundred acres planned for a future shopping center west of town for $2,000,000 or a site of exactly the same size, exactly the same distance east of town, along the same highway, for $200,000. Which property is she likely to try to buy? Suppose that she successfully obtains an option on the property on the east side and then goes to the local government, asking that it change the plan and allow the shopping center east of town. She will point out that the proposed site is along the highway where the community wants a shopping center and exactly the same distance away as the planned center; because the community really wants a shopping center, it is very likely to approve that change to its plan.

Some communities actually elect not to map such future uses as shopping center sites for precisely that reason. In such communities, the plan may contain written policies suggesting the type of location suitable for such a unique use but leaving it up to developers to seek designation of a particular site for that purpose.

Another significant difficulty with future land-use planning is that it typically designates the maximum intensity of a land use that can take place, but the community needs greater certainty about what will happen there and when. Thus, most communities that plan an area for "low-density residential, up to four units per acre," for example, have nothing in the plan or regulations to prevent a developer from building a project with only one unit per acre. Similarly, at a site designated for "regional commercial," it may be possible for someone to build a convenience store. In both cases, the actual development would appear to have less impact on the community than what would otherwise be permitted and thus to be desirable. Neither is a desirable result, however. The convenience store is likely to take the prime corner in the site designated for "regional commercial" and by doing that may so limit the visibility of and access to the site that it becomes undesirable to the sort of shopping center developers the community hoped to attract to the site.

More complex is the issue of residential development built below the planned level. There really are two problems involved. First, remember that the engineers who plan roads, sewer and water lines, and drainage typically rely on the comprehensive plan to determine how much development will take place in an area and to size their facilities accordingly. In the given example, responsible infrastructure providers would have built lines and roads adequate to serve development at four units per acre; if actual development occurs only at one unit per acre, 75 percent of the infrastructure capacity is wasted—that is expensive. Second, the lower-density development increases land consumption and sprawl. If one considers this issue from the perspective of the site—suppose that it consists of 100 acres—less development on the site (one hundred units instead of four hundred) may seem better. Suppose, however, that this site is part of the area intended to help the community provide for four thousand new dwelling units over the next ten years. At four units per acre, those four

After an owner decides to sell, land-use change will occur only if someone agrees to buy the land and then build something on it.

thousand units would require a total of 1,000 acres of land; because one hundred units have used up one hundred acres of land, the total to handle the four thousand units will now be at least 1,075 acres. If all of the residential development occurs at one unit per acre instead of four, the total land necessary to accommodate the residential development will be four thousand acres, or nearly five square miles more land than the community had planned for conversion to residential use. In an agricultural area, that means that there will be five square miles less agricultural land than was planned.

Oregon has led the nation in beginning to establish minimum expectations for development as well as maximums. More and more communities are beginning to consider this important issue both in their future land-use plans and in the related zoning regulations.

There is one more market complication, however. From looking at a "low-density residential classification" on a future land-use map, it is typically impossible to tell whether the property consists of:

- an existing residential development,
- a new residential development that is under construction,
- a new residential development that has been proposed but for which construction has not started, or
- vacant or agricultural land that may (or may not) some day become residential.

In short, what is missing from most future land-use maps is any indication of the timing of the proposed development. If the school board wants to acquire a new school site, it would like to know whether the planned residential development to the east will occur before the similar development planned on the west side of town. Although the community can try to encourage development in a particular direction by investing in roads and sewer and water lines in that direction, there is no way to know that development will occur there first—the land may not be for sale, the price may be too high, or a major developer may already own land in another location.

Do all of these problems make future land-use planning irrelevant? Absolutely not. It is better to have a plan than not to have a plan, even if the future does not happen exactly as the plan suggests. Many students start out with a four-year study program sometime in their first year of college; most of them will wind up taking some of the designated courses in different years than planned and substituting other courses for some listed on the program—nevertheless, by following the basic elements of such a program, a student can ensure that he or she completes the requirements of a proposed major, as well as related general studies requirements, within a reasonable period of time.

Although this chapter suggests some general principles that influence the land market, the only factor that is important to a particular community plan is the local land market. Consulting with major local developers, Realtors, and financial experts about the dynamics of that market can yield valuable information to help planners develop land-use plans that make sense in the context of that market—and that seem likely to influence it in the desired ways.

Conclusion

The purpose of describing the relationship of the private land market to planning in this chapter is to help planners incorporate this understanding into the planning process. Effective planners understand the land market and use a variety of implementation tools (described in the next chapters) to encourage development to take place, not just to suggest what ought to take place. Public-private partnerships are increasingly common in the creation of new industrial parks and other types of development that are central to long-range plans of communities. The next four chapters discuss some of the tools available to local government to ensure that development of the community conforms to its long-range land-use plan.

EXERCISES

1. Learn something about the prices of vacant land around your community. Read newspaper ads or go to a local real estate office and ask to review the listings of vacant land. If there are "for sale by owner" signs on land around the community, call some of those owners and ask what price they are asking per acre. Can you find any relationship between their asking prices and other data that you have? What?

2. You have just taken a job with a major (and very responsible) developer of shopping centers. You have been assigned to find a site of at least 60 acres in your community. What would you look for? Is a good site available? What extra expenses would be necessary to make that site suitable for your new employer's purposes?

3. Now undertake the same exercise for a big housing developer seeking a location for a large new project of houses that will be reasonably affordable for families with parents in their thirties. You need a site of at least 60 acres, but the company would accept a site of up to 120 acres. What would you look for? Is a good site available? What extra expenses would be necessary to make that site suitable for your new employer's purposes?

4. Ask a representative of a developer or real estate investor in your community to come to class and talk about how he or she makes decisions that change land. Ask their opinions of the community's future land-use map.

DISCUSSION QUESTIONS

1. Do developers in your community seem to be following the future land-use plan? If not, why do you think they are not following it? This is an

important question, to which the answer may not be as simple as you think—ask a developer.

2. Get out the exercises that you did for chapter 6, dealing with the future land-use plan. Do your initial recommendations still make sense? What would you change after reading this chapter and undertaking the exercises suggested above?

FURTHER READING

Miles, Mike E., Emil E. Malizi, Marc A. Weiss, Gayle L. Berens, and Ginger Travis. 1991. *Real Estate Development: Principles and Process.* Washington: Urban Land Institute. Designed as a teaching text, this is an excellent introduction to the field.

Miller, Ross. 1996. *Here's the Deal: The Buying and Selling of a Great American City.* New York: Alfred A. Knopf. A colorful story of deal making and its interaction with planning in Chicago's Loop, written by a journalist and carefully researched.

Weiss, Marc A. 1987. *The Rise of the Community Builders: The American Real Estate Industry and American Land Planning.* New York: Columbia University Press. An interesting and scholarly treatment of this subject.

Chapter 10

....

Controlling the Use of Private Land

Zoning was the first widely adopted form of regulatory implementation of planning and remains the most widely used and most widely discussed. It is a fairly simple technique that is based solidly on the concerns that led to its adoption. The essence of zoning involves the division of the community into districts, or zones, with different rules for different districts. Within each district, local governments typically regulate the following:

- the *use* of land or buildings;
- the *intensity* of that use, regulated by lot size, height limits, and, in some cases, direct regulation of intensity through floor-area ratios or limits on the number of dwelling units per area; and
- the *height and bulk,* or extent, of that use, regulated both directly and indirectly, through requirements that portions of the lot be maintained for yards or setback.

Although legislation in most states provides for regulation of other and related matters, the three items in the list above are the issues most commonly addressed through zoning ordinances around the country. This chapter discusses zoning as a tool of plan implementation.

Regulating Use

Zoning regulations typically define districts by uses and by intensities. The basic use categories in most communities are:

- agricultural
- residential

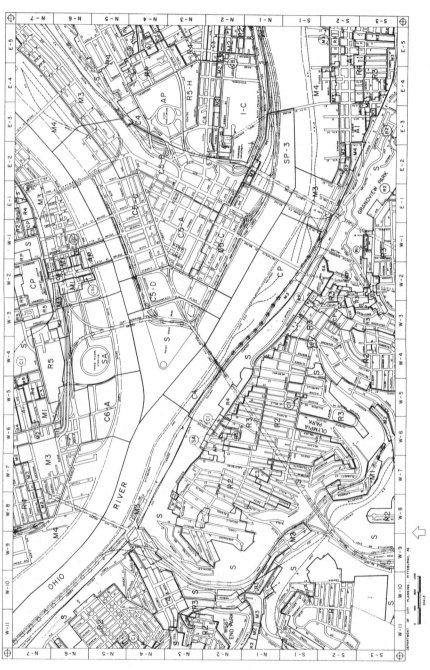

This portion of a zoning map for a diverse area of Pittsburgh shows a variety of residential (R), commercial (C), manufacturing (M), public/school (S), specialty planned (SP), and institutional (I) districts. Source: City of Pittsburgh zoning atlas.

- commercial (or business)
- industrial (or manufacturing)

Subcategories of industrial uses typically focus on the intensity of the use, with the heaviest industries (e.g., steel mills, foundries, slaughter houses) in one district and the lightest (e.g., warehousing and light assembly) in another; some communities have three or four industrial districts, with varying degrees of intensity.

Subcategories of commercial uses address both issues of intensity and issues of orientation. Thus, a community may allow sit-down restaurants in some districts where it does not allow fast-food restaurants, because the fast-food restaurants generally draw more customers and more traffic and thus constitute a more intensive use. Many communities separate "highway commercial" uses into their own district; that district may allow some of the same kinds of uses allowed elsewhere (e.g., hotels, gas stations) but apply different setback, parking, and other rules to them. Some communities use zoning to separate auto-oriented commercial uses (e.g., lumberyards, gas stations, drive-through banks) from pedestrian-oriented ones (boutiques, ice-cream shops) for simple reasons of land-use compatibility.

Some communities create one or more separate districts for office uses, recognizing that offices are business oriented but that many offices are far less intense (particularly in traffic generation) than retail stores. All but the smallest communities have two or more districts for retail uses; most zoning ordinances now include one or more districts that allow shopping malls, allowing the stores to be connected in one building and to share parking, something that has been common for office buildings since the first communities adopted zoning but is a fairly recent (1960s) development for retailers.

Zoning typically distinguishes residential districts based on the type of dwelling unit and the intensity of the use allowed, a topic discussed in the next section. The uses are all residential, although there are often citizens involved in planning who believe that mobile homes, modular houses, high-rise apartments, and even duplexes are different "uses" than the traditional single-family house.

When communities have multiple agricultural districts, it may mean that some of those districts are disguised forms of large-lot residential zoning; such zones often require minimum lot sizes of five or ten acres. Lots that size are far too large to be reasonable for an individual home but far too small to be a viable agricultural parcel, except in select areas where growing kiwifruit or other high-value crops may be practicable on that scale. Some communities create separate agricultural zones for agricultural service establishments such as grain elevators and chemical dealers. Others are beginning to address the issue of intensive animal agriculture (large cattle feed lots and large poultry and hog operations) as a form of agri-industry that ought to be separated from

Table 10.1. Zoning Districts, Fargo, ND

District Label	Description
AG	Agricultural district
SR-1	Single-family, 16,000 s.f. min. lot
SR-2	Single-family, 8,000 s.f. min. lot
SR-3	Single-family + duplex, 5,000 s.f. min. lot
SR-4	Single-family + duplex, 3,600 s.f. min. lot
MR-1	Multi-dwelling district
MR-2	Multi-dwelling district
MR-3	Multi-dwelling district
MHP	Mobile home park district
NO	Neighborhood office district
NC	Neighborhood commercial district
GO	General office district
LC	Limited commercial district
DMU	Downtown mixed-use district
GC	General commercial district
LI	Limited industrial district
GI	General industrial district

Source: Unified Development Ordinance, Article 20 of the Municipal Code, prepared for the City of Fargo by Duncan Associates, Austin and Chicago (1997).

other agricultural uses, just as heavy industry is separated from many other types of business.

Small communities may have as few as four different use districts, one representing each of these general categories. Larger communities will have more. A typical community of 100,000 or so today probably needs at least two or three industrial districts and three or four commercial ones, in addition to some range of residential and agricultural districts. Table 10.1 shows the zoning districts of Fargo, North Dakota.

Cumulative and Noncumulative Zoning

One of the basic principles underlying early zoning ordinances was the primacy of the single-family house. The purpose of the regulations was primarily to protect one-family homes from other uses; but, because they were a preferred use, single-family homes were often allowed in all or most zones. Such early zoning regulations were pyramidal, or cumulative, creating a one-family (or sometimes one- and two-family) district at the top of the pyramid and allowing in each successive district all uses allowed in those above it plus some additional uses; thus, at the bottom of the pyramid would typically be what amounted to the local industrial district, often called a "general" district, allow-ing most if not all possible land uses. Although most people wanted to have homes in residential districts, some with a pioneering spirit, or a lack of under-standing of industry, built their homes in industrial and commercial districts, often before there were businesses or manufacturing establishments in the area; when businesses later moved in, the residents had to deal with the impacts of those businesses on the neighborhood.

Many communities subsequently removed residential uses from commer-cial districts. This type of regulation had the effect of prohibiting the very common pattern of residential uses above small commercial buildings, a pat-tern that characterized healthy downtowns throughout the Midwest and else-where when zoning was adopted. Subsequently, more and more communities removed residential uses from industrial districts, because modern plant man-agers do not want nearby residential neighbors any more than residents of nice neighborhoods want nearby industry. Nearby residents represent the potential for complaints about noise and odors and, more seriously, the risk of injury and subsequent litigation in case of an accidental fire, chemical spill, or other event at the industry.

Many communities retain the cumulative nature of zoning in residential districts, allowing single-family homes in every residential district, allowing duplexes in all but the most restrictive residential district, and so on. Some also have office districts that permit some residential uses, creating an opportunity for transitional uses along major roadways. Today some communities are once again allowing the mixture of residential and commercial uses in downtowns and some other commercial areas.

Regulating Intensity

Intensity is the measure of the quantity of a particular use allowed at a partic-ular location. There are four basic measures of intensity in zoning:

- residential intensity measured in *dwelling units per acre;*
- *minimum lot sizes* for single-family homes, which create an inverse calcula-tion for the number of dwelling units per acre (a quarter-acre minimum lot size implies a density that will not exceed four dwelling units per acre);
- commercial and industrial intensity measured in *floor-area ratio* (FAR), which is the maximum number allowed for the ratio of the floor area of the pro-posed building to the land area of the lot on which it will be built (thus, a FAR of 2 would allow a building with twice the floor area of the lot); and
- indirect intensity regulation through *maximum height restrictions,* which are discussed in more detail in the next section (if a building can be only two stories high, that imposes a significant limit on the total intensity of use at that location).

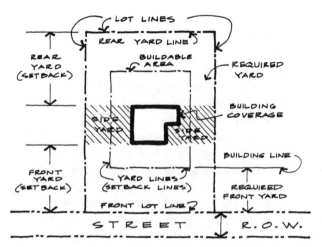

This drawing illustrates how some key dimensional standards in zoning are measured. Courtesy of Duncan Associates, Austin and Chicago (1999).

Intensity varies by zoning district. It is intensity of use, as well as unit type, that distinguishes one residential district from another. Thus a community may have three single-family residential districts, allowing development on one-acre, half-acre, and quarter-acre lots, and three multifamily districts, allowing eight dwelling units per acre, twelve dwelling units per acre, and sixteen dwelling units per acre.

Although FAR is the basic measure of quantity for uses in commercial and industrial districts, it is not necessarily the best measure of impact. Traffic is in many ways a better indicator of impact on the neighborhood, and that is often a key factor in determining what uses are allowed in which commercial districts. FAR regulations in commercial and industrial districts become design controls that vary by district but typically do not define the characteristics of particular districts.

Regulating Dimensions

The third principal piece of zoning regulation focuses on the dimensions of lots and buildings: lot width and depth, building height, building bulk, and yard and setback requirements. These regulations play an important role in defining the skyline and the streetscape of a community.

Lot width and depth standards usually prevent the creation of strangely shaped lots. Some communities impose an absolute minimum lot width or depth requirement in a particular district; others simply specify a maximum ratio between the two. For example, in a district requiring lots of 10,000 square feet (a 100' × 100' square would meet that exactly), one community might specify a minimum lot width of 60 feet, another might specify a maximum lot depth of 150 feet, and a third might specify that the ratio of depth to width not exceed 2. All three want to avoid the creation of a lot of long, skinny lots or "flagpole" lots, which have only 10 or 12 feet of frontage on the street—enough for a driveway—with the bulk of the lot nested in with others away from the road.

Building height standards are straightforward and simple. Although some communities express height standards in stories, most use feet. Allowing for space between floors, a safe way to convert height limits expressed in feet to building stories is to divide by ten. As noted above, building height standards serve to regulate intensity as well as to define the skyline and streetscape. Height does not always vary directly with intensity, however; a community may limit buildings in an intensive highway-commercial district to a maximum height of 30 or 35 feet, comparable to many residential districts. In larger cities, height is often the defining characteristic of a zone—and one can easily determine the maximum height restriction by visually drawing a line across the tops of rows of buildings. In smaller communities, many buildings do not reach the maximum permissible height.

Bulk standards define the maximum size of a building in directions other than height. Some communities regulate bulk directly, providing that a building may not cover more than a specified portion of the lot. Others depend on yard and setback requirements, discussed in the next paragraph, to address the issue of building bulk. A few impose maximum dimensional limits on buildings, and some larger cities (led originally by New York City) have "wedding-cake" regulations, which require that a building essentially become smaller as it grows taller.

Yard and setback standards are very similar but serve slightly different purposes. Both prohibit building within a specified distance of the front, rear, and side lot lines. For example, it is common in residential areas to require that buildings be set back 25 or 35 feet from the front line, 5 or 10 feet from each side line, and 5 feet from a rear property line. In residential districts, such regulations are typically expressed as "yard" regulations, requiring a "front yard" of at least 35 feet and a "side yard" of at least 10 feet. In commercial and industrial districts, this standard is often expressed simply as a "setback" standard of 5 feet or 10 feet. The principal difference between a yard and a setback area in communities that use the language carefully is that parking is allowed in a setback area but not in a yard. In principle, the purpose of the setback is simply to set the building back away from the street, alley, or adjoining property, while the purpose of the yard is to create open space. Not all communities make this distinction, however, and some allow parking in yards, while others prohibit parking in setback areas.

Design Implications of Zoning

There are a number of design implications of zoning. Although a broad discussion of urban design is beyond the scope of this book, it is important to understand how zoning has helped to shape cities and suburbs.

The Engineered Community

Professionals and academics sometimes refer to *Euclidean zoning,* a phrase with a double meaning: it refers to Euclid, Ohio, the city in which zoning was first upheld by the U.S. Supreme Court in 1926;[1] and it refers to the geometric nature of zoning. Clearly, the easiest way to create lots that meet all of the basic requirements of zoning is to create a series of rectangular lots on rectangular blocks. Most zoning ordinances do not require rectangles, but developers who want to put into a particular parcel the maximum number of lots meeting the minimum size requirements quickly discover that the easiest way to do that is with rectangular lots and rectangular blocks.

Even if a developer creates a satisfactory development design with something other than rectangles, builders in that development discover that it can be very difficult to meet all of the yard and setback requirements on an odd-shaped lot. That is another reason that developers tend to prefer rectangular, or nearly rectangular, lots in new developments.

The resulting pattern of urban development is very much an engineered design. Creating that pattern of development often requires extensive earthwork, because the earth in its natural form does not lend itself to rectangles and straight lines; obviously, where farmers have previously created rectangular fields, creating rectilinear developments within them will be easier. In other cases, however, it is often more environmentally responsible and cheaper to "design with nature," as Ian McHarg has suggested.[2] Developers who create subdivisions that fit easily into the natural environment, however, often discover that they must increase the size of their lots to ensure that they meet all of the dimensional requirements of zoning and that they leave enough room for building sites that will meet all applicable yard and setback requirements.

Some communities have adopted "cluster," "planned unit development," and other more flexible forms of zoning (discussed below) to give developers more freedom to design with nature. But in many communities, zoning still creates an engineered-looking city rather than a natural one.

Suburban, Auto-Oriented Commercial Areas

Although zoning began in an urban context (New York City), contemporary zoning practice includes a strong suburban flavor. Most zoning ordinances require that buildings be set back from the front lot line and that commercial establishments provide off-street parking, usually in front of the establishment. That is quite different from what traditional urban environments and even small-town downtowns looked like. Urban neighborhoods and down-towns typically allowed buildings to be built right up to the sidewalk and right up to each other, with both building owners and community leaders anticipating that customers and sometimes residents would park on the street or in public parking lots. The resulting streetscape was pedestrian-oriented and created a friendly sort of commercial area in which pedestrians enjoyed walking down the street and peering in a series of store windows, just as they do in shopping malls today. That sort of urban streetscape has been lost from many communities.

In contrast, businesses set back from the street, with parking lots in front of them, create an environment that is hostile to pedestrians. There is nothing for pedestrians to look at along the street, except the backs of a lot of parked autos. Worse, pedestrians have the street on one side, a parking lot on the other, and cars trying to go from one to the other across the sidewalk. That is not an environment in which people want to walk. Thus, most of them choose to drive, and they reinforce the auto-oriented character of the newer commercial areas. Many businesses that people consider auto oriented in the suburbs also thrive in more urban environments, serving as many pedestrians, including people who park nearby and make several stops along the way, as they might in the mall; examples are ice-cream and yogurt stores, branch banks, small grocery stores, and card shops.

Zoning requirements have defined some of the worst aspects of suburban commercial development, but the implications are even worse when similar standards are applied to existing urban areas. Some major cities and many small communities have adopted suburban-style zoning even for the traditionally urban parts of the communities, requiring off-street parking and front set-backs. In those contexts, building owners sometimes choose not to remodel, because by seeking a permit to remodel, they may be asked to tear down part of their buildings to create off-street parking. Someone may build a new building between two old ones, with the new one set back 25 feet, using the interim space for parking; that not only breaks the uniform streetscape of buildings, but also creates a hazard, with cars trying to come out of a lot that is "blind" on both sides because of the surrounding buildings.

Certainly, along busy roads and in other areas it is both necessary and appropriate to require that buildings be set well back from the road and that the intervening space be used for parking. That is not appropriate in all contexts, however, and those using planning and zoning to create neighborhoods need to consider carefully how they use those tools.

Strip Commercial Development

Zoning created the "strip commercial" development that most people hate. As purists used zoning to separate uses, they gradually created new neighbor-hoods without the corner grocery store and other walking-distance services

Strip commercial developments are typically designed to serve autos rather than pedestrians.

with which many people grew up. This placed convenience uses beyond easy walking distance for most people and necessitated making them easily accessible by automobile. Making those businesses easily accessible by automobile in turn implied that they should be along major roads, with lots of convenient parking. Placing them along major roads with parking in front, of course, created environments that were unfriendly to pedestrians, even for those who happened to live nearby.

At the same time, planners faced a problem. Often there would be a busy street running through an otherwise quiet residential area. Sometimes the land along the busy street remained vacant and sometimes there were houses, usually built before traffic became so heavy. Clearly, no one chooses to live on a busy street, particularly not in a smaller community. Thus, even in an otherwise residential area, it made little sense to plan or zone the land along that street for residential uses. Some communities compromised by zoning for apartment buildings or offices along those streets, but others decided that those streets would be the perfect location for the commercial uses necessary to serve the surrounding, service-free, residential areas. Many comprehensive plans and zoning maps prepared in the 1950s, 1960s, and 1970s addressed this problem by zoning for commercial uses along a strip of land, usually one-half block to one block (150 to 300 feet) deep, along each side of major thoroughfares through residential areas. Not surprisingly, commercial developers began to build there.

Typical early stores in such zones were "strip centers," rows of small shops, often anchored by a convenience store or sometimes by a supermarket—

The overwhelming dimensions of many contemporary supermarkets and discount stores has led to the generic name of "big box" stores. Courtesy of Pflum, Klausmeier & Gehrum, Cincinnati.

although those early supermarkets were only about one-fourth the size of many built in the 1990s. Gradually, some operators, particularly in the discount-store field, saw the opportunity to serve even more customers, and they began to build larger stores along some of those strips. Supermarkets expanded. Then retailers in pet food, books, music, bedding, and clothing discovered the wonders of "big box" marketing.

Today, big boxes on commercial strips have become a defining feature of the suburban landscape. Neighbors often protest them, planning commissioners worry about them, planners criticize them, but few remember that it all began with zoning. It can also stop with zoning. Nothing requires a community to create strip commercial opportunities. Few communities will want to tell retailers that they cannot build "big boxes," which are popular with consumers; however, any community can tell retailers to build them in mall-like complexes or clusters and not spread out along a strip.

The Zoning Map

A zoning map applies a community's zoning districts to particular areas of the community. Zoning maps are always property-specific, making it possible for a property owner or public official to determine exactly what set of district regulations applies to a particular piece of property.

The planning commission recommends the original zoning map to the governing body, which then adopts the map as part of the zoning ordinance, or local law. Changes to the map require review and recommendation by the planning commission as well as by the governing body.

In principle, the zoning map should be consistent with the future land-use map of the comprehensive plan (chapter 6). In practice, it often is not. Even in a community that takes planning very seriously, it may be difficult to update the zoning map to match a new plan. Although citizens—even property owners—often take the planning process seriously, they do not necessarily take it personally—few seem to lie awake at night or get very upset with city officials over the color of their land on the future land-use map. In contrast, most property owners recognize that zoning directly affects value. People often take any proposal to change the zoning of their land very personally, as well as very seriously. Thus, a proposal to update the zoning map to match a new comprehensive plan may bring out massive protests, including some from property owners who paid very little attention to the planning process and who otherwise may have little interest in local government or public policy.

Whether it is important to update the zoning map depends heavily on how most undeveloped land in the community is zoned. If there are large areas zoned for industrial uses but planned for future residential uses, or large areas zoned as commercial strips along busy highways where the plan calls for a nodal pattern of development, updating the map is important; otherwise, developers may take advantage of the relatively intense zoning available on some undeveloped property and significantly damage the prospects of implementing the proposed land-use pattern.

If, in contrast, most of the undeveloped areas are zoned for agricultural or large-lot residential uses, there is little risk in leaving them alone. Farming or ranching is a desirable use for undeveloped land, and scattered residential development typically will not cause great harm—unless the future plan for the area calls for industrial development. When the zoning of undeveloped areas is very low intensity, most development proposals will begin with a request to change the zoning, allowing the local government to bring the zoning map into conformity with the future land-use plan at that time. One factor to consider in all this is that only a small percentage of the undeveloped area is likely to be developed (and thus require any change in regulation) over the planning horizon used, but any attempt to rezone property is likely to affect and perhaps offend owners of the whole area.

For those reasons, we, and many other experienced professionals, recommend that communities not undertake the politically challenging task of updating the zoning map unless there is a real risk that development incompatible with the plan (note the use of the phrase "incompatible with" rather than "different from") will occur under the current zoning.

Rezoning

For reasons explained in chapter 9, it is very difficult to create an accurate future land-use map. Establishing principles that should guide future development is fairly easy (e.g., "any new regional shopping center should be within one-half mile of the current edge of the community, located along Highway 9, on a site of at least 100 acres"), but picking a particular site that will turn into that use is much more difficult. Zoning can prevent an owner from making particular uses of a piece of property, but zoning cannot force an owner to build something the owner does not want to build—nor can it force the owner to build anything at all.

Zoning maps work very well in established neighborhoods. They protect the existing patterns of use and thus maintain stability. In contrast, zoning on undeveloped land often bears little resemblance to logical future uses of the land, to planned future uses of the land, or to anything that makes economic sense. Even in communities that update the zoning map to match the future land-use map, the zoning map has the same risk of judgment error as the future land-use map, and it is still unlikely to be correct. Working in a community of 100,000 people that was growing very slowly, one of the authors of this book made a study and informed members of the governing body that they had approved 102 changes in the zoning map during the previous twelve months. They immediately became defensive and started to explain the reasons for each of the changes. The point of the study was to help those city officials understand what a common activity it was for them to rezone land and to encourage them to use the comprehensive plan as a frame of reference for such changes in the future.

Like that community, most communities of any size regularly consider and often approve changes to the zoning map. Such changes require a recommendation of the planning commission and final action by the governing body. In some states, the governing body can override a negative recommendation of the planning commission only with an extraordinary majority (five of seven votes, a two-thirds majority, or a majority of the entire body—not just a majority of those present and voting). All state laws require a public hearing on the proposed change and some form of notice of the public hearing, usually involving a mailed notice to surrounding landowners, combined with a sign posted on the property, a legal notice in the newspaper, or both. Although one public hearing is enough to satisfy the law in most places, in some communities both the planning commission and the governing body hold hearings on proposed rezonings.

Most rezonings are initiated by the owners of the property involved. Local planning offices typically provide application forms and charge a fee for handling the application. In many communities, hearing rezoning cases is one of the principal activities of the planning commission.

In principle, and by law in most states, local governments should follow the comprehensive plan when considering a change to the zoning map. Many do, but some do not. A city council member in a college town once remarked, "We do a very good job of following the plan, until two or three neighbors come in to protest what we are doing, and then all the rules go out the window." Actually, many local planning commissions and governing bodies ignore the plan as often to help a well-regarded local business person or developer as to help neighbors.

How can public officials ignore the plan? In Oregon, Florida, and a handful of other states, the law clearly says they cannot. In most others, the law is less clear. One of the problems is that the zoning map is itself a law—part of the local ordinance or other legal enactment that governs land use. When an individual applies to a government office for a driver's license, or approval of a subdivision (see the next chapter), the public official handling the matter is working within the law; either the proposed application conforms to the law, in which case it should be approved, or it does not conform to the law and should not be approved. In contrast, when considering a zoning matter, the local governing body is considering a change to the law. Like state legislatures and Congress, local governing bodies have broad discretion to adopt and change laws, sometimes doing things that are downright silly or that even interfere with the public purposes they are supposed to support. Nevertheless, within broad limits established by the Constitution and by state laws creating local governments, governing bodies are free to do as they please when they are making or changing the law.

Clearly, changing the zoning map ought to be a little different from the typical change in the law. Most changes in the law affect a broad classification of people (e.g., everyone over twenty-one, all students under eighteen, everyone owning dogs, everyone parking at a meter downtown, everyone with a car up on blocks in their yard); most proposed zoning changes directly benefit a particular individual, something that might be called special legislation in other contexts. Further, that particular individual usually has a specific goal in mind—much like the applicant for a driver's license or subdivision approval. Legislatures and courts have tried to establish some guidelines for zoning changes, recognizing that they are different from other amendments to local laws; those guidelines typically require or suggest some sort of conformity with a comprehensive plan. Practically and legally, however, most local governments retain a good deal of discretion to balance their broad legislative authority to serve the needs of the community against any duty to follow an adopted plan.

One problem in holding governing bodies precisely to a plan is that the plan may not always be so specific or so clear that it is obvious how the plan should affect a particular proposal. One local governing body turned down a proposal for a factory outlet mall on a site planned for "regional commercial" on the theory that the plan contemplated a more traditional mall, serving a smaller "region" than that from which the outlet mall might draw. Industrial developers today sometimes seek zoning for *flex space,* a term used loosely to apply to a combination of office and warehouse, typically providing for nice sales offices connected to warehouse space. A local government may have to make a judgment about whether such a use belongs in an area designated for industrial use or in one designated for commercial. Further, plans sometimes contain policy statements that seem perfectly consistent but that, when applied to a particular case, suggest unanticipated results. Thus, there is often a need for some discretion in the interpretation of the plan.

Cluster Zoning and Planned Unit Development

Planned unit development regulations evolved in the 1970s in response to the desire of some larger developers to deal comprehensively with the plan for a large parcel of land, rather than simply planning for it lot by lot, and by a related desire to mix uses and to create developments that were more interesting and more compatible with the land than traditional rectangular developments. Developers began to propose to communities that they be allowed to mix apartments and single-family homes and even some businesses. They also proposed clustering, or density averaging, that computed the number of homes that could be built with the specified minimum lot size but then clustered them; thus, instead of building four hundred houses on quarter-acre lots under the zoning ordinance, a developer might propose to build the four hundred houses on slightly smaller lots on eighty acres of a parcel and to reserve the other twenty acres as common open space, partly for recreational purposes and partly to buffer different uses from one another.

Local officials often responded positively to such proposals but found them practically and philosophically inconsistent with local zoning ordinances. Thus evolved cluster zoning and planned unit development ordinances, now commonly used across the country. Cluster zoning typically allows the same uses and the same unit types otherwise allowed on the property but creates some flexibility in lot sizes. Some cluster zoning ordinances allow or even require that the developer create a certain amount of open space to be commonly owned by the purchasers of units in the project, with each lot reduced in size proportionately. Thus, if the basic zoning for a twenty-acre site required lots of one-quarter acre each, clustering might allow the creation of eighty smaller lots (no change in the total number) with two acres kept as common open space.

Planned unit development ordinances generally create more flexibility in site planning and mixing uses than is allowed under typical zoning ordinances, and the best of them blend the review of use and intensity issues (typically under zoning) seamlessly with the consideration of site development issues. Mixtures of unit types (e.g., apartments, townhouses, and single-family houses) are more common than mixtures of uses. Some communities accomplish clustering through planned unit development ordinances, and some allow only very limited mixing of uses and unit types. The technique is not always well understood, by either planners or developers, so not all planned unit developments enhance the communities in which they exist. In principle, however, planned unit development offers a flexible alternative to traditional zoning that can, if properly administered, result in developments that are more compatible with the landscape and with the lifestyles of humans who live in them.

Variances

Zoning is simple, but it is also rigid. That rigidity concerned the people who invented zoning, so they built in a form of relief. They realized that there would be some circumstances where, for reasons beyond the control of a landowner, she or he might not be able to meet all of the minimum requirements of zoning. Classic "hardship" situations for which the drafters of zoning laws thought there ought to be relief include:

- *Preexisting, undersized lots.* Many lots existed before zoning; when zoning first came to a particular community, all of the lots existed before zoning. Usually, public officials chose an average or typical lot size as the "minimum" to apply to a neighborhood. For example, in a neighborhood in which most lots are one-half acre, but a few are three-quarters of an acre and a few are a little less than one-half acre, the local government might choose to zone the area for a half-acre minimum lot size. The purpose of that regulation would be to ensure that all future development would create lots no smaller than one-half acre, but everyone involved always recognized that someone who had a lot smaller than one-half acre before zoning came to town ought to be able to use it.
- *Preexisting strangely shaped lots.* Meeting all of the setback requirements on a triangular lot can be difficult indeed, unless the lot is very large. Drafters recognized that there could be problems in meeting certain dimensional requirements on existing lots, even when the lots themselves met the minimum size requirements.
- *Unusual topography.* Suppose that a particular zoning district requires a minimum lot size of one acre and a setback of 60 feet; suppose also that there is in that zone a lot that is 250 feet wide by 150 feet deep (exceeding the minimum size requirement) but that the back 75 feet of the lot is in the floodplain. In that case, the owner would have only 15 feet between the front setback line and the floodplain, which is not enough room for much of a house; both the community and the property owner would benefit from allowing the owner to build a house closer to the street and out of the floodplain.

The tool through which communities address problems like this in zoning is called the *variance*. In most states, the power and duty to consider variances fall to a separate body called either the board of adjustment or the board of appeals (sometimes including *zoning* somewhere in the name, also, such as zoning board of appeals or board of zoning adjustment). The original concept behind the variance was that if a landowner in one of the situations described above applied for a building permit to do what seemed to make sense (like building out of the floodplain) and the local government denied the permit (because it violated the zoning), the owner could then appeal to the board of adjustment or board of appeals, which would have the power to "vary" the detailed terms of the ordinance to provide relief in such hardship cases.

Although sound in concept, the variance process today is overused and often abused. Some states actually allow "use" variances, which flies in the face of both planning and zoning. The theoretical basis of a variance is that it allows a minor deviation from the regulations that resolves an individual hardship in a way that is consistent with the overall purpose of the regulations and patterns of use established by them; if through a variance, the zoning board can change the use of land, it can create a conflict both with the purpose of the regulations and with the established patterns of use. Many local boards of appeals or adjustment will grant variances because they feel sorry for the applicant or because the applicant convinces them that it would be more profitable for him to have a variance—perhaps allowing the construction of a duplex where zoning will permit only a single-family home. The idea behind variances remains sound, if they are used for their original purpose—to solve hardship problems inherent in the piece of land and not created by the current owner.

A great deal of zoning law and, in some communities, too much zoning practice, focuses on the variance. Our treatment is intentionally short, because it has little to do with planning and in fact often thwarts the purposes of planning.

Special Exceptions, Conditional Uses, Uses by Review

Two of the basic principles of zoning are simplicity and predictability. The use of every piece of land can be determined quickly and easily with the use of a map and the accompanying zoning ordinance.

Those implementing zoning in its early days, however, quickly discovered that some things are not so simple. For example, how should zoning treat a utility substation, such as an electrical transformer station or a major pumping station for the water system? Utilities typically determine the locations of such facilities through engineering analyses of the utility systems, not through land-use studies. If the engineering analysis indicates that a supplemental pump is essential to good water service in a particular residential area, no one would seriously oppose building the pumping station. Few people, however, would be happy with a zoning ordinance that allowed "single-family residences and utility facilities" in the zoning district—what if some other utility decided to build a nuclear power plant there?

Similarly, there are complex, high-impact uses for which it is difficult to write all of the rules in advance. Quarries and waste disposal sites are good examples. Both of those illustrate another point. Quarries must locate where there is a rock or gravel supply. Sometimes communities know exactly where those are, but often they do not; it is difficult to pre-zone for such uses when the location of the site-determining resource is unknown. Federal and state laws define the geological and soil specifications of sites that are suitable for waste disposal sites; few communities know exactly what areas will meet those criteria, and most wait for someone to conduct an engineering study to identify a site. Thus, it is difficult to create zoning districts for quarries, waste disposal sites, and some other intensive uses in advance of an application for that use at a particular site.

Most zoning ordinances include some sort of provision for "uses by review." Uses by review may also be called special exceptions, conditional uses, or special uses. The concept behind all of them is that some designated local body (usually either the governing body or planning commission) must review any application to establish that use on a particular site. Typically, zoning districts include a list of "uses by right" (those uses requiring no further review) and uses by review (or other local term). Thus, in most communities no one could apply for a quarry use in a residential area; that would typically be a use by review in specified industrial and agricultural areas. Communities often use this review process to establish particular conditions for access, buffering, and environmental management, to ensure that the use is reasonably compatible with its surroundings. The local water utility in one community built a pumping station that looked like a house—complete with drapes in the windows.

Conclusion

One of the great attractions of zoning is its simplicity. Someone can look at a map to determine what zoning district affects a particular piece of property, then look up the rules for that district and know exactly how the property can be used and what sort of building can be built on it. It creates a solid sense of predictability that induces confidence in many users, especially when applied to established, healthy areas of the community.

When applied to developing areas of the community, however, the uncertainties inherent in having public bodies plan for the future use of private land (see chapter 6), make zoning a less effective tool. Most of the emphasis on zoning in developing areas is on changing it—is on rezoning. Thus, rather than a map that creates real predictability, zoning becomes a set of floating rules, with the political process (hopefully influenced by the comprehensive plan) determining which set of rules (which zoning district) will apply to a particular location.

The Role of the Professional Planner

Planners, and their colleagues in zoning and building offices, make zoning work every day. Many new planners begin their careers working "at the counter," where they respond to citizen and property owner inquiries. Although zoning changes draw the most public attention, the zoning of most property does not change in a particular year, and far more people are affected by existing zoning than by zoning changes. It is the professionals who administer the zoning ordinance who explain it to citizens and help citizens conform with it as they make plans to use their property.

In some communities, professional planners play a role in enforcing the zoning ordinance. In other communities, that duty falls to a code enforcement office, which may also have responsibility for enforcing building codes. Although most people voluntarily comply with zoning and other local rules, enforcement remains important; if someone clearly ignores the zoning ordinance and the local government takes no action, others may learn by example and begin to ignore the ordinance, also.

In dealing with rezonings, the zoning activity of most interest to most people, the professional planner is a technical advisor to the planning commission (which makes recommendations) and to the governing body (which makes the final decisions). The professional planner often plays the role of the conscience of the body, also, reminding both the commission and the governing body about the existence and the content of the comprehensive plan as it relates to a zoning proposal. In many communities, professional planners make specific recommendations regarding zoning map amendments, but those recommendations are only one factor among those that influence the bodies that decide zoning cases.

Uses by review, planned unit developments, and cluster developments often raise complex issues. In dealing with such cases, professional planners play a particularly important role in advising decision makers about the nature of the issues involved and potential solutions to issues that may arise.

Although the practice varies from community to community, there is surprisingly little involvement of planners with the variance process. Many boards of adjustment and boards of appeals meet without planning staff present and with little or no technical support; some receive support from an enforcement or code officer but not from a professional planner.

Planners make zoning work, but they are not always at their most effective when dealing with the most controversial rezoning cases.

The Role of the Individual Citizen

More than 95 percent of the U.S. population lives in zoned areas. Thus, the primary contact of most citizens with zoning is that of living with both its burdens and its protections.

Citizens typically play very little role in the enforcement and administration of zoning, activities that take a great deal of the time of professional planners. When proposed rezonings, variances, and uses by review are under consideration, however, affected residents and landowners always have the right to testify. The concerns of citizens significantly influence decision makers. At their best, interested citizens remind public officials that they should follow the community's adopted plan; at their worst, interested citizens, like other interest groups, may persuade local government to ignore both its plan and its principles. It is safe to say, however, that local officials are far more likely to follow an adopted plan when citizens are interested and watching.

EXERCISES

Note: There are many exercises suggested here, all laying a foundation for the discussion question. In a class setting, it may make sense to break into small groups, with each group taking one or two of the exercises and then sharing the results with the class as a basis for the discussion.

1. Get a copy of the zoning map for your community. If you live in a large community where the zoning map comes in sections, get maps of three or four sections with which you are familiar, including some developed areas and some developing ones. Compare the zoning map to the future land-use map from the comprehensive plan. How well do they match in developed areas? How well do they match in developing ones?

2. Find your house or some residential area with which you are familiar on the zoning map. Look up the zoning rules for that district. What other uses are allowed there? Are any uses by review allowed? Are you surprised by any of the uses that are permitted?

3. Look through the zoning ordinance for your community and determine in what districts you could establish the following: a bowling alley; an adult bookstore; a bar; a movie theater; a church that seats three thousand people and may show movies in its auditorium on weeknights; a homeless shelter; a video rental store. Now find locations on the zoning map(s) where you could establish these uses. Are these logical locations for these uses? Why or why not?

4. Attend a meeting of the zoning board of adjustment or board of appeals and watch that body in action. Do the members grant variances just to alleviate true hardships related to the land, or do they follow other criteria? Check the zoning ordinance—are those criteria in the zoning ordinance?

5. Attend a meeting of the planning commission when it is considering one or more applications for rezoning. Do commission members seem concerned with the comprehensive plan? Does their recommendation in each case seem to conform to the comprehensive plan?

6. Although this makes a lot of meetings, try to attend the meeting of the governing body at which they consider the cases that you saw before the planning commission. If you call the clerk's office, you may be able to determine what time they are likely to consider the zoning matters. Do the members of this body seem concerned with following the comprehensive plan? Do they do so?

7. Find the commercial district that applies to the area that you consider downtown. Do the rules for that district resemble the current development? Do they require off-street parking? Do they require building setbacks? Do they allow people to live above stores? Do you think that these rules make sense?

CLASS DISCUSSION EXERCISE

Consider the results of the exercises above. Could you, as a class, recommend some improvements to the local zoning ordinance? Do those conform to the plan? Do you want to recommend some improvements to the plan, also?

FURTHER READING

Babcock, Richard F. 1966. *The Zoning Game: Municipal Practices and Policies.* Madison: University of Wisconsin Press. A classic. Highly entertaining, very readable. It may look old, but the game has changed little since the book was written.

Babcock, Richard F., and Charles L. Siemon. 1985. *The Zoning Game Revisited.* Cambridge, MA: Lincoln Institute for Land Policy. A good sequel.

Kelly, Eric Damian. 1988. "Zoning," in *The Practice of Local Government Planning,* 2nd edition, Frank S. So and Judith Getzels, eds. Washington, DC: International City Management Association. A more detailed treatment of the topic of zoning, in a standard reference work.

Mandelker, Daniel R. 1971. *The Zoning Dilemma: A Legal Strategy for Urban Change.* New York: Bobbs-Merrill. Another classic, this one an open critique. Again, the date may be old, but the issues have not changed a lot.

Porter, Douglas R., Patrick L. Phillips, and Terry J. Lassar. 1988. *Flexible Zoning and How it Works.* Washington, DC: Urban Land Institute. An excellent introduction to clustering, planned unit development, and other techniques designed to bring flexibility to zoning.

REFERENCES

Kelly, Eric Damian, ed. 1998. *Zoning and Land Use Controls.* New York: Matthew Bender. Original author is Patrick Rohan. A ten-volume reference set on zoning and land-use law. It treats topics like variances in great depth.

Lerable, Charles A. 1995. *Preparing a Conventional Zoning Ordinance.* Planning Advisory Service Report No. 460. Chicago: American Planning Association. A very practical guide for local planners and a useful reference for those studying the subject.

NOTES

1. *Euclid v. Ambler Realty,* 272 U.S. 365 (1926).
2. Ian McHarg, *Design with Nature,* New York: John Wiley (1992). This topic is discussed in more depth in chapter 4.

Chapter 11

....

Controlling the Development of Land

Zoning regulates primarily the *use* of land; subdivision regulation addresses the *development* of land—the creation of lots and blocks, streets and sidewalks, and the linkage of those to the larger community. This regulatory process, at its best, addresses three related sets of issues:

- design of the internal streets and utilities of the subdivision and the resulting layout of lots and blocks
- relationship of the streets and utilities in the subdivision to those of the larger community, ensuring the continuity of streets, management of stormwater, and logical connections of utilities
- construction of the actual streets, utilities, and other improvements within the subdivision

Concept and Substance of Subdivision Regulation

The regulation of subdivisions evolved out of concerns with public roads. Many states still require that a local government adopt a "master street plan" or similar document before it can regulate subdivisions.

In the 1920s and 1930s, as subdivision regulation began, communities had two sets of concerns, one related to design and construction of the road itself and the other focused on the relationship of a new road to the network of roads in the larger community. The construction issue is fairly simple. Developers then (and even, occasionally, now) would simply take a road grader or maintainer and scrape away vegetation and topsoil to give the appearance of a road. Some added a couple of inches of gravel or even a thin layer of blacktop. That kind of road construction is certain to fail, usually within a year or two in a wet climate and probably within three or four years in a drier one. The result is a road full of potholes and other hazards. Many of these poorly designed roads had low places that allowed water to stand, and that water would turn into hazardous ice in the cold months. Developers who managed their costs by building inferior roads often built roads that were too narrow, also; many of these roads did not have room for two vehicles to pass.

Cities and counties have no legal obligation to take care of a road unless it is a public road, and no road can become a public road without the consent of the governing body of the city or county. Most of these early, inferior roads were built without any consent or even knowledge of public officials. Thus, city and county officials could have told residents who called to complain about these roads, "Gee, I'm sorry to hear that you bought a home from a poor-quality developer who did not even put in adequate roads. I hope you can find a solution to it."

Although public officials did not (and do not) always yield in response to the first call, eventually the legitimate concerns of constituents and taxpayers win out. For that reason, and often under a scenario much like that described here, most substandard private (or unauthorized) roads become public roads. Many public officials saw the folly in allowing developers to create new developments with inferior roads, with the local government and its taxpayers then bearing the burden of fixing the problems. That was one impetus for subdivision regulations.

Street offsets like this one create awkward and potentially dangerous traffic movements, as drivers trying to proceed along a single street must make two quick turns to do so. Most modern subdivision regulations prohibit the creation of new situations like this one, which dates from the 1960s.

The other local government concern that led to subdivision regulation related to street patterns. In most communities, there is a major road that has a jog or offset in it—where a driver proceeding along the road must make a quick left turn followed by a quick right turn, or vice versa, simply to continue along the same road. Examining a map of the community typically shows that the two sections of the road are parts of two separate grid systems (which represent two separate subdivision plats) and that the two do not line up. Thus, another major purpose of early subdivision regulations was to ensure that the streets of the new subdivision integrated logically into the street system of the community—that new streets would line up with existing streets, that new neighborhoods would connect with old, that a city with a grid street pattern would maintain that pattern, and that major new roads would feed onto roads that could handle the traffic.

The creation of roads in this way is a part of the larger system that consists of the business of land development. Few states allow local governments to regulate development directly; most address the issue of "subdivision," which is a subset of development. Typically defined as "the division of a tract or parcel of land into two or more lots or parcels," subdivisions make up most, but not all, new development in the United States. It was logical to make subdivision the fulcrum of this new type of development regulations for a couple of reasons: first, the act of subdividing almost always involves recording a deed or a plat (a concept discussed below), creating an opportunity for public contact with the act of development and thus an opportunity for control; second, only through subdivision does a developer create roads that have the potential of becoming public.

For these historic reasons, development regulation in the United States hinges on the act of subdivision. Although there are gaps in the regulation because of types of development that are not subdivisions—and are thus exempt from regulation—subdivision control has evolved very effectively to meet contemporary needs. Local subdivision ordinances today continue to address the design and construction of roads but also include standards for such other essential public facilities as:

- sewer and water lines
- fire hydrants
- drainage systems;
- sidewalks
- street signs and street lights
- items such as bus stop benches, street trees, and subdivision identification signs

For all of these facilities, good subdivision regulations establish basic requirements (for example, there must be sidewalks on both sides of the street) and include minimum design and construction standards. In short, subdivision regulation establishes both the pattern of development and the quality of development.

Issues in Subdivision Design

Like zoning, subdivision regulations solve some problems but may create others. Certainly, every community needs subdivision regulations, but not all subdivision regulations are good.

Street Grid or Street Hierarchy?

The older parts of most communities from Ohio west—and in many communities east of that—have a relatively simple grid system of streets. There are several reasons the grid evolved. First, it created a logical subdivision of the national survey system used as a reference framework for all land from Ohio west. Second, many of the communities were originally laid out by railroad surveyors, who, with their engineering training, viewed the grid as a logical way to divide the rectangular parcels of land allocated to the railroads for development. Third, it created a simple pattern with essentially unlimited potential for expansion. With the grid, in theory, every street is a "through" street, and any street can become a major street.

During the 1960s and 1970s, developers began to propose new developments with hierarchical street systems, designing a limited number of through streets, which provided connection through the development and to other parts of the community, and creating a number of subordinate streets that, because of their design, would handle only local traffic. The cul-de-sac (a street designed as a dead-end street, usually short, with a turning circle at its end) is an easy example, but many developments included partial loops, "eyebrows" (arched, wider sections of street providing access to two or three lots), and even portions of modified grids. With a hierarchical street system, through streets are designated in advance and designed accordingly. An extreme form of a hierarchical street system is the gated community. It is difficult to close off a grid, but putting guarded gates on a limited number of access points within a hierarchical street system is relatively simple. Many other developments lack gates but use a hierarchical street system to discourage through traffic.

The philosophy behind the hierarchical street system is really a planning philosophy, designing certain roads for heavy traffic and creating other roads that, because of their position in the circulation system, will never carry significantly increased traffic.

Today, there is a vigorous debate in planning over the merits of the grid compared to the hierarchical street system. Advocates of the grid argue that:

• because every street is a through street, the grid balances traffic loads among streets;

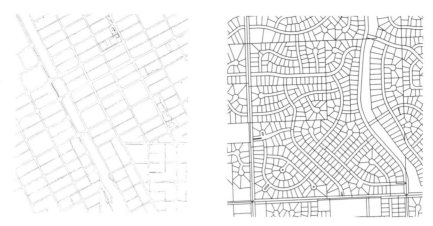

These simplified drawings compare a traditional street grid to a hierarchical pattern, planned to place residential uses on streets that do not carry major "through" traffic. The top drawing shows a small section of a traditional grid system, modified slightly to address local issues of topography, while the bottom drawing shows a hierarchical pattern of streets. Courtesy of Pflum, Klausmeier & Gehrum, Cincinnati (1998).

- the grid is pedestrian friendly, because it generally provides the shortest possible distance from one point to a variety of other points;
- the grid provides both rapid access and an infinite variety of alternative means of access for emergency vehicles; and
- the grid is "neotraditional" and associated with things like front porches and human-scale development.

Advocates of a hierarchical street system respond to all of those arguments. The last one is probably the only spurious one; it is fully possible to build front porches and walkable human-scale communities with a street hierarchy. More important, advocates of a hierarchy argue that:

- as the grid expands outward and streets nearer the urban core carry more traffic, the traffic load becomes so heavy that it interferes with residential uses on many streets;
- under those circumstances, most cities improve a few streets through the grid as the major arterials and collectors, thus creating a hierarchical street system in an area that was not designed for it;
- with a grid system, the community must require excessive rights-of-way and pavement widths on all streets to allow for the fact that traffic will increase on some or all of them;
- with a street hierarchy, traffic should never grow significantly on local streets, allowing them to be designed to an appropriate level; in contrast, the

community can reserve very large rights-of-way along the major streets on which growth may indeed occur;

- the local streets in a hierarchy create ideal residential environments, much better than streets along a grid with growing traffic; and
- with a street hierarchy, it is possible to plan for offices, apartments, or back-yards to line the major streets, eliminating the problem of having front doors and driveways on busy streets—something that occurs commonly in a grid.

As with most such debates, the "right" answer probably includes elements of both designs, resulting in a large-scale grid of through streets, with a hierarchy of other, more local, streets within each sector of that grid. The following are some of the considerations in creating such a situation:

- Most planners and engineers agree that developments with a single entrance and without links to adjacent developments are undesirable from a community perspective; considerations range from pedestrian routes to emergency vehicle access and to a general sense of community. The large-scale grid linking developments together at multiple levels addresses this issue.
- Some developments with hierarchical street systems include additional pedestrian and bicycle paths, providing more direct links than the street system; in some communities, those trails are wide enough and sturdy enough to handle emergency vehicles, thus offering an alternative form of ingress and egress.
- The modified hierarchy avoids the long-term conflicts that inevitably arise as traffic increases through older parts of a grid, making some formerly local streets undesirable as locations for individual residences.

Right-of-Way Compared to Street

A street right-of-way is the strip of land containing the street. Although early rights-of-way arose from use and thus largely corresponded to the actual street or road, rights-of-way today are created separately and are almost always wider than the street.

The most common use of right-of-way besides streets is for sidewalks and drainage facilities. Sidewalks are almost always on the public right-of-way and sometimes define its limits. In many urban areas, the streets, with curbs and gutters, serve as the drainage collection systems, but in other areas, swales and ditches alongside the road collect stormwater; those, also, are typically in the public right-of-way.

Through the 1950s, many developments in the United States included alleys. It was common to bury sewer and water lines in the alley and to run utility poles containing power and telephone lines down the alleys, also. Although advocates of neotraditional development urge the return of the alley, alleys use land and cost money to build and maintain and have largely fallen

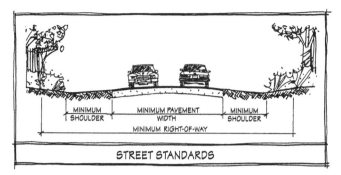

The street right-of-way typically includes land for sidewalks, utilities, drainage, and snow storage (in northern climates), as well as the street itself. Courtesy of Duncan Associates, Austin and Chicago (1998).

out of favor. Thus, most communities today allow extra land along the street for utilities. The extra strip allows for separation of sewer and water lines from each other and from the electric, telephone, and cable lines that are often buried now, also. It remains relatively common to bury sewer and water lines, which rarely require much service, under the streets; operators of telephone, electric, and cablevision systems, however, prefer to have their lines more accessible, under grass or other landscaping adjacent to the street itself.

In northern climates, there is one additional and very important reason for the local government to want right-of-way beyond the street paving—that is for the storage of snow. Although some people might not mind having snow pushed into their yards, for legal reasons, local governments prefer to control the property where they push heavy snows.

Street profiles in the 1950s and before typically included sidewalks at the outer edge of the right-of-way, with a landscaped "parking strip" separating the sidewalk from the traveled street. Today, the economies of the combined roll-curb and sidewalk, and concerns of traffic engineers that the trees planted in parking strips might be hazardous to cars, have led most communities to move sidewalks up to the street. With such a design, it is often difficult for the casual observer to know where the public right-of-way ends and private property begins; most people maintain part of the public right-of-way along with the rest of their front yard and consider it their own. Typical rights-of-way along residential streets are fifty feet or sixty feet, or fifteen to thirty feet wider than the paving.

Street Design

Traffic engineers have traditionally designed streets to optimize safety for automobiles at some designated design speed; in residential areas, engineers often use a speed of twenty-five or thirty miles per hour, or some other speed designated as the default speed limit in areas not otherwise posted. Those design considerations have, in most communities, resulted in the construction of wider, flatter, straighter streets in newer parts of the community. Planners have long argued that straighter, wider, flatter streets actually encourage drivers to drive faster, thus reducing safety on those streets—at least for pedestrians, children, and pets, and, in many cases, for the automobiles for whom the streets were designed.

In the 1990s, many communities, and their traffic engineers, became interested in techniques of "traffic calming." The most dramatic and most violent form of traffic calming—and the least safe—is the speed bump. Other techniques include narrower streets, visual encroachments (such as trees) along the street, physical encroachments (islands in the middle of the street and bumpouts in the curb); in areas with many pedestrians or other considerations suggesting low-speed traffic, some communities use grooves or other indentations in the pavement to give speeding cars a "rumble" effect. Planners fully support optimal design of major streets for speed and safety, but many today urge alternative designs in residential areas.

There are two other arguments for creating wide streets. Many communities design local streets to meet the hypothetical need of allowing two trash trucks to pass each other on a cul-de-sac with cars parked on both sides, or allowing a fire truck to make a U-turn without using reverse gear. There are,

Pedestrians as well as cars use this street, which has no sidewalks along it. The narrow street, encroaching vegetation, and regular presence of pedestrians discourages fast driving. The sign on the right is less important to slowing traffic than the curving, narrow street design, which appears even narrower because of the trees growing close to the street.

of course, other solutions. Although some trash trucks and fire engines are very wide, with wide turning radii, more maneuverable units are easily available. Further, almost all fire trucks and all trash collection trucks have reverse gears. In a worst-case scenario, a fire truck on a narrow street might have to make a U-turn that ran up on a curb and damaged some grass or even knocked down a mailbox. Although there is some cost in replacing grass or a mailbox, many communities require that developers spend hundreds of thousands of dollars a year to make streets wide enough to ensure that those small costs never arise; the city then has to maintain the wider street, sweeping it, clearing snow from it, and, ultimately, replacing it. Everyone would be better off if each developer simply contributed a few dollars to a "mailbox replacement fund."

Another consideration in designating street widths is parking. Most communities have some older neighborhoods of homes with one-car garages and shared driveways, located along streets that are only twenty feet wide; at twenty feet, a street has room for parking on one side plus one and one-half lanes of traffic. In reaction to the problems in such neighborhoods, these communities require that new residential streets be thirty-two or even thirty-six feet wide, allowing room for parking on both sides and two lanes of traffic. There is another difference between these neighborhoods and the old ones, however—all include large areas for off-street parking. Most new homes built in the United States after about 1960 include a two-car garage, with a two-car driveway; the driveway often extends over a twenty-five-foot or thirty-five-foot front setback requirement plus another fifteen feet of right-of-way, leaving room for an additional four cars in the driveway. In short, the need for off-street parking in these newer neighborhoods is minimal. At one point, one of the authors of this book lived in such a neighborhood, along a thirty-six-foot-wide cul-de-sac with eleven houses along it; there were at most eight or ten cars per hour traveling the street (meaning that it was rare for cars to pass each other), and, on most days, there were no cars at all parked along the street. Certainly, every neighborhood needs some overflow parking for parties and other special events, but those needs can easily be accommodated with eyebrows, bump-outs, or other design features that are far less costly than wider streets.

Note that the issue of street width relates directly to the idea of traffic calming. Other considerations include these:

- wider streets cost more money, both to build (usually paid by the developer and passed on to the consumer) and to maintain (almost always paid by taxpayers);
- wider streets use more land than narrower ones; and
- streets hold and throw off heat in the hot months, and wider streets throw off more heat.

Private Streets

Developers sometimes propose that they include private streets in their developments and create a homeowners' association to maintain the streets. There are three reasons that developers propose private streets:

- gated developments must have private streets;
- sometimes developers of prestige developments without gates use private streets as a technique of discouraging traffic other than that of residents; and
- in some cases, developers propose private streets to avoid having to comply with what they perceive as excessive local subdivision design requirements.

Some local officials find the idea of homeowners maintaining their own streets to be relatively attractive. The problem is that most homeowners' associations do not adequately maintain streets or other major facilities over the long term. They may keep the snow cleared and potholes fixed, but few maintain the "sinking funds" or replacement reserves necessary for major maintenance every ten or fifteen years. When a poorly maintained street begins to fail, residents of the development often demand that public officials take over the streets and solve the problems. Although local officials may want to say, "That is not the way it was supposed to work," they often recognize that the residents of that development pay just as much in taxes as those in developments with public roads.

For that reason, we typically recommend that communities insist that private roads be built to the same standards as public ones; such construction provides the local government with a better starting point if it becomes necessary

Streets within a gated development are always private; no private group has the authority to block a public street with a guardhouse.

to take over maintenance of those roads. We also urge, however, that local governments review the reasonableness of their construction requirements for public and private streets.

Drainage Design

The standard urban drainage system in the United States consists of surface collection along streets (using the curbs to hold the water on the street) and movement of the collected water to underground storm drains, which in turn carry it to a nearby river or stream. That is essentially the only kind of system that will work in a highly urbanized area like New York City. In smaller communities and suburbs, however, there are alternatives.

There are some serious problems with the traditional drainage system design. They include the following:

- the paving on the streets and the hard surfaces of the underground drains accelerate the flow of the water, thus potentially increasing downstream flooding;
- the system itself may carry the water far from where it would, more naturally, have soaked back into the ground and recharged underground aquifers and nearby streams;
- it is an expensive system; and
- because most communities gradually expand upstream, the demand on downstream facilities constantly increases as new development takes place, thus requiring constant expansions or massive oversizing of facilities.

Some developers today propose more natural drainage systems, using combinations of drainage swales (usually gradual ditches, planted with grass) to carry the water, and ponds to detain (short-term) or retain (long-term) water. The swales carry the water more slowly than paving and pipes, thus limiting the peak flood problem; further, well-planted swales allow some water to soak back into the ground, where it would have gone before the land was developed.

Detention ponds simply hold water after a major storm and release it slowly, thus helping to reduce flooding problems in exactly the same way a reservoir does. A detention pond usually has a wide inlet, accepting lots of water quickly, and a small outlet, something like the overflow drain on a wash basin. Many detention ponds look like ponds, but others are simply low places in parks or even parking lots, used temporarily to hold the excess runoff from an unusually large storm. Retention ponds hold the water until it evaporates or soaks into the ground; many become aesthetic or even recreational features in a development.

Developers like these more natural drainage systems because they are typically much cheaper to build than traditional systems of storm drains. Further,

This pond serves as a retention pond for stormwater from the surrounding patio home development, but it also creates an amenity for the development.

if integrated into the development design, they can become aesthetic enhancements to the project. Environmentalists also generally like such systems, because they get water back into the ground, recharging the aquifer (although some environmentalists have concerns about possible contamination of this water by lawn chemicals and other pollution). Local government engineers often do not like these systems, however, because they require much more maintenance and management than streets, curbs, and pipes. The engineered systems are likely to handle stormwater without much attention (other than routine street maintenance) for forty or fifty years. In contrast, swales must be mowed and cleared of trash regularly, and ponds and their dams must be maintained.

There are clearly advantages to and appropriate uses for both systems. Planners ought to understand both.

Subdivision Review Process

In the early days of controlling subdivisions, planning commissions adopted "regulations" that established the standards and review procedures for new subdivisions. Today, almost all local subdivision controls are local ordinances or laws, adopted by the governing body. The term *subdivision regulation,* however, remains in common use, and the planning commission still has the primary responsibility for subdivision review.

In most states a proposal for a subdivision is called a *plat,* and it typically goes through two stages of review, one that examines broad design issues and one that is largely technical, dealing with precise engineering details; these are often called "preliminary" or "tentative" and "final." In most states, the planning commission is the primary reviewer of plats, although many plats ultimately go to the governing body to consider proposed dedications of streets and other public facilities. Plat review in general is a technical review against standards contained in the ordinance or regulations and is thus widely viewed as ministerial.

During preliminary or tentative plat review, the planning commission determines:

- whether the proposed lots conform with the applicable zoning;
- whether the layout of proposed lots and blocks also conforms to requirements in the subdivision regulations, which may contain additional standards dealing with this issue;
- whether the layout and width of the proposed streets conforms with the subdivision regulations;
- whether the proposed streets conform to the adopted master street or circulation plan for the community; and
- whether the drainage, sewer, and water systems for the proposed subdivision will connect appropriately to the systems of the community.

Subdivision review is often called a "ministerial," or administrative process. If the proposed plat conforms with standards listed above, or any others included in the local regulations, the planning commission must approve it; if the application does not conform to the regulations, the planning commission may not approve it. As a practical matter, many planning commissions grant conditional approvals to preliminary subdivision plats, using conditions to require that the subdivider cure any deficiencies identified in the review process.

If the planning commission does not approve the preliminary plat, the process ends, subject to certain appeal rights. If the planning commission approves the preliminary plat, the subdivider then submits a final plat. The final plat also goes to the planning commission, although at this stage it must depend heavily on its professional staff for technical review. Standards for approval of a final plat usually include:

- whether the final plat is consistent with the approved preliminary plat and any conditions imposed on it;
- whether the proposed engineering details of the project meet technical standards included in the regulations;
- whether the proposed design and construction of streets and other public facilities (thickness of paving, size and composition of lines) meets standards included in the regulations;
- whether the proposed locations of street lights, street signs, and other items conform to the regulations; and
- whether the community can be assured that the developer will complete the required facilities (see next section).

Drawings submitted at the final plat stage should show exactly what will be built and how. Measurements are shown in tenths of degrees and tenths of feet, establishing an engineering precision that can be used by contractors in the field. It is relatively rare for a planning commission to disapprove a final plat; there should be no new substantive issues at this stage, and technical issues are usually resolved with a phone call from the professional staff asking that the developer's engineer or other consultant make appropriate corrections to the plat proposal.

If the proposed plat includes public roads or utility easements, it must go to the governing body for review. The act of creating public roads or easements is called "dedication," which is short for "dedication to the public." If anyone who wished could simply give things to the government without any consent, governments around the country would own endless numbers of dilapidated buildings, pot-holed driveways, and contaminated land. That cannot happen, however, because the law of every state provides that a dedication to the public is not effective unless some governmental entity accepts it. Only the governing body of a community can commit the community to major contracts, and accepting new land or new roads is potentially a major commitment to expenditures for maintenance over a period of time. Thus, only the governing body can accept dedication of the roads and easements on a plat.

In most states, the only issue officially before the governing body in reviewing a plat is the issue of dedication. If the planning commission has

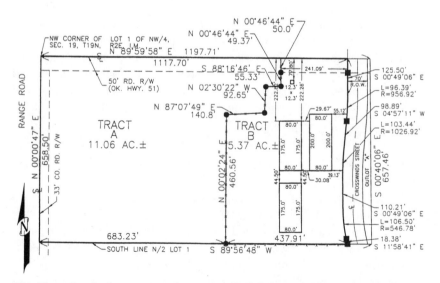

This illustration depicts a portion of an approved subdivision plat, showing streets, lots, easements, and engineering measurements. The dotted lines show the boundaries of easements for utilities and road rights-of-way.

approved the plat, the governing body may reject dedication of some or all of the facilities but may not reverse the action on the plat; in that case, the developer would have a choice between proceeding with the project with private roads or amending the proposed dedication in some way to try to persuade the governing body to accept it.

There are two other elements to the subdivision review process, and it is important to understand both to understand the process and the risks that attend it.

Recording the Plat

Every state has a system of land records. A good set of land records contains a chronological history of the ownership of every piece of property—and such records exist for most of the country. Typically called the clerk or clerk and recorder, the recording official is usually found in county or township government. It is the records of that office to which people turn to determine ownership of property. An automobile dealer assumes that anyone who has a car title and a matching piece of identification has the right to sell that car. In real estate, however, simply having a physical deed is not enough; anyone dealing in real estate wants to be certain that the land records show that the person selling the property actually owns it. Although having a physical deed may be useful under some circumstances, in case of doubt the land records usually determine ownership.

Land ownership in this country (as in most) follows a chain of title. Thus, if John sells a piece of property to Sarah who sells it to Brenda who sells it to Tommy, it is very important to Tommy that Sarah ensured that the deed from John was placed in the land records and that Brenda ensured that the deed to her from Sarah was placed in the land records. If that did not occur, the land records may not show that Brenda owns the property; if she does not own it, her deed to Tommy may be worthless. Suppose that the transactions above all occurred but that Sarah forgot to record the deed from John and in the meantime someone recorded a deed saying that Georgia sold the same property to Samson, who now has a deed to it. But, according to this chain of title, Georgia did not ever own the property, so she had no right to sell it; nevertheless, her deed in the land records creates considerable confusion. Suppose, however, that Brenda sold the property to Tommy one day and then decided to sell it to Diane the next day? If Diane records her deed immediately and Tommy does not, Diane may have a superior claim to the property—even though, in principle, Brenda had already sold the property to Tommy and thus had nothing to sell her.

Why does it matter to planners how land titles are transferred in the United States? It matters because the system of subdivision regulation is injected into the process of transferring title to land.

Most parcels of property in the country today exist because of several divisions of land over the years. Jonathan may have owned 160 acres and sold 40 of those to Andrew and 120 to Roberto. Andrew may then have sold his 40 acres to Alice, who split it into four 10-acre parcels and sold them to four different people, including Oswald.

People can divide land simply by granting a deed for part of the property to someone else: "I sell the east half of my land to George." That is a land division and, under the laws of many states, is considered a subdivision. Today, most states require that most land divisions go through the process of public subdivision approval. In most states, however, it is the duty of the recording official to record any piece of paper brought into the office with the appropriate fee; a student could record her high school transcript in the land records of most states. Thus, if someone brings a deed dividing property into the office and records it, she or he may effectively create a subdivision without any sort of public approval. A few states actually make it unlawful for the recording official to accept for recording a document that will create a subdivision unless there is on record evidence that the subdivision has been properly approved or was for some reason exempt from approval.

The recording office becomes important in another way, however. Suppose that Andrea purchased 40 of Roberto's 120 acres, perhaps the northeast quarter of the northeast quarter of Section 32, and she now wants to subdivide it and sell the property. The simplest way to refer to a lot in her subdivision is by referring to "Lot 22, Block 3, of Andrea's Subdivision," for example. That description will have meaning, however, only if the subdivision plat is part of the land records. By placing the plat in the land records, Andrea legally notifies the world (or at least anyone in the world who is interested) that her 40 acres is now known as Andrea's Subdivision. Further, placing an approved subdivision plat in the land records demonstrates that the local government has accepted dedication of the roads and easements. Buyers (and their lenders) often want to be sure that the lots they purchase have direct access to an accepted public street; a recorded plat, with an accepted dedication, establishes that fact.

For exactly those reasons, the recording of the approved plat is the last step in the subdivision approval process, but it is a very important step indeed.

Construction of Improvements

Communities expect developers to complete the public improvements that make a subdivision operational. Most developers understand that the construction of roads, sewer and water lines, and other subdivision improvements is a cost of doing business.

There is a timing problem in the system, however. The developer typically does not want to invest in building the improvements until the local government has approved the subdivision; on the other hand, once the local government has approved the subdivision, it may have little control over whether the developer completes the improvements.

Local governments use two techniques to address this issue. Some require that the developer post a bond or letter of credit equal to the cost of completing the improvements; such local governments usually make approval of the final plat conditional on the actual posting of that bond. If the developer fails to complete the improvements, the local government can draw against the bond or the letter of credit for the cost of doing the work that the developer omitted.

The alternative is to withhold the final plat from recording. Some local governments grant approval to the final plat at a public meeting, where it is a matter of record. These local governments then withhold the physical plat, so that it cannot be recorded in the recording office until all of the improvements are complete to the satisfaction of the local government. Until the plat is recorded, the developer cannot legally sell lots in the subdivision, so withholding the plat gives the developer a powerful incentive to complete the required improvements.

The construction standards in subdivision regulations are meaningful only if there is an effective enforcement mechanism. Most communities use one or the other of these; those that do not often find themselves with unhappy residents living in subdivisions with inadequate or incomplete facilities.

Exactions

Subdivision regulations address the issue of improvements on a particular site. They do not address the closely related issue of improvements serving other parts of the community as well and typically located off that site. For example, a proposed subdivision may comply fully with the community's requirements for internal roads but may have access only by an inadequate, largely unimproved rural road. Or a subdivision may have excellent internal stormwater collection facilities that dump into a channel that already floods.

Further, some community facilities that are affected by development are rarely part of a subdivision—the most common examples are parks and schools. Every residential subdivision has an impact on those facilities, but it is rare for a residential subdivision to include voluntary provision for either.

Through exactions, local governments attempt to require developers to provide or pay for the off-site and other improvements that serve both the particular development and the larger community. These can range from neighborhood facilities like parks and schools to community-wide facilities like sewage treatment plant expansions, to site-related improvements like turning lanes or traffic signals at nearby intersections or paving improvements to an access road.

Conclusion

Zoning and subdivision regulations are the fundamental land-use controls in the United States. The public is often most interested in zoning because of the politics of land use; it is subdivision regulation, however, that in many ways defines the quality of the community in the future. It is through subdivision regulations that a community ensures that the street, sewer, water, stormwater, and other systems in a new development are adequate to serve that development and that they integrate easily into the comparable systems of the larger community.

The Role of the Professional Planner

Subdivision review is highly technical. Most of the responsibility for subdivision review falls to professional planners and their colleagues in engineering. Although the planning commission must act on the application for plat approval and the governing body must consider any proposed dedications of land or facilities, it is the professional staff that conducts most of the review that informs the decisions of the public officials.

The more important role of the planner, however, is working with the community to develop the planning basis for its subdivision regulations and then to implement those plans. Subdivision regulations, like zoning regulations, often simply evolve over time. One engineer suggests making all the streets wider, another engineer suggests new drainage standards, and a planner suggests adding sidewalk requirements. As part of any planning effort, the community ought to consider the types of development that occur under its current regulations and compare those to the types of development that it would like to have. The question of whether a community ought to develop along a rigid grid or a hierarchical system or some combination is a fundamental policy question—it ought not to be left to planners and engineers. Similarly, questions about street design, accessibility, and even drainage involve policy issues that ought to be governed by the plan.

It is the job of the professional planner to facilitate the consideration of these issues in the process of planning the community. Once the plan is adopted, the planner often has the responsibility of proposing amendments to the subdivision regulations to implement the new plans.

The Role of the Individual Citizen

Because the subdivision review process is largely technical, there is relatively little role for the individual citizen. Neighbors sometimes use hearings on subdivision plats as opportunities to protest a particular development. What most such neighbors mean is that they do not like the type of project that the zoning allows. If the project conforms with zoning, the planning commission cannot deny subdivision approval on the basis of neighborhood objections.

Thus, individual citizens, like planners, must consider the policy implications that underlie subdivision regulations. First, when a community adopts a new plan, interested citizens ought to check to see that the zoning in their neighborhoods is reasonably consistent with the new plan. If it is not, citizens ought to insist that the local government consider changing the zoning map to conform to the new plan (but see the discussion of the difficulty of doing that in the previous chapter). In addition, interested citizens ought to work with professional planners to ensure that the issues of quality of development are considered as part of any planning effort and that the resulting policies are implemented through appropriate amendments to the subdivision regulations.

EXERCISES

1. Find an older residential neighborhood with a grid development pattern near downtown in your own community; if your community has fewer than 25,000 people, it may be more meaningful to do this exercise in a larger community nearby. Is traffic evenly balanced over the grid in this area, or are some streets busier than others? Were those streets designed adequately to handle today's traffic load? Do you think a hierarchical street system might have served this area better? Why or why not?

2. Drive down an older, narrow, residential street with cars parked along it; drive at what feels like a safe speed and then look down at the speedometer to see how fast you are going. Now do the same exercise in a new residential area with wide streets. In which location were you going faster? Does that tell you anything about street design? About traffic calming?

3. Find a cul-de-sac in a new part of town, if there is one. Try to be there at rush hour, about eight in the morning or five in the afternoon—or whenever your local peak hour is. Watch the traffic flow for thirty min-

utes. Look at the parking along the street. Watch for heavy trucks. Is the street too wide? Too narrow? Just right?

4. Are there neighborhoods where you particularly like to walk or ride your bike? What makes them attractive for that? Do they have a grid street system or a hierarchical one? Are the sidewalks next to the street or set away from them? How wide are the streets? How fast do cars drive?

5. What kind of drainage system does your community have in the older areas? In the newer ones? If you do not know, drive around and look— it should not take you long to figure it out. Do you find one of them more aesthetically appealing than the other? Which one? Why?

CLASS DISCUSSION EXERCISE

Divide the class into two teams. One group will be advocates for the grid pattern of development; the other will be advocates for a hierarchical street system. After each group spends some time looking at developments of each type and reading more background on each type, have a debate. Invite members of the local planning commission or other interested citizens to serve as a jury. Ask the jury to develop a brief policy statement on the grid vs. hierarchy issue, allowing them to select any combination of solutions that they may wish.

FURTHER READING

Frank, James E., and Robert M. Rhodes, eds. 1987. *Development Exactions.* Chicago: Planners Press. An excellent collection of essays covering the policy and practical issues involved in exactions; even the legal chapter essentially predicted how the law in the field has evolved since then.

Freilich, Robert H., and Michael Shultz. 1995. *Model Subdivision Regulations: Planning and Law,* 2nd edition. Chicago: American Planning Association. An excellent discussion of subdivision law from a very practical perspective, with model forms.

Listokin, David, and Carole Walker. 1989. *The Subdivision and Site Plan Handbook.* New Brunswick, NJ: Rutgers University, Center for Urban Policy Research. A much more complex model than the Freilich one, this goes well beyond basic subdivision design.

Morris, Marya. 1997. *Subdivision Design in Flood Hazard Areas.* Planning Advisory Service Report No. 473. Chicago: American Planning Association. A technical report that is very useful in dealing with this subject.

Chapter 12

Controlling When and Where Development Takes Place

Creating the future land-use plan does not make it happen. Because developers and others make key decisions about the future of the community, a simple commitment by the local government to the plan is not enough. Communities have long used zoning and subdivision regulations as tools of plan implementation. Just as subdivision regulations are incomplete in addressing a community's planning needs for public improvements, zoning does not fully address issues related to the intensity of use. Its major flaw is that it really does not give the community the sort of predictability that the early engineering supporters of zoning thought it would. By looking at a zoning map, an engineer can determine what in theory is permitted (perhaps homes on quarter-acre lots) but cannot tell whether such homes have been there for fifty years, were recently built there but are not yet occupied, or are under construction there; whether the land is for sale and a homebuilder may soon buy it, or the long-time owner is growing seed corn there. Neighbors, traffic engineers, and sewage plant operators all would like to have a greater degree of predictability regarding the timing of development at particular locations.

Some communities now regulate that issue directly through a variety of growth management techniques:

- *Adequate public facilities* (APF) regulations add to other local land-use controls a requirement that there be express findings regarding the availability of adequate road, sewer, water, and other critical facility capacity to serve the proposed development. The net effect of such controls is typically to keep development more compact and contiguous to existing development, or to cause it to locate in nodes around other service providers. Because such controls tie so directly to issues of public health and safety, they are easily defensible.

Florida has a statewide program based on APF concepts and calls it "concurrency," relating to the concurrent provision of public services for new development.

- *Phased-growth programs* typically identify areas of the community to target for growth, often moving out from the center of the community in somewhat concentric rings, based on presumed availability of services. Because rarely do all services originate from the center of the city, and because the availability of services typically varies wildly, with one part of town having good capacity in its street systems and another part having a brand-new school but overcrowded streets, this type of program can become disconnected from its apparent purpose. For that reason, such a program is less defensible than a purer form of APF controls. The obvious appeal of such a system is that it can preserve the concept of mapped growth, a concept that arose from zoning, and that it is simpler to administer than an APF review of every proposed project.

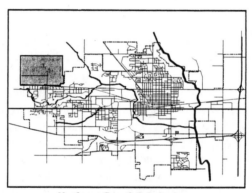

Northwest Growth Priority Area

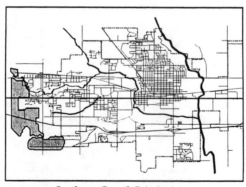

Southwest Growth Priority Area

These two maps show the "priority growth areas" in which Ames, Iowa, is investing in major infrastructure and encouraging development. Source: *City of Ames and RM Plan Group, Nashville (1996).*

- *Rate-of-growth programs* impose on the community a predetermined, level growth rate, sometimes expressed as a percentage increase in the number of dwelling units and sometimes simply as a number. Such programs are relatively rare and are seldom tied directly to public service issues. They raise serious issues of social and fiscal equity when imposed arbitrarily by one community in a larger metropolitan region.
- *Urban growth boundaries* are just what they sound like. They have evolved rather naturally from the logical determination of public sewer and water providers that there are geographical limits within which they can provide service much more easily. The difficulty with urban growth boundaries is that if they are drawn too tightly, they can seriously distort the land market and resulting development patterns (leading to significant "leapfrog" development to other communities); but if they are drawn too loosely, they may permit far more scattering of development than an APF program. There have been few if any serious tests of their defensibility.

Growth management is really a logical evolution in land-use control and one that is adopted by a few additional communities each year. Although it will never become as common as zoning, it will become rare to find a metropolitan area without some form of such controls in some rapidly growing communities.[1]

Local governments make other decisions that affect the management of growth. Another tool with significant implications for growth management is the annexation of land by cities, discussed later in this chapter. Further, decisions about where and when to invest in major infrastructure, discussed in detail in the next chapter, can have a significant influence on where and when growth occurs.

Adequate Public Facilities Controls

Adequate public facilities controls have common-sense roots. A basic set of APF controls provides that development shall be approved only if the approving body makes explicit findings that:

- there is, or will be at the time of actual development, an adequate supply of water to serve the needs of the project;
- there is, or will be at the time of actual development, adequate capacity to collect and treat wastewater (sewage) from the project;
- there is, or will be at the time of actual development, adequate road capacity to handle traffic to and from the project;
- there is, or will be at the time of actual development, adequate capacity in stormwater drainage systems to handle stormwater runoff from the project.

The standards themselves are simple enough, although interpreting and implementing them is somewhat more complicated.

Water

There are three separate concerns in dealing with water: quality of the water for drinking and other household use; adequacy of the supply of water to serve household, commercial, and industrial needs (usually measured in "gallons per day"); and adequacy of the delivery system and short-term supply to maintain a specified pressure for the use of fire hydrants in fighting a fire.

A system of state and federal regulations addresses the quality of drinking water. Where a proposed project will connect to a public water system, quality is not generally a serious issue. With private wells and some very small systems, however, it can be an important issue; fortunately, state and federal regulations provide excellent guidelines regarding water quality and thus establish a basis for local regulations.

Most water utilities and local water departments track figures on water capacity and demand by unit (usually tracked separately for industrial uses and counted on a per-household basis for residential use). These agencies can usually provide accurate figures on the current available (excess) supply to serve new development. It is typically safe to project that new development will consume water roughly in proportion to existing development.

Either the local water department or the fire department should track water pressure for fire-fighting purposes. The Insurance Services Office (a trade organization) controls a rating system for the fire protection available in communities; the ratings influence the insurance rates charged in each community. Communities try to maintain or improve their fire ratings and thus strive to maintain fire-fighting capacity in their water systems. Pressure is in significant part a function of elevation. Most water systems pump water uphill to storage tanks or, in communities with hills, to reservoirs on high locations; the effects of gravity on water create the pressure necessary to drive the system. Locations much lower in elevation than the storage site will generally have excellent pressure, but pressure will decline as elevation increases and the effects of gravity are smaller. Thus, there is always some line in a community that defines the elevation above which the water system cannot provide adequate water pressure to meet local standards. This line is often a major factor in creating "urban service area boundaries," discussed below.

Obviously, water pressure is also affected by the supply of water and by pipe size. A very tall storage tank that is empty will provide no pressure, and a system starting with good pressure feeding into a two-inch line will provide serviceable pressure only for the first two or three users on that line, below which there will be little water left to pressurize. In general, the eastern half of the United States and some other wet areas typically have enough water to fill a system, but the supply of water is an important issue in very arid states like Nevada, New Mexico, Colorado, and Arizona. Most modern systems have lines that are sized adequately to provide good pressure throughout a system, but there are many situations where, to reach new development, water must flow through an older system that may not have adequate size.

Residents of communities usually expect good water pressure for showers, laundry, and other domestic purposes. That is rarely a controlling factor in creating APF regulations, however, because a system that has adequate standby pressure to fight fires will always have reasonable pressure for domestic use, at least in most of the system. The principal contact that consumers may have with pressure and delivery issues occurs in arid states where lawn irrigation is common; in such states, communities often address short-term problems by limiting or even prohibiting irrigation.

Most water system operators monitor their water quality, water flow, and water pressure constantly. Staff or consulting engineers can project with reasonable accuracy the impacts of adding more users to the system. In short, the question of whether an existing system has adequate capacity to serve additional development is one that can be answered.

Wastewater

Although most consumers use the term "sewage," professionals prefer to use the word "wastewater" when dealing with this by-product of society. There are two critical issues in dealing with wastewater capacity: treatment capacity and collection capacity.

Treatment capacity is a function of the ability of a treatment plant to remove harmful bacteria, chemicals, and other matter from a wastewater flow; the objective of the system is to remove enough of these substances to ensure that the water going back into the stream meets federal and state water-quality standards. Historically, the defining factor in determining the size of a wastewater treatment plant is its capacity to handle *biological oxygen demand* (BOD)—in other words, to remove bacteria from the waste stream. Sewage treatment has long focused on bacteria because of the direct and obvious harmful effects of such sewage-borne bacteria as *e coli*. Today, however, sewage treatment plants must remove phosphates, nitrates, and other organic substances to comply with water-quality standards. The important thing to understand in dealing with all of these capacity issues, however, is that the capacity of the plant is really a function of the amount of waste, not the amount of water. For example, using water-saving toilets or showerheads may help address water supply problems in a community, but such measures are of no benefit to the sewage treatment plant, which must handle the same amount of waste as before. Although small deviations in the amount of water going into a wastewater treatment plant do not make a significant difference in its waste-handling ability, large deviations can. Older systems in some communities still combine stormwater and sewer systems; in such systems, water from a heavy rain can overwhelm the treatment plant, allowing untreated waste to escape

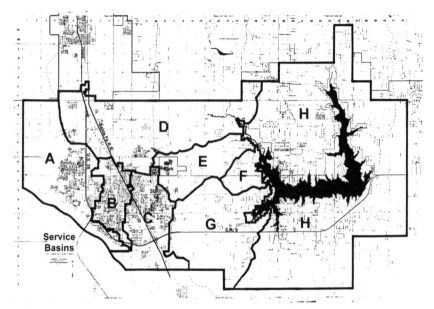

Capacities within individual water and sewer service basins often define the limits of facility capacity. The internal lines show the boundaries of the drainage basins, which are labeled A through H. Source: City of Norman and the Burnham Group, Cincinnati, Little Rock, and Birmingham (1996).

into a stream, as the flow of combined wastewater exceeds the physical capacity of the treatment plant (or elements of it) and flows around or over it.

Collection capacity is also an important link in the system. Today, most wastewater collection systems are designed to carry significant capacity beyond projected demand; undersized pipes in older systems, however, can lead to backup of sewage into basements, bathtubs, and storm drain outlets—creating both a real and a perceived nuisance.

As with water, determination of the available capacity in a sewer system is a fairly straightforward engineering calculation. Determining whether that capacity is adequate to serve the demand from a new development is simply an extension of that engineering analysis.

Stormwater

Addressing the adequacy of physical systems to handle stormwater is more complex. Historically, natural systems have handled stormwater quite nicely. It is only when humans intervene with development that additional management measures become necessary.

The earliest programs and regulations to address this issue dealt with floodplains. One of the ways that nature handles large storms and the resulting stormwater runoff is with floods. Unfortunately, many human settlements have been established in areas that flood after major storms. The U.S. Army Corps of Engineers and other agencies have created massive systems of dams, dikes, and other structures to control flooding that affects settled lands, and most local governments have now adopted floodplain regulations to limit the types and locations of development in floodplains.

This is a complex and dynamic system, however. Another of the tools that nature uses to manage stormwater is the wetland. Wetlands serve as giant sponges, absorbing rain from major storms and, like a wet sponge left on the kitchen counter, allowing the gradual release of the water, which then flows down the stream after the peak flow from the storm is over, a topic discussed more in Chapter 11. Local stormwater management is simply a smaller-scale view of the same dynamics. Communities grew up along rivers because they needed water for domestic and industrial use and because, in many areas, water represented a means of transportation. An unintended consequence of locating communities along rivers, however, was to place portions of those communities in or near floodplains. Limiting the location of new development in the floodplain works only if the location of the floodplain is known. Unfortunately, the floodplain itself is dynamic—and, in most growing communities, it also is growing. Land in its natural state typically has some sort of vegetative cover—grass and trees that absorb some water directly and hold other water in their leaves and around the plant bases until it can seep into the ground. As developers replace that vegetation with buildings and paving, the water that once went into the ground runs off—thus increasing the total amount of runoff from a particular area and, as a direct consequence, increasing the size of the area that will be flooded in a major storm.

There are two very different approaches to ensuring the adequacy of stormwater facilities. Some communities use a combination of the two, but it is easier to understand them separately:

- *Traditional, structural.* The traditional approach to managing stormwater is entirely structural, using a combination of urban streets (curbs are not just tire-stops for young drivers—they actually turn the street into a stormwater channel) and pipes to carry the stormwater to the nearest stream. Engineers like the certainty of such a system and like the fact that it consists largely of durable, publicly owned elements. Thus, a developer simply needs to have consulting engineers compute how much new stormwater will be created by a proposed development and then calculate whether facilities downhill (which is really downstream) can handle the flow; many communities expect developers to pay for any improvements or enlargements necessary to create adequate downstream capacity.
- *On-site.* Some communities, and some developers, prefer an "on-site" solution. If the developer can handle development-related increases in stormwa-

ter on site, then the flow of stormwater coming off the site should be no greater than historic flow. Because existing streams and systems are already handling the existing flow, such an approach should result in little or no impact on the volume of stormwater to be handled downstream. Typical design elements used to achieve such a performance goal include: reducing paved areas where practicable, to reduce runoff; using drainage swales (ditches) as part of the collection system, thus allowing some water to seep into the ground through the dirt bottom of the swale; creating detention ponds, to hold temporarily the excess flow from a major storm and release it gradually to flow downstream after the storm has passed; or adding retention ponds to hold some water until it either evaporates or soaks into the ground. Lower areas of parking lots or even ballfields can be used as detention ponds, because they will be under water only a few days in a typical year; retention ponds often serve as water-feature amenities in new developments.

The attraction of the on-site system is more than just environmental. Engineering a traditional system for a growing community creates significant challenges. Because they started along rivers or streams, most communities grow uphill. That means that new development will be on higher ground than current development, and the drainage from new development will flow through current development. Thus, stormwater lines and other facilities in a new development must be large enough to handle historic flow plus flow from the new development plus possible new flow from development upstream. But how much development will there be upstream? Will the community build all the way to the top of the drainage basin? Will it do so on all sides of the existing community or just some? Without answers to those questions, it is impossible to determine the appropriate size for traditional facilities. Engineers make estimates, but those estimates are based on land-use plans and population estimates that are part art and part science; as with any connected system, the weak link defines it, and there are several potential weak links in this one.

That sort of concern makes the on-site system relatively attractive. The difficulty with the on-site system is that it creates many separate, often individually owned stormwater management facilities, with no long-range maintenance or management plan. One community in Oklahoma pushed this policy to such an extreme that it had hundreds of retention and detention ponds on private property, some serving sites of an acre or less. As individuals fail to maintain or even fill (or build in) their pieces of this complex drainage system, its capacity will be diminished and the system will fail to serve its purpose.

Thus, many communities use a combination of the two systems, relying on traditional systems to collect the stormwater from residential neighborhoods and small commercial sites but requiring that large commercial developers include on-site stormwater facilities in their projects. Either a structural or on-site approach can ensure the adequacy of these facilities, but it is important to understand the differences. Stormwater, like water and wastewater, is a tangible, measurable commodity; to the extent that it is practicable to project development patterns, it is possible to predict with reasonable accuracy the amount of stormwater likely to result and the size of the facilities necessary to handle it.

Streets and Roads

Streets and roads are critical links in people's lives, as well as in the communities they inhabit. Although roads have both physical and functional capacity limitations, in many ways road capacity is a psychological phenomenon. Functional road classification systems focus on the extent to which congestion impairs smooth travel and thus creates "traffic jams" or an effect like rush hour. Those systems are objective, but the context in which traffic functions is not entirely objective. People in Chicago expect heavy traffic and significant delays, particularly at peak hours in the morning and afternoon. In Peoria, however, a much smaller city one hundred or so miles to the south, people are not accustomed to much congestion and may become very frustrated if they have to sit through a traffic signal cycle two times. But even Peoria has heavy traffic when compared to small midwestern farm communities, where the very installation of a traffic signal would lead to complaints about the growing traffic problem.

Why do planners consider traffic impacts if the issue is so complex? Very simply, because some level of service is so bad that it is unacceptable in a particular community. The road system differs from the water-related systems in that its capacity is only theoretically finite—as a practical matter, the acceptable capacity varies with the circumstances. While the goal with a water or sewer system is to ensure that it is never overloaded, with a road system the goal is to ensure that it is never overloaded *to an extent unacceptable in that community*. That distinction is critical in dealing with traffic capacity issues.

It is also important to think about how traffic works. Although traffic engineers often talk about the capacity of roads and lanes, most actual traffic problems occur at intersections, where traffic-control devices and turning movements interrupt what may be a fairly smooth flow of traffic on open sections of the same roads. Further, most traffic problems occur during "peak hours," which are the busiest hours of roadway use—usually morning and evening rush hours. Sometimes more than 10 percent of traffic on a road will occur during either the morning or evening rush hour. Offsetting those periods in the computation of average traffic flows are the wee hours of the morning, when there may be little traffic on a particular road.

Thus, if a road is heavily congested at peak hours but operates smoothly at other times, a proposal to locate a new office building (which will generate or attract rush-hour commuting) along that road may increase congestion to an

*Traffic problems are often signifi-
cant factors in leading communities to consider the adoption of
adequate public facilities controls.
Photo by Jennifer Greig.*

unacceptable level, while an alternative proposal to put a twelve-screen cinema
complex at that location may actually make efficient use of road capacity that
is underutilized at the time that people want to go to the movies.

Measuring traffic capacity and demand is a complex process, discussed in
more detail in chapter 7. Of these four basic considerations related to land
development—sewer, river, drainage, and traffic—traffic is the most complex
(and least certain) to model and evaluate. At the same time, to most residents
of a community, it is probably the most important of the four. Thus, streets and
roads are usually one of the first types of facilities for which a community
adopts adequate public facilities controls. Because of the complexity of modeling the system and because of the value judgments inherent in determining
demand (see the capacity classification system reflected in table 7.1 and
accompanying text), traffic is also the system for which it is most difficult to
set standards of adequacy.

Other Facilities

Some communities also develop adequate public facilities standards for
schools, fire service, emergency medical service, libraries, and parks. Obviously,
all of those facilities have somewhat more elastic capacities than the pipes that

carry water or wastewater. Adding an extra row of desks across the back of a classroom or having a few more users in a particular library branch is not likely to push it beyond capacity. That is one reason more communities do not base APF standards on those facilities.

The other reason is that it is often difficult to correlate the capacity problems directly with any particular land development. If schools are on double session or the library is completely overcrowded, that condition has probably resulted from many years of growth—and births among the current population—not from the effects of one or two developments. When the capacity problem has arisen over many years from many causes, it may be difficult—both politically and legally—to deny approval to a particular development, particularly when it is clearly possible to handle the additional impact of that development in the existing facility simply by incurring some extra crowding.

Other Levels of Service

Few local governments try to set required levels of service for telephone, electricity, cablevision, and natural gas. Those services are typically provided by private utilities, or sometimes by public entities. In general, the law in most states and the policy of most utilities state that a utility with the right to operate in a particular area (often called a franchise) has the obligation to serve all users that it can reasonably accommodate. Thus, the underlying assumption in the development process is that these services will become available as needed. Although there are certainly exceptions, including some large-scale subdivisions in the Southwest that lack both electricity and wired telephone service, the exceptions are rare enough that it is not a topic that planners often address. Some local governments do set level-of-service standards for schools, parks, and fire protection. Many communities include in their plans at least general discussions of the levels of service for those facilities, as well as for libraries, police, and general government services. There are several reasons that many adequate public facilities systems do not include these important public service systems among their criteria for development approval:

- Their capacities are, or at least appear to be, somewhat flexible. Adding ten homes to the area served by a park or a school is unlikely to have a noticeable effect on the usage of either the park or the school. In contrast, adding ten homes to a particular water or sewer line may push it past its capacity. For a police department or a library, even the addition of one hundred homes will not have a big impact; one hundred homes may have twenty library users who check out one hundred books in a year; those same one hundred homes are likely to involve less than a mile of new street, which would add two or three minutes to a police car's driving "beat" through a sector of town.

- Schools, fire departments, parks, and libraries generally expand only in very large increments, typically serving many hundreds of homes. Because growth in the number of residents and the number of homes tends to follow a sloping line while these facilities expand in stairsteps, it is likely that sometimes there will be excess capacity in the system (right after a new school opens for example) and at other times the system will be temporarily somewhat overcrowded.
- None of these facilities is as essential to day-to-day living as sewer, water, drainage, and road systems. Although everyone wants the assurance of fire protection, few homeowners need the fire department in a particular year. Many people buy in new developments knowing that they are far from the nearest parks, schools, and fire stations.

All of these facilities are important, and most communities address the expansion of these facilities as part of a comprehensive planning process. That is not the issue here, however. The issue here is whether a temporary capacity problem in a particular facility ought to result in the denial of approval to a particular proposed land development. In most communities, capacity problems in these facilities will not lead to such a denial.

Phased-Growth Programs

A good APF system requires constant monitoring of capacity and demand— every time a family moves into a new house, the available capacity in the system shifts slightly. Some communities have preferred the simplicity of a "phased-growth" program, a simplified geographic application of the concept of adequate public facilities.

In a phased-growth program, a community encourages development in areas where basic infrastructure already exists. That is a very logical approach to planning and one that developers immediately understand. There is one problem with it, however. Rarely is there excess capacity in all infrastructure in the same part of town. The community may have an underutilized road system on the north side of town, lots of extra sewer capacity on the south side of town, and some ability to absorb more water customers on the west side of town. Where does such a community designate the phases for growth?

Ramapo, New York, came up with a system that gave points for each part of the infrastructure available to a particular site. Those developments achieving a designated number of points (essentially representing full availability of at least three of five infrastructure elements considered under the system) received approval. Although the system remained in effect for only a few years, it established the principle of growth phasing and has been widely discussed.[2]

Hawaii has essentially applied the growth-phasing principle to the entire state, through a system that classifies all land in the state in four categories:

urban (allows many kinds of urban development, subject to local control); rural (allowing rural communities with some services for rural areas); agricultural (allowing agriculture and closely related activities); and conservation (allowing very little development). The derivation of the phases is somewhat different from that of the Ramapo program, but its operation is similar in concentrating development in areas with planned or existing services.[3]

Rate-of-Growth Programs

A few communities have established significant limits on their total rate-of-growth. The most famous of those are Petaluma, California, which, in the 1970s, established a growth limit of five hundred dwelling units per year (with some exceptions); and Boulder, Colorado, which has used a variety of related techniques to hold its growth in the range of 2 percent per year.

The two are quite different in one sense. Petaluma adopted its program in response to a surge in development, which pushed it past five hundred new units in a year; that was the last time for many years that its growth even approached the limit, meaning that the absolute limit in the program did not really result in turning away any development proposals.[4] In contrast, demand for housing in Boulder, a university town with a lot of high-tech jobs, has remained high, and the city has constantly strained at its growth limit; one result of the Boulder growth program has been a lot of leapfrog sprawl, as people who work in or near Boulder but cannot find housing there have moved into surrounding communities.[5]

Although many communities consider growth phasing in the planning stages, few have adopted regulatory programs implementing rigorous growth phasing. Another way to accomplish growth phasing is with a comprehensive plan, implemented through public investments in infrastructure in the priority-growth areas, complemented by effective adequate public facilities controls that make development in lower-priority areas unattractive or expensive.

Urban Growth and Urban Service Area Boundaries

There is a certain satisfaction in drawing boundaries. Communities that have suffered from adverse effects of unmanaged growth may find a boundary a particularly attractive alternative. Some have tried a technique called *urban growth boundaries,* which usually set regulatory limits to urban growth.[6] Probably the most famous urban growth boundary in the United States is the one drawn around Portland, Oregon, under a state law that requires major metropolitan areas to set such boundaries.[7] Lexington and Fayette County, Kentucky, jointly adopted one of the first urban growth boundaries in the country, to protect the famous horse farms around the city.[8] Boulder has complemented its rate-of-growth system with an open-space purchase pro-

gram that has created a publicly owned growth boundary around the city.[9] The
Hawaii state law described above essentially creates such boundaries around
major cities. They are also increasingly popular in California.

A tool that is somewhat more common elsewhere is the *urban service area
boundary.* As the name suggests, such a boundary limits the expansion of urban
services without necessarily setting an absolute limit on growth. Sewer and
water systems almost always have an inherent service-area boundary at any
given time, based on the maximum or minimum elevation that can be served.
The concept of service area boundaries differs from urban growth boundaries
in two respects:

1. Urban service area boundaries are deliberate, planned boundaries that
   may drive the location and sizing of infrastructure, whereas other limits
   may be a side effect of engineering-driven decisions about building
   sewer and water lines.
2. Urban service area boundaries attempt to consider the availability of all
   major, location-specific infrastructure (or at the very least, both sewer
   and water service), in contrast to limits of individual services, which
   rarely coincide.

Boulder's earliest growth management efforts involved the use of a "blue
line" designating as early as the 1950s the highest elevation at which the city
would provide water service;[10] this was really a form of urban service area
boundary. The effect of urban service area boundaries on growth patterns
depends in significant part on whether other sources of services are available.
Where suburbs or special sewer and water districts are available to provide services, the fact that the dominant city draws a service line will have little effect
on the pattern of growth. On the other hand, Lincoln, Nebraska, which has
no real suburbs, has been very effective in managing growth through tight
controls on extensions of utilities. Note that a locally adopted urban growth
boundary can have exactly the same problems, as the Boulder experience with
leapfrog sprawl illustrates; other communities in the region can simply serve
and absorb the development that the growth-limiting community does not
want. A state-mandated growth boundary, reinforced with legislative limits on
the ability of other communities to take that growth, can be considerably more
effective.

Annexation

City limits in most states can move outward. The process through which a city
(or, in some cases, a town) expands its boundaries is called *annexation.* Laws concerning practice of annexation vary by state, but it exists in most states outside
New England and some of the Middle Atlantic states. Annexation is a tool available to "incorporated municipalities," which include most cities, many towns,
and, in some states, even villages. Townships, some towns, and some organized

villages are generally considered municipalities but not incorporated ones, and they typically have a different range of powers than their incorporated sisters.

The concept of annexation is simple. Land in the states that allow annexation is either in an incorporated municipality or it is not. Subject to limitations and rules spelled out in state laws, an incorporated municipality can add to its territory certain land that lies in the "unincorporated area" around it. Today, citizens and planners often talk about land being either in the city or in the county, but annexation makes more sense if one considers land as being either in the city or not in the city. For the first 150 or 160 years of this nation's history, urban-scale development took place almost entirely in cities. For land to develop, it was annexed to a nearby city. That city provided the water service, fire protection, and other services essential to urban development. Only with such services available was land reasonably developable for urban uses or at urban densities. Thus, annexation and development historically followed the same geographic patterns. In fact, in many states, land was platted (subdivided) at the time of annexation—and the resulting parts of the city would be called things like "Smith's Addition to the City" or "the Brown Addition."

Today, the system has become more complex. Although counties and, in much of the Midwest, townships once served primarily as branches of state government, carrying out few independent functions, their role has changed. Today, counties in many states can offer sewer and water service, street lighting, animal control, and other urban services. In some states, a variety of special districts and even private utilities can provide essential services to new developments. Thus, it has become possible to develop land without having it annexed to a city.

At the same time, some cities annex land for reasons other than to facilitate its development. Norman, Oklahoma, annexed many square miles of land surrounding Lake Thunderbird, because the county lacked the land-use controls necessary to protect the water quality in the lake and its drainage basin,

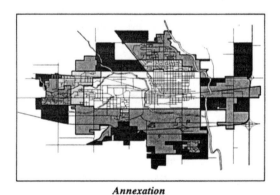

Annexation

☐ 1930   ▨ 1950   *This map shows the recent annexation*
history of the City of Ames, Iowa. Source:
▦ 1975   ■ 1994   *City of Ames (1996).*

and the city wanted to protect it. The desire to control development or to restrict certain types of fringe land uses (liquor stores and adult entertainment establishments are common examples) often leads cities to annex property. Suburbs in rapidly growing parts of metropolitan areas around Denver, Des Moines, Columbus, Albuquerque, and other cities have engaged in annexation "wars," annexing far more territory than they can serve at the time of annexation simply to prevent other nearby cities from annexing the same land and thus gaining control of its development.

Local governments typically have certain legal obligations to provide services to newly annexed territory on a timely basis; that is often reinforced by political pressure from the new taxpayers who are owners of that land. Further, annexation does facilitate development, and most people whose land is annexed expect to see it developed. Thus although the system has become more complex, annexation still should—and really does—relate to land development. Both through their decisions to annex certain lands and through their decisions not to annex other lands, cities can use annexation as a tool for addressing the timing and location of growth.

Growth Shapers

As the discussion of infrastructure planning in chapter 7 suggests, the construction of sewer and water lines and roads is a powerful force in shaping growth. The next chapter discusses how those infrastructure-building decisions influence the timing and location of growth.

Conclusion

Growth management is an essential tool for the effective implementation of planning. Unfortunately, many communities today do not use it. Individual growth management techniques range from the very common-sense adequate public facilities controls to more complex programs of development rating and phasing. The comprehensive plan should indicate what growth management techniques will be useful to a community in implementing its plan.

The Role of the Professional Planner

A major role of the professional planner in dealing with growth management is education, helping public officials to understand the importance of the technique. Public officials may believe that they already have the ability to refuse to approve developments that lack adequate public facilities, but it is important for the planner to work with them to put a formal program in place, consistent with the comprehensive plan, and with clear standards to guide both developers and decision makers.

There is a good deal of technical work involved in designing and implementing a growth management program. Much of that work typically falls to the professional planner, in cooperation with engineers and others involved in dealing with infrastructure and other growth-related issues.

Finally, a growth management program typically requires administration, much like a program of zoning and subdivision regulation. Again, that responsibility is an appropriate one for the professional planner.

The Role of the Individual Citizen

Most interested citizens who learn about growth management promptly conclude that it is an essential tool for implementing plans. Because plans typically focus on the development of the urban fringe, citizens expect their local governments to have tools like these in place.

Thus, citizens can play an important role in persuading a local government that does not have growth management tools to implement such a program. In some communities, citizens do that indirectly, expressing frustration over the symptoms of growth—traffic problems and over crowded public facilities, and leaving it to public officials and the professional planners who advise them to devise a growth management program to address those issues.

EXERCISES

1. Designate a representative of your class or group to contact your local government to determine the currently available capacity of the local sewer and water systems to absorb more growth. At today's rate of building, how many more years of growth can each system handle? Does the local government have plans to upgrade or expand those systems before they run out of capacity?

2. Ask the same student representative also to obtain maps or descriptions of: the maximum service elevation for water that will meet current fire-flow and pressure standards in your community; the limits to the drainage basins that have gravity flow to the sewage treatment plant.

Using USGS (or other) topographic maps, locate the two boundaries and the related service areas. How do the two compare to each other? To emerging development patterns?

3. What level of traffic congestion is the maximum that people will tolerate in your community? Use the criteria in table 7.1 to evaluate major roads in the community to help you in answering this question. Can you identify intersections or road segments that have a lower level of service than the one that you think most people will accept? Has there been recent development activity that affects those intersections or segments? Has that development increased the problem or simply used up available capacity at odd hours?

4. Has the largest city in your area annexed territory recently? Can it? Should it?

Discussion Question

Should your community attempt to manage the timing .and location of growth? If so, why? If not, why not? If it had begun managing growth five years ago, how might it be different today?

Further Reading

Kelly, Eric Damian. 1993. *Managing Community Growth: Policies, Techniques and Impacts.* Westport, CT: Praeger Publishers. A practical treatment of techniques discussed in this chapter, providing more depth and a number of examples.

Nelson, Arthur C., and James B. Duncan. 1995. *Growth Management: Principles and Practices.* Chicago: American Planning Association. A broad-based assessment of local growth management programs.

Porter, Douglas R. 1997. *Managing Growth in America's Communities.* Washington, DC: Island Press. An excellent and very current treatment of the subject by an author who has written on the subject for more than twenty-five years.

Notes

1. On growth management programs in general, see Eric Damian, Kelly, *Managing Community Growth: Policies, Techniques and Impacts,* Westport, CT: Praeger Publishers (1993); and Arthur C. Nelson and James B. Duncan, *Growth Management Principles and Practices,* Chicago: American Planning Association. (1995).

2. See Kelly, ibid., pp. 30–31.

3. See David Callies, *Regulating Paradise: Land Use Controls in Hawaii,* Honolulu: University of Hawaii Press (1994).

4. Kelly, note 1, pp. 31–35, 54–58, 203–204, 208–209.

5. Ibid., pp. 202, 209–210.

6. See V. Gail Easley, *Staying Inside the Lines: Urban Growth Boundaries,* Planning Advisory Service Report No. 442, Chicago: American Planning Association (1992).

7. Described in Arthur C. Nelson, "Oregon's Urban Growth Boundary as a Land-

mark Planning Tool," in Carl Abbott, Deborah Howe, and Sy Adler, eds., *Planning the Oregon Way,* Corvallis: Oregon State University Press (1994).

8. Nelson and Duncan, note 1, p. 80.

9. Kelly, note 1, pp. 95–99.

10. Ibid., pp. 53.

Chapter 13

Deciding When and Where to Build New Public Facilities

Among the most visible and obvious functions of local government are the building and maintaining of public facilities. Public facilities planning and policies are tied to a capital improvement program (CIP) process in many communities. The CIP is the detailed plan for capital (major investment) expenditures for construction, maintenance, improvement, and replacement of a community's physical system. It is the link between the comprehensive plan and the local budget process. Examples of capital improvement projects include:

- construction of a new sewage treatment plant;
- installation of a new water tower;
- acquisition of land and construction of a new regional park;
- construction of a major new boulevard or other important road;
- construction of a new fire station;
- widening and upgrading of an existing major road; and
- expansion of a public library.

Policy and Political Issues

The classic decision-making method used for such programs is cost-benefit analysis, a subject that future planners will study in more depth in a later course. Cost-benefit analysis is rooted in economic concepts of efficiency, evolving from a philosophy known as utilitarianism. The underlying notion of utilitarianism is that, with given resources, society ought to try to achieve the greatest good for the greatest number of people.[1]

Cost-benefit analysis weighs the economic costs of a particular project against its benefits and then compares that ratio to the cost-benefit ratio of competing projects. The factors used in the computation need not always be dollars—they may be households or people or reduced driving time—but they are always quantifiable factors. For example, if a community can either expand a branch library to serve 3,000 new users or build a new soccer complex that will serve eighteen hundred players and their families, for the same amount of money, the governing body can use that data to choose between the projects.

Public policy is more complex than simply making cost-benefit analyses, however. It is an important part of the political process because it allocates the community's limited resources among different interests; the governing body may have to choose between expanding the library on the west side and building a new park on the south side, between widening an overburdened north-south thoroughfare and extending a loop road around the north side of the city. Chambers of commerce, neighborhood associations, and other organized interest groups all lobby actively to persuade the local government to invest in capital projects that will advance their respective interests. Often the geographical balancing of investments within the community becomes the dominant element in the CIP process.

If only powerful political interests are heard when the community is making its investment decisions, poor areas of the community may remain poor. Advocate planners often urge that the community invest the most money in the poorest areas, to try to make them better. Philosophically, this is directly related to the thinking of John Rawls, whose *Theory of Justice,* as mentioned in the introduction, urged that society in general should spend the most on those who have the least.[2] There are many examples of such investment policies. Some communities have used well-funded "magnet schools" to attract students to public schools in poor areas. An increasing number of local governments today recognize the need to invest extra money in upgrading parks, replacing sidewalks, maintaining drainage systems, and generally improving some of the poorest neighborhoods of the community. In some communities, however, the big investments go to the new areas or to those inhabited by influential residents. The governing body that makes such decisions may not even be consciously aware of the lack of equity in those decisions. An important role of the planner and the planning commissioner in this process can be to ensure that the equity issues are at least considered in the budgeting process.

Unfortunately, communities are not left alone to decide what public facilities projects are going to be done, rescheduled for a future time, or completely dropped. Federal and state laws require that local governments maintain water quality at a particular level, solve certain drainage problems, pave streets if necessary to maintain air quality, make public buildings accessible to most people, and otherwise invest in matters determined to be public policy priorities by Congress or the state legislature. Although most people accept the merits of most such programs, the effect of these so-called unfunded mandates may be to usurp the ability of the local government to set its own priorities.

Communities often compete for economic development, for tax base, and for other private investment with surrounding communities and the surrounding county. If services or facilities such as construction and maintenance of roads in one community are noticeably poorer than those in others, citizens will choose to live in other areas. While this promotes greater efficiency, this type of competition is often difficult for communities, especially if they have a poor tax base. This is one reason that many communities have found it difficult to redevelop their inner cities. Incorporated communities typically have newer public facilities, so as residents migrated out to those suburban communities, the very revenue base that would have made rehabilitation possible left with them.

Link between CIP and Planning

The capital improvements program process can be an important means of linking the comprehensive plan to an important implementation tool. Comprehensive plans contain goals, objectives, and strategies. Typically some of those goals, objectives, and strategies focus on particular geographic areas of the community: for example, encouraging residential growth to the south, industrial development to the east (along the rail line), and continued agricultural production to the west and north. As discussed in the previous chapter, and explored more here, the community can reinforce those patterns by building facilities important to residential development to the south and facilities essential to industry to the east. The community can, often with equal ease, thwart its own plans by building a major new road to the west or the north and cooperating with the school district in locating a new school to the north.

The capital improvements program, or CIP, is the tool through which a local government should show its plan for capital improvements. Sometimes a CIP is little more than a "project list," without a map and without any clear relationship to goals and strategies. Priorities on the project list may come from many sources other than the comprehensive plan: an attempt to equalize distribution of funds among council wards or other geographic areas of the community; a response to citizen complaints about potholes or bad water pressure in some part of the community; a safety recommendation of the community's engineer or risk manager; conditions of a grant; or simply a very old plan that identified a project that has never been built and that thus remains on the list. Ideally, capital improvements are based on the CIP and the CIP is based on the comprehensive plan. In many communities, however, the CIP process primarily involves engineers from a public works department and representatives from the finance department. Firefighters, librarians, and other constituent groups within government may lobby for their own projects.

Often, engineers respond to what they perceive as immediate needs in the physical operation of the community.

This lack of guidance from the comprehensive plan is most apparent in communities where rapid growth is occurring. The land-use element of a comprehensive plan often directs growth in one direction, while it actually occurs in another direction. This is often the result of upgrades and improvements being made at the request of the utilities department because of a pressing need to better serve certain areas. In turn, these improvements allow for greater land use where facilities already exist, even if it is in a more fragile environment or if future extensions will be more costly than in the area chosen for this higher land use. Thus, the very essence of the comprehensive planning process is lost since it is not guiding growth and development; rather the decisions made by other government departments are guiding growth and development.

An effective CIP includes a physical plan that (1) shows how projects to be built in a particular year relate to those built in other years, (2) shows the geographic relationship among investments in different infrastructure (schools, roads, sewer, water, parks), and (3) relates directly to the future land-use element of the comprehensive plan. Ranking of projects need not be based entirely on the comprehensive plan—improvements needed to address public health and safety issues often must take priority over other projects—but the CIP should show how it all fits together and how even the public health and safety improvements also relate to the comprehensive plan.

A CIP typically includes two to four different levels of projects:

- those projects to be built this year and thus to be included in the current budget;
- other projects to be built from currently available funding (usually a multi-year grant from a state or federal agency, or a bond issue);
- projects planned to be built over the next four or five years if current projections of tax revenues and other expenditures are accurate, but subject to adjustment through the annual budgeting process; and
- projects that are a priority for the community but for which no specific source of funding has been identified or which the community probably cannot afford within five years.

Unlike most comprehensive plans, most CIPs are "rolling" CIPs. That is, a community that uses a five-year CIP planning period updates its plan each year, dropping off the previous year and adding one more year at the end of the cycle. That technique differs from the way most comprehensive plans are updated, which is to rely on the twenty-year plan for several years and then to prepare a major update.

How the community plans for its investments in public improvements is critical to the success of comprehensive planning and to the public's perception of the effectiveness of planning. Often, the completed public facilities are the most visible, tangible results of any local government planning process.

It is important that planners participate in the preparation of the CIP if the community is to be guided by the comprehensive plan. Decisions dealing with money are means of implementing plans. As resources grow more scarce, it becomes increasingly important for planners to play a major role in the CIP process. Choices will have to be made with very long-term effects. The planner participating in the capital improvements program process can help focus priorities on those projects already established as important to citizens through the planning process.

The corollary of this principle, however, is that the constituent groups within government who manage or control capital facilities ought to be included in the comprehensive planning process. A comprehensive plan with a broad base of citizen participation but no involvement from the streets and public works departments it not likely to be very effective. Representatives of these in-house constituent groups must be involved in the plan for two reasons: first, to be effective, the plan must respond to their needs, and those constituent groups are the best ones to present their own needs; second, as with any other constituency group, a certain amount of political acceptance of the plan comes from involvement in the planning process.

In some communities, the CIP itself goes to the planning commission for review and verification for consistency with the comprehensive plan. That is an important step in the process, but it is equally important that planning staff be actively involved in the preparation of the document that goes forward to the commission and other groups.

Sustainability, or Shaping Growth to Fit the Plan

The discussion in chapters 3, 7, and 12 illustrates the important role of public facilities in shaping growth. If a community builds a major new road to the west side of town and supplements that with extensions of sewer and water lines, a disproportionate share of new growth in the community is likely to go to the west side.

Historically, planning for public facilities has been responsive to actual or perceived demand, with some considerations of economic efficiency. That is, engineers proposed building roads where there were existing traffic problems or where their projections showed that there would be increases in traffic in the future. Wastewater engineers similarly proposed sewer extensions to serve areas likely to grow, but typically only to the extent that those areas could easily be served by gravity flow to the sewer plant. Effects of these facilities in shaping growth were incidental and often contradictory, with the local government possibly investing in roads to the west, sewers to the north, and water lines to the east.

Today, communities must recognize the powerful growth-shaping influences of their investments in public facilities. One of the best ways to make a future land-use plan come true is to use investments in public facilities to reinforce the plan. The community should invest in new roads, sewer and water lines, and other public facilities in areas where it wants growth to occur. It should refuse to make major investments in areas where it does not want growth to occur. Although a community may have to make some investments in other areas to avoid public health or safety hazards, it can allow traffic congestion to grow to a point of inconvenience and refuse to provide new parks and other facilities in areas where it wants to preserve agricultural land or otherwise discourage growth.

This desire to shape growth can guide a community's capital improvement policies in two other ways. Generally, local government engineers recommend "oversizing" new facilities to allow some extra capacity. Although good sewer or water engineering design typically includes 20 or 25 percent extra capacity as a safety factor, engineers may propose laying a line that is two or three times as large as that necessary to serve present demand. Their logic in making that recommendation is that it will be needed someday and it is cheaper in the long-run to lay one large pipe now than to go back later and dig a second trench to lay another pipe parallel to the first. They are correct in their logic. If, however, the community wants to limit its growth to the west to land inside the current beltway, it is bad public policy to build sewer and water lines that will handle more development than can reasonably occur within that beltway; the extra capacity will facilitate extra growth, which may well take place outside the beltway.

Investments in infrastructure are generally far more powerful than zoning, subdivision, or growth management regulations in influencing growth. Communities must recognize the power of this tool in implementing plans. Sometimes these issues of growth and sustainability will override traditional infrastructure planning criteria. Perhaps the most efficient way to help the small, outlying rural community is by extending sewer and water services to it through prime agricultural land; an alternative way to serve it, however, without creating growth pressure on that land, is to offer to help it construct and manage a small water treatment system and package sewer plant to meet its own needs. Engineers prefer to let sewage flow downhill and not to use pumps in sewage collection services; but if a community can avoid running a new line through a wetland by adding a pump, that may be a good decision from the perspective of implementing the plan, even if it does not represent optimal efficiency.

Communities that want to limit sprawl, preserve open space, protect agricultural land, and/or provide public services at a reasonable cost need to manage growth. Most communities concerned with long-term sustainability address some or all of those issues in a plan. The techniques discussed in the

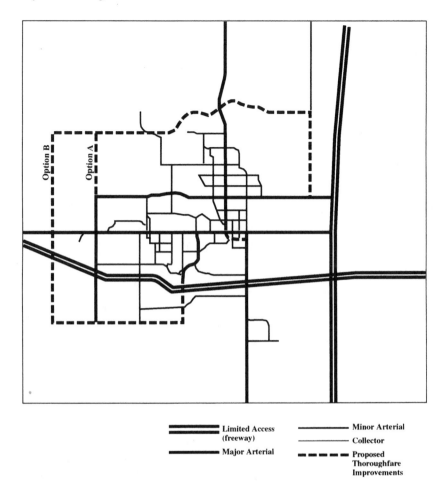

Limited Access (freeway)	Minor Arterial
Major Arterial	Collector
	Proposed Thoroughfare Improvements

The intersection of the two limited-access roads has attracted much new growth around Ames, Iowa, southeast of the city. New roads planned as part of a coordinated land-use and transportation plan will help to draw growth to the easily served southwest and northwest areas. Option A shows an alternative extending an existing road (solid line) further north to connect to a new northern boundary road; Option B shows construction of an entirely new north–south road at the western edge of the city, again connecting the northern boundary road to the southern link. Source: City of Ames and RM Plan Group, Nashville (1996).

previous chapter are useful in managing growth, but the most powerful tool a community has to shape its future is its investment in public facilities. It must use that investment to guide its growth and implement its plan. For that reason, the comprehensive plan must provide a solid and practical basis for the CIP, and the CIP must follow the comprehensive plan.

Capital Improvements Programs

Because the CIP is both a budget and a planning document, it is typically adopted either as part of the regular budget process of the community or in a separate capital budget process. Although the typical local government budget covers only one year, the capital improvements program usually covers a longer period, often as much as five years.

The capital improvements program is typically developed from individual project proposals, which ideally come from a comprehensive plan and departmental plans. Since the budgeting process is annual, the CIP is part of the normal annual budgetary process of local government. The current year of the CIP is often simply called the capital budget and shows up as a part of the community's annual adopted budget. The CIP itself should cover a longer period, often five years or so. There are several reasons for that longer time horizon. First, some projects will simply require longer to complete than one year. Second, some projects will require more funding than the local government can afford in a particular year. Third, the longer time frame allows the community to build projects in logical sequences, perhaps acquiring the land for a park in one year and beginning to improve it the next. Fourth, the longer time horizon addresses some of the political issues inherent in the capital improvements programming process; for example, governing body members can assure the neighborhood group that will receive no benefits this year that their new park is included in the CIP three years from now.

Because they extend over a long time, CIPs require scheduling and coordination. Some of the projects will take more funds in the early stages of development and construction, and others will take more capital as the project nears completion. For that reason, budgeting has to be planned for the entire duration of the project to insure that the funds are available to complete something that is started. Other projects, such as building a new airport farther out of town than the existing airport, require coordinating a number of related projects. In this example, a new airport will require roads, sewer and water, utilities, and other public facilities. However, it will not need all of these things at the beginning of the project. The different projects—road building, laying sewer and water lines, putting in utilities—have to be coordinated so that the largest expenditures for each project do not come in the same budget year but are all completed as needed.

Coordinating different projects requires a cost estimate for each project so that these costs can be budgeted for the life of the project. The further away the project is, the less reliable are the cost estimates. This is understandable considering how quickly the costs of supplies, land, and labor fluctuate. However, good cost estimates might make the difference in a project being accepted or rejected. If costs are overestimated, the project might be postponed indefinitely due to inadequate funds; and, if they are underestimated and exceed the budgeted amount by too much, the project might have to be abandoned.

Selecting Projects

Ideally, selection of projects for a CIP is based on the comprehensive plan. In addition, to that, there are often political and policy issues involved in the selection process. Beyond all of that, however, it is necessary to set priorities within the CIP. The comprehensive plan may suggest nearly $100,000,000 in new capital improvements, but the local government may be able to afford only about $8,000,000 per year. Thus, even if it follows the plan, it must make choices.

Many local governments have established criteria for evaluating capital improvement program requests. Typical criteria address the following issues:

- *Risk to the public health and safety.* Projects to correct serious risks are almost always at the top of the list. A project in this category typically addresses a clear and immediate risk to the public health and safety. For example, if after a heavy rainstorm part of a street is washed out, the condition of the road is an issue of public safety.
- *Completion of approved projects.* A major public building, a sewage or water treatment plant, or even a large park or highway interchange is likely to require funding from the capital budget for several years. Once a project is begun, finishing it becomes a very high priority.
- *Linkage to approved projects.* Some projects become a high priority simply because they are linked to another high-priority project. For example, if a community decided to build a new hospital and the road leading to the project is being widened and improved, it would be efficient and less costly to schedule the sewer project to coincide with the street reconstruction so that the street is under repair for a shorter period of time.
- *Equitable provision of facilities.* Sometimes investment is necessary to ensure that facilities or services are built or established for neighborhoods or groups that are undeserved in comparison to the rest of the community. Or groups with special needs, such as the elderly, deserve special facilities or services.
- *Scheduling of systematic replacement.* Equipment and facilities need to be replaced or upgraded periodically. For example, improvements in telecommunications help emergency response teams, such as ambulance crews, do their jobs even when storms have torn down utility lines.
- *Maintaining deteriorating facilities.* Equipment and facilities deteriorate, so communities have to plan for reconstruction, replacement, or extensive upgrading to avoid or postpone replacement. For example, it might be less expensive to outfit an existing ambulance with new life-saving technology

than to replace the ambulance with a new one to gain the needed technology.

- *Improvement of efficiency.* With new advances in technology, it may be possible to extend the life of an existing facility rather than replace the facility. For example, rather than build a whole new sewer treatment plant, it might be possible to expand the existing facility to meet projected demands on the system.
- *Addition of new facilities or equipment.* Sometimes this is a conscious decision, such as building a new arena downtown to help redevelop the downtown while providing a facility to keep the team in town. Other times it might represent elusive opportunities, such as a hockey team negotiating to move to a community if the community will provide a new arena that will seat twice as many people as the existing arena.
- *Protection and conservation of resources.* Projects might be built to protect the environment; for example, sewer and water lines might be extended to developments not on existing systems to protect the groundwater. Rehabilitation or upgrading might be necessary because existing facilities are at capacity. This is fairly common, particularly in areas experiencing rapid growth.
- *Encouragement of economic activity and increase in job opportunities.* Often communities need to encourage economic activity, especially to increase the existing tax base. For example, a major plant might be willing to come to the community if the community will provide the enlarged sewer and water lines necessary for its product production.

These are examples of criteria used by communities to assist in ranking and selecting projects. Although some of these criteria are common to most CIP selection processes, each community must develop its own list.

Note that these selection criteria can provide the basis both for selecting projects for inclusion and for establishing priorities among projects. There is rarely enough money in any capital budget to carry out all planned projects. Thus, even within projects included in the CIP, it is necessary to set priorities. Setting priorities is not always based on a simple analysis derived from a list of criteria, however. If the current capital budget is $8,000,000 and the first five items will use $7,500,000 of that, the sixth item on the list costs $3,000,000, and the seventh costs $350,000, it is very likely that the local government will skip the sixth item and pick up the seventh that year, leaving item six to become a high-priority item the following year.

Capital budgets are sometimes funded from different sources. Thus, the priority list may establish different priorities for different funding sources. A new road project may be number one on the list for the use of state highway funds but number fifteen if it is to be locally funded.

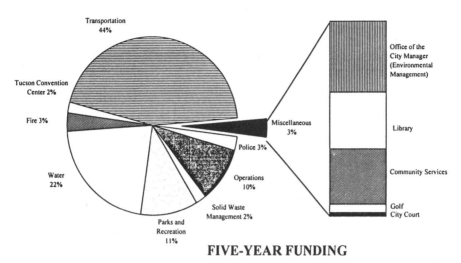

FIVE-YEAR FUNDING

This chart shows Tucson's priorities for spending the capital funds available to it. Source: *City of Tucson, Approved Five-Year Capital Improvement Program, July 1, 1998–June 30, 2003, Vol. 3 (1998).*

Financing the CIP

Most governments do not have sufficient annual tax revenues to finance all their public facilities projects. However, for many communities, current revenues finance a significant portion of CIPs. When communities use current revenues to fund projects, those funds are often accumulated in a reserve account until there are sufficient funds available to carry out a project.

Communities often have dedicated funds for capital improvements. Impact fees or other fees collected from developers may be accumulated in an account for the expansion of a particular facility. Sometimes a portion of user fees from sewer or water systems is specifically designated for capital investments.

Bonds are another means of financing capital improvements projects. Bonds are financial instruments that represent debts. A local government may "sell" $1,000,000 in bonds. The "buyers" of the bonds give the local government $1,000,000. Under the terms of the bond, the local government agrees to repay the holder of the bond the full principal amount of the bond along with interest at an agreed rate. Through bonds, local governments can usually borrow money at lower rates than those available to individuals.

Just as with individuals, when communities borrow money, they must pay it back. That is why capital budgets must include debt service payments. CIPs do not normally show principal and interest payments, but annual operating budgets must show them. After the initial year of budgeting for the CIP, projects will be scattered throughout the annual budget depending on expendi-

Table 13.1. Sources of Funding (in thousands of dollars) for Capital Projects, Tucson, Arizona, July 1, 1998, to June 30, 2003.

Department	Prior Years	Carry Forward	New Funding	Year 1 Total
RECURRING REVENUES				
Capital Contributions and Agreements	61,053.2	3,949.8	59,506.3	63,456.1
Central Arizona Project Reserve Fund	5,408.0	—	1,132.0	1.132.0
Convention Center Fund	630.0	—	720.0	720.0
General Fund	8,365.6	1,688.3	2,512.0	4,200.3
Golf Fund	28.9	—	—	—
Highway User Revenue Fund	2,820.8	530.0	1,350.0	1,880.0
Highway User Revenue Fund, Restricted	4,882.8	1,452.0	9,506.0	10,958.0
Mass Transit, Local	694.0	53.4	1,868.0	1,921.4
Mass Transit ISTEA, Local	—	—	191.0	191.0
Solid Waste Management Fund	2,990.6	—	—	—
Water Revenue and Operations Fund	31,555.1	—	30,071.0	30,071.0
BONDS	62,165.7	26,243.8	38,273.3	64,517.1
General Obligation Bonds	35,779.2	9,732.2	9,769.3	19,501.5
Street and Highway User Revenue Bonds	8,706.8	5,041.0	14,640.0	19,681.0
Water Revenue Bonds	17,679.7	11,470.6	13,864.0	25,334.6
FEDERAL GRANTS	7,058.8	3,189.5	17,939.3	21,128.8
Community Development Block Grant	125.3	359.7	—	359.7
Federal Highway Administration ISTEA	1,459.0	160.0	6,940.0	7,100.0
Mass Transit, Federal	4,404.5	1,077.7	7,467.0	8,544.7
Mass Transit ISTEA	—	—	1,524.0	1,524.0
Miscellaneous Federal Grants	1,070.0	1,592.1	2,008.3	3,600.4
OTHER	2,261.0	928.9	11,328.5	12,257.4
1994 Bond Interest	—	—	3,363.0	3,363.0
Library Settlement	18.5	—	—	—
Miscellaneous Nonfederal Grants	1,042.5	428.9	974.0	1,402.9
Pima County Bonds	—	—	1,844.0	1,844.0
Certificates of Participation	1,200.0	500.0	5,147.5	5,647.5
Total Funded	132,538.7	34,312.0	127,047.4	161,359.4

Source: City of Tucson.

tures and if interest payments are being made. Some communities maintain cross references of accounts on their annual budgets so that they can easily account for expenditures and keep financial accountability of specific projects.

Roads are often major elements in local capital improvements programs. A good deal of funding for construction of major roads comes from state gas tax revenues, which are typically shared with local governments under a formula. Many local governments have an entirely separate priority list of projects to be built with state highway tax money.

Sometimes local governments have a "wish list" of capital projects that they want to build but that are not high priorities for the use of local money. Government agencies often seek grants from federal, state, or private sources to pay for such projects. Expansions to zoos, extensions of greenway trails, fountains, and public art and other amenities are the types of projects that local governments may keep on such a wish list. Although the wish list is typically a part of the capital budget, the items on it may carry a very low priority for local funding unless a particular grant proposal is approved.

Conclusion

Investments in public facilities guide growth and otherwise define the future of a community. They determine which areas can grow easily and which will not. They influence which neighborhoods thrive and which wither. In many ways, they define the quality of life. They are probably the most important long-range decisions made by most local governments. If a local government follows its comprehensive plan in developing a CIP and follows the CIP in investing in public facilities, many of the goals of the comprehensive plan are likely to be realized. If a local government ignores its comprehensive plan as it spends its own money, the community can hardly expect that others will follow the plan or that the plan itself will much influence the future of the community.

The Role of the Professional Planner

The professional planner should be directly involved in the preparation of the CIP. In many communities, however, the mayor or city manager relies on the city's engineer and finance director to prepare the CIP. The CIP typically involves significant engineering considerations and major expenditures of funds, so it is logical to include those individuals, but it is important for the planner also to be included to ensure that there is a link back to the comprehensive plan.

Where the professional planner is involved in the process, his or her major role is to inform or remind participants in the CIP process about the priorities of the comprehensive plan and then to check their recommendations against the comprehensive plan priorities. Others involved in the process may rely heavily on the professional planner to provide them with trend information and projections of future population and future land-use patterns. The professional planner may play a role in creating a map or other graphic representation of the recommended CIP.

Note that it is not just the professional planner who ought to be involved in this process—it is all the representatives of the comprehensive plan. Thus, the final role of the professional planner in this process is to make certain that the planning commission has the opportunity to comment and make recommendations on the CIP before it goes to the governing body for approval.

The Role of the Individual Citizen

Many local governments treat capital improvements programming as a technical and financial exercise in which there is little public involvement before the public hearing on the community's entire budget. Individual citizens may directly influence that process without realizing it when they complain about drainage problems or water pressure in their neighborhoods—if enough people complain about the same problems, the solutions to those problems may become major elements of the CIP.

For the citizen who is interested in planning, however, it is important to try to become more involved—to make public officials recognize that the CIP is one of the most powerful implementation tools of public policy and not simply a technical exercise about which citizens should be left in the dark. If the discussion of the CIP focuses on engineering details, itemized costs for projects, and the technicalities of state tax and bonding law, it may be very difficult for individual citizens to participate. If, however, the discussion focuses at a policy level, the individual citizen—and her elected representatives—can participate much more effectively. The questions in which citizens should be engaged ought to be framed as in the following: "We have $20,000,000 to spend on capital improvements next year. Of that, $2,500,000 must be spent to correct serious safety problems and another $3,750,000 must be spent to bring the sewage treatment plant into conformance with state regulations. That leaves $14,750,000 to spend on other projects. What are our priorities?"

EXERCISES

1. Contact your local sewer and water provider(s). Obtain maps, or rough sketches, of areas to which they have extended service in the last five years. Look at what has happened in those areas. Compare these extensions and the related development activity to the community's future land-use plan.

2. Does your community have a capital improvements program? To find out, contact the local government finance office, or the office of the mayor or other chief executive. Ask for a copy of the summary version of the CIP. Compare it to the comprehensive plan. Do they make sense? Do they reinforce each other?

3. Ask a representative of the local sewer and water provider to come to your class and talk about how that entity makes decisions about line extensions. Is the comprehensive plan a factor that they consider?

4. Contact the planning office and ask for a copy of the most recent regional transportation plan, the one used by your state department of transportation in making its decisions about new projects. Compare it to the comprehensive plan. Do they reinforce each other, or are there differences or even serious inconsistencies?

DISCUSSION QUESTION

Based on what you have learned so far in this course, and on what you discovered in the exercises for this chapter, what do you think are the dominant forces determining the pattern of growth in and around your community? Do you think that your local planning commission and public officials fully understand that? If not, how would you educate them about these issues?

FURTHER READING

Bowyer, Robert A. 1993. Capital *Improvements Programs Linking Budgeting and Planning.* Planning Advisory Service Report No. 442. Chicago: American Planning Association. A practical treatment of a complex subject, from the planner's point of view.

Brevard, Joseph H. 1985. *Capital Facilities Planning.* Chicago: Planners Press. Although the date on this may concern some readers, the basic principles have not changed significantly.

Kelly, Eric Damian. 1993. *Planning, Growth and Public Facilities: A Primer for Public Officials.* Planning Advisory Service Report No. 447. Chicago: American Planning Association. This report is just what it says it is—a treatment of the subject of this chapter from a policy perspective.

Petersen, John E., and Dennis R. Strachota, eds. 1991. *Local Government Finance: Concepts and Practices.* Chicago: Government Finance Officers Association. An accessible treatment of the principles of government finance that underlie the subject of this chapter.

Robinson, Susan G., ed. 1990. *Financing Growth: Who Benefits? Who Pays? And How Much?* Chicago: Government Finance Officers Association. A collection of essays on financing the costs of community growth.

NOTES

1. For a defining essay on utilitarianism, see that of John Stuart Mill, available in a variety of collections of essays. One is H.B. Acton, ed., *Utilitarianism, Liberty, Representative Government: Selections from Auguste Comte and Positivism / John Stuart Mill,* Rutland, VT: C.E. Tuttle (1984).
2. John Rawls, *A Theory of Justice* Cambridge, MA: Belknap Press of Harvard University (1971).

Chapter 14

Fitting All These Plans Together

Planning in the United States is largely a function of local governments. There are more than thirty thousand local governments of general jurisdiction (primarily cities, towns, and counties) in the United States. That suggests the opportunity for a lot of planning, but it also represents the potential for a lot of confusion if all of those plans are developed separately.

The problem is more dramatic in metropolitan areas. Metro Denver, which is the fifteenth largest metropolitan area in the United States, has a population of more than 1,000,000 people. Of those, only about 500,000 live in Denver. The others reside in a six-county metropolitan area that includes one other city with more than 250,000 people, two or three others with more than 100,000 each, at least four more with populations of more than 50,000, and more than a dozen other small cities, including one that is little more than an incorporated shopping center and one so small that a handful of bars and adult businesses appear to dominate the economy. Des Moines, Iowa, is in the center of a much smaller metropolitan area, with a total population of only about 300,000; yet that metropolitan area includes four counties and more than a dozen cities. In both cases, the population in the dominant cities has remained relatively stable for two decades or more, but the suburbs have grown rapidly, absorbing regional population growth and creating sprawl.

Some of the nation's largest metropolitan areas are even more complex. Chicago has more than one hundred local governments of general jurisdiction in its metropolitan area. The Philadelphia metropolitan area spans the Delaware River and includes parts of New Jersey, covering more than ten counties, well over one hundred townships, and dozens of incorporated cities and towns. The New York metropolitan region expands into three states, with major suburbs in both New Jersey and Connecticut. Some Washington, D.C., commuters now live in parts of West Virginia, making it effectively the fourth state in a metropolitan region that already includes five counties and many cities in Virginia and Maryland.

This chapter examines the issue of planning at a regional—or larger than local—level in the United States.

A Historical Perspective

Three types of government dominate planning and land-use controls in the United States. Understanding how they evolved helps to understand why there are so many of them.

Municipalities

In all states, incorporated cities and towns provide zoning, land-use control, and other public services in urban and suburban communities. Created under authority of state constitutions and supplemental enabling acts, these entities developed as the primary providers of everything from water service to police protection. There are some odd creatures, like the City and County of Denver, Nashville-Davidson County, and Indianapolis-Marion County, but the typical example is a Binghamton, Bismarck, Boise, or Burbank, a city that is an identifiable place with a local government that serves a largely developed area around the heart of that place. Early cities and towns were sometimes created by the simple act of a railroad or land promoter filing a plat for the town in the county land records, creating a pattern of streets, blocks, and lots that define the centers of many cities and towns today. By the mid-twentieth century, creation of an incorporated city or town in most states required some sort of petition or vote by a number of people already residing in the area and stating their desire to form an independent local government.

Not surprisingly, early cities and towns developed as market and service centers for a largely rural population, often engaged in agriculture, mining, or some other relatively dispersed activity. Although there are certainly examples of cities like New York and Boston that evolved as very urban areas, there are far more cities today that began life as relatively small towns, serving the market, transportation, health care, and recreational needs of a region. Most of today's cities of 100,000 or more, and many others, first developed when people traveled primarily by horse and by train. Thus, many small communities evolved in what seems today to be close proximity; in wondering why they are all there, it is important to consider that a trip that may take a half hour by car would easily take a half day on a fast horse or a day or more by wagon.

As these small towns grew into larger towns and cities, they often grew together. Boston actually consists of more than a dozen cities, brought together by a special act of the Massachusetts legislature more than a century ago: Roxbury and Jamaica Plain, now considered neighborhoods of Boston, were once independent municipal governments. New York's five boroughs and several cities that now form Philadelphia were similarly merged by legislatures in those states. Colorado created the City and County of Denver to offer a form of government adequate to serve the growth needs of the region, a plan that worked well until the region exceeded the practical capacity of that relatively small geographical area. Nashville and Davidson County in Tennessee and Indianapolis and Marion County in Indiana merged in the last half of the twentieth century to create some semblance of metropolitan government, although both, like Denver, have additional suburbs today.

With those and a handful of other exceptions today, however, the nation's metropolitan areas consist of multiple cities and towns, and there are many other cities and towns scattered around the states. Although such complex metropolitan areas occupy only a small fraction of the land area of the United States, 75.2 percent of the population lives in or very near them, with 63.6 percent living in the urbanized areas.[1] In virtually all such areas, each local government has its own planning function and its own plans.

Counties

In western, most midwestern, and most southern states, the county is the fundamental unit of government that serves and governs areas outside cities and towns. Counties evolved as subdivisions of state government, created to bring state government close to every citizen, in most cases long before telephones, automobiles, and airplanes made state capitals themselves more accessible. Every inch of land in these and most other states falls in a county.

Although counties in urbanizing areas today often act much like cities in the same areas, the original purpose of counties was quite different and quite limited. As subdivisions of the state, counties typically provided: law enforcement services, through a sheriff; law administration, through a prosecuting attorney and some sort of connection to the state judicial system; and roads, often the state roads plus local roads serving areas outside cities and towns; administration of property taxes; and maintenance of land records. The fact that the seat of county government is typically in the "courthouse" while the seat of city government is in "city hall" tells a lot about the history of counties. Today counties often provide local offices for such state services as automobile licensing and serve as the operational units for implementation of state policies for welfare, mental health, and other services.

County boundaries today often seem to make little sense. Iowa, which has a population of about 3,000,000 people has ninety-nine counties. Colorado has twenty counties with populations of less than 5,000 people and two with populations of less than 1,000. Nebraska has ten counties with populations of less than 1,000. More than half the counties in North Dakota have fewer than 10,000 people in them. The criterion for county size when several midwestern states developed was to place everyone within a half day's wagon ride of the county seat, which is generally found near the middle of the county. Although the county seats in such counties once served as market and service centers, in many cases today, people drive an hour or two to another county to shop and obtain medical care. Were legislators or constitutional conventions to create county boundaries today, it seems likely that they would create fewer counties serving the much larger areas served by today's regional market and medical centers. There is little likelihood of legislators forcing existing counties to merge or disappear, however. Just as the county serves as a branch of state government, in most states, county office holders and their allies typically form the backbone of the state's political parties. Thus, counties represent far more power in state legislatures than one might expect if considering only the portion of the population that is significantly dependent on county government for services.

Historically, counties had no real police service and no general regulatory power. Laws enforced by the sheriff were, historically, state laws—originally focusing on major crimes but gradually evolving to include infractions such as violations of state speed limits. A hundred or even fifty years ago, few counties provided local infrastructure other than roads or bridges. People living on farms and ranches did not need sewer and water service and did not expect government to provide fire protection; volunteer groups often provided some of these services in rural areas.

As urban growth expanded outside the boundaries of cities and towns, counties began to deal with urban problems. They also began to deal with former urban residents who were accustomed to such urban amenities as trash collection, streetlights, emergency medical services, and stormwater management. Thus, counties began to seek an expansion of their legal authority, allowing them to become more than just a branch of state government—to become real local governments. Today counties in many states have the authority to provide sewer and water service, trash collection, and fire and emergency medical services. In some states, counties even have the same "ordinance power" as cities and towns, permitting them to adopt local laws on such matters as loose dogs and overgrown weeds.

With the expansion of county powers and activities has come a significant increase in planning and zoning activity by counties. Of the first one thousand zoning ordinances adopted in the United States, only a handful were in counties. Today most urban counties have basic zoning and subdivision regulations, and almost all counties in the southeastern and western United States have zoning and planning authority; Texas counties and certain counties in a handful of southern states are the exceptions.

In most states, land that becomes part of a city or town, either through incorporation or annexation, remains part of the county, also (Virginia is the clear exception to this rule). In those states, within cities and towns, the county continues to provide those original state services—enforcement and administration of state laws, management of land records, management of the property tax system, welfare, and mental health—while the municipal government becomes the government of general jurisdiction within its boundaries, handling planning, zoning, utility services, fire protection, and other local services.

To go back to the examples of Denver and Des Moines, almost all the incorporated cities and towns in those metropolitan areas have zoning ordinances, and so do all the counties. Many also have their own plans and other related tools and controls, creating a huge patchwork quilt of plans and regulations in each of those and most other metropolitan areas. Although there are only a few counties in each of those metropolitan regions, each of the incorporated cities and towns has its own planning and zoning authority within its boundaries, leaving to the counties only those areas not included in any city or town.

Townships

There are counties in every state (with the exception of Louisiana, which calls a similar unit of government a *parish*). In some states, however, there is another active layer of general local government, and that is the township. The township exists primarily as a mapping reference in western states, where it typically defines a square that is six miles on each side and contains thirty-six sections of land. In New England, some of the mid-Atlantic states, and a few midwestern states, the township exists as a separate governmental entity. In those states, every square inch of land falls in a township or in an incorporated town or city; all land also falls in counties.

Although the patterns vary slightly, in the strong township states, the county government often serves as the branch of state government, and the township evolves as the unit of local government outside cities and towns. Thus, in most of those states, state law enforcement and administration, as well as welfare services, fall to the counties, but it is the townships that deal with local roads, some utilities, and, in many cases, planning and zoning.

Note that other states have townships with limited local government roles. In Iowa, many townships operate cemeteries and fire services. In Indiana, townships play a significant role in administering the social welfare and property tax systems. In those states, however, the township is more like a special district, serving defined purposes, than it is like the townships that serve as units of general local government in states like New Jersey, New York, and New Hampshire.

Townships in the strong-township states make metropolitan areas even more complex than they would be with just counties, cities, and towns. New Jersey has only twenty-one counties, but it has hundreds of townships. Thus, a major reason that the Philadelphia and New York metropolitan regions must cope with hundreds of units of local government while Denver has only three dozen or so is that the states including those eastern metropolitan areas have

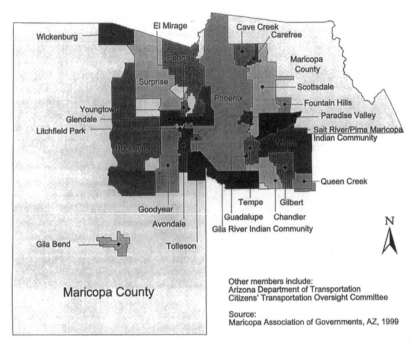

Even relatively new metropolitan areas often include a large number of local governments. This map shows the local governments of general jurisdiction in the Phoenix, Arizona, metropolitan area. Copyright 1999 by Maricopa Association of Governments. Used with permission.

townships. Further, because townships in those states evolved more rapidly into providing general government services than did counties in some southern and western states, people in those townships have been less inclined to form cities or to seek annexation to existing ones. Resulting from this pattern of evolution of government are the crazy quilts of jurisdictions and plans that surround the major, and even minor, cities of the northeastern and mid-Atlantic states.

The Challenge and the Opportunity

One Illinois county that includes a number of residential suburbs of Chicago assembled a meeting of planning commissioners from the municipal governments in the county. All brought their plans with them, and planners at the meeting laid them out and tallied some figures. Although this area was largely residential, and most of its current growth was residential, planners found that, if all of the plans were carried out, the county would become a major employment center within twenty years and that more than 100,000 workers per day would have to commute into the county. It also found that the total development projected by all local governments would bring the road system to gridlock well before the end of the twenty-year planning period. The state and county planned for continued road construction, but each of the municipal governments developing its own plans assumed that it could consume as much of that road capacity as it wished; although the development projected by each local government fell within the capacity of the planned road system, the total demand from all of the local governments would have far exceeded the capacity of that system. Roads are not the only issue of concern; local governments in that same county wound up before the U.S. Supreme Court in the 1970s, arguing over the allocation of sewage treatment capacity.

That county is not particularly unique. Examining in depth the development trends and long-range plans of local governments in suburban counties in many major metropolitan areas would identify similar issues and concerns. The problems are even more complex than that, however.

Infrastructure is a major factor. Logically, infrastructure should function as a system, serving a region. Planning for federally funded highways generally occurs on a regional level, but planning for most local and some state roads remains relatively provincial, creating effective networks of roads within particular jurisdictions but lacking logical connections for the region. Sewer systems typically serve the units of local government that own them, rather than the drainage basins that geographers and engineers would suggest as their logical service areas. In some metropolitan areas, competing water systems serve areas that interlock like pieces of a jigsaw puzzle. Although fire departments in some metropolitan areas cooperate under "mutual aid" agreements, it is not uncommon for a fire department to arrive at a fire, discover that it is in another city, and simply notify that city of the fire, rather than trying to fight it.

Clearly, building multiple, overlapping, and often competing infrastructure systems in a metropolitan area is expensive. It is usually cheaper to build one large system than several small ones. With good operating practices, it is also cheaper to operate one large system. Some small cities and towns have discovered that it has become very expensive to operate their sewage systems, because the effect of current state and federal environmental regulations is to require essentially full-time monitoring of the system. For a city of 100,000 to keep a qualified operator on duty overnight is not a large per-user burden, but for eight cities of 12,000 people each to keep an operator on duty overnight is obviously eight times as expensive and costs eight times as much per user.

Land use and planning are certainly part of the equation. Some cities have incorporated or annexed territory to provide better planning and zoning than advocates believed the county offered to them. In states with local-option licensing for alcoholic beverages, people have incorporated cities or towns simply to be able to permit, or deny, such licenses in a jurisdiction with which they disagreed. Some local governments place their least desirable land uses on their borders, sharing the negative impacts of salvage yards or heavy industry with another city or an adjoining county. Regulation in counties is sometimes more liberal than in cities; in such cases, it is fairly common to find an array of bars, adult entertainment establishments, pawn shops, and other urban-oriented but sometimes unpopular uses located right on the border of the more restrictive city.

Local governments within a metropolitan area often compete in ways that seem to make sense from the perspective of each local government but do not serve the region well. Competition often centers around potential tax revenue. Many local governments depend heavily on property taxes and thus seek high-value uses like industries and office buildings. In states with local sales taxes, shopping malls, discount stores, and other retail outlets are fiscally desirable land uses. The local governments in the Illinois county described above all wanted industry, undoubtedly because of the potential tax revenue; the most likely scenario for the county is that there will be far less industrial development than the amount for which the communities have individually planned and they will thus compete for it. It is very difficult to plan the road and infrastructure network to serve the county, however, when the communities within it lack a commonly accepted plan showing where new industry, shopping, and employment centers ought to go.

Sometimes the competition within a metropolitan area is simply for land, particularly in those states with relatively liberal annexation laws. Cities sometimes annex territory that they do not need and have no plans to serve simply to keep other cities from grabbing the same land. In some states, cities can (and do) annex a narrow finger of land that involves little obligation on the part of the city but creates a boundary that blocks annexation attempts by another city. Competition for land can lead to annexation of land wildly in excess of the current needs of the city and even further in excess of its ability to provide services in the foreseeable future.

Cities or counties with good plans may establish growth areas or other development priorities. A city can encourage development in designated growth areas by annexing the territory and extending roads and sewer and water service to it. Equally important, that same city can discourage growth on steep slopes, on prime agricultural lands, in wetlands, or along a scenic seashore by refusing either to annex or to provide services to such areas. Where that city is the only city and the only service provider in the region, those tools can be very powerful. In a metropolitan region consisting of a number of cities and counties, however, another city, or even a county, may provide the essential services to an area in which the well-planned city wanted to discourage growth. Understanding that principle sometimes leads a city to annex territory that it does not want developed, because it believes that only with full local planning control can it protect the land; unfortunately, as discussed in chapter 12, the act of annexation often leads to both political and legal pressures to develop the new territory.

When people say Denver, most of them mean the metropolitan area that includes Westminster, Aurora, and Greenwood Village. When people say Chicago, they usually think of an area that runs along Lake Michigan from Indiana almost to Wisconsin and extends several miles to the south and west. However, for reasons outlined in this section, and for many others, the most logical way to plan for the future of Dallas, Des Moines, Denver, and Durham is to plan for the entire region of which each is a part.

Regional Planning in the United States

Purists, theorists, and political (and planning) novices sometimes suggest that the real solution to the planning issues raised above and to fundamental issues of the efficiency of government is to consolidate the local governments in a metropolitan region. The question of whether that is desirable is beyond the scope of this book, because it is not a likely scenario. Nashville and Indianapolis are the only contemporary examples that even approach that model; and neither of those included the entire region, and the Indianapolis model is far from a complete consolidation.

People are simply too attached to their local governments to give them up easily. Even if advocates sold a majority of the people in a region on the merits of regional government, selling them on the idea of giving up their own local government—with its local police and fire departments and local zoning authority—would be far more difficult. Leaders or interested citizens may still pursue that model in selected regions. It is certainly an alternative worthy of consideration in a particular community but one not likely to find wide enough acceptance that it is worthy of further discussion here.

Thus, the rest of this chapter examines some of the approaches to regional planning used in the United States today. Most require voluntary cooperation among local governments to be effective, and a handful of state laws mandate such cooperation, at least for specific local governments or under particular circumstances. The discussion below moves from the traditional, voluntary models to some with more force.

Regional Planning under the Model Acts

Comprehensive planning, zoning, and subdivision controls all evolved from model enabling acts developed in the 1920s and then widely published and adopted as the basic framework for planning law in all the states. Those model acts included provisions for regional planning. Like the rest of the acts, however, those provisions were entirely voluntary and basically encouraged intergovernmental cooperation.[2]

Regional Plan Association

The New York metropolitan region has a long history of regional planning through a process facilitated by a private entity with no official role in government, the Regional Plan Association.

Note that the provisions in the model enabling acts do not provide adequate authority for true regional planning in New York, Washington, or Philadelphia, because all of those metropolitan regions cross state lines and the respective enabling acts are effective only within the boundaries of the states that have adopted them.

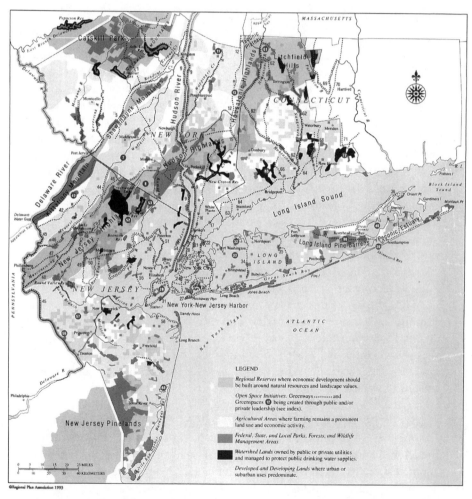

The Regional Plan Association has recently completed its third regional plan for the New York–New Jersey–Connecticut metropolitan area. Copyright 1993 by the Regional Plan Association. Used with permission.

Intergovernmental Agreements

Many states have laws permitting local governments to enter into contracts with other local governments to cooperate in carrying out a variety of governmental functions. These laws typically allow cooperation in providing services of all kinds and are often used as a basis for cooperation in building sewer and water plants and in providing fire protection services, either directly or through mutual aid agreements. Many of the laws are broad enough to allow local governments to plan jointly, but few would extend far enough to allow local governments to merge their regulatory implementation—such an approach would require special legislation in almost all states.

In a variation on this approach, some states specifically allow counties and cities within them to form joint city-county planning commissions. Typically, such joint commissions provide the planning and advisory functions of a planning commission to both the county and the participant cities, with each of those jurisdictions otherwise maintaining separate structures of local government. Charlotte and Mecklenburg County in North Carolina and Muncie and Delaware County in Indiana are two examples of communities with such combined planning commissions but entirely separate local governments. Both share planning staffs.

Federal Requirements and Incentives

Congress has recognized the value of regional planning and sometimes included in federal funding programs requirements for some sort of regional planning.

During the 1970s and into the 1980s, the federal government provided extensive funding for the construction of local sewage treatment plants. All of the programs required a long-range service and facilities plan for the entire service area of the entity receiving the funding. For several years late in the 1970s, the federal government also provided funding for the development of regional plans for the management and treatment of sewage. Unfortunately, many of the individual facility plans preceded the regional plans for the same area, limiting the effectiveness of the regional plans in some areas. The program, nevertheless, led to some excellent, environmentally based regional plans.

The federal government provides billions of dollars for construction and upgrading of the interstate and federal-aid highway system, which includes most of the major, non-toll highways in the country. One of the conditions of receiving funding for projects in metropolitan areas is the existence of a metropolitan-wide transportation plan, to be developed by a designated metropolitan planning organization, often just called an MPO.

Georgia's Regional Development Commissions

Georgia created an interesting variation on the traditional, voluntary model of regional planning. Under a state law passed in 1989, it created the authority

for "regional development commissions." Although those commissions significantly resemble traditional regional planning commissions, the law shifts the
emphasis from "planning" to planning for "development," with particular reference to economic development.[3]

The difference between the Georgia law and many others is that it
requires that every local government belong to a regional development commission; but, unlike laws in a handful of states such as Oregon, the Georgia law
does not specify which regional development commission a particular local
government must join. Although a local government near the center of a
region clearly must join the commission for that region, local governments on
the border have a choice. The concept increases the apparent local autonomy
and is an approach that many local governments may find more attractive than
a no-choice model, although the differences are small.

Tennessee Mandates County-Wide Plans

In 1998, Tennessee adopted a law that requires local governments to cooperate in planning at a county level.[4] Basically, the Tennessee law established a
"sphere of influence" around municipalities, protecting them from annexations by other municipalities or incorporations of new ones within that territory.

What is more important to the discussion here is that the law set a tight
deadline by which all local governments in the state had to enter into county-
wide growth plans, designating areas that will develop, areas that will be held
in reserve for future growth, and areas that will remain rural. If local governments within a county are unable to agree on such a county-wide plan, they
will lose state funding for roads and other infrastructure, a financial risk that
few local governments in the country would take.

Municipal Planning and Zoning beyond Municipal Boundaries

Several states grant municipal governments some planning and regulatory
authority beyond municipal boundaries. There are several variations on this
technique:

- *Extraterritorial subdivision regulation* allows municipal governments to regulate
  subdivisions within a specified distance of the city limits. The logic underlying such laws is that since most subdivisions near a city will probably
  become part of the city, it thus makes sense to have the city, rather than the
  county, regulate the design and construction of subdivision improvements
  for which the city is likely to have long-term responsibility.
- *Extraterritorial zoning regulation* allows municipal governments to use zoning
  to regulate land use within a specified distance of the city limits. The foundation for this law rests in concerns that counties may fail to zone or may
  have relatively loose zoning that allows the accumulation of undesirable or
  unpopular uses along the municipal boundary.

- *Conditional extraterritorial zoning regulation* gives a city extraterritorial zoning control only if the surrounding county does not have zoning at the time that the city decides to adopt the control. Under some models, the county may supersede municipal regulation by adopting its own zoning controls, but, under others, the city controls remain in place once adopted.
- *Sphere of influence* laws allow a city to prevent the formation of a new city or the annexation of territory by a competing city within a specified distance of the city limits. Such a law eliminates both the need and the opportunity for most "defensive annexations" of the type described previously.

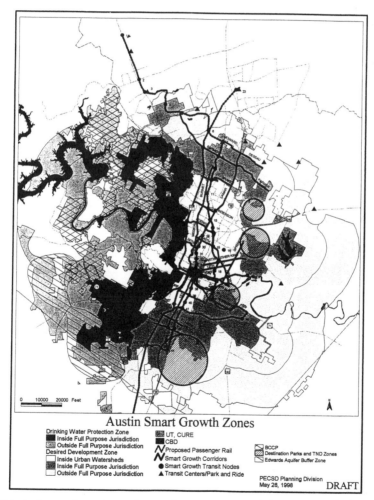

This draft map shows the city limits of Austin, Texas, and the area over which it has xtraterritorial land-use authority. Source: Planning, Environmental and Conservation Services Department, City of Austin, February 1999; available on the Web at http:// www.ci.austin.tx.us/smarthgrowth/images/smarthgrowthmaplg.jpg.

There are variations on all of these techniques, and some states allow the use of more than one of them. Most are accompanied by some related planning authority. They reflect the evolutionary pattern of local government, acknowledging that municipal governments are in some sense the preferred form of local government. The laws recognize both the need for these preferred governments to control their destiny beyond their borders and their power to exercise authority on land that otherwise falls within the jurisdiction of another local government.

Areas of State Concern

A model law developed in the 1950s by the American Law Institute (ALI) proposed a new planning and regulatory structure for local and state governments to use in dealing with land-use issues.[5] Although no states have adopted the entire model and it has had far less impact than the model planning and zoning legislation of the 1920s, one part of it has drawn more attention than the rest—that is the concept of "areas of critical state concern." Although there has been periodic interest in a strong state and even a national role in land-use planning, the focus of land-use regulations in most states remains at the local level.[6] The ALI model recognized this preference for local control and placed most powers and duties at that level. One of the powers that it placed at the state level, however, was the power to designate areas of particular concern. The theory was to allow each state to establish its own criteria for making those determinations and to designate its own areas of concern.

The law provided for special regulation around major new public facilities (such as highway interchanges); significant environmental, historic, or natural resources; sites of new towns; or land within the jurisdiction of a local government that has no land-use regulations in effect.[7] The effect of the state designation does not shift the regulatory responsibility for the area but simply forces the local government to adopt special regulations, addressing the issues identified in the state action designating the area. This model has served as the basis of laws adopted in Florida, Colorado, Connecticut, and Maryland and has probably had more influence than any other part of the model code.[8]

Developments of Regional Impact

Also originating in the ALI model code is the concept of "developments of regional impact."[9] Working from the basic belief that most control should be local, the drafters of the model code recognized that facilities like large shopping centers, sports stadiums, and other major traffic attractors have an impact far beyond the borders of any particular local government. Thus, the model code mandated a regional review process—still emphasizing local control—for such large-scale developments. Although not as widely adopted as the provisions regarding areas of critical state concern, this part of the model serves as the basis for parts of the state law in Florida and New Hampshire.[10] As in the concept for areas of state concern, final land-use control remains with the local government, but local regulations for such projects are subject to state review, and the project itself must undergo a regional review process.[11]

Special Laws for Special Places

Several states have built on the model of areas of state concern but have designated such areas and created control schemes for them through direct legislation. Examples include: the Pinelands area in New Jersey, which includes a great deal of privately owned, environmentally sensitive land west of Atlantic City; the Adirondack Park in New York, a large area in east-central New York State, including a combination of public park and private land; and the Tahoe region surrounding Lake Tahoe, which is actually the subject of an interstate compact between California and Nevada.[12] All three of these programs involve powerful regional agencies that preempt or override many local land use controls; all involve land-use policies that are a good deal more restrictive than typical local land-use controls.

Cross-Acceptance in New Jersey

New Jersey's state legislature developed an elegant solution to the problem of regional planning. In addition to making local planning mandatory, it required that the more than seven hundred municipal governments in New Jersey each obtain "cross-acceptance" of their own plans from adjoining local governments and others likely to be affected by those plans. At first consideration, local officials of City A may be horrified at the idea that City B could veto its plan—but the elegance of the system is in the fact that City A could also veto City B's plan. Thus, they need each other and must work together on issues of mutual interest. That leads to a kind of grassroots regional planning that addresses some of the governance issues inherent in other discussions of the subject.

Tax-Base Sharing in Minnesota

One of the major issues that leads to regional land-use conflicts is that of tax base. In states where local governments depend heavily on the property tax, those governments compete to attract large industries. Because industries typically involve a great deal of investment in facilities (resulting in large property tax collections) and generate no students, they are extremely attractive fiscally—both to local governments and to schools. In states where local governments can levy sales taxes, shopping centers and big-box retailers represent major fiscal benefits to local governments, although not to schools. At the other end of the spectrum are large apartments, which often have relatively low value for tax purposes and may house many children, which places a fiscal burden on local schools. Thus, it is not unusual in a metropolitan area to find local governments competing for industry and shopping centers and reluctant to take apartments and other types of affordable housing.

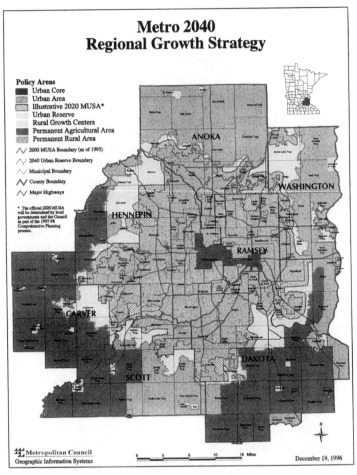

The Minneapolis–St. Paul, Minnesota, metropolitan area has a long history of regional planning, of which the tax-base sharing program is a part. MUSA in the legend stands for "metropolitan urban service area," which is the Metropolitan Council's designation for its growth area. Source: *Metropolitan Council (1998).*

Minnesota has addressed that issue directly through a program of tax-base sharing in the Twin Cities (Minneapolis and St. Paul) metropolitan area. The program, called *metropolitan revenue distribution,* spreads property tax revenues from industry in the seven-county metropolitan area among local governments based on a formula; that formula retains reasonable incentives for local governments to want industry but shares the benefits among the many local governments that provide housing and other public and private facilities that directly or indirectly support the industrial development.

A Note on Larger Regions

Certainly the issues that affect planning go beyond even a metropolitan region. There have been eloquent arguments for regional planning at a much larger scale, perhaps including multiple states.[13] Although there are strong geographical and environmental arguments in favor of such an approach, the political odds against a kind of planning that would affect multiple states seem overwhelming at this time. A true national approach to planning of this type was last considered in the 1960s and has not been presented as a serious alternative since. Some conceived the Tennessee Valley Authority, now best known as a provider of electric power, as a model for a strong regional agency that would plan and promote the region and invest in the development of its resources.[14]

If one were writing a briefing paper for a member of Congress on issues in planning, broad-scale regional planning would be an important issue to address. In a textbook focused on planning practice as it exists in the United States, it is not a topic that justifies much space because it does not exist in this country in any effective sense.

Conclusion

The patterns of development that affect people's lives are regional. Conducting local planning in some ways misses the point. The issues occur at many levels. One community may dump its heaviest traffic or major stormwater outfalls on another community. A county may allow undesirable land uses to sprout up along the city limits, perhaps next to nice residential neighborhoods. A major thoroughfare in the city may not connect with one elsewhere in the county. A new mall or strip commercial development in one community may siphon activity from the downtown of another. Cities may engage in virtual wars over the annexation of territory or the capture of new industry or business likely to generate significant tax revenue.

Only in the context of effective regional planning can local planning make much sense. Regional planning in much of the United States remains entirely voluntary, but it is essential. Accomplishing it is a political challenge.

The Role of the Professional Planner

Where there is any interest in (or mandate for) regional planning, the professional planner plays an essential role in facilitating and providing technical support for such a plan. The process itself is very similar to that described in the front part of the book for an individual community, but it is made more complex by the number of entities involved.

Where there is no official commitment to regional planning, the professional planner can do the next best thing, which is to gather the kind of information that would be used in a regional plan. With that information, the planner can inform local decision makers about activities in surrounding communities and how those will affect their own community. In addition, the planner can alert public officials to major proposed actions in adjoining communities, encouraging those officials to consider contacting the decision makers in those other jurisdictions. If the public officials are not interested, the media may be.

Finally, at some levels, professional planners can coordinate plans among jurisdictions, even without official sanction. Although public officials decide the locations of major roads, for example, planners in adjoining communities can cooperate to ensure that roads line up as well as possible and that there is some consistency among plans for other infrastructure investment.

The Role of the Individual Citizen

Because they can step back and consider the big picture and are not bogged down in the day-to-day concerns of government, citizens sometimes have a better grasp of regional issues than do public officials of individual local governments. In that role, citizens can lobby to make regional planning happen.

EXERCISES

1. Do you live in a metropolitan region? If so, how many cities, towns, and counties are part of that region? Do all of them have plans? Is there a regional plan? Do local plans conform to that regional plan? Do local plans fit together into any kind of logical whole?

2. If you do not live in a metropolitan region, how many other local governments make decisions that would seem to affect your community directly? Do all of them have plans? Is there a regional plan?

3. Are one or two communities dominating the new development activity in your region? Can you determine why? Look at recent infrastructure investments in the region. What other issues might influence that pattern?

4. Go to the library or talk to the local planning office to see if there has

ever been a regional plan for your region—many were funded by federal and state agencies in the 1970s. If you can get a copy, see if it still seems like a good plan. Is it better than what has happened?

Discussion Questions

Why is there not more regional planning in this country and/or in your community? What are the arguments that local officials might make against regional planning? What arguments might individual citizens make against regional planning? Who would create the regional plan? Who would ensure that local governments followed it?

Further Reading

Branch, Melville C. 1988. *Regional Planning: Introduction and Explanation.* Westport, CT: Praeger Publishers. A classic work by a leader in the field.

Buchsbaum, Peter A., and Larry J. Smith. 1993. *State & Regional Comprehensive Planning: Implementing New Methods for Growth Management.* Chicago: American Bar Association, Section of Urban, State & Local Government Law. A collection of essays about successful regional planning efforts in selected regions in the United States, with one Canadian example.

Rothblatt, Donald N., and Andrew Sancton, eds. 1993. *Metropolitan Governance Perspectives: American/Canadian Intergovernmental Perspectives.* Berkeley: University of California Press. An examination of the broader issues involved in metropolitan areas, issues that regional planning alone can only partially address.

Rusk, David. 1993. *Cities without Suburbs.* Baltimore: Woodrow Wilson Center/Johns Hopkins University Press. An excellent study of the differences between cities without suburbs—cities that are essentially their own regions—and similarly sized regions consisting of multiple communities.

Notes

1. Bureau of the Census, 1990 Census of Population, Table STF1, P004; percentage calculations by author.
2. Standard City Planning Enabling Act, Title IV, "Regional Planning and Planning Commissions," Washington, DC: Department of Commerce (1928).
3. For summaries of state land-use laws, including this one, see chapter 53 in Eric Damian Kelly, ed., *Zoning and Land Use Controls,* New York: Matthew Bender (1998), 10 vols. For an early description of the Georgia program, see chapter 7, "A Growth Strategy for Georgia: Consensus-Building at Its Best" in John M. DeGrove, *The New Frontier for Growth Policy: Planning and Growth Management in the States,* Cambridge, MA: Lincoln Institute for Land Policy (1992).
4. Tennessee *Acts 1998, ch. 1101,* codified at Tenn. Code Ann. §§6-58-101, *et seq.* (1998).
5. American Law Institute, *A Model Land Development Code,* Washington, DC: Amer-

ican Law Institute (1975), with an introduction by Alison Dunham, chief reporter; hereinafter called ALI.

6. See, for example, Fred Bosselman and David Callies, *The Quiet Revolution in Land Use Control,* Washington, DC: Council on Environmental Quality (1971). This landmark work examined current state activity in land-use planning and regulation and suggested a trend that has evolved far more slowly than the authors—and many others—anticipated at that time.

7. See ALI, note 5, §7-201.

8. For summaries of state land-use laws, including these, see chapter 53 in Kelly, note 2.

9. See ALI, note 5, §7-301.

10. For summaries of state land-use laws, including these, see chapter 53 in Kelly, note 2.

11. See ALI, note 5, §§7-203-204.

12. For summaries of state land-use laws, including these, see chapter 53 in Kelly, note 3; for descriptions of the Pinelands and Adirondack Park, see, generally, Douglas Porter, ed., *Growth Management: Keeping on Target?* Washington, DC: Urban Land Institute (1986).

13. See, for example, Melville C. Branch, *Regional Planning: Introduction and Explanation,* Westport, CT: Praeger Publishers (1988); and Benton Mackaye, *The New Exploration: A Philosophy of Regional Planning,* Urbana: University of Illinois Press (1962).

14. See Arthur E. Morgan, *The Making of the TVA,* Buffalo, NY: Prometheus Books (1974); and Julian Huxley, *TVA: An Adventure in Planning,* Cheam, England: Surrey Architectural Press (1943).

Chapter 15

Preserving Open Space

Preservation of open space today is a major priority of many local governments. The National Recreation and Parks Association, which once published guidelines for parks and recreation, now publishes *Park, Recreation, Open Space and Greenway Guidelines*.[1] The Urban Land Institute, a membership organization serving primarily major land developers, in 1997 published a major book, *Urban Parks and Open Space*.

The emphasis of such planning was once on formal parks and areas suitable for such active recreation uses as softball, soccer, tennis, and picnicking. Federal Works Progress Administration and Civilian Conservation Corps projects during the depression added many such formal parks to cities around the country. Those parks are often recognizable by the use of local fieldstone and other native materials in the construction of walls, buildings, shelters, and other facilities. Planners once recommended a typical community standard of ten acres of park for every thousand residents of the community.[3]

Parks remain important. The National Recreation and Park Association recommends that local governments develop level-of-service standards (a concept discussed in more detail in chapter 12, under "Adequate Public Facilities Controls") for different levels of parks, including mini-parks, neighborhood parks, community parks, and regional parks. The guidelines also recognize the importance of other types of open space and greenways. A 1996 plan for Ames, Iowa, calls for five acres of park land for every thousand residents and an additional five acres of "woodlands/open space" for every thousand residents.[4]

Classification of Parks and Open Space

Table 15.1 shows the classifications of parks, greenways, and open spaces published by the National Recreation and Park Association in 1996. This table provides a general description, location and size criteria, and level of

Table 15.1. Classification of Parks, Open Spaces, and Pathways

PARKS AND OPEN-SPACE CLASSIFICATIONS

Classification	General Description	Location Criteria	Size Criteria	Application of LOS
Mini-Park	Used to address limited, isolated, or unique recreational needs.	Less than a 1/4-mile distance in residential setting.	Between 2,500 sq. ft. and 1 acre.	Yes
Neighborhood Park	Neighborhood park remains the basic unit of the park system and serves as the recreational and social focus of the neighborhood. Focus is on informal active and passive recreation	1/4- to 1/2-mile distance and uninterrupted by nonresidential roads or other physical barriers.	5 acres is considered minimum size. 5 to 10 acres is optimal.	Yes
School Park	Depending on circumstances, combining parks with school sites can fulfill the space requirements for other classes of parks, such as neighborhood, community, sports complex, and special use.	Determined by location of school district property.	Variable, depends on function.	Yes, but should not count school-only uses.
Community Park	Serves broader purpose than neighborhood park. Focus is on meeting community-based recreation needs, as well as preserving unique landscapes and open spaces.	Determined by the quality and suitability of the site. Usually serves two or more neighborhoods and 1/2- to 3-mile distance.	As needed to accommodate desired uses. Usually between 30 to 50 acres.	Yes
Large Urban Park	Large urban parks serve a broader purpose than community parks and are used when community and neighborhood parks are not adequate to serve the needs of the community. Focus is on meeting community-based recreational needs, as well as preserving unique landscapes and open spaces.	Determined by the quality and suitability of the site. Usually serves the entire community.	As needed to accommodate desired uses. Usually a minimum of 50 acres, 75 or more acres being optimal.	Yes

Natural Resource Areas	Lands set aside for preservation of significant natural resources, remnant landscapes, open space, and visual aesthetics and buffering.	Resource availability and opportunity.	Variable.	No
Greenways	Effectively tie park system components together to form a continuous park environment.	Resource availability and opportunity.	Variable.	No
Sports Complex	Consolidates heavily programmed athletic fields and associated facilities to larger and fewer sites strategically located throughout the community.	Strategically located community-wide facilities.	Determined by projected demand. Usually a minimum of 25 acres, 40 to 80 acres being optimal.	Yes
Special Use	Covers a broad range of parks and recreation facilities oriented toward single-purpose use.	Variable, depends on specific use.	Variable.	Depends on type of use.
Private Park/ Recreation Facility	Parks and recreation facilities that are privately owned yet contribute to the public park and recreation system.	Variable, depends on specific use.	Variable.	Depends on type of use.

PATHWAY CLASSIFICATIONS

Classification	General Description	Description of Each Type	Application of LOS
Park Trail	Multipurpose trails located within greenways, parks, and natural resource areas. Focus is on recreational value and harmony with natural environment.	Type I: Separate or single-purpose, hard-surfaced trails for pedestrians or bicyclists and in-line skaters. Type II: Multipurpose hard-surfaced trails for pedestrians, bicyclists, and in-line skaters. Type III: Nature trails for pedestrians. May be hard of soft surfaced.	Not Applicable.

(continues)

Table 15.1. Continued

PATHWAY CLASSIFICATIONS

Classification	General Desciprtion	Description of Each Type	Application of LOS
Connector Trails	Multipurpose trails that emphasize safe travel for pedestrians to and from parks and around the community. Focus is as much on transportation as it is on recreation.	Type 1: Separately or single-purpose, hard-surfaced trails for pedestrians or bicyclists and in-line skaters *located in independent r.o.w.* (e.g., old railroad r.o.w.). Type II: Separately or single-purpose, hard-surfaced trails for pedestrians or bicyclists and in-line skaters *typically located within road r.o.w.*	Not Applicable.
On-Street Bikeways	Paved segments of roadways that serve as a means to safely separate bicyclists from vehicular traffic.	Bike Route: Designated portions of the roadway for the preferential or exclusive use of bicyclists. Bike Lane: Shared portions of the roadway that provide separation between motor vehicles and bicyclists, such as paved shoulders.	Not Applicable.
All-Terrain Bike Trail	Off-road trail for all-terrain (mountain) bikes.	Single-purpose loop trails usually located in larger parks and natural resource areas.	Not Applicable.
Cross-Country Ski Trail	Trails developed for traditional and skate-style cross-country skiing.	Loop trails usually located in larger parks and natural resource areas.	Not Applicable.
Equestrian Trail	Trails developed for horseback riding.	Loop trails usually located in larger parks and natural resource areas. Sometimes developed as multipurpose with hiking and all-terrain biking where conflicts can be controlled.	Not Applicable.

Note: LOS = level of service, r.o.w. = right-of-way
Source: James D. Mertes and James R. Hall, Washington, DC: National Recreational and Park Association (1996), pp. 94–95. Copyright 1996 National Recreation and Park Association. Used with permission.

service for these lands. A more general classification of those lands would include:

- recreation structures (swimming pools, community recreation centers, sports arenas);
- open space for active recreation (including ball fields, playing courts, picnic areas);
- open space for formal but passive recreation (traditional formal parks);
- open space for informal or natural active recreation areas (primarily hiking and biking trails in greenways);
- natural areas, not for recreation (undeveloped greenways, undeveloped nature preserves, wetlands); and
- linkages in the system, with or without significant open space (trail linkages along streets or sidewalks, connecting other parts of the open-space and greenway system).

Note that there are two other ways to think about these separate parts of an open-space and recreation system: by ownership and access; and by general physical character. These lands may include lands in private ownership as well as in public ownership. Some land in private ownership may allow public access (certain nature preserves or greenways in some subdivisions are examples), and some land in public ownership may prohibit or limit public access (wetlands are a common example).

In general physical character, these lands fall into three general categories:

- Covered with buildings or other improvements (note that swimming pools and tennis courts, although often open to the air, remove the natural character of the land);
- open but covered with formal, human-designed plantings that are often not native (typical formal parks); and
- natural or relatively natural (wetlands, forests, and many greenways).

The different character of the land responds to different needs. Swimmers and tennis players generally prefer courts and pools built by humans to accepted design standards. Soccer and baseball players happily use grass and open lands, but they want level land without trees, bushes, and other obstructions to running and ball playing. Bicyclists and hikers typically want improved trails (although runners and mountain bikers may accept or even prefer unpaved ones), but those trails can go through land that can otherwise be either natural or improved. Few users care who owns the land they use, provided that they can gain access to it without significant cost. A local government, which must pay the costs of acquiring and building public parks, typically welcomes the additions of private open space and recreation facilities to the local system.

The accompanying figure shows the neighborhood and community parks in Ames, Iowa, in 1995, along with their respective service areas. This map does

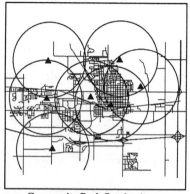
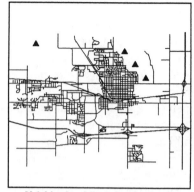

Community Park Service Areas   **Neighborhood Park Service Areas**

These two maps show the existing community and neighborhood parks in Ames, Iowa, with their respective service areas. Source: *"Land Use Policy Plan," City of Ames and RM Plan Group, Nashville (1996).*

not reflect all open space in the community, which includes the large campus of Iowa State University, much of which is open, and its significant agricultural land holdings around the city. The terms used in these different classification systems vary somewhat, but the principles are very similar. All of them function on some combination of the nature and use of the land.

All of this discussion ignores one form of open space that many suburban residents prize, and that is agricultural land. Much of the attraction of the suburbs is the perception of adjacent open space. Much of the concern about "sprawl" today is as much about the perceived loss of the open-space buffer around the city as it is about the character of the development that replaces it. The preservation of agricultural land is often an important issue to urban and suburban residents who have little knowledge of what grows on that land or how it affects the local economy. People simply value the aesthetic and apparent environmental contributions that the agrarian border provides to the urban area.

The quantity of agricultural land is shrinking, particularly around urban areas. According to the U.S. Department of Agriculture, from 1982 to 1992 the nation lost 38,600,000 acres of cropland, 6,000,000 acres of pasture, and 10,000,000 acres of rangeland.[5] That amounts to a total of more than 71,000 square miles of land in just that ten-year period. In most regions of the country, more than two-thirds of the land lost from agriculture was converted to residential use, with 14 to 18 percent going to commercial use and small amounts to recreation, transportation, and other uses. In the region including the upper Great Plains and northern Rocky Mountains (Montana, the Dakotas, Wyoming, Nebraska, Colorado, and Kansas), 37 percent of the lost agricul-

Richard Hedman on agricultural land as open space. Copyright by Richard Hedman.
Used with permission.

tural land was converted to transportation use; in those states, the only significant form of transportation construction is for highways.[6]

Farmers and other rural landowners are not always as enthusiastic as urban residents about preserving agricultural land, particularly in areas where there is significant development pressure. Like anyone else with a valuable asset, a farmer who can choose between selling land at $2,000 per acre for use as a farm or $20,000 (or more) per acre for development is likely to prefer the higher price. Many farmers consider their land their pension plan, expecting to retire on revenues from its sale. Although some farmers may choose to keep farming, it is unrealistic for urban and suburban residents to expect farmers to provide open-space buffers around communities without some form of compensation or other incentive to do so.

Community Needs and Perspectives

A 1998 planning document of the City of Stillwater, Oklahoma, representing the conclusions of community-wide participation in development of a new plan has eleven well-focused goals, two of which generally address issues related to recreation and open space.[7] Under the heading "Visually Appealing Community," the document states a broad general principle, followed by one specific goal and a total of a dozen objectives:

> Our vision for Stillwater involves the ideal of a physically attractive community through better design, integration with the natural environment and property maintenance. In enhancing our ideal, we

further envision visually appealing gateways that provide a sense of arrival and wayfinding.

Goal No. 1: Our goal for Stillwater involves being a *steward of a visually appealing environment.*

Under the heading "Community Linked through Education, Recreation, Neighborhoods and Commercial Services," there are two goals, one of which refers directly to open-space issues.

Our vision for Stillwater involves the ideal of a well-connected community that includes linkages for educational and recreational provisions, neighborhoods and commercial services. Our ideal also includes linking people through these provisions.

Goal No. 1: Our vision for Stillwater is *an open space greenway/park system linking community components such as neighborhoods, Downtown, OSU [Oklahoma State University] arboretum and equine center, outlying lakes and creeks.*

Some of the specific objectives in the Stillwater plan illustrate the broad concerns with open space. In reviewing these, it is important to remember that these evolved from a citizen participation process that included elements of issue identification followed by goal setting.

Objectives relevant to open space that were included under the "Visually Appealing Community" heading are as follows:

- Stillwater seeks to identify arrival within the community by establishing gateways and related design improvements.
- Stillwater needs to create an integrated corridor appearance in conjunction with gateways through the use of tree-lined streets, uniform signage, and street furniture.
- Stillwater seeks unified entries and tree-lined corridors.

Under the second goal listed above, that refers directly to recreation, there are the following objectives pertinent to recreation and open space:

- Stillwater seeks to provide community-wide pathways that link parks, schools, water bodies, open space, cultural centers, and trails.
- Stillwater seeks to link its streamways, natural resources, and other environmentally sensitive areas in creating a community-wide greenway system.
- Stillwater seeks to expand its types of parks to include a large citywide recreational area and nature center.
- Stillwater seeks to promote the inclusion of private provisions for recreation and open space in new development through zoning and design incentives.

- Stillwater seeks to provide parks as community gathering places through the use of facilities and activities that are targeted toward user preference and through increased accessibility.
- Stillwater seeks to provide places for youth to gather through the use of facilities and activities that are targeted toward user preference and through increased accessibility.
- Stillwater seeks to improve recreational opportunities for the elderly and persons with disabilities through enhanced facilities and activities and through increased accessibility.

Under the general heading of "transportation" are two more objectives for Stillwater that relate to open space:

- Stillwater seeks to provide a recreational trail system within appropriate greenways that is compatible with pedestrian, biking, and elderly/disabled activities.
- Stillwater seeks to provide a bikeways system utilizing designated streets and specially designed bikeways to serve leisure and work/school commuting activities.

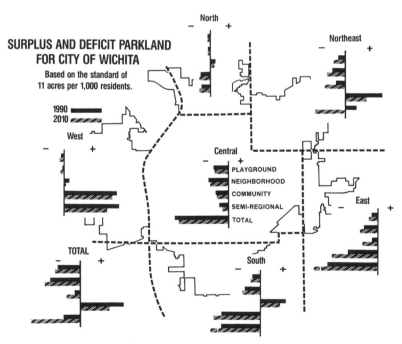

This bar chart shows how seven separate sectors of the Wichita, Kansas, area measure up to a designated level of service of eleven acres of parkland per thousand residents. Source: *Metropolitan Area Planning Department (1993).*

- Stillwater seeks to provide sidewalk and other pedestrian improvements within neighborhoods, within appropriate activity centers, and that link these neighborhoods and activity centers.
- Stillwater seeks to link recreational trails, bikeways, and sidewalks in creating an integrated, community-wide system.

Every community is different, but the Stillwater planning effort is interesting because it identifies such a broad range of community interests in open space. Stillwater has had relatively slow growth, which may be a reason there is no reference to the preservation of agricultural land or creation of an open-space buffer around the community.

The Value of Open Space

The most obvious and traditional public purpose of open space in a community is to serve the active and passive recreation needs of the community. That is the purpose of public parks. The tradition of public parks in this nation is a long one, with historic parks like the Fenway in Boston, Central Park in New York, and Fairmont Park in Philadelphia providing classic and historic examples. Note that the historic definition of parks as part of the open-space system has included paved areas such as playing courts and even streets within the park. The traditional focus was on recreation and public use rather than on the character of the land.

Open space serves many other purposes for a community. As the excerpts from the Stillwater plan suggest, some of those are purely aesthetic. People like looking at open space. It serves as a buffer between developments and between communities. It provides a green break in a densely populated community. It varies the urban skyline, interrupting blocks of buildings with trees and open spaces. Manhattan Island has a very different character with Central Park dominating its center than it would have without that important open space. Further, the excerpts from the Stillwater plan suggest the importance of open space in providing linkages among parts of the community. The Ames, Iowa, plan also included provisions for:

> a greenway system that encompasses portions of environmentally sensitive areas. These streamways and natural resources are recommended for protection and use as passive recreational areas. Linking them together with the City's existing parks and open space creates a greenway system serving the entire community.[8]

The statement from the Ames plan identifies two other purposes of open-space preservation: one is to use the open-space system as a context for preservation of environmentally sensitive areas; the second is the creation of greenways, a topic discussed below.

In a later section of the plan, Ames identifies environmental purposes for this system of open space:

We envision a community that protects its resources, conserves its energy and recycles its products. Our environmental priorities include the following:

- Natural streamway preservation and water quality enhancement for supporting human and aquatic life;
- Stormwater run-off management through land use design and other protective measures;
- Air quality preservation through the avoidance of pollutant emitting uses;
- Energy conservation through the use of more efficiently operating transportation systems and alternative modes;
- Vegetation maintenance and enhancement for its beautification, air cleaning, water run-off reduction and climate modification qualities; and
- Natural resource areas conservation.[9]

That is a good list of environmental reasons for preserving open space, but it omits two important ones: preservation of wetlands and floodplain areas; and preservation and restoration of wildlife habitat and corridors.

Development on floodplains creates obvious hazards for the people and property located there. Further, that development in some cases impedes and in other cases accelerates the flow of floods, in both cases increasing the level of flood damage to other land, property, and people. Repeated major floods, particularly in midwestern communities, have convinced most people of the seriousness of the problem. Although there is continuing debate over the extent to which government agencies should go to force people already in floodplains to move, there is little question that preserving undeveloped floodplains in their natural state is beneficial to the community at large. Communities have traditionally treated floodplains as a negative factor in the community, where development should be avoided. Thinking of them as part of an open-space and greenway system recognizes their positive value if preserved, while addressing the negative concerns associated with development of them.

Modern approaches to managing stormwater and flooding recognize the value of wetlands as nature's sponge (see discussion in chapters 3 and 7). During a major rain, wetlands fill up, retaining much of the water that falls on them or flows into them. After the rain, they release that water gradually, serving as a sort of detention facility that mitigates the peak-flow problem that causes floods in rivers and drainage channels. That is a purely engineering value for wetlands, but wetlands have many other values to society. Perhaps most important, they contribute to biodiversity.

Planners increasingly recognize the importance of biodiversity. All living things are part of a larger system that makes up the earth. Most people recognize that plants add back to the air the oxygen that is so important to human existence, but most do not recognize the many more subtle contributions of other species to the health of the global environment on which we depend. Even scientists do not understand the complete operation of this complex system. The harm caused by the loss of biodiversity is clear, however, and many planners at all levels are concerned with trying to reduce or even reverse the loss of species. Accomplishing that requires the preservation of habitat, including such biologically diverse areas as wetlands.

Preserving habitat in isolation accomplishes little, however. Many species of animals migrate, and providing them with a summer or winter home without access is a little like providing a family a house with no road leading up to it. Greenways and natural corridors can provide the access among habitat areas and between urban habitats and rural areas (which are often rich in natural habitat) that is essential to effective planning for the preservation of wildlife. Even plants depend to some extent on migration. Many plant seeds are "designed" to be carried by the wind or by animals from one location to another, allowing the plants to spread and propagate. As with animals, there must be routes along which that plan propagation can occur.

The desire to provide trail linkages for humans, connections among habitat areas, and visually defining green linkages among parts of the community has led to a growing interest in planning for greenways. In its 1997 land-use and transportation plan, Norman, Oklahoma, set out the following policies for a new greenbelt system, policies that also reflect their purposes:

1. Use greenbelts to protect environmentally sensitive lands that are generally the least suitable for development.
2. Encourage the use of lot clustering in areas not served with sanitary sewers as a means to develop the greenbelt system.
3. Use the greenbelt system to link existing recreation areas.
4. Create a multipurpose greenbelt corridor that:
   • creates a unique greenway character for Norman;
   • protects the environmentally sensitive areas of the city and serves as a wildlife habitat;
   • serves as a stormwater management resource for urban runoff and regional detention needs;
   • provides recreation opportunities for bicycling, walking, and jogging;
   • preserves agriculturally sensitive lands; and
   • provides suitable locations for sanitary sewer easements and facilities.
5. Use greenbelts to provide open-space areas adjacent to highways and major streets for sound buffer zones and protection from incompatible land uses.

6. Develop a natural landscape planting and maintenance program for city-owned properties and rights-of-way of major streets and highways.[10]

Boulder, Colorado, has created a greenbelt of publicly controlled land around the entire city, a technique it implemented as part of its larger growth management plan. The land remains in private agricultural use. Although it serves other purposes, also, much of the purpose of the Boulder greenbelt is to define an edge to the city.[11]

Ownership and Acquisition of Open Space

Traditional parks are owned by local governments or related parks boards. Local governments can acquire public parks and other open space by purchase, gifts, or development exactions, through which developers give the city land for park expansion based on some formula related to the number of residents (and park users) the development will add to the community (exactions in general are discussed in chapter 11).

Many people think of open space as public property, but there are many other forms of open space. First, it is important to recognize that there are many forms of public property besides those owned by a local government. In a number of western states, the federal government owns from one-third to one-half of the land. Although much of that land is in mountainous and rural areas, some of it is near or even in communities. Although the federal government uses some of its land for federal purposes, other federal land is likely to remain part of an open-space system for many years. Certainly, any community located near a national park or national monument can count on that open space continuing to exist through any reasonable planning horizon.

Similarly, many state governments have parks and other public open space that help to serve the recreational needs of people in communities. A community with easy access to a state park can depend on that park to meet some of its open-space needs. State and federal agencies sometimes also own large parcels for which there are no immediate planned uses. The so-called mainstreaming of many mental health patients has left underused campuses that once housed large populations of people with mental problems at "state hospitals." Closed military bases provide another example. Although some land previously used for institutional purposes may be contaminated and may have more environmental problems than opportunities, other land associated with such institutions remains in relatively natural condition. Where such lands exist, local planners and officials ought not to assume that they will continue to remain open and unused; they ought to inquire about the possibility of acquiring parts of those lands for use as part of a public open-space system. Even where state- or federally owned lands are not ideally located for a planned greenway or park system, it is sometimes possible to arrange trades of those lands for valuable private property.

University and other campuses provide another example of valuable open lands. They may or may not be publicly owned and may or may not allow full public access for recreational purposes, but large and open campuses can serve many of the other purposes of open space. Any local planning for open space ought to recognize the significant value of this open space and evaluate the risk that some of it may be sold or built on for other institutional purposes.

An increasing number of communities benefit from a variety of private open-space preservation efforts. The Nature Conservancy acquires important natural sites around the country, and some of those are in or near cities; all are slated for long-term preservation and, in some cases, restoration. An increasing number of state organizations with similar purposes seek to acquire strategic environmental or open parcels and arrange for their long-term preservation. Many of these organizations are part of the "land trust" movement, although many different kinds of profit and nonprofit organizations actually can preserve open space and other land. A community including such privately owned open space in its plans should evaluate carefully the prospects for its long-term preservation. Where it is important to have public access to such property, as part of a trail system, for example, local planners must evaluate whether public access is now allowed and whether future public access can be denied or limited.

Modern cluster and planned unit developments often include open space. As with other forms of open space, its value to the community depends on both its nature and its location. Where the open space is internal to the project or heavily developed with playing courts and swimming pools, it may have significant value to the development but little open-space value to the community. On the other hand, some developers use (and some local regulations require that they use) clustering to keep development out of floodplains and wetlands, maintaining those valuable resources as open space. Particularly where the development plans also include greenway linkages from those resources back to the larger system of the community, such private open space can have great value to the community.

Note, however, that private greenways often do not allow general public access. Thus, a private greenway that provides an attractive visual linkage and valuable wildlife corridor may not accomplish the community's purpose of creating a community-wide trail system. A community planning a linked trail system must ensure that it obtains easements or other legal rights to extend trails through privately owned parts of the greenway system.

Publicly controlled open space need not be publicly owned in the classic sense. Today many government agencies acquire "scenic" or "conservation" easements in land. Such easements are based on the traditional concept of roadway easements, which provide person A with the right to drive (or ride or walk) across person B's land, while the person B still owns the land. Simi-

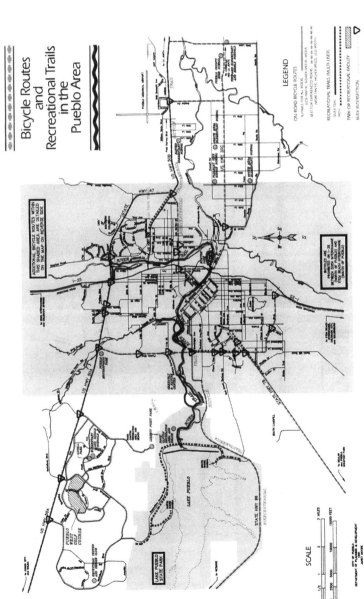

This map shows the 25-mile main arteries of a biking and walking trail system in Pueblo, Colorado; land crossed by the trails is owned by several different public and non-profit entities. Source: City of Pueblo (1991).

larly, with a conservation or scenic easement, the landowner keeps the property but gives the public (or sometimes a private entity) certain rights to keep it from developing the property. Such programs are sometimes called *purchase-of-development-rights programs,* although the legal device used to control the property is almost always a form of easement. People can even give government agencies or nonprofit groups scenic easements across their land, take a tax deduction for the value of the gift, and still keep the property.[12]

A more complex method for protection of open space is used in Montgomery County, Maryland, and a few other places. It is called *transfer of development rights.* Under such a program, one landowner essentially acquires a conservation easement in another owner's land and then "moves" the development that would take place on that land to another parcel, elsewhere in the community. Although sound in theory, there are some very difficult issues involved in implementing the technique, and it has not been widely used.

Successful plans often include a variety of ownership techniques. Pueblo, Colorado, has a twenty-five-mile trail system that links the University of Southern Colorado, at the city's northeastern corner, to the Pueblo Reservoir and State Recreation Area, west of the city (see map on previous page). Along the way, it passes through many residential areas, near the historic downtown, along the edge of the city's largest park, through a nature center managed by the university, and through a variety of ecosystems located along the Arkansas River and a tributary to it. Land along the route includes floodplain land owned by the city; land in a flood channel owned by the Pueblo Conservancy District; land owned by the university; land owned by nonprofit organizations and used in connection with the nature center; privately acquired greenway lands; state highway right-of-way; city-owned parkland; state parkland; and other state-owned land. That basic spine connects to trails along city streets and state highways, to other parks and schools, and to an additional ten miles of trails in the state park. Local leaders brought the basic system together in less than twenty years, in significant part because they were able to use land in so many different forms of ownership.

Conclusion

Preservation of open space serves many purposes for communities today. Communities have long included provisions for park and recreation areas in their plans. Today, many communities also plan for the preservation of wetlands, wildlife habitat, passive recreation areas, woodlands, nature preserves, and greenway linkages. Community leaders and individual citizens today recognize the environmental, economic, engineering, aesthetic, and recreational values of preserving open space. Communities and other organizations use an increasing variety of creative acquisition and ownership techniques to control and preserve parks, greenways, and other forms of open space.

The Role of the Professional Planner

The role of the professional planner in planning for parks and open space is similar to that of the professional planner in dealing with other aspects of planning that combine technical analysis with policy making. Some of the work is objective and is best handled by a professional:

- inventory of existing conditions, especially existing parks and open space
- assessment of current levels of service
- comparison of levels of service to those in similar communities
- conduct of citizen surveys of needs/wants
- identification of lands that are a priority for preservation
- identification of possible methods of funding

From there, this type of planning, like many others, moves into the policy-making arena. Because there is a great deal of judgment involved in determining appropriate levels of service for a community, and because meeting those levels is usually a direct function of money, any workable plan must emerge from a good policy-making process.

Note that some parks departments have their own planners, many of whom are trained as landscape architects. A few local governments even have staff open space planners. This is a field in which planners are most effective if they work closely with landscape architects, in their own offices, in other offices or in consulting firms.

The Role of the Individual Citizen

Policymakers ultimately respond to citizens. Thus, citizens play a critical role in shaping plans for parks and open space.

Demand for parks and other facilities for active recreation varies a great deal by community. Some communities have many soccer teams, while softball is dominant in others. Golf courses are more popular in some communities—and climates—than others. Interested citizens can help to ensure that policy-makers support—and fund—the types of parks and recreational facilities that the citizens want and will use.

Almost all communities have some sort of park, and most have a plan or program for expansion of the park system as the community grows. Today, only a small percentage of communities actively preserve greenways and other open space. Some clearly view such preservation as unnecessary, and others seem to consider it a luxury that local taxpayers cannot afford. Citizens must help their own elected officials to make open space an appropriate local priority and to provide funding that supports that level of priority.

EXERCISES

1. Make an inventory of the important open space in your community; if it is a large community, pick one part of it and make an inventory for that part. How is that open space used? Who owns it? Is some of it simply unused private land that may develop in the future?

2. Does your community have a greenway system? Should it have? Can you suggest some routes that such a system might follow? Would those routes include any floodplains or wetlands? Would they provide good human connections within the community?

3. Do new subdivisions in your community include open space? Is that open space accessible to people who do not live there?

4. Are you aware of serious unmet park, recreation, or open-space needs in your community? What are they?

5. Are there private land trusts or other groups involved in open-space acquisition and preservation in your community? If you do not know, have someone in the class contact the local parks department or planning office and ask them.

DISCUSSION QUESTIONS

1. Does your community value open space? How can you tell? Does the local government regularly invest in expanding the open-space system?

2. If there is a land trust or private open-space group active in or near your community, ask a representative of that group to come to your class and describe its activities. While that person is visiting, ask her or him to comment on some of the questions raised in the exercises for this chapter.

FURTHER READING

Arendt, Randall. 1994. *Rural by Design: Maintaining Small Town Character.* Chicago: Planners' Press. Discusses methods for creating "conservation subdivisions" with open space, as well as other methods of encouraging development that is compatible with environmental values.

————. 1996. *Conservation Design for Subdivisions: A Practical Guide to Creating Open Space Networks.* Washington, DC: Island Press. This books goes into more practical detail on actual subdivision design than the previous one, with a heavy emphasis on the preservation of corridors.

Calthorpe, Peter. 1993. *The Next American Metropolis: Ecology, Community, and the American Dream.* Princeton, NJ: Princeton Architectural Press. A good argument for environmentally responsible development practices, with the inclusion of open spaces.

Endicott, Eve, ed. (Lincoln Institute of Land Policy). 1993. *Land Conservation through Public/Private Partnerships.* Washington, DC: Island Press. An excellent set of descriptive case studies, with concluding "how to do it" chapters.

Garvin, Alexander, Gayle Berens, and others. 1997. *Urban Parks and Open Space.* Washington, DC: Urban Land Institute and Trust for Public Land. An excellent discussion of the value of open space, with a number of good case studies. Well illustrated.

Kellert, Stephen R. 1996. *The Value of Life: Biological Diversity and Human Society.* Washington, DC: Island Press and Shearwater Books. A significant discussion of the relationship of biodiversity to human life.

Mertes, James D., and James R. Hall. 1995. *Park, Recreation, Open Space and Greenway Guidelines.* Alexandria, VA: National Recreation and Park Association. Although this is a useful reference book, with worksheets and guidelines, it is also a highly readable text.

Porter, Douglas R., and David A. Salvesen, eds. 1995. *Collaborative Planning for Wetlands and Wildlife: Issues and Examples.* Washington, DC: Island Press. An excellent collection of essays with case studies and analysis of methods for preserving wetlands and habitat.

Strong, Ann L. 1973. *Private Property and the Public Interest: The Brandywine Experience.* Baltimore: Johns Hopkins Univ. Press. A detailed case study of a relatively early private effort to preserve open space in the environmentally and aesthetically valuable Brandywine River Valley.

REFERENCES

Baskin, Yvonne, ed. 1997. *The Work of Nature: How the Diversity of Life Sustains Us.* Washington, DC: Island Press. With a foreword by Paul Ehrlich, this book includes practical but scientific analysis of how the decline in diversity of species affects human society.

Diehl, Janet, and Thomas H. Barrett. 1988. *The Conservation Easement Handbook: Managing Land Conservation and Historic Easement Programs.* Washington, DC: Trust for Public Land and Land Trust Exchange. A handbook on using this important technique.

Land Trust Alliance. 1990. *Starting a Land Trust: A Guide to Forming a Land Conservation Organization in Your Community.* Another useful handbook.

Mertes, James D., and James R. Hall. 1995. *Park, Recreation, Open Space and Greenway Guidelines.* Alexandria, VA: National Recreation and Park Association. The standard reference in the field of park and open-space planning, it contains formulas and guidelines and replaces an earlier publication that suggested numerical standards for ratios of parkland and other facilities to local population.

Whyte, William H. 1959. *Securing Open Space for Urban America: Conservation Easements.* Technical Bulletin 36. Washington, DC: Urban Land Institute. A landmark work that defined the concept of conservation easements. It is still a relevant text on how to use the technique.

NOTES

1. James D. Mertes and James R. Hall, Washington, DC: National Recreation and Park Association (1996).
2. Alexander Garvin and Gayle Berens, Washington, DC: Urban Land Institute and the Trust for Public Lands (1997).
3. Mertes and Hall, note 1, p. 57. For an earlier publication from the same organization containing this "standardized" approach, see Roger A. Lancaster, ed., *Recre-*

ation, Park, and Open Space Standards and Guidelines, Alexandria, VA: National Recreation and Park Association (1983).

4. City of Ames, *Land Use Policy Plan,* Ames, IA: RM Plan Group (Nashville) and City of Ames (1986).

5. Natural Resources Conservation Service, *America's Private Land: A Geography of Hope,* Washington, DC: Department of Agriculture (1996), p. 30.

6. Ibid.

7. City of Stillwater, "Comprehensive Community Service, *America's Private Land: A Geography of Hope,* Washington, DC: Department of Agriculture (1996), p. 30.

8. City of Ames, note 4, p. 88.

9. City of Ames, note 4, p. 109.

10. City of Norman, "Norman 2020: Land Use and Transportation Plan," Norman, OK: The Burnham Group (Cincinnati) and City of Norman (1997), from Goal 5.

11. Open Space Department, City of Boulder, CO, "Boulder's Open Space Then and Now" (1992) and "Some Facts about Boulder's Open Space" (1992).

12. Code of Federal Regulations, Title 26, °1.170A-14, "Qualified conservation contributions" (1997).

....

Part IV

Plans for Special
Topics or Areas

A comprehensive plan provides the best context for addressing broad issues about the future of a community. Every community should have a comprehensive plan, but some communities may also want more specific plans for particular systems or for certain geographical areas of the community. Common subjects of such separate plan elements include:

- transportation and infrastructure plans (discussed in chapter 7)
- neighborhood plans
- corridor plans
- downtown plans
- housing plans
- economic development plans
- park and recreation plans (discussed in chapter 15)
- annexation plans (discussed in chapters 12 and 14)

Plan elements like these provide greater detail for particular systems or parts of the community or for addressing related issues that go beyond those included in the comprehensive plan. The comprehensive plan may focus on the park and on open spaces related to "parks and recreation," but a plan element specifically addressing parks and recreation may also include plans for softball tournaments, swim classes, and other recreational programs; similarly, the comprehensive plan may designate lands for industrial development, and an economic development plan may include marketing programs, job training, and tax incentives to be used in attracting industry to the community.

The types of plans discussed in this part are often developed and adopted separately from the comprehensive plan. Planning for parks or housing is a relatively specialized task that requires different expertise from general comprehensive planning and that may interest different constituent groups in the community. Thus, there is considerable logic in preparing these plans separately. The comprehensive plan, however, should provide the context for all of these plans and should represent the link that connects them all as part of a cohesive system of plans.

This part of the book addresses these special types of plans—for specific systems or geographical sections of the community—plans that at their best, form more detailed elements of a larger comprehensive plan. Chapter 6 introduced the concept of the plan for future land use. Some people view the future land-use plan as almost synonymous with the comprehensive plan. It is such an essential element of a comprehensive plan that it is almost always incorporated into the comprehensive plan document itself.

Similarly, transportation is such a central element of community planning that the specialized plans related to streets, highways, and other transportation systems are typically a part of the primary plan document; this topic, also, was addressed earlier, in chapter 7. That chapter also described planning for other kinds of infrastructure ranging from sewer systems to fire stations. Although many communities address plans for all of the physical infrastructure together, others may treat transportation and land use as part of the basic plan and then create separate plans for sewer, water, drainage, and other infrastructure. In that context, it may be useful to review chapter 7 briefly in relation to this part of the book.

Chapter 16 builds on this base with a more detailed examination of the issues involved in attempting to plan separately for a particular geographic part of the community. Chapter 17 focuses that concept on older, established neighborhoods. Although much of the change in a community occurs on its fringes, where there is vacant land, some of it will occur in older areas. Change in older areas can consist of simple decline and abandonment. On the other hand, change can involve redevelopment, some of which may reinforce the character of such an area and some of which may change it significantly.

Housing is the focus of chapter 18. Housing is one of the most important elements in people's lives. Unlike sewer and water services and parks and libraries, however, it is largely provided in this country by the private sector. Thus, public plans for housing take on a very different character than public plans for public facilities.

The economy is the lifeblood of a community or a region. Effective comprehensive plans relate closely to local economic development efforts. The bottom line in economic development efforts is jobs—employment opportunities for residents of the community. Thus, chapter 19 examines planning for jobs and economic development.

Chapter 16

Planning for Particular Geographic Areas

Many communities adopt plans for specific geographic areas within the community. Typical subjects of such plans include neighborhoods, sectors, downtowns, historic districts, and corridors along roads. Planning for only a portion of a community is more manageable than creating a community-wide comprehensive plan, allowing evaluation of the future of the area in detail. Some neighborhood plans show very specific uses for every separate parcel of land.

Geographically focused plans may deal with many of the same subjects as a comprehensive plan but they differ from the comprehensive plans in some specific ways:

- The most obvious difference between such a plan and the comprehensive plan is the limited geographic area included in it.
- Because of the narrower focus of such a plan, it typically encourages greater participation by property owners, residents, and business operators.
- Also because of the limited geographical scope of such a plan, it often includes a much greater level of detail than a community-wide plan would show for the same area.

These differences can be both strengths and weaknesses. While the area involved in such a plan is well defined, it must be considered in the context of the community as a whole. Neighborhoods are systems that are part of the larger system of the community. Rare is the neighborhood that is self-contained. A particular neighborhood may lack a grocery store, hardware store, or some other service that is essential to the community but not a necessary part of every neighborhood. Similarly, the community as a whole must depend on all of its neighborhoods collectively to participate in providing locations for such high-impact uses as utility substations, shopping centers, and middle schools. Although the allocation of such uses can occur easily as part of a community-wide, comprehensive planning process, it is difficult to achieve a comprehensive result from a collective of individual decisions made by planners considering only one neighborhood at a time.

The small scale that creates strong emotional support for a planning process in a neighborhood may also lead to a loss of objectivity. People may fail to see the community for the neighborhood, just as some fail to see the forest for the trees. A commission looking at an entire community is likely to recognize those neighborhoods that need additional investments and those that are in good health. In contrast, typical neighborhood planning processes lead to the conclusion that each neighborhood is one of the finest in the city with the only thing standing between it and a great future is an inadequate level of investment by the local government in parks, libraries, and other services.

Neighborhood and other sector plans involve many of the steps taken in the comprehensive planning process, but they differ in the level of detail. For example, mapping the existing uses of each parcel of land is often practicable at a neighborhood level, although it is much more difficult to accomplish the same task community wide. The land-use map may also be more specific—although the community-scale land-use map may simply show that a parcel is "commercial," a neighborhood-scale map may show that the same parcel is a "grocery store." Chapter 6 suggests the hazards of future land-use mapping, however, and the greater specificity often found in a neighborhood land-use plan increases those hazards. The neighborhood may really want a bowling alley and may plan one for a specific parcel of land. The owner of that parcel may decide to open a video store instead. The video store may be a useful commercial-recreational use for the neighborhood, but what happens to the bowling alley now that the land planned for it has found another use? Certainly it could go to some other site appropriate for commercial uses, but the very detailed neighborhood plan may not suggest that alternative.

Such risks of over specificity can be minimized and the strengths of sector planning reinforced by conducting such planning in the context of a community-wide comprehensive plan, using it to provide a context in which to address neighborhood, district, corridor, or other limited-area issues. Some communities take a different approach, collecting a series of limited-area plans and blending them into a community-wide plan by linking major elements of each separate plan such as circulation (transportation), parks, and infrastructure. Consistency is easier to achieve when these smaller plans develop in the context of an existing comprehensive plan.

Neighborhood Plans

Many communities place high priority on planning for individual neighborhoods. Neighborhood plans are for involving citizens in considering their

Many new subdivisions have a strong sense of neighborhood identity, reinforced with entrance treatments like this.

future and effective tools for examining a community at a detailed level. Because of the obvious self-interest of those involved in neighborhood planning, these are also the type of limited-area plans that carry with them the greatest risk of inconsistency with community-wide planning efforts.

The goals of neighborhood planning are noble. At best, a neighborhood ought to be a partially self-contained mini-community, including within it many of the public and private services needed by its residents on a daily basis and providing good transportation links to allow residents to reach other services in the rest of the community.

The character of neighborhoods changes over time, both in principle and in practice. Forty or fifty years ago, many communities placed a high priority on neighborhood parks, often located adjacent to elementary schools. Today, there is far more demand in most communities for large softball and soccer complexes than for neighborhood parks. To allow the inclusion of such amenities as full auditoriums and sometimes even swimming pools and language labs, newer elementary schools are typically large enough to serve two or three times as many students as elementary schools did forty years ago. Further, because there are fewer people in each family today than there were then, there are no longer enough students living in the homes in many of these 1950s neighborhoods to fill the elementary schools that once served them. The identification of neighborhoods is not as strong as it was when the neighborhood defined the scope of many daily activities. Today, children may ride a bus a mile east to the elementary school and then carpool two miles west to the soccer complex, while their parents satisfy convenience shopping needs at an all-night store located where there once was a filling station.

Nevertheless, neighborhoods remain an important focus of many local planning efforts. The first step in neighborhood planning is organization of neighborhood residents, creating a planning body or other method for establishing collective goals and objectives for the neighborhood. Planners provide the technical services. The success of neighborhood plans rests primarily on the commitment of residents to the neighborhood and its leadership. Advocates of neighborhood planning urge that these plans represent the best level of planning since they address the daily lives of citizens.[1] Neighborhood plans are most effective when the boundaries of the neighborhood are readily recognized in the community.

Some communities have such a strong neighborhood structure that the planning agency has a wall map showing the precise boundaries of neighborhoods and a mailing list for organizations representing those neighborhoods. Neighborhood planning is fairly easy in such a context. In other communities, people refer to themselves as residents of the "east side" or of a particular high school district but have little sense of neighborhood beyond that. Organizing a neighborhood planning effort in such a community is considerably more difficult. The most challenging situations sometimes arise in those communities where a few neighborhoods are clearly identified and well organized but many people live in other areas with less identity and little organization; in such a community, the risk of neighborhood planning is that it will create special opportunities for those neighborhoods that are best organized, not necessarily for those that need it most. Successful planning director Bruce McClendon used that technique as a motivational one in Fort Worth, encouraging neighborhoods to bid for the privilege of city support of their plans. The currency used in the bid was largely that of proposed organizational and other volunteer effort from the neighborhood.[2] Often in such communities the best-organized neighborhoods will be the newest subdivisions, areas that may need the least planning and the least help.

Implementation of neighborhood plans often depends heavily on the private sector, because neighborhood goals are as likely to focus on the need for additional commercial services—such as grocery stores and movie theaters—as on public facilities. Thus, it is particularly important that neighborhood planning efforts ensure the involvement of neighborhood business people and the owners of properties designated for commercial uses in the neighborhood; the community can plan for and even encourage a particular commercial use, but in most cases the decision actually to build or open such a use will fall to someone in the private sector. A neighborhood planning committee that meets weekly for a year will find that many business people and landowners will drop out early in the process, significantly decreasing the likelihood of implementation of a plan. It is thus important to ensure that the energy of a few neighborhood advocates does not take over the process to the extent that it effectively excludes people who are interested in the neighborhood but too busy to attend dozens of meetings.

The best neighborhood plans reinforce the position of the neighborhood within the community, recognizing and improving on the neighborhood's identity while also building into the plan the interconnectedness of the neighborhood with surrounding neighborhoods and with commercial and employment centers that serve the larger community.

Communities may reinforce neighborhood identity with entrance signs to neighborhoods and even with banners or specially designed street signs to provide identity to a particular neighborhood. St. Louis, Missouri, has been a leader in using neighborhood banners, and Cary, North Carolina, is a community where nearly every subdivision has its own entrance sign.

District or Sector Plans

Some communities use district or sector plans.[3] In a few communities, a district plan is simply a different name for a neighborhood plan. Most communities that use one of these terms, however, apply it to one of two types of areas: a collection of neighborhoods; or a segment of the community that is discrete and identifiable but cannot logically be called a neighborhood.

Larger communities may use district or sector plans as a bridge between neighborhood plans and the community-wide comprehensive plan. At the district or sector plan level, the community can address major transportation links to the rest of the community and facilities that serve more than a neighborhood but less than the entire community—facilities like branch libraries, middle and high schools, supermarkets, and shopping centers in the 100,000–250,000 square foot range. Albuquerque, New Mexico, has developed an effective method of linking neighborhood and sector plans to the community-wide plan; it has used the working names Rank 1, Rank 2, and Rank 3 to refer to the categories of plans.

Other types of districts for which communities may develop specific district or sector plans include:

- downtowns (discussed in the next section of this chapter)
- historic districts (also discussed in a later section of this chapter)
- other major commercial areas
- industrial parks
- areas around airports
- agricultural areas
- sensitive environmental areas such as floodplains

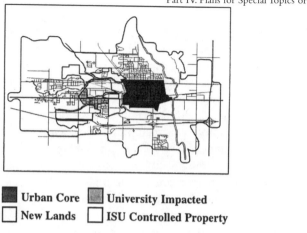

■ Urban Core   ▦ University Impacted
☐ New Lands   ☐ ISU Controlled Property

The 1996 plan for Ames, Iowa, identified these special planning areas. ISU represents Iowa State University. Source: City of Ames and RM Plan Group, Nashville, (1996).

The purpose of the types of district or sector plans listed above is somewhat different from the purpose of a neighborhood plan. Each of the kinds of areas listed above has unique characteristics that are likely to make it different from the rest of the community. Although most people believe that their own neighborhoods are unique, neighborhoods actually have many characteristics in common. In contrast, a community is likely to have only one downtown, and each agricultural or industrial district is likely to be distinguishable from others in many ways. Further, a downtown or an industrial area has many characteristics that are entirely different from those of the rest of the community, and the planning issues for such areas are quite different from the planning issues for the rest of the community.

Thus, providing a separate planning mechanism for such areas is often useful and at times essential. A community-wide planning effort often cannot give to an area like a historic district the detailed attention necessary to create a workable plan for its future.

One significant difference between district plans of this sort and neighborhood plans is that a comprehensive plan can often build on and incorporate a previously prepared plan for a downtown or for a particular historic district. With district plans, the question of whether the limited-area plan or the comprehensive plan comes first is often not critical—as long as all planning bodies involved ultimately review both plans to ensure that they are both consistent and compatible.

Downtown Plans

Many communities have separate plans for their central business districts or downtowns. The nature of downtowns in the United States, particularly in the northern half of the country, has changed significantly in the last forty years.

Fifty years ago, downtown was where one went shopping and where many fathers went to work. Today, regional shopping malls have replaced many of the retail functions of typical downtowns, and outlying business parks in many communities provide the base for more office jobs than the downtown. Walk-up apartments that once provided inexpensive housing above stores in the downtown have now been turned to storage uses, professional offices, or abandoned space as people have moved away from the city center and toward the greener pastures of the suburbs.

Weather is clearly a factor. Shopping in downtown Omaha, Nebraska, or Peoria, Illinois, in January can be downright unpleasant, with bitter cold and blowing snow. Given the choice between going to a climate-conditioned mall and a traditional downtown in a northern climate, most people will choose the mall several months out of the year. Both because their stores need business year-round and because two of the biggest shopping months (November and December) are also two of the coldest months, many merchants in such communities have chosen to relocate from downtown areas to malls.

In many communities, major banks, government offices, law offices, and title companies remain downtown. The combination of such office and professional uses creates a good deal of activity downtown from perhaps 7:30 in the morning to 5:30 or 6:00 at night. Most planners and downtown developers agree that a viable downtown must be lively at least fifteen or sixteen hours a day. With the extended hours of activity, nice restaurants become viable, there is sufficient revenue to support the level of parking that is necessary during the day, and a variety of small retailers begin to reopen in the district. Jane Jacobs, an interested citizen who wrote an important and influential book based on observations of her own neighborhood (Greenwich Village in New York City), helped planners and public officials to recognize the importance of day-and-night activity to the vitality of neighborhoods.[4]

Communities have experimented with pedestrian-only open malls, skywalks (a notable success in Minneapolis), festival marketplaces, and other concepts to revitalize downtowns. Still others have brought in athletic facilities (Cincinnati and Indianapolis are good examples), major visitor attractions (an aquarium in Baltimore, the Rock 'n' Roll Hall of Fame in Cleveland), and a variety of entertainment opportunities to the downtown—often using public-private partnerships, tax incentives, and other tools to encourage these uses. Many communities have placed an increased emphasis on encouraging residential uses in the downtown, something that was once common when merchants lived in or rented out the walk-up apartments above their stores. The purpose of all of these efforts is to bring people downtown.

Clearly, a downtown is so unique that it makes sense to create a separate plan for it. A comprehensive plan can create the context for a downtown, but most planners will cheerfully build a new comprehensive plan around a good downtown plan—if there is one in existence.

Historic District Plans

The French Quarter in New Orleans; the heart of Old Savannah, Georgia, and the Plaza in Santa Fe, New Mexico, are outstanding examples of historic districts that truly define their communities. Many other communities contain historic districts that are less famous but extremely important to local culture and heritage.

Because the issues involved in historic districts are unique, it is usually both necessary and desirable to have a separate plan for the historic area to serve as the basis for creating regulations to protect it. Designating an area as historic only initiates the process of protecting it. Through a plan, the community defines the values that it wishes to protect. A single-family neighborhood in a Los Angeles suburb is likely to benefit from the same types of regulations that protect the suburbs of Des Moines. In contrast, the French Quarter is very different from the Plaza in Santa Fe. It is through planning that a community defines the value of a particular historic district and establishes the principles for protecting it.

Like downtown plans, historic district plans can be developed separately from a comprehensive planning process, either before or after the preparation of the comprehensive plan. In many communities, a separate historic commission in responsible for planning for—and often for regulating—historic districts.

Historic districts such as the Union Avenue Historic District in Pueblo, Colorado, are often the subject of special plans.

When the downtown area or a particular neighborhood is historic, the two planning processes typically merge—that is, the neighborhood or downtown plan is also the historic preservation plan for that area.

There are some unique legal issues involved in protecting historic areas that are discussed to a limited extent in chapter 10, on zoning, but that are largely beyond the scope of this book.[5]

Plans for Agricultural and Sensitive Environmental Areas

Humans and their activities define most districts or sectors that are subject to special plans, but the character of the land typically defines the most viable agricultural areas and the most sensitive environmental areas.

Thus, communities that prepare plans for such areas typically start with an environmental opportunities and constraints analysis, based on the work of Ian McHarg.[6] Through mapping soil, subsurface geology, hydrology, vegetation, slopes, and sometimes other factors, a community can define those special areas of land and water that it wants to protect.

Further, the same analytical and mapping techniques used to define sensitive agricultural lands and other environmental areas can also define their most important characteristics and provide some of the most essential elements of a plan. Wetlands have value as wetlands only if they remain wet—a principle

This aerial view shows the encroachment of a residential subdivision into an agricultural area. Courtesy of Pflum, Klausmeier & Gehrum, Cincinnati.

objective in planning for wetlands. Agricultural soils serve agriculture best if left undeveloped, again providing an obvious planning goal. Planning for such areas is not always as simple as it might seem, however. Many communities are built in or near river bottoms, surrounded by the excellent agricultural soils deposited by the river over the years; for such a community to expand in any direction may require development on some agricultural lands. Further, lands that are good for agriculture are usually good for urban development, also. Planning bodies dealing with these issues must make policy choices in their planning, but information available from land analysis will help the planning bodies and the professionals who assist them in applying those policies to the land.

Plans for Other Types of Districts

A community may develop a special plan for an industrial park, for an area around its airport, for the ski mountain or beach area that creates much of the economic base of the town, or for a former military base now abandoned by the government and available for redevelopment.

Such plans are in many ways self-defining and self-explanatory. The goals for these sectors are often implicit in the plans themselves—the goal of a plan for an industrial park is to attract certain types of industry, and the goal of a reuse plan for a military base is to create a new use for the land and buildings, replacing some or all of the jobs once provided there by the military operation.

Such specialized plans need not interfere with the comprehensive planning process in any way. They can supplement the plan after its preparation or help to define it as it is being prepared. The need for such a plan is usually obvious to a community, and there is often a good base of political and financial support for the preparation of such focused plans.

Corridor Plans

A corridor in community planning is a strip of land on both sides of a major access way to or through a community—usually along a highway or other major road. Corridors include community entrances and exits, links among neighborhoods and between neighborhoods, pathways for community-level services, and connections between suburbs and city. Because most people enter a community along a highway corridor, that corridor often provides people with their first—and, in many cases, most lasting—impression of the community. And because people within a community use major corridors daily, those corridors often form one of the dominant impressions of citizens about their own community or metropolitan area.

There are two reasons for planning for corridors: (1) to preserve and protect the few good ones; and (2) to fix the many poor ones. What makes a good

Corridors like this one in Arizona may be the subject of special plans to enhance both their efficiency as transportation corridors and their aesthetic appeal. Photo by Jennifer Greig.

corridor? A good corridor serves its primary function well—providing for safe and efficient travel—and at the same time provides users with a pleasing aesthetic experience.

When asked to describe a major local transportation corridor, most people will describe a busy street, interrupted by many traffic lights, with lots of driveways in between, decorated with a plethora of billboards and advertising signs and bordered largely by parking lots. Those are corridors at their worst. A visitor to Hilton Head Island, South Carolina, finds corridors lined with trees and low-profile, conservative signs identifying adjacent businesses. Henrico County, a more typical suburban area surrounding Richmond, Virginia, has achieved a similar effect along its major corridors, hiding parking lots behind wooded strips that define corridors, punctuated only by attractive signs identifying shopping centers, office buildings, and residential developments.

While some are well-defined land areas that have significant design elements, making them attractive and distinctive, many corridors in the United States are commercial strips with little character or interest. Because of a lack of planning, with too many driveways and too many intersections, these commercial strips are often dysfunctional as well as ugly; cars turning into the driveway at one business impede traffic bound for other businesses farther down the strip.

Corridor plans usually have dual goals: (1) improved transportation; and (2)

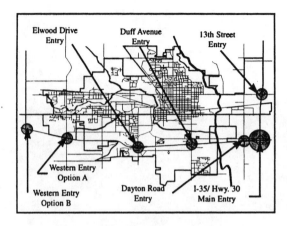

The 1996 Ames, Iowa, plan included this identification of gateways to the community; gateways often receive special treatment within corridor plans. Source: *City of Ames and RM Plan Group, Nashville (1996).*

enhanced appearance. By limiting the number of driveways (or "curbcuts") along the corridor, adding turning lanes to those that exist, using more traffic signalization and signage, and eliminating distracting visual clutter, transportation planners can significantly increase the effective traffic-handling capacity of a road without widening it. By adding landscaping, reducing paved parking in front of businesses, and managing signage and utility poles, planners can help to create a more pleasing entrance or link along the corridor.

Corridor plans often lead to special regulations and implementation mechanisms along a particular corridor. A community may use unique street signs or lighting or add special landscaping to a planned corridor while imposing on private property owners in that corridor special rules regarding signage, parking, and landscaping on their own properties. Corridor plans typically provide a greater level of detail than a comprehensive plan for aesthetic and technical issues but rarely conflict with or even differ from the comprehensive plan on basic issues such as land use or circulation patterns.

Planning for Neighborhoods, Districts, and Corridors

Creating plans for neighborhoods, districts, and corridors begins, as comprehensive planning begins, with data collection, followed by an analysis of existing conditions. Data gathering and analysis efforts for neighborhood and sector plans typically focus on transportation and circulation, land use, and current development trends, although all of the data gathered and analyzed for a community-wide plan an often relevant to a sector plan. This analysis provides a baseline for the assessment and comparison of alternatives and for development of the plan. Community participation and support is as essential in this process as it is in comprehensive planning—and it is often easier to achieve, because the scope of the plan keeps it "close to home."

Many communities appoint committees or task forces to work on a sector plan, usually advising the planning commission and governing body on consideration and adoption of the proposed plan. To make such a neighborhood or other sector plan an official document, most communities adopt it as an element of the comprehensive plan. Such an action requires a vote by the planning commission and, in many states, also by the governing body.

The tools for implementing such limited-area plans are typically the same tools used for the rest of the comprehensive plan, a combination of regulatory tools and community investment, all discussed in part III of this book.

Conclusion

A comprehensive plan is essential but sometimes is not enough to help a community achieve its goals. Thus, many communities use special plans for neighborhoods, districts, corridors, or other defined sectors. Such plans can provide useful detail for the implementation of a comprehensive plan and in some cases can actually serve as part of the basis for a comprehensive plan. Simply compiling a group of such plans, however, will not create a comprehensive plan. The community must create the comprehensive plan and use it to provide context for these limited-area plans, regardless of the order in which they are prepared.

The Role of the Professional Planner

The role of the professional planner in preparing sector plans is a dual one:

1. First, the planner must perform all of the technical, analytical, and communication tasks that are performed in the comprehensive planning process.
2. Second, the planner must serve as a sort of collective consciousness for the planning body, reminding it of the pertinent parts of the comprehensive plan and how it provides context for and thus should define the limited-area plan.

It is easiest for the professional planner to play the second role when she or he is also involved in the comprehensive planning process. Some communities have separate planning staffs for neighborhoods, and others have positions devoted just to planning for a downtown or a historic district; planners with such narrow duties must be particularly careful to study the comprehensive plan and to ensure that their own, specialized work links logically to it.

Note that here, as with the comprehensive plan, it is the designated planning body and not the individual planner that makes the policy decisions that create the plan—the best planners facilitate that process in such a way that the planning body and other participants in the process are convinced at the end that the result is truly their own plan and not the product of the planning staff or a consultant.

The Role of the Individual Citizen

Individual citizens often play a much more active role in development of limited-area plans than they do in preparation of a community-wide comprehensive plan. The scope and scale of the plan for a limited geographical area make it more practical for a planning body composed of individual citizens to manage the process and be directly involved in every step of it. Although sometimes the preparation of a neighborhood, district, or corridor plan involves the same level of staff support used in a comprehensive planning process, typically the citizen's responsibility is far greater in preparing the limited-area plan.

As with any planning effort, individual citizens not directly involved in the planning body should have ample opportunity to offer questions, comments, and suggestions to those preparing the plan. Where the process is largely handled by volunteer citizens, they are likely to do much of their work in meetings that are open to other interested citizens, thus providing an excellent chance for those who are interested to understand and influence the process.

Because the staff support for such an effort is often limited, it is sometimes possible for volunteer citizens essentially to take over the process. Although that may be satisfying for those who like volunteer work and enjoy policy making, it is important to maintain the involvement of the professional planners, who can provide essential technical background and logical links back to the comprehensive plan for the community.

EXERCISES

1. Identify three limited geographic areas in your community for which it would be useful to have special plans. Are the boundaries of those areas clear? Is each of those areas relatively unique, or are there other parts of the community like it?

2. Does your community have clearly defined neighborhoods? Can you name some of them? Can you identify them on a map of the community?

3. Identify two or three major corridors in your community. Now, working in a group or alone, pick one of those and conduct a strengths-and-weaknesses analysis on it. What might be some basic policy elements of a plan to improve that corridor?

4. Send representatives from your class or your group to your local planning office and find out what neighborhood or sector plans exist for your community. Obtain copies if possible. Are they consistent with the comprehensive plan?

DISCUSSION QUESTION

Does your community have a plan for its downtown? Does it need one? What would you do to make the downtown the "heart" of the community, as most downtowns once were? How would those plans relate to the comprehensive plan for the community?

FURTHER READING

Bishop, Kirk R. 1989. *Designing Urban Corridors.* Planning Advisory Service Report No. 418. Chicago: American Planning Association.

Gil, Efraim, and Enid Lucchesi. 1988. "Citizen Participation in Planning," in *The Practice of Local Government Planning,* 2nd edition, Frank S. So and Judith Getzels, eds. Washington, DC: International City Management Association. An important discussion of the role of citizens in developing a plan.

Jacobs, Jane. 1961. *The Death and Life of Great American Cities.* New York: Random House. A landmark book about neighborhoods; although written by a nonplanner, it has greatly influenced planning thought and practice.

McClendon, Bruce W., and Ray Quay. 1988. *Mastering Change: Winning Strategies for Effective City Planning.* Chicago: Planners Press. A leading work on the role of professional planners in facilitating the planning process and managing the planning function of local government.

REFERENCES

McBee, Susanna, with Ralph J. Basile, Robert T. Dunphy, John M. Keeling, Ben C. Lin, David C. Petersen, Patrick L. Phillips, and Richard D. Wagner. 1992. *Downtown Development Handbook,* 2nd edition. Washington, DC: Urban Land Institute. A standard reference for the development industry.

McHarg, Ian. 1992. *Design with Nature, 25th Anniversary Edition.* New York: John Wiley. Original publication 1969, Garden City, NY: Natural History Press for the American Museum of Natural History. A landmark work that used the techniques of landscape architecture at a regional scale to define opportunities and constraints based on the character of the land and the natural environment. A work that redefined regional planning.

Sedway, Paul H. 1988. "District Planning," in *The Practice of Local Government Planning*, 2nd edition, Frank S. So and Judith Getzels, eds. Washington, DC: International City Management Association. A good description of a process for planning for part of a community.

NOTES

1. See, for example, Bernie Jones, Neighborhood Planning, Chicago: American Planning Association (1990).
2. Bruce W. McClendon and Ray Quay, *Mastering Change: Winning Strategies for Effective City Planning*, Chicago: American Planning Association (1988).
3. See, for example, Paul H. Sedway, "District Planning," chapter 4 in Frank S. So and Judith Getzels, eds., The Practice of Local Government Planning, 2nd edition, Washington, DC: International City Management Association (1987).
4. Her book is called *The Death and Life of Great American Cities*, New York: Random House (1961); it is available in paperback.
5. See chapter 7, "Landmark and Historic Zoning," in Eric Damian Kelly, ed., *Zoning and Land Use Controls*, New York: Matthew Bender (1998).
6. Ian McHarg. *Design with Nature, 25th Anniversary Edition*, New York: John Wiley (1992).

Chapter 17

Planning for Change in Established Neighborhoods

The maintenance and revitalization of the physical fabric of communities has attracted the attention of Americans over the last century. Often attention has been focused on improving conditions for the poor, but most efforts have ultimately been focused on slum clearance for the purpose of economic development. Over the last fifty years, Congress and some state legislatures have created significant programs for urban regeneration. Each has had some successes as well as some problems.

Buildings age, but with maintenance and appropriate remodeling and updating, they can remain vital, safe, and healthy environments for living and working for centuries, as they do in many countries. In the United States, however, the emphasis on replacement of buildings rather than on rehabilitation has often resulted in abandonment of buildings. As several buildings are abandoned in an area, the area begins to deteriorate, remaining owners cease to maintain and reinvest in their properties, and more and more properties are abandoned.

In theory, the market ought to address this, and it does so very well in some cities. In the hearts of cities like Manhattan and San Francisco, there is a constant market for old buildings that can be renovated or removed, creating sites for new buildings. In many communities, however, the free market has failed to revitalize such areas, leading to continued deterioration and the creation of slums and "bad areas" of the community. There are several reasons for this trend, including changes in manufacturing techniques, changes in shipping, creation of shopping malls, difficulties in land acquisition, and federal policies encouraging suburbanization.

Many early industrial plants were multistory buildings located in the core of urban areas. People often lived near their work. Automobiles and heavy machinery, as well as small items, were assembled in those plants. As industry gradually shifted to the use of the assembly line, however, such plants were inadequate. At a typical auto plant today, a bare chassis starts down the line on a belt and has parts added until it reaches the other end of the line as a complete car. The only efficient way to operate such a process is in a straight line, on one level. It was simply not possible to retrofit the old multistory factories for use with these assembly lines. Further, urban sites were limited in size not only by surrounding buildings but also by the grid pattern of streets, which effectively limited building length to four hundred or five hundred feet on a site. Unable to meet their physical needs easily in an urban environment, many factories moved out of the core of the cities, to areas where they could find more land.

At the same time, there has been a significant shift in shipping techniques for industry. Industries that once depended almost entirely on rail and built private sidings into their plants now often use trucks to ship the same goods. Bringing large numbers of trucks into heavily urbanized areas was simply not practical. The trucks often blocked streets while loading or unloading, thus antagonizing local officials, as well as potential customers. Traffic congestion and odd street patterns delayed trucks going in and out, resulting in increased costs. This change in shipping techniques affected warehouses as well as factories and gradually led many major warehouses to move from the urban core to outlying areas with better highway access, again leaving behind vacant buildings.

People who worked in the early, urban factories and warehouses often

Industrial plants like this, located in urban areas on parcels interrupted by the street grid, often do not meet the current needs of industry.

lived in the neighborhoods near them and walked to work or rode a bus or subway for a short distance. As the factories moved, these residents had less incentive to stay in those neighborhoods. In urban areas, many of these industry-oriented neighborhoods consisted largely of row houses and apartments, with little if any parking. As the jobs moved out, residents often needed cars to go to and from work. Not only did they not have places to park the cars in their old neighborhoods, but they realized that, with a car, new housing choices opened up to them. Thus, many of them moved out of the core, again leaving behind empty buildings. Although other people might have moved into a particular residential building, the residents moving into those dwelling units often came from worse areas of the city, abandoning other units elsewhere and thus resulting in net new vacancies in urban residential units.

Zoning and building regulations also contributed to urban flight in some smaller cities. Early zoning regulations forced industry out of primarily residential areas, thus improving the quality of residential life but sometimes complicating commuting. Later, with the advent of environmental regulations and increasing concerns about environmental litigation, industry proactively sought separation from residential uses.

In many U.S. cities and towns during the first half of the twentieth century, the typical downtown residence was a second-floor walk-up apartment above a store. Many communities later adopted zoning regulations that prohibited the location of dwelling units and commercial activities in the same building (based on the principle of separation of uses, discussed in chapter 10), thus forcing people out of those units. The lack of parking for those units additionally impaired the market for them. Those who wanted to remodel their buildings were often told that to get a building permit, they would have to create off-street parking spaces to comply with new zoning regulations; the practical effect of such a requirement was often to suggest to a building owner that he or she tear down part of the building (to create parking) in order to get a permit to remodel it. Similar regulations may make perfect sense in a suburban environment, but many communities have made the mistake of trying to retrofit such regulations onto older areas of the community that developed in very different patterns—patterns that do not match these regulations.

Facing this "urban flight," urban landlords lost much of their motivation to maintain their buildings. Many realized that the shelf life of their buildings as marketable goods was fairly limited, and they began to try to recover their investments before the market went away. One way to do that was to increase profits by reducing expenditures on maintenance.

As people left, some of the stores and restaurants that they supported also left, creating a further ripple effect in the economy. Reinforcing the abandonment of some areas of the city was the emergence of the enclosed, climate-controlled shopping mall, a trend that began in earnest in the 1960s. Once people in most of the United States discovered the pleasures of shopping out

Ames, Iowa, solved its downtown parking problem by replacing buildings and vacant land on the rear half of blocks facing its main street with parking lots. The lots create convenient parking without disrupting the urban streetscape, but they also make the downtown itself an "island." The parking lot pictured in top photo is at bottom center of bottom photo; see similar lots in blocks to each side. (City of Ames file photos)

of the rain, the sleet, the snow, and the heat, it was hard to get them back downtown. Although communities in parts of Florida and Southern California have climates conducive to year-round shopping outside, in most U.S. communities, there are months of the year in which the weather strongly encourages mall shopping. As shoppers abandoned downtown shopping for the malls, the merchants went with them, leaving many downtown areas with only banks, stock brokers, government offices, and lawyers. Those downtown areas, of course, lost their life at night, when the workers went home. Thus, downtown movie theaters and major restaurants also moved to the suburbs.

At the same time all of these forces encouraged both merchants and residents to look elsewhere for shelter, the federal government adopted housing and highway-building policies that facilitated flights to the suburbs. Discussed in more depth in chapter 13, these policies made it easier to get financing for new suburban homes than for older ones in the city and made those suburban homes accessible with excellent roads.

The combination of these forces left behind in many urban areas abandoned buildings and, in some cases, entire abandoned neighborhoods. Some owners tore down their buildings. Some buildings were lost to fire or collapse. Other owners allowed the local government ultimately to acquire title to them for unpaid taxes.

Some developers and other entrepreneurs realized that vacant buildings and vacant land represented opportunities as well as problems. Some developers actively acquired land and buildings in such areas, intending to redevelop. Many owners of property in these areas were eager to sell, but no one had to sell. If a developer wanted to acquire an entire block as a location for a new building, he might acquire property from twenty-five of the twenty-six owners on the block and then discover that the last owner was unwilling to sell or willing to sell only at an outrageous price. Although developers like Donald Trump and Bill Zeckendorf in New York persevered and acquired large areas for redevelopment, others were thwarted by holdouts—and many simply never began the process because of the difficulty and risks involved. For all of these reasons, as the suburbs grew and prospered after World War II, the hearts of many cities withered and some died.

The Shifting Federal Role

After World War II, urban renewal efforts accelerated. Congress adopted a series of laws, starting with the Housing Act of 1949, that created public housing projects. In addition to creating new housing programs, a topic discussed in chapter 18, these early housing acts focused on slum clearance. Later laws added the urban renewal program. The typical urban renewal project bulldozed blocks, replacing them primarily with roads and businesses.[1] Federal subsidies were used to renew deteriorated portions of urban centers. Although

Urban renewal and similar programs left large vacant sites in the core areas of many communities.

the original intent of the federal government was to rebuild new housing for low- and moderate-income families, over the years slum clearance changed to focus on downtown redevelopment and industrial development. States, responsible for passing federal funds to local communities, encouraged an emphasis on economic development.

One of the attractions of the urban renewal program was that it used the local government's power to acquire property to facilitate the acquisition of large sites. Under the power of eminent domain, a government agency has the right to force someone to sell his or her property to the government for a public purpose, provided that the government pays a fair price. With eminent domain, there was no longer a risk of holdouts (someone who refuses to sell a critical parcel necessary for a new development), and it became practical for those who wanted to develop or redevelop in the urban core to do so. Although sometimes abused, the power of effective land acquisition remains a strength of the urban renewal laws. Those laws still exist in most states, although they are not extensively used because of the lack of federal funding for property acquisition and clearance.

By the mid-1960s, it was evident that these massive urban renewal efforts, funded and encouraged by the federal government, had caused more problems than they had solved. The sweep of urban renewal was so broad that it eliminated sound buildings along with dilapidated ones, and it wiped out older but vital neighborhoods along with slums. The scope of projects was also so vast that it often created more vacant land than the community could possibly redevelop in a reasonable period of time. Thus, much of the cleared land sat vacant for years, creating wastelands in the urban core.

One of the most significant negative impacts of urban renewal programs was the displacement of low-income families. The elimination of blighted neighborhoods sometimes had the effect of eliminating housing opportunities for those who needed it. In the face of such social concerns, Congress amended the laws funding urban renewal projects to require effective opportunities for participation by residents in preparing urban renewal plans.

As neighborhood and civic leaders reacted to some of the unanticipated effects of urban renewal and to some apparent abuses of the program, Congress learned and gradually eliminated the programs of slum clearance, replacing them with aid assistance for rehabilitation rather than demolition. Perhaps the most lasting institutional effect of the urban renewal program has been the federal government's requirement of building and housing codes, which are now common in major cities. Prior to the mid-1950s, most cities lacked codes, but the federal government required codes for urban renewal projects. Today these codes (discussed in more detail in chapter 18) are an effective means of helping protect the health, safety, and welfare of citizens.

As Congress moved away from slum clearance into programs of revitalization, the new efforts were included in President Lyndon Johnson's War on Poverty, requiring increased public participation in decisions about urban revitalization. In a related initiative, Congress created a new cabinet-level agency, the Department of Housing and Urban Development (HUD). Into this new department Congress placed such continuing programs as the Federal Housing Administration mortgage insurance, public housing funds, and block grant programs, as well as many of the new War on Poverty programs, focused around the Model Cities program. The Model Cities program targeted specific areas for a comprehensive approach to poverty. The federal government provided 80 percent of the funding, requiring local matching funds of only 20 percent. With only a small share of the Model Cities program's funding specifically going to housing, major efforts were put into projects for education, health, skills training, economic development, and an assortment of social services. Federal money was given directly to local governments rather than passing it through the states. The Model Cities program lasted for only a short period, but it had some lasting effects. Citizens became aware of the importance of community-based organizations and even stable, moderate, and middle-income neighborhoods began to organize. Neighborhood planning became a viable and accepted form of planning.

In 1974, HUD consolidated all its programs into the Community Development Block Grant (CDBG) program. Local communities were directly given lump sums of money to use in a variety of urban development efforts. Aimed at cities with populations over 50,000 and counties of over 200,000, the funding required less documentation than previous programs. The CDBG programs were based on an entitlement formula with fewer restrictions than before. While eliminating urban blight and improving housing stock was part of the objectives of the program, emphasis was placed on expanding and improving community services and employment and economic opportunities for low-income households. Part of the formula in qualifying for these federal funds was based on existing housing conditions.

The Urban Development Action Grant (UDAG), to aid cities in economic and physical distress, was established in 1977 by the federal government. The grant was created to supplement private investment by leveraging capital for development projects. Today, UDAG has disappeared, and the CDBG program is greatly reduced, as funding was continually cut through the 1980s and 1990s. However, the UDAG program did prove that private and local initiatives are effective in creating viable solutions to local problems.

Current Trends and Programs

Today efforts in preservation, revitalization, infill, and renewal reflect the withdrawal of the federal government from pushing a specific agenda. Instead, public-private partnerships at the local and state levels are driving investments by communities, businesses, not-for-profit organizations, and individual households, supplemented through subsidized loans and through public investments in land and special regulations. Each strategy is unique in its aims and outcomes.

Brownfields

One of the unanticipated side effects of the environmental laws passed by Congress beginning in the 1970s was the abandonment of a number of industrial sites in cities. Those laws, particularly the one that created the Superfund program for cleaning up contaminated lands,[2] created statutory liability for landowners for environmental pollution. The liability passes on to subsequent owners, meaning that the purchaser of an urban site could become legally liable for cleaning up problems caused by owners who had used the property years, or even decades, before. Often this apparent risk was compounded by a lack of knowledge of what the extent of the contamination might be. The early programs essentially mandated full cleanup of a site, even if it were simply to be paved over and used as a parking lot.

Through so-called brownfields legislation, the Congress and many states have offered relief from that liability for subsequent owners and developers. One of the provisions of such laws eliminates the requirement that contaminated sites be cleaned to a nearly pristine state; when the site will be reused for industry or paved over for parking, the law focuses on the containment of pollutants to ensure that they do not flow or blow off site, where they might cause harm to residents or their water supplies.

Cleaning up sites like this one can be prohibitively expensive, often leading to the abandonment of the sites; brownfields legislation has reduced the cleanup requirements for property not to be used for residential purposes, thus facilitating reuse of these sites.

The effects of the brownfields laws are just beginning to be felt. They should gradually result in increasing interest in developing abandoned industrial sites located in cities. Those sites are often attractive for development because they already have a full range of urban services and may be available for sale at a reasonable price after sitting unused for many years.

Gentrification

Gentrification is a trend that has had significant impacts in many cities. It is a process that began in the 1960s as individual, middle-income households began reinvesting in low-income neighborhoods by buying and renovating older and sometimes dilapidated homes. All levels of government have encouraged this form of renewal, although it is not entirely clear what has made it succeed. Local communities use rezoning, flexibility in codes, subsidized loans, and tax incentives, while state grants and federal tax subsidies also help to encourage this form of private investment. Although this form of public-private investment has contributed positively to the revitalization of some deteriorated areas, it has also created further displacement. People tend to select marginal but not abandoned areas for gentrification. Although the first people into an area may take over vacant or dilapidated units, late arrivals often buy marginal rental units, evicting the tenants and restoring the buildings to owner-occupancy status. Even residents who own homes in the area may suffer from increased assessments and higher taxes triggered by the upgrade to the neighborhood.

Many local governments encourage gentrification, as the restoration of housing stock and the expensive shops and services that are established in these areas bring in new taxpayers. This trend began in large cities, but it has become increasingly popular in smaller communities where it has served as an economic development tool by increasing tourism. Today, local governments often encourage gentrification of designated areas by repairing and replacing deteriorated streets and sidewalks and sometimes adding new neighborhood parks, library branches, and other amenities. Banks are more willing to loan on such properties than they once were, in part because they face scrutiny of their policies in inner-city neighborhoods (and elsewhere) under the Community Reinvestment Act.

Revitalization

A more common form of public-private urban revitalization occurs when local residents, business people, and developers invest in upgrading existing property. They may use grants or funds from local government or agencies and their personal funds to renovate their property. These projects range in size from individual homes, with the help of low- or no-interest loans, to malls. Under some local programs, community-oriented design centers provide suggestions on the design of new or restored facades, new landscaping, and other improvements to the streetscape. Local governments typically reinforce these efforts with investments in basic infrastructure and such aesthetic improvements as neighborhood-appropriate streetlights, street signs, and street furniture.

Revitalization projects can also be a combination of structural reuse and new construction to create large-scale, mixed-use development. Some of the best-known revitalization projects in the United States include the Faneuil Hall Marketplace in Boston, the Horton Plaza in San Diego, and Pike Place in Seattle. An early success story in revitalization is that of San Antonio, where the civic investment in its famous River Walk has led to significant revitalization along that historic channel. One of the leading developers of such projects is a spin-off of the Rouse Corporation, which developed Columbia, Maryland, a new town. That company uses profits from its "festival marketplaces" in part to subsidize innovative housing projects. Baltimore and Norfolk are among the early communities with festival marketplaces. These markets, like the one in Faneuil Hall, include a variety of boutiques, restaurants, and informal eating places in a setting intended to convey a continually festive atmosphere—banners abound, and the operators try to provide frequent live entertainment, both formal and informal.

Many of these private revitalization projects have been remarkably successful, particularly in attracting tourists and adding to the prestige of cities. Such large-scale projects are normally located on strategic sites such as the old wharf area in Baltimore, where they do not displace residential neighborhoods. In situations where some residents are affected by redevelopment efforts, negotiations between developers and residents can ensure gains for residents in the form of promised opportunities for job training, guaranteed percentage of employment, and even construction of some affordable housing units near the development.

While the efforts of both individuals and major developers have shown that this form of renewal can be very successful, it is a slow process. In many cities, such isolated efforts have created scattered islands of revitalization within areas of decline. The greatest success can be achieved when several projects of varying land use occur simultaneously in a relatively confined area of a city.

Historic Preservation

An active and organized movement for historic preservation evolved in this country late in the nineteenth century and continues today. It began when industrialization caused the physical environment in cities to undergo rapid change. Demolition of buildings occurred to make way for new construction, often eliminating historic or architecturally significant buildings. Early preservation efforts were undertaken by community groups, such as the group of women who created a museum out of George Washington's home at Mount Vernon. These individual efforts saved a small number of buildings and homes with historic, and often architectural, significance.

By the end of the 1970s, all states and many communities had put into

Effective historic district regulations ensure the compatibility of new development with the historic character of the area. This 1990s gas canopy provides a stark and unfortunate contrast to the historic homes in the area, some of which are framed by the canopy in this photo.

place landmark and architectural preservation laws. New York City, which had allowed the destruction of half of the exterior of Grand Central Station for the construction of the then-named Pan Am Building, prevented the owner from destroying the other half of it.[3] Today, preservation is part of a larger movement to maintain and conserve existing physical and social networks by rehabilitation of buildings. Many people actively seek listings for their property on the National Register of Historic Places, an entirely voluntary action that results in certain restrictions on the property—as well as certain tax benefits for the property owner. Most states and many local governments maintain their own official lists of historic buildings and places, and many of those are certified by the secretary of the interior and state historic preservation officers as meeting specified federal guidelines.

Interest in preserving the historic and architectural heritage of the United States, from the national to the local level, has grown significantly in the last quarter of the twentieth century. Individual citizens, property owners, and public officials recognize it as a means of preserving the past because of its intrinsic value, and as a means of slowing down sprawl by putting valuable sites and buildings to economically viable use. Local governments typically use a combination of carrots (tax and cash incentives, plus loan programs) and sticks (restrictive zoning ordinances) to encourage the preservation of historic structures and the character of historic districts.

The economic use of historic resources became very popular during the 1980s. Cities such as St. Louis, in an attempt to regain population in the central city, led the use of investment tax credits and other financial and regulatory incentives to rehabilitate older buildings. A number of developers such as the Rouse Corporation, which rehabilitated St. Louis's Union Terminal into a marketplace and hotel, have taken advantage of these opportunities to create successful mixed-use developments. These public-private partnerships have gained momentum over the last twenty years as communities continue to find ways to promote reuse.

Local communities have gone beyond tax and funding incentives by creating innovative zoning ordinances for historic preservation. New York City was a pioneer in the use of *transfer of development rights* as a tool of historic preservation. Under such a program, the owner of a small historic building on a site that might profitably be developed with a much taller building can sell the extra "development rights"—the difference between the development actually on the property and the total development that would be allowed on the property under current regulations—to other landowners, who then can build more on their property than would otherwise be allowed. The New York City program limits transfers to adjacent properties. Chicago adopted a similar program but permits transfers anywhere within a defined area essentially contiguous with the Loop, the popular name for Chicago's central business district.

The most visible preservation efforts are usually those focused on individual buildings. Such programs typically require that the owner preserve the building and that any remodeling be used to bring it back to its original, historic character. Thus, the owner of a Victorian building covered by an aluminum front may not be pressured to remove the false front immediately, but if the owner seeks a building permit for any sort of remodeling—inside or outside—one of the conditions of the permit might be that the false front be removed and the original facade restored.

Historic preservation efforts for a building can involve every possible form of intervention, from mere repainting to full-scale restoration or reproduction. While the term *preservation* implies maintaining a structure in its original state, most historic structures have become so outdated that their use would be impracticable without some adaptations. Those structures maintained in their original form are usually good for museums, as other uses are often impractical or impossible. The use of old buildings as museums or historic house museums has limits in terms of community support and the ability to save enough structures to have any meaning.

It is not possible to use a structure built in the 1830s for offices without providing plumbing and electricity necessary for today's standards. Therefore, most communities also maintain standards that must be followed when restoring structures for reuse. Adaptive use involves structural and cosmetic changes, which must be regulated so that the structure maintains its original architectural integrity. Local and state entities have established commissions that determine the appropriateness of intended renovations and oversee these changes.

Many communities also create special historic districts. Special district zoning designation has long been used in preservation. Among the earliest historic districts created are the famous French Quarter in New Orleans and the Plaza in Santa Fe, New Mexico. Historic district designation allows communities to impose special architectural controls in an area to integrate historic preservation of specific buildings and ensure that any new construction is based on certain standards. Those standards usually include specifications for building materials and colors, proportions of buildings, setbacks, roof treatments, facades, signage, porches and entries, and other architectural detailing. The emphasis of these regulations is on ensuring that new development and remodeling within the district is compatible with its most important historic features, recognizing that not every building or site within such a district is itself of historic importance.

The number of historic districts is growing as communities realize their importance, not only in terms of maintaining the unique culture and heritage of an area, but for economic development purposes. Historic districts attract tourists to the area's cultural heritage and create a unique identity. Unfortunately, in many communities the richest cultural areas were demolished in earlier renewal eras. However, even a handful of buildings are used to create his-

toric districts because special restrictions can then be placed in the areas surrounding a district. Some communities help stabilize neighborhoods surrounding districts by preventing certain kinds of development and land use
within a designated area encircling a historic district.

Historic preservation is a particularly valuable aspect of urban revitalization because it encourages revitalization and long-term preservation of an area
in the character in which it was built. Historic preservation does not work
everywhere—there are older neighborhoods that are not historic and historic
buildings that are in such disrepair that they are probably not worth saving—
but it is one important tool in implementing plans for older areas.

Infill Development

Infill development has also become an important tool in urban revitalization.
The term *infill* applies most aptly to the construction of individual buildings
or small projects on vacant tracts in established areas that are already served by
utilities and surrounded by urban development. It provides a way of helping
communities maintain or restore existing areas, reduce infrastructure investment, and improve the tax base. While infill normally constitutes only a small
proportion of the development in a community, it can help communities
reduce sprawl.

Following World War II, communities grew significantly while the population density declined. Developers found it more cost effective to use large
tracts of land at the fringe of communities than to build within the existing
city center. This also meant that developable land was left vacant or underutilized within the city. Into the 1970s, local governments contributed to
sprawl by providing the necessary infrastructure of roads, schools, water and
sewer systems, electric and gas lines, and neighborhood parks. However, by
the mid-1970s, as federal funding decreased, communities found it more and
more difficult to finance sprawl, particularly when existing infrastructure
needed more funding for maintenance and upgrading. As older schools
became vacant, inner-city parks too dangerous to use, roads more congested,
and tax rates high, communities began looking for alternatives to sprawl. This
became particularly critical in older cities totally enclosed by incorporated
communities. One solution to sprawl has been to make infill a more attractive option.

Infill requires either vacant or underused land, and most cities contain significant amounts of such land. Sometimes these parcels were the sites of buildings that have become dilapidated or even been destroyed. Sometimes they are
overlooked parcels that seemed overpriced to developers who could find
cheaper, larger tracts of land at the urban fringe. Some tracts remained vacant
for many years due to neighborhood opposition to proposed development on
them. Other tracts are vacant because they have had stubborn or greedy owners who always held out for a higher price than the market would offer.

Undeveloped urban land is cause for increasing concern among local government offices, developers, businesses, and property owners. The continued decentralization of development causes further suburbanization of jobs and a disproportionate amount of new services outside the city, often beyond the suburbs. The costs of sprawl are significant, and the empty spaces left behind create many problems of their own.

For infill development to occur, developers must be willing to develop vacant or underutilized land. Developers are, above all, experts in local real estate market conditions. They understand which locations in town are best suited for development. The key to successful development for them is the timing of construction, sales, and payments. For developers to be interested in infill, they must have assurance that they are buying land in a stable area and that they have neighborhood approval. There also has to be some assurance that they can make a profit comparable to what they would make in fringe development, which often means that communities must be willing to streamline the regulatory process.

Whether infill occurs or not is in part a regional function. Where there is cheap land with good access and public sewer and water service in outlying areas, infill is relatively unattractive. Where the land market is tight, the suburbs are nearing capacity in their infrastructure, or commuting times have reached levels that are unacceptable to many people, infill becomes much more attractive. Thus, antisprawl policies (discussed in chapter 12) are also pro-infill policies.

Not all vacant parcels are reasonably developable. Some are owned by speculators or continue to be owned by landowners who simply do not want to sell at a reasonable price. Some are entangled in estates or bankruptcies that take years to resolve. Some have environmental problems that may be so expensive to cure, there is little profit potential left (although brownfields legislation at both federal and state levels mitigates some of that potential burden).

Successful infill also depends on effective neighborhood participation in community planning decisions. Unfortunately, conflicts between developers and neighborhood groups are common, particularly in developed areas. Most homeowners do not want higher-density development in or next to their neighborhoods; some residents oppose any change whatsoever. Citizens perceive that infill has the potential of infringing on their way of life. Neighborhood complaints tend to focus on concerns about traffic, design compatibility, parking, and maintaining property value. While a very serious obstacle, neighborhood opposition is not insurmountable. Most people would like to see improvements to their neighborhood. If people participate in preparing a plan that creates neighborhood improvements including infill, they may well support the new projects. Where there is neighborhood opposition, local planners, acting as mediators, can help groups with differing interests to find common ground.

Typically there are five approaches to infill development:

1. A pilot project consisting of a single commercial building or a few model homes to determine if infill is economically viable. This method lends itself well to residential infill projects where small sites are available.

2. A cluster project that provides amenities on the fringe of the development parcel. This technique requires a larger parcel, but it is popular because it combines modern amenities found in suburban developments with the convenience of living closer to employment and services.

3. The niche market approach. Often developers find a market that is underserved. A niche market may exist for gallery-studio-apartment combinations for artists, high-tech home offices (with high-speed data lines to every unit), or a small entertainment area to serve a gentrifying neighborhood.

4. Affordable housing. This is a common form of infill. This method usually relies on some form of government or not-for-profit assistance or a public-private partnership (concepts discussed in more depth in Chapter 18).

5. A piecemeal approach. Individual city lots are purchased and homes or offices are built for the builder's use or on speculation. This piecemeal approach generally involves individual lots, small-scale builders,

This map shows opportunities for additional development and areas that should be conserved in their present condition in core areas in Stillwater, Oklahoma. Source: RM Plan Group, Nashville, for the City of Stillwater (1998).

and individual landowners. Often it simply reflects the free market in operation, with the small builder using a lot when time and money allow.

Most of these techniques require a plan and at least tacit cooperation from the neighborhood, allowing the local government to grant rezoning or other regulatory accommodations for the infill project. Certainly, a small pilot project or a series of piecemeal buildings is possible with no action by the city (and thus no particular concern with neighbors), but such projects are most likely to occur in relatively healthy neighborhoods where infill is natural but not essential to survival of the area.

To date, the greatest success in infill efforts has occurred in older communities in the North and East. Newer communities in the West and Southwest still have the ability to expand their borders. Their rapid growth in the last few decades has lent itself to large tract development at the urban fringe. Most of these communities in areas of rapid growth are looking at ways to encourage infill before their unique environments are consumed by expansion and the negatives of urban sprawl create unwanted impacts.

Neighborhood Preservation and Stabilization

Sometimes communities discover deterioration in older areas before it becomes serious. When that occurs, the problems are more subtle, as are the remedies. When a once solid neighborhood begins to show signs of deterio-

Even modest older neighborhoods can remain vital with the help of neighborhood stabilization programs. A problem often faced in older neighborhoods is that of parking. Homes like these typically have garage space for only one car, requiring that multiple-car households create more parking in their yards or on the streets.

ration—reduced quality of maintenance on some properties, decrease of owner occupancy, abandonment of some residential properties, vacancies in some commercial properties—it is often time for the local government to undertake a stabilization effort.

Neighborhood stabilization involves many of the same techniques as other development techniques for older areas: a good plan and incentives to encourage its implementation. One of the issues to be addressed in planning is the cause of the deterioration. Sometimes it is just age, but sometimes there are other factors such as increased traffic on a major road through the area, adoption of zoning regulations that discourage rehabilitation of properties, the closure of a school, or the abandonment of other public facilities in the area. Sometimes the local government can reverse or mitigate the decisions that have contributed to the decline—by rerouting some of the traffic on the road, reopening a branch library or establishing a community center in the old school, or amending the zoning or other codes to encourage rather than discourage reinvestment. In other cases, it may be impossible to reverse a decision to close a school or otherwise change the neighborhood, and the local government must then work with neighbors to develop countermeasures. Local investment in visible infrastructure is almost always both useful and essential to success.

Issues of Social Equity

Land developers, owners of major businesses, Realtors, and even neighborhood associations typically have the ability to take care of themselves in the planning process. Such groups have the time, energy, knowledge, and political contacts to ensure that their interests are carefully considered and, usually, protected. Not everyone can do that, however. Many people are left out of the process because they lack the means, the time, the connections, or the confidence to participate. One of the critical roles of professional planners in comprehensive planning is to ensure that plans are equitable to all the groups in the community; planners should strive to ensure that even those not involved heavily in the process are treated fairly.

Social equity issues have dealt historically with income, social opportunities, access to various institutions and services, and health and welfare opportunities. Among the many national efforts has been the provision of free public education, benefits from the Social Security system, health insurance through Medicare and Medicaid, and unemployment insurance. In the last fifty years, planners have taken an increasingly important role in meeting social needs and mitigating social consequences of policies. All planning has social implications, so it is not surprising to find planners assuming the role of social planner in all of their work.

It is the job of the practicing planner to create better communities. That concept means different things to different people, because there is a diversity of needs within any community. For planners, it has very specific meaning. The American Institute of Certified Planners has adopted a code of ethics, which provides, in part, that:

> A planner must strive to expand choice and opportunity for all persons, recognizing a special responsibility to plan for the needs of disadvantaged groups and persons, and must urge the alternation of policies, institutions and decisions which oppose such needs.[4]

As simple as that seems, it is a challenge. For decades cities experienced rising crime rates, areas of economic decline, and even riots. At the same time the United States has an aging population and an increasing percentage of families with a single head of household. As the economy has changed from one with a manufacturing base to one with a service and information base, urban conditions have deteriorated with a growing disparity between the wealthy and the poor. Thus, planners must not only consider the equitable distribution of resources, they must also seek to reduce the impacts of decisions and policies on any disadvantaged group.

Addressing the issue of social equity requires that planners view comprehensive planning from a very different perspective than the purely analytical one suggested in much of this book. Social impacts must be considered in planning decisions just as environmental or economic impacts are. One of the first ways that planners began to bring social equity into the planning process was through the public participation of traditionally underrepresented groups.

Paul Davidoff, in his theory of advocacy planning, and Norman Krumholz, in the *Cleveland Policy Plan Report,* led the efforts to deliberately create policies aimed at redistribution of resources and to create means of enhancing participation in the decision-making processes. Davidoff was concerned that planners approached policy decisions in terms of technical solutions and that there was a persistence of inequitable distribution of resources due to a reliance on the private market. In the mid-1960s he proposed that planners should act to attract resources for disadvantaged groups rather than continue to act as neutral agents.[5] He further argued that all decision making, including planning, is laden with values. Thus, the values of the planner should be made clear, and planners should act as proponents of specific solutions that represent specific interest groups. The goal of advocacy planning is to make the client group politically powerful. As an advocacy planner, the planner educates the group being represented on how to be a part of the planning process, as well as helping the group articulate its own ideas.

Krumholz and his co-workers in Cleveland embraced the concept of equity planning in the 1970s, when they created the *Cleveland Policy Plan Report.*[6] By working closely with groups, particularly neighborhood groups forming at that time, they were able to open up the planning process to greater citizen participation. Their primary goal was to create city policies that provided choices for disadvantaged groups.

The theories and actions of the 1960s and 1970s gradually gained popularity, and conscious attempts were made to create policies to redistribute resources in favor of the least powerful groups. Traditionally, planners have presented decision makers with choices, but with equity planning, planners have sought to distribute resources to include the disadvantaged rather than hope for decisions from policy makers that would cause redistribution.

Unfortunately, as planners became more aware of social equity issues and the political realities of their communities, cities became increasingly diverse and the concepts of shared governance became more difficult to achieve. At the same time, groups that began as advocates for specific disadvantaged groups or neighborhoods evolved into recognized community organizations. By the early 1990s, fiscal austerity served to emphasize issues related to this growing diversity and representation. Therefore, today there is an increasing dependence on coalitions of allied community organizations as economic and demographic inequities continue to grow. Just as in the past, government has been the entity to respond to issues of social equity; today, society increasingly depends on partnerships between the public and private sectors to realize these social goals. It is these coalitions that will be leading in the political arena.

A number of elements in the comprehensive planning process relate directly to social planning. The most obvious ones are housing, transportation, economic development, and citizen participation. However, this subject also touches on areas such as human services and environmental planning. Planners address social equity issues through the planning process and the policies and programs that are an outcome of that process. Therefore, there should be an understanding of the issues and techniques related to social equity that form the foundation of social planning.

Note that the issue of social equity cuts across many of the issues discussed in other parts of this text: in transportation, it is important to recognize that some people depend on mass transit as their primary form of transportation; in economic development, plans should include opportunities for those with limited skills and limited choices; and affordable housing is a critical need in many areas.

Established Areas and Sustainability

Chapter 3 introduced the concept of sustainability in the context of existing conditions analysis. A key element of any plan for a sustainable community is to continue to make use of established areas. Land in developed areas has already been taken from agriculture and other natural uses and cannot easily be restored to those purposes. Typically, there is infrastructure such as roads, sewer, water, and schools available in established areas, eliminating the need for major new investment in those elements.

Further, development in established areas is a part of the established urban fabric, depending upon and reinforcing existing shopping centers, libraries, parks, and other essential community facilities. As new suburbs move outward, it is necessary to replicate those facilities. To the extent that redevelopment occurs within established areas, the community can continue to use those facilities.

Travel distances to jobs, shopping, and recreation are usually shorter from established areas than from new suburbs, reducing the dependence on autos and other forms of transportation. Infill development at its best may include both the adaptive reuse of buildings and the preservation of some valuable historic ones. It can maintain social balance in the schools, instead of leaving poor people in the city while richer ones move out; there need never be a cycle of gentrification if areas are never abandoned by middle- and upper-income groups.

Further, it is clear that keeping people in the city is essential to basic safety issues and to the general quality of life. There really *is* safety in numbers, and having people live in the heart of the city keeps people there twenty-four hours per day, not just during the working day. With more people in town, restaurants can stay open for dinner as well as lunch, stores will stay open in the evenings, suburban shoppers may return to the city to visit specialty stores, and there will be at least the beginnings of a critical mass of activity to support movie theaters and other forms of entertainment.

The goals of sustainability, in making continued use of developed areas, are entirely compatible with the long-standing planning objectives of maintaining healthy and vital neighborhoods and shopping areas in older parts of the community. A commitment to sustainability simply increases the number of reasons to pursue those objectives.[7] Note that the "new urbanists" advocate recreating "traditional" neighborhoods (houses with front porches on smallish lots, served by alleys and relatively narrow streets with sidewalks, all located in a traditional grid of streets).[8] Seaside, Florida, which served as a set for the 1998 movie called *The Truman Show,* is perhaps the most famous of the creations of the new urbanists.[9] Existing neighborhoods in many communities already have such traditional characteristics; continuing to include them achieves these "new" objectives, as well as the objectives of sustainability and urban revitalization.

Conclusion

While there are many critics of early efforts of urban renewal, those efforts, spearheaded by the federal government, brought the issues of deteriorating inner areas to general public attention and began efforts to stabilize neighborhoods. Citizens gained an important role in the planning process with the recognition of the value of their participation. Valuable tools also were put in place as local governments were forced to standardize building and housing codes and create innovative incentives to guide growth and development. Unfortunately, low- and moderate-income families were often displaced, and much of the social fabric of urban centers was destroyed at the same time.

In response to some of the drastic actions of urban renewal, efforts today involve a slower process that calls for longer planning horizons and is driven by local and individual efforts. It will take many years to erase the decades of decay and abuse. Communities are responding to diminishing resources by developing creative approaches to financing. Efforts to conserve and improve the existing stock of housing, industrial and commercial structures, and public facilities are now dependent on negotiation and mediation by planners and the flexibility of communities in administering and encouraging various conservation and redevelopment efforts. The success of these public–private partnerships will determine the extent to which inner cities can be preserved and used.

The Role of the Professional Planner

Planners must play four critical roles in dealing with development in older areas:

- *Urban planner.* Redevelopment, revitalization, stabilization, and preservation all require good plans as a starting point;
- *Facilitator and coordinator.* As this chapter suggests, success in revitalizing, stabilizing, or preserving older areas requires a complex combination of techniques; blending and managing those techniques over time is a hands-on management task and one that often falls to the planner.
- *Mediator.* New development in older areas almost always raises concerns from neighbors, and those concerns can easily become opposition—often irrational opposition. The planner as mediator can help prospective developers modify project designs to respond to legitimate neighborhood concerns and can help neighbors understand the benefits, as well as the threats, of new investment in older areas.
- *Advocate.* The role of the planner as advocate becomes particularly important in planning for change in older areas. Otherwise, those who are not well represented in the political system (often the poor and underemployed) may suffer unfairly for the community's gains in revitalization.

The Role of the Individual Citizen

Unfortunately, the typical role of the individual citizen in dealing with older areas is to ignore the problems and oppose the solutions. People living in other parts of the community may choose to ignore deteriorating areas. Those who live in or near older areas often fall into two groups: those who are eager to get out and thus do not particularly care about change; and those who are happy with their own situations (sometimes on the edge of the deteriorating area) and are opposed to any change that increases the number of people or amount of traffic in their neighborhood. Although the opposition of the latter group to change is understandable, without revitalization and other forms of change, many such older areas will die.

Thus, the appropriate role of the individual citizen in dealing with the future of older areas is to help plan constructively for the future. An analysis of strengths and weaknesses (see chapter 2) can be a particularly effective technique in older areas. Neighbors can use such an analysis to establish a goal of preserving the strengths and attempting to mitigate the weaknesses. Because it is usually the strengths of the area that attract developers to it, their goals are likely to be similar.

Once having participated in a planning process, responsible neighbors ought to support publicly proposed changes consistent with the resulting plan. Other neighbors may still fear and oppose change, and the public support of more thoughtful neighbors may be essential to the success of the plan.

EXERCISES

1. Pick an older area of your community. Working with a group, assess its strengths and weaknesses, opportunities and threats. Is it deteriorating? If so, can you tell why? What could local government do to make that area more attractive to private investors?

2. Drive, bicycle, or walk around that same older area or another one and pick a site where you think a rational developer might want to build something—then decide generally what you would want to build if you were the developer. Now go to the local planning office and check on zoning and other development regulations. Will the regulations allow you to build what you would like to build there? Are all of the rules reasonable? Are they consistent with the existing pattern of development? Did you check the rules on off-street parking and loading?

3. While driving around, pick out an older building that you think might be available cheap, as a "fixer-upper." Go to the building office and find out what you would have to do to use the building, besides putting it back in good structural condition with safe plumbing and electrical systems. Would you have to add parking? An elevator? Other accessibility features? Would it still be feasible to undertake the project? (*Note:* If you are doing this exercise in a class, assign a couple of people to go to the building office, so that dozens of students do not descend on that office asking the same questions.)

4. Is there an area in your community that is undergoing gentrification? If you are not sure, ask a local Realtor. What has made it attractive? Does the gentrification appear to be displacing other people? Where are they going?

5. How does your community address the housing needs of those who cannot afford housing on the open market? Did you know anything about this before you read this chapter and came to this exercise? Why or why not?

Discussion Questions

What can be done to revitalize your community's downtown? How much of the effort would be public? How much would be private? Who owns most of the property? Are they the kinds of owners who seem likely to participate in a revitalization effort? Is there one owner with a lot of property that might be part of a large project, or are there many small owners? Even if your knowledge of ownership patterns is not complete, does it provide you with useful information regarding the probable success of a revitalization effort?

Further Reading

American Planning Association. 1994. *Planning and Community Equity: A Component of APA's Agenda for America's Communities Program.* Chicago: Planners Press. An interesting and insightful collection of short articles that address the basic issues involved in social equity.

Bartik, Timothy J. 1991. *Who Benefits from State and Regional Economic Development Policies?* Kalamazoo, MI: W.E. Upjohn Institute. A good text on economic development programs. The appendices have good models of causal relationships.

Beatley, Timothy. 1994. *Ethical Land Use: Principles of Policy and Planning.* Baltimore: Johns Hopkins University Press. An excellent discussion of social equity issues and land use, with particular emphasis on environmental issues; Beatley applies Rawlsian principles to the consideration of environmental impacts on different socioeconomic groups.

Byrum, Oliver E. 1992. *Old Problems in New Times: Urban Strategies for the 1990s.* Chicago: Planners Press. This book presents persuasive arguments for social planning for central cities. It shows how physical, economic, and social issues are integrated and suggests means of solving a number of social issues.

Camon, Naomi. 1997. "Neighborhood Regeneration: The State of the Art." *Journal of Planning Education and Research* 17, no. 2: 131–144. An excellent review of the three cycles of urban renewal over the last 50 years.

Davidoff, Paul. 1965. "Advocacy and Pluralism in Planning." *Journal of the American Institute of Planners* 31, no. 6:331–337. The classic work that defined advocacy planning and laid the foundations for contemporary consideration of social equity issues in planning. Old but still very relevant.

DeGrove, John M. 1992. *Planning & Growth Management in the States.* Cambridge, MA: Lincoln Institute of Land Policy. Good case studies of how communities around the United States have attempted growth management.

Fisher, Peter S., and Alan H. Peters. 1998. *Industrial Incentives: Competition Among American States and Cities.* Kalamazoo, MI: W.E. Upjohn Institute. A clear and interesting quantitative analysis on the effectiveness of incentive programs in creating local and state economic development. It is an excellent reference book because it covers both fiscal and regulatory incentives.

Krumholz, Norman, and Pierre Clavel. 1994. *Reinventing Cities: Equity Planners Tell Their Stories.* Philadelphia, PA: Temple University Press. An interesting book with a great deal of insight into social planning. The format of the book combines case studies and interviews with key figures in the case studies.

McGuire, Chester C. 1979. "Maintenance and Renewal of Central Cities," in *The Practice of Local Government Planning,* Frank S. So, Israel Stollman, Frank Beal, and David S. Arnold, eds. Washington, DC: International City Management Association, 469–498. A basic text with a solid chapter on the history and status of urban renewal efforts through the 1970s. The second edition did not include a chapter on this issue. A third edition is now in the works, and such a chapter may again appear.

Miller, Ross. 1996. *Here's the Deal: The Buying and Selling of a Great American City.* New York: Alfred A. Knopf. A well-documented story of largely failed redevelopment efforts in Chicago.

Weiss, Marc A. 1987. *The Rise of the Community Builders: the American Real Estate Industry and Urban Land Planning.* New York: Columbia University Press. A scholarly but highly readable account of real estate development in big cities.

NOTES

1. See, for example, Martin Anderson's indictment of the urban renewal program in *The Federal Bulldozer: A Critical Analysis of Urban Renewal, 1949–62.* Cambridge: MIT Press (1964).

2. The critical step came in 1986, when Congress enacted amendments to the Comprehensive Environmental Response, Compensation and Liability Act (abbreviated as CERCLA but commonly referred to as the Superfund act because of its creation of the superfund for cleanup of abandoned sites); the 1986 amendments increased the number of parties who might be liable for cleanup and enhanced the remedies available to the federal government.

3. The Supreme Court upheld the city's decision in *Penn Central Transp. Co. v. City of New York,* 438 U.S. 104, 98 S. Ct. 2646, 57 L. Ed. 2d 631 (1978).

4. American Institute of Certified Planners, "Code of Ethics and Professional Conduct," number A.5, under "The Planner's Responsibility to the Public."

5. Paul Davidoff, "Advocacy and Pluralism in Planning," *Journal of the American Institute of Planners* 31, no. 6:331–337 (1965).

6. Krumholz describes the Cleveland plan and the efforts behind it in, Norman Krumholz and John Forester, *Making Equity Planning Work: Leadership in the Public Sector,* Philadelphia, PA: Temple University Press (1990).

7. See, generally, Diane Warburton, ed., *Community and Sustainable Development: Participation in the Future,* London: Earthscan (1998); and Peter Calthorpe, *The Next American Metropolis.* Princeton, NJ: Princeton Architectural Press (1993).

8. See William Fulton, *The New Urbanism: Hype or Hope for American Communities?* Cambridge, MA: Lincoln Institute for Land Policy (1996).

9. Its designers, Andres Duany and Elizabeth Plater-Zyberk, wrote *Towns and Town-Making Principles,* London: Rizzoli (1991).

Chapter 18

Planning for Housing

Housing in the United States is largely a private commodity. In the United States in 1993, about 64 percent of housing units were owner occupied, and most others were rented from private landlords by private individuals.[1] Yet housing is a critical part of what makes a community. The history of civilization shows repeatedly that a society that is ill housed and ill fed is one that is ripe for revolution.

Fortunately, most families in the United States are very well housed indeed. U.S. housing features space and amenities unimaginable to any but the wealthiest individuals in most other countries. Yet housing costs have skyrocketed in some communities, pricing home ownership out of the range of many working families and forcing others to choose between living in a distant exurb or living in quarters far smaller than those of their parents at the same stage of life. Market-rate housing is completely unaffordable for the lowest-income wage earners in many communities, and a growing homeless problem is attributable at least in part to the costs of housing. At the same time, many consumers who can afford housing want large houses on large lots, creating an image of abundance in the housing market, although others remain homeless or severely underhoused.

Housing is the largest consumer of land in our communities and one of the most important factors in the lives of people. It directly affects our quality of life—our health, safety, and welfare. The earliest efforts to regulate land use through zoning resulted from a combination of housing concerns. One set of concerns was that of housing reformers, who sought to ensure that all housing units had windows, with direct access to light and air, and indoor plumbing to serve sanitation needs. Another set of concerns came from residents of established neighborhoods, who sought protection from the encroachment of

Many people in the United States are very well housed. Such developments as this one are not typical of the housing stock available to most people, however.

industrial uses into residential areas. Housing long has been and continues to be a central concern in community planning. It is quite different from many of the other facilities for which planners plan—government provides roads, sewer and water systems, schools, and parks and can easily implement its plans for such facilities. In contrast, private developers and builders provide most housing units, creating a challenge for government to plan for the provision and delivery of a service that it typically does not provide.

Planning Principles

Local planners analyze supply and demand as the basis of planning for housing. The basic question is whether the projected supply in the market is adequate to meet the projected demand. The housing market area, usually defined as the local community or the metropolitan region, is the region within which housing is generally competitive because of the employment and service structures that link the region. Consumers are tied to certain locations, and thus to certain housing markets, because of jobs and family, which are linked to transportation systems, trade centers, and educational and health facilities.

Demand for housing is largely a function of population, as divided into households. Population projections take into account both the natural increase and the migration of people into a given market area. In the last few decades, the decline in births, the increase in life span, and the rise of single and divorced households has caused housing demand to increase faster than population in almost all areas of the country. Areas experiencing rapid growth often have trouble keeping up with housing demands. Even in declining and static areas, the change in the size of average households has created increased housing demand. When there were 3.1 people per household in the 1970s,[2] about 30,300 dwelling units were required to house a city of 100,000; with household size at 2.63 people in the 1990s,[3] that same population needs 37,000 dwelling units. Data on population trends and household sizes are usually based on the census, adjusted with any locally available data that are more current. Local planning offices sometimes have census updates, and some state agencies provide updates.

The supply side of housing consists of existing and projected housing units. Most people are generally aware of the construction of new housing units in a community, but it is important to remember that there is also a constant loss of housing units in most communities. Some housing units may be purchased (or condemned) and demolished because they stand in the way of some new public or private development project. Other units may be demolished because they have deteriorated to the point that they are unsafe or otherwise not useful for habitation. Natural disasters, like floods and tornadoes, and human-related accidents, most notably fires, eliminate other housing units. In some communities, the adaptive reuse of commercial buildings into "loft" or other living units, or the conversion of large, old homes into multiple dwelling units bring some additional new units on line. Projecting the available supply of housing requires analysis of current (and probable future) trends in all of these areas.

Planning for housing begins with the same basic step as planning for any other system in the community, with the gathering and analysis of data. Essential data to gather include:

- housing types
- housing condition
- vacancy rates
- housing costs
- new housing construction
- population and population trends
- household size
- household income

All of these data are available from the Bureau of the Census,[4] except data on new housing construction, which should be available from the local building or zoning office. The local planning office or housing authority may have a more current survey of vacancy rates and housing conditions. The local organization of Realtors often tracks housing costs and vacancy rates, also.

These graphs provide a valuable combination of baseline housing data for Delaware County, Indiana. Source: HNTB Corp., Indianapolis (1998).

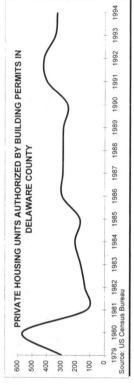

OCCUPANCY AND TENURE

	Renter Occupied	Owner Occupied
Delaware County	19%	81%
City of Muncie	43%	57%
Indianapolis	43%	57%
Anderson	36%	64%
Columbus	38%	62%
South Bend	34%	66%
Bloomington	66%	34%
Kokomo	37%	63%
Indiana	30%	70%

Source: 1990 Census

PRIVATE HOUSING UNITS AUTHORIZED BY BUILDING PERMITS IN DELAWARE COUNTY

Source: US Census Bureau

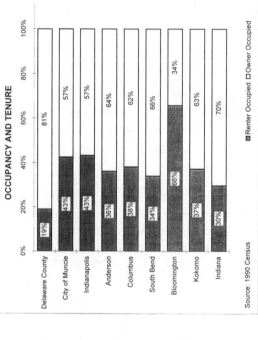

UNITS IN STRUCTURE
(Percent of Total Units by Location)

City of Muncie   Delaware County   Indiana

■ 1-unit detached   ■ 1-unit attached
□ 2 to 4 units   □ 5 to 9 units
■ 10 or more units   ■ Mobile home, trailer, other

Source: 1990 Census

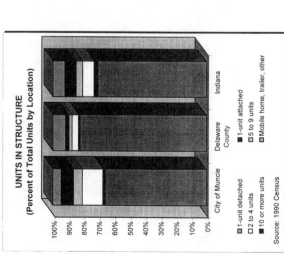

DELAWARE COUNTY HOUSING TRENDS

	1970	1980	1990
Population	129,219	128,587	119,659
Dwelling Units	41,455	47,583	48,793
Households	39,572	44,724	45,177
Persons per Househol	3.27	2.88	2.65

Source: US Census Bureau

From population trends and household size, planners can project housing demand or need. Table 18.1 shows housing projections for Norman, Oklahoma. By factoring income data into the equation, planners can project housing demand by price range. It is important to make the adjustment for income because in some markets there are plenty of units but not enough affordable ones. A typical measure of affordability used in federal programs is the percentage of households that can afford the median-priced house, assuming that they spend 30 percent of their income on housing (including rent or mortgage payments, applicable taxes, insurance, and utilities). Income data typically must be based on the last census and adjusted for changes in the cost of living since it was taken.

Census data include information on the types of housing units, the types of buildings in which they are located, and their general condition; the census identifies particularly dwelling units that are dilapidated or lack indoor plumbing. Some communities have field surveys of housing conditions that are more current and sometimes more detailed; see the description of methodology of conducting housing surveys in chapter 3. Otherwise, local planners can adjust census data by adding to it dwelling units constructed since the census and subtracting units demolished. All of that data can be derived with reasonable accuracy from permit files in the office that issues building (and demolition) permits. This calculation yields the total number of available housing units, a number that can be compared to projected need. The result is often shown as a "vacancy rate," reflecting the percentage of local housing stock that is not occupied at any given time.

Note that a low vacancy rate may suggest that demand exceeds the supply, even if the current housing stock appears adequate for the current popu-

Table 18.1. Projected Housing Needs for Norman, Oklahoma, by type, to 2020.

Type of Structure	1995 Occupied Units		2020 Occupied Units	
	Number*	Percent	Forecast	Net Increase
Duplex	1,212	9.85%	1,705	493
Triplex/quadriplex	2,240	18.20%	3,151	911
Townhouses	1,330	10.80%	1,870	540
Multifamily	7,528	61.15%	10,586	3,058
Total-two or more	12,310	100.00%	17,312	5,002
Single-family	22,788		30,331	7,543
Total-all households	35,098		47,643	12,545

Note: 2020 breakdowns: single-family total calculated at same percentage of net increase as previous 25 years; remainder (multiple-unit structures) allocated in same percentage as 1995 mix by structure type.

Source: The Burnham Group, Cincinnati (1996).

lation; a high occupancy rate may indicate that some people cannot find housing locally and are commuting into the community to work. An absolute shortage of housing units is an important issue for a local government to address, as is a shortage of any particular category or price range of housing.

The study of housing costs is complex. Published figures typically show average cost of new houses, average cost of houses sold, or average construction cost. None of those are particularly meaningful figures, because most housing is not new. A 1993 report found that only 3 percent of rental units and 7 percent of owner-occupied units had been built nationally within the previous four years.[5] The cost of new housing tells little about the cost or resale price of those houses. That is particularly true of many communities in the 1990s, when a large percentage of new houses being built have been large luxury homes that are in no way comparable to "average" homes in the same market. An "average cost of houses sold" (a figure often published by local associations of Realtors) is not much more useful, because there is no way of knowing if the houses sold in a particular year are representative of the market as a whole. In general, very low-priced houses may be less likely to turn over in a particular year, because their owners may have few other housing choices available and thus may hang on to what they have.

What planners would like to know is the *average market value* of houses in the community. Although property tax data may provide a basis for that, most local tax assessment systems have so many twists and turns to them that the data from them are not particularly useful except perhaps in comparing them to housing values in other communities in the same state. Another approach to the housing cost issue is to pick some "typical" housing units—perhaps a 3-bedroom, 1-bath, 1920s bungalow (or other local style) with 1,100 square feet plus basement; a 4-bedroom, 2-bath, 1970s two-story with 2,200 square feet; and a 3-bedroom, 1 1/2-bath, 1 1/2-story 1980s unit with 1,800 square feet—and compare recent sales of units meeting those descriptions to income data for the market and to the costs of similar units in other markets. This provides some basis for determining if there is a shortfall of housing supply and, if so, in what categories it exists.

Many communities make a gross sort of average affordability analysis by determining what percentage of the local population can afford the median-priced local home. That data can be made more useful by establishing, at least for planning purposes, some benchmark, minimum-priced home (such as the 3-bedroom bungalow described above) and determining what percentage of the local population can afford that unit. Planners can complete that analysis by then determining if there are rental units or other habitable alternatives available in the market to serve the rest of the population.

The housing plan then is simply a strategy for meeting the housing needs of the community and, in particular, filling any obvious gaps. Sometimes the strategy can be fairly simple. A particular suburb may discover that it has a statistically inadequate supply of apartments and townhouses, while nearby suburbs have adequate supplies; those data suggest that the market is willing to provide such units but there may be a shortage of available land for such units in the community developing the plan. A community can cure a shortage like that easily, simply by planning and zoning more land for apartments and townhouses. There are actually older, blue-collar suburbs in metropolitan areas that have decided that they do not have enough higher-priced housing. Such communities may develop land-use and zoning strategies to encourage larger homes on larger lots; but such strategies will work only if the community has land with good views, waterfront locations, or other amenities likely to attract upper-income home buyers. Sometimes such a community provides encouragement or even incentives for a developer to build a golf course or other defining amenity for such a project.

Often, however, the unmet housing needs go beyond what the market can provide. An issue that has been growing over the last decade is that of housing the homeless. This is a problem that typically falls to local governments and to local social welfare agencies. Homeless people rarely qualify for federal and state programs, most of which are place-based. The homeless problem is complex and not well understood. It is unclear, for example, whether the homeless problem has grown worse in the last quarter of the twentieth century or has simply become more visible. The homeless are not a homogeneous group. Some are homeless by choice, like the colorful hobos who once rode the rails for adventure, or those modern hobos who follow particular rock groups around the country. Other people are temporarily homeless due to fire, flood, or the loss of a job. Some are homeless because of mental illness, domestic violence, or other personal problems, including divorce. Obviously, society must respond to those different groups differently. Most measures now in place, however, are stopgap measures, simply providing rescue services for mothers with young children and temporary places for the homeless to sleep during the worst weather.

In many communities there are also working poor who cannot afford local housing. In major metropolitan areas, those people may be able to find more affordable housing in other parts of the region, and a good mass transit system may be an effective solution. In some cases, however, there are no free-market solutions to the homeless problem. It is in those cases that only government intervention can close the gap in delivery of this private commodity that is so essential to life.

The Role of Local Government

Local government has always had the most direct impact on housing through regulation and provision of services. More recently, some local governments have joined with private industry in the provision of housing.

Local regulations begin at the most basic level with building and housing codes. Building codes establish standards for construction and remodeling, while housing codes establish standards of maintenance. Virtually all cities and towns and most counties have adopted building codes. Because there is philosophical resistance to such government intervention in some rural areas, some counties do not have building codes (a few are still not permitted by their states to adopt them), and others have simply exempted agricultural buildings from the codes. Housing codes are more common in larger cities, but college towns and others with a high percentage of rental housing sometimes adopt them, in addition to building codes.

Most local governments adopt a standard building code by reference. There are currently three model building codes in use in most of the United States: one produced by the Building Officials and Code Administrators (generally known as the BOCA Code); another produced by the Southern Standard Building Code Conference (known, not surprisingly, as the Southern Building Code); and the Uniform Building Code, produced by the International Conference of Building Officials (ICBO). These code organizations and a small number of other groups also publish and update codes for plumbing, electrical, and mechanical systems, as well as for fire safety. Recently, the three code organizations have been actively working to merge their efforts and their products; the result should be a single national model building code sometime around the year 2000.

These codes have standardized the requirements for and quality of construction of all housing regardless of the type or ultimate price. Although there is little question that the codes have ensured that all newly built housing (and other buildings) will be safe for its inhabitants, some critics have argued that the codes are so detailed and so rigid that they have inhibited technological innovation in housing and have artificially inflated costs. It is interesting to compare the changes in technology in housing to those in transportation and communications. Oldsmobile, Chrysler, Ford, and others who were pioneers in the automobile business would recognize today's vehicles for what they are but would be astonished at the changes in technology ranging from such basics as automatic starters (early cars were hand-cranked) to electric seats with memories, multispeed automatic transmissions, and automatic traction control. Marconi and Edison, pioneers in communications, might not even recognize what they were seeing if they went into a modern electronics store. Although those inventors would understand the basic principles on which cell phones and pagers work, the technology is radically different in size, performance, and cost from anything with which they worked. Communications is a fascinating example, because costs have declined as quality has improved.

In contrast to transportation and communications, someone who built homes for those pioneers could build today's houses with little retraining. Modern homes have more insulation, plastic pipe instead of metal, and some new flooring and countertop materials, but there is little fundamental, technological change in the house itself. Building codes certainly play an important role in society, but it is interesting to contemplate what might happen if the housing industry had more flexibility in creating its product.

Housing codes typically deal with maintenance and usually apply only to multifamily or other rental housing. These codes provide a useful tool that government can use to ensure that landlords keep their buildings safe and that they make such simple safety additions as smoke detectors and battery-powered exit lights. Some housing codes are enforced on a complaint basis, others on an inspection cycle in which every building is scheduled to be checked at specified intervals (such as every four or five years), and still others require an inspection whenever there is a change in tenants. Housing codes are fairly common in larger cities but extremely rare in small towns and essentially unknown in rural areas.

Beyond building and housing codes, local governments regulate housing through zoning (chapter 10) and subdivision regulations (chapter 11). Zoning has become increasingly complex in the last four decades, but it remains the basic means by which local government separates land uses. Through zoning, communities determine the areas in which housing will exist and the characteristics of those neighborhoods—the size of the lots, the mixture (if any) of dwelling unit types, and the other kinds of uses allowed in the same neighborhood. Zoning can have adverse effects on housing by excluding apartments or low-cost housing from part or all of the community; it is generally called *exclusionary* when it has these effects, because the result is the exclusion of some socioeconomic groups from those parts of the community.

Through subdivision regulations, local governments determine the quality of developments in which housing will exist. Well-designed subdivisions include adequate streets, good drainage, sidewalks, street signs, streetlights, and other basic necessities; the absence of any of these, or obvious deficiencies in them (standing water in neighborhoods, potholes in relatively new streets), is typically an indication of weak subdivision regulations or poor administration and enforcement of them.

The combination of zoning and subdivision regulations can directly affect the cost of housing. Developers invariably try to pass on the costs of land development to consumers, so any increased requirements are likely to affect housing costs. A development with wider streets, some parkland or open space, and better drainage will involve higher development costs than one that omits those. Over the long term, consumers need good drainage, and the quality of life will be improved if residents can enjoy parks. Beyond some point, however, wider streets create no particular benefit. Similarly, oversized drainage facilities and poorly located parks serve little public purpose. One of the goals of local governments in development regulation must be a reasonable balance between cost and quality in new development.

Local governments play another important role in dealing with housing.

They provide many of the services on which housing depends—sewage collection and treatment, stormwater management, treatment and delivery of water, fire protection, street and sidewalk maintenance, and construction and maintenance of parks and other public facilities. To the extent that local government invests in quality facilities in areas where it wants to encourage new housing, it provides positive reinforcement for housing investment. Where it lags in providing services, it may discourage housing investment. As the discussion in chapters 11 and 12 suggests, some local governments today try to pass on some or all of the cost of constructing new infrastructure to builders and developers; obviously some or all of those costs get passed through to buyers, resulting in higher housing costs. Thus, the policies of local government in dealing with infrastructure and public services play an important role in the housing market.

Today an increasing number of local governments go beyond assessing housing needs and attempt to implement programs to provide an adequate amount of low- and medium-cost housing. Some local governments regularly evaluate land-use and housing regulations to assess their impact on the supply and costs of housing. The costs associated with developing residential neighborhoods include the rising land costs resulting from local land-use or environmental restrictions; shortages of land with local services; rising construction costs due to increases in labor, materials, and equipment; and financing charges incurred during the permit processes. For example, many communities have streamlined the site plan approval process so that processing delays do not increase the costs that developers will pass on to consumers. Some communi-

Public housing projects like this one filled a crucial role in the housing market, but many have failed to become viable neighborhoods.

ties allow reduced subdivision standards (often narrower streets with smaller lots) for developments focused on lower-cost housing. This approach raises serious questions. A local government should not encourage the construction of any housing in substandard developments, and particularly not housing for lower-income individuals who may have few choices of places to live; if the narrower streets or other reduced standards are indeed adequate for public safety, those standards ought to be applied community wide, saving everyone money.

Most local governments in communities of significant size have local housing authorities. Funding for housing authorities has largely come from federal programs, described below. These authorities have been direct providers of housing, historically in notorious "projects." The spectacular demolition of the failed Pruitt-Igoe high-rise public housing project in St. Louis drew negative publicity a number of years ago, and today many housing authorities are quietly eliminating this old-style public housing, which in many ways created public ghettos—forcing everyone in need of public housing into one area. At the end of the twentieth century, much of the emphasis on new public housing is on "scattered-site" housing integrated into neighborhoods, thus dispersing public-housing families throughout the community. Although that approach has clear benefits in terms of community integration, the scattered-site housing sometimes takes public-housing tenants away from bus lines and other public and private services on which they may depend. Further, where public housing projects have been occupied by recent immigrants or others with a common ethnic or other background, they have provided support systems for each other and created a critical mass necessary to support ethnic groceries and other important services. While the creation of subsidized ghettos is clearly undesirable, the creation of communities of common interest and support systems can be very desirable indeed. The problem is finding a balance, an issue with which public housing authorities are now struggling.

As housing costs have continued to increase, the affordability issue has affected more and more working families and others who would have been easily housed by the private market thirty or forty years ago. Many communities offer a variety of private and public-private programs to create lower-cost, good-quality, market-rate housing. Typical programs include those in which the local government provides free land (sometimes from old school sites, sometimes lots acquired years earlier when people did not pay their taxes) and nonprofit groups or even local builders agree to construct relatively low-cost housing on them. Special financing is often available for such units from mortgage pools created by local banks and from state housing finance agencies; some states even provide down-payment loans or subsidies for first-time home buyers. One of the "secrets" to creating these lower-cost homes is keeping them relatively small and simple. Builders typically create such homes to have 1,000–1,200 square feet, one or one and a half baths, and either no garage or a one-car garage. Such homes are much smaller than typical new suburban homes, which in the late 1990s are in the range of 1,800 square feet, with at least two baths and a two-car garage, but they are very typical of average new homes built sixty or even forty years ago.

Using the concept of sweat equity and largely volunteer labor, Habitat for Humanity builds this type of home for a similar market, requiring that future owners help to earn their homes by working on those homes and others with the local Habitat group. Habitat also finances the homes, usually without interest. Habitat has become one of the world's largest home builders. Some larger cities have created "urban homesteading" programs, allowing individuals to acquire abandoned and dilapidated houses (often claimed by the local government when the owner quit paying taxes) for one dollar and packaging the acquisition with bank financing, allowing the buyers to restore the units.

Communities can apply for federal grants for affordable housing, but they must have a specialized plan as the basis for such applications. Previously, communities were required to have a Comprehensive Housing Affordability Strategy (CHAS), but late in the 1990s, the CHAS was combined with submission and reporting requirements for several HUD grant programs into the Consolidated Plan. That plan is now used consistently for all major HUD grant programs, although it is still referred to as CHAS. The Consolidated Plan is itself a comprehensive plan incorporating all housing and community development needs, as well as the strategies for addressing those needs. Like other compre-

Habitat for Humanity uses the concept of sweat equity to help bring lower-income families into the housing market. Photo by Jennifer Greig.

hensive planning processes, it includes citizen participation along with elements such as housing and homeless needs assessments and housing market analysis. The CHAS is a three- to five-year strategic plan with priority needs and strategies that can include related issues such as economic development and land use.

CHAS helps to focus community efforts on the provision of affordable housing. For example, when creating the housing market analysis, planners have to describe concentrations of minorities and/or low-income families; show the condition of public housing units; inventory homeless facilities; and describe barriers to affordable housing. Each year, communities submit an action plan that is based on what has been achieved and what is planned for the next year. Thus, communities are held accountable for what is working; what is not working and why; and the next priorities to be addressed. Among the requirements and restrictions for funding is affirmative action for fair housing. This is particularly important in the citizen participation efforts. There is also recognition by the federal government that past housing efforts have resulted in dissolution of neighborhoods and displacement of residents. All affordable housing strategies and policies must include plans for relocating or avoiding displacement of existing residents.

Local, state, and federal planners are beginning to recognize the need to include citizen participation in planning. The requirements put forth in CHAS make it imperative that planners work closely with not-for-profit agencies, housing departments, and community organizations to coordinate viable, fundable plans. While the federal government is withdrawing from directly providing public housing, it is assisting in increasing alternatives in low-cost housing.[6]

A few communities and at least one state (New Jersey) have created "inclusionary" or "fair share" housing programs, attempting to create more balance in the private housing market by ensuring a better mix of housing types and price ranges.[7] At a minimum, such programs typically encourage the construction of apartments and townhouses in suburban areas that might usually attract only detached, single-family homes. Oregon has adopted a statewide policy intended to force all local governments to increase the percentage of their housing stock that consists of apartments and townhouses.[8] Some local governments actually require that individual developers include a certain percentage of specified lower-cost housing in their developments. San Francisco has used a high demand for office space in the city as leverage to require that office developers also provide housing or contribute to a fund that will do so.

There are a number of good programs, but the problem of housing those at the low end of the income scale is a growing one. Planners should seek continued expansion of existing programs and experimentation with new programs to meet these local needs.

The Role of State Government

States have joined the efforts to address housing problems typically through financing. Most states have some sort of a state housing finance agency, usually a quasi-public agency that borrows money by selling bonds and uses that money to make relatively low-interest loans to low-income people, first-time home buyers, and other target groups. Some states have separate programs to provide down-payment subsidies and loans. It is often the lack of a down payment that prevents people from moving from rental units into their first owner-occupied unit; mortgage payments may run little more than rent. State agencies sometimes assist with planning costs and other background studies to address lower-cost housing needs. In some states with unique housing problems, such as Hawaii, state housing agencies take an even greater role in the provision of housing.

States also have some indirect impacts on housing. The growth of state regulations has been cited as contributing to the rising cost of housing. Environmental regulations to protect groundwater, conserve wetlands, manage stormwater, prevent or limit flood damage, and control sediment are mandated by the federal government and instituted and carried out by the states.[9] All these regulations are designed to protect the public health and safety, but many also have secondary effects on development costs. While some of those cost increases involve additional site improvements and other direct costs, there are also indirect costs from such programs, including the fees and other costs associated with additional permitting requirements. States have moved to protect the consumers of housing by passing legislation protecting renters and buyers of newly constructed homes and establishing laws for converting apartments to condominiums.

The Role of the Federal Government

Since the 1930s, during the height of the depression, the federal government has played a significant role in housing in the United States. Although the federal government receives the most publicity for its programs to help low-income groups with subsidized housing, its greatest impact has been in encouraging and facilitating the ownership of single-family homes, typically in the suburbs.

Two issues brought the federal government into housing during the depression: financing housing and housing the poor. When the depression was at its height, large numbers of mortgages were defaulted, and remaining banks were reluctant to lend money either for construction or for mortgages. The Housing Act of 1934 was passed to guarantee bank deposits and insure mortgages. Through a series of federal housing laws, of which the next notable one was adopted in 1948, the federal government created the Federal Housing

Administration (FHA), which provided mortgage insurance. After World War II, Congress created the Veterans Administration (VA) home loan program, which guaranteed low-interest, long-term mortgages with low down payments. The practices of the FHA and VA changed mortgage lending by insuring long-term loans for housing. Prior to the FHA, mortgage loans were short term, with relatively high monthly payments, thus limiting the number of people eligible. Both the FHA and VA programs also reduced the need for down payments. Under federal banking rules, banks and thrift institutions have typically been limited to making mortgage loans for a maximum of 80 percent of the value of a home; that meant that the buyer of a $100,000 home needed a $20,000 down payment. In many cases, finding the down payment has been far more difficult for the buyer than finding the monthly cash to meet the mortgage payments.

Although the two programs operate differently, both the FHA and the VA programs reduce the down-payment requirement (in the case of VA, to zero) by guaranteeing to the bank the payment of the amount of the loan over 80 percent of the value of the home. Neither program is subsidized; in both cases, the buyers pay a small premium for the mortgage insurance, and that premium creates the pool of funds from which the agency covers the small number of losses that arise. The available mortgage funding through these two programs started a period of rapid expansion of suburban housing development and home ownership in the 1950s. Today, private mortgage insurance has largely replaced these two programs, but they had enormous impact on housing by changing mortgage lending practices and making home ownership the norm within the United States.

Through these programs, the federal government began to redefine housing. During the years after World War II, the FHA published an increasing number of guidelines and regulations for homes that would receive insurance through the program. Those regulations at times went beyond building codes in requiring amenities like entry closets that did not serve any particular health or safety purpose. In addition, the FHA published standards for subdivisions for new homes, standards that showed a strong bias toward suburban, single-family developments. The VA typically adopted the FHA standards. Although neither the FHA or VA is a big factor in the housing market today, some of the standards that they once imposed have been adopted by the Federal National Mortgage Association (FNMA, commonly called Fannie Mae). FNMA is a large mortgage pool (obtaining its money by selling bonds to investors) that is the largest buyer of home mortgages in the United States. Many local mortgage "lenders" are not really long-term lenders—they simply process loans. They sell most of those loans to FNMA. Even banks that may own some mortgage loans want to make loans that can be sold to FNMA if the bank ever suddenly needs cash (if, for example, many depositors suddenly want to withdraw their money). Thus, most mortgage loans in the United

States today meet FNMA standards, which are, in part, carryovers from the FHA standards.

The concept of public housing was also redefined by the federal government. The Housing Act of 1937 provided financing for local public housing authorities with the power to build, own, and maintain public housing. With the Housing Act of 1949, the emphasis of urban programs shifted from the delivery of low-cost housing to the clearance of slums. The urban renewal program created by the Housing Act of 1949 focused on redeveloping residential slums. It was quickly expanded to include commercial, industrial, and institutional redevelopment of decaying city centers. Through the years, all these programs have changed and been modified to meet the needs of the era.

By the end of the 1960s, so-called categorical grants to local and state governments replaced some of the older federal programs. In 1974 the Community Development Block Grant (CDBG) program was created to increase the participation of local governments in the use of federal funds. For the first time, the federal government used rent supplements as well as home ownership incentives. Within a few years (in 1977) the federal government created the Urban Development Action Grant (UDAG) to stimulate private investment in low-income housing, which for the preceding fifty years had been the responsibility primarily of the federal government. While UDAG is gone and the CDBG program has very reduced funding levels, the federal government continues to address issues of low-cost housing provision. However, the drive to reduce federal social spending in the 1980s left these programs with very limited funding.

The federal government still plays a significant role in housing finance and investment. The regulation by the federal government of financial institutions regulates and provides funding for mortgage credit. The Government National Mortgage Association (GNMA) buys mortgages backed by the FHA and VA, and the Federal National Mortgage Association (FNMA) buys and holds mortgages, while the Farmers Home Administration (FmHA) gives direct loans for rural housing and community development.

The major role that the federal government has in housing in the United States is best demonstrated by HUD—the United States Department of Housing and Urban Development. While the federal role in housing was fairly weak after World War II, the Housing and Home Finance Agency coordinated public housing and urban renewal. After the Watts riots in Los Angeles in 1965, riots which resulted from dissatisfaction of some residents of a relatively poor, African-American part of the city, the federal government began a more aggressive role by creating HUD. HUD was unique from its inception since it was created as a cabinet-level department and its first secretary, Robert Weaver, was the first African American to head a cabinet-level department. Throughout HUD's existence, it has dealt with complex issues affecting housing, many of which represent conflicting interests. For example, the Urban Renewal Program is focused on slum clearance, often eliminating low-rent housing, yet HUD continues to focus on providing low-income housing. Over the last decade, HUD has consolidated and privatized many of its programs while placing more responsibility on state and local governments. Its central program remains HOPE, Homeownership and Opportunities for People Everywhere, which privatizes public and subsidized housing. HUD's powers, funding, mandated programs, and structure have changed over the decades, but it continues to reflect the federal government's interest in housing for low- and moderate-income families in the United States.

Congress has intervened in the housing market in another way. Through the Fair Housing Act,[10] it has created a federal policy banning discrimination in housing. Although the primary effect is on landlords and professional Realtors, as a practical matter the act applies to everyone. More recently, in 1990, Congress adopted the Americans with Disabilities Act (ADA),[11] which also applies to many types of housing—particularly multifamily housing. The ADA requires increased accessibility for at least some units in larger projects. One of the practical effects of the ADA, however, has been an increased interest in "universal design" principles, intended to serve all people better. Advocates of universal design generally suggest wider doors (to be wheelchair accessible), levers for door handles (most people can push down on a lever, while the young, the old, and people with problems with their hands may have difficulties with knobs), and gently sloped ramps to raised entrances (essential for wheelchairs and easier than steps for many people). There are critics of the intrusion of the federal government into such areas as housing design and the real estate market, but there are few if any public advocates for eliminating the Fair Housing Act or the accessibility provisions of the ADA as they apply to new construction.

In some ways the greatest impact that the federal government has had on housing is not from its housing programs but from its tax policy and its road-building program. The federal income tax has long included a deduction for mortgage interest and for property taxes. For a taxpayer in the 22 percent tax bracket choosing between paying rent of $750 or making a mortgage payment of $850, the tax deductions make all the difference. A typical $850 monthly mortgage payment is likely to include $125 in property taxes, $700 of interest, and $25 in principal. That means that $825 of the mortgage payment is deductible, resulting in a tax savings of about $180 per month, making the effective, after-tax cost of the mortgage payment only $670, or $80 less than the rent. That policy has encouraged a broad pattern of home ownership in the United States.

Dwight Eisenhower, who led the Allied victory in Europe, admired at least one German achievement, which was the construction of its advanced highway system, called the Autobahn. When he became president of the United States in 1953, he led the federal government in creating what has become today's interstate highway system. Its original purpose was defense oriented, to provide high-speed transportation for soldiers and equipment among all U.S. metropolitan areas, but it was that system more than anything else that opened up the suburban development of the 1950s and created the sprawl of the 1970s and beyond.

Conclusion

The average housing situation in the United States is probably the best in the world. More than 100,000 individual home builders and a number of apartment developers and other private entities deliver a remarkable variety of safe, habitable, and often luxurious housing to U.S. residents. Yet there is an increasing part of the population that is inadequately served by the private housing market. Efforts to plan for housing focus on that underhoused or homeless group, trying to understand its needs and create plans for meeting those needs effectively.

The Role of the Professional Planner

Most housing in this country is provided by the private market. Nevertheless, local governments plan for housing for several reasons: to be eligible to participate in certain federal grant programs; to provide a context in which to adopt zoning and other regulations for the protection of neighborhoods; and to define deficiencies in the housing market that may require intervention by local government. Good housing programs are based on good housing plans, which, in turn, should relate to an adopted comprehensive plan.

Developing a housing plan is highly technical. The professional planner has the largest role in developing the analytical background for a housing plan and in identifying appropriate and workable strategies for the plan. Many local planning offices, particularly in larger communities, have at least one person who spends full time on housing issues. Some local governments have separate offices for planning for housing. Some housing authorities have their own planners.

Planners also play a critical role in implementing housing plans. The emphasis of most housing plans is on meeting the needs of those at the lower end of the income scale. Meeting those needs typically involves seeking state and federal funding and state mortgage financing, as well as identifying available property and units that might be redeveloped and creating partnerships with the private sector. All of

---

those are relatively technical tasks that are likely to succeed only with significant effort from professional planners.

As the box on the role of citizens suggests, however, there is a significant policy role in housing planning, and, at that stage, individual citizens as well as public officials must become involved. Another role that many planners play is that of advocacy for those with particular needs, recognizing that people whose circumstances price them out of the housing market may have (or feel that they have) limited influence in the political process.

The Role of the Individual Citizen

Professionals must conduct the complex analyses necessary to determine the extent and scope of the housing problems in a community. Citizens should, of course, provide a reality check on such studies, verifying that the statistical analyses and field studies show results that are generally consistent with the experience of individuals involved in the market.

Once the problem is understood, however, the most serious policy decision involves the extent to which a local government will involve itself in solving housing problems. Some local governments that discover a shortage of housing for lower-income groups create additional zoning for apartments and do nothing else. Others develop truly comprehensive strategies, including public-private partnerships, to deliver more housing to the part of the market needing help. Interested citizens can and should play a key role in helping the local government decide what role it should take in addressing local housing issues.

Individual citizens often play a key role in the enforcement of housing policies, also. It is impossible for local, state, and federal agencies to inspect regularly every housing unit to ensure that it complies with all applicable codes and to monitor every housing transaction to ensure that it is indeed a "fair housing" transaction. Thus, citizens who encounter a housing situation that appears unsafe or unsanitary, or new units that appear not to meet ADA, or ads or marketing practices that are clearly discriminatory should report them. If uncertain about whether a particular situation is a violation, the interested citizen can simply give the facts to the appropriate agency and let case workers there determine whether those facts justify further action.

EXERCISES

1. Interview several recent graduates of your college who are working in your area. Ask them how well the housing market serves their needs. Ask them if they have bought homes or if they expect to be able to buy homes anytime soon. What do the results of this informal survey tell you about your local housing market?

2. If you are living in a dorm or sharing an apartment with a group of students or are otherwise not really a part of the housing market, do a little shopping for housing, at least from ads. Find out how much a starting salary would be in your field. Subtract about 20 percent for taxes. Assume that you can afford to spend 25 to 30 percent of what is left for your monthly housing costs, including utilities. Now look at the ads and see what you can afford. What do these findings tell you about your local housing market?

3. Find out if your community has a Consolidated Plan housing element for its comprehensive plan, or other local housing plan. Check with the planning office, the housing office, or, if in doubt, the office of the mayor or other chief executive. Borrow a copy and review it. What are the local housing problems? How difficult will they be to solve?

4. Evaluate the accessibility of your own housing unit. Borrow a wheelchair (a medical supply store is likely to be happy to loan you one for a day or two) and try to get around in it—try to get into the bathroom and then get up to the sink to wash your hands. How hard would it be to make your existing unit more accessible? How hard would it have been to build the unit originally to be more accessible?

DISCUSSION QUESTIONS

1. How serious is the homeless problem in your community? What is the community doing about it? Is that a good approach?

2. Invite one or more of the following guest speakers to come to class and discuss issues in this chapter: a representative of a large landlord, a local Realtor, a representative of the public housing authority, an advocate for people with disabilities.

FURTHER READING

Culhane, Dennis P., Chang-Moo Lee, and Susan M. Wachter. 1996. "Where the Homeless Come From: A Study of the Prior Address Distribution of Families Admitted to Public Shelters in New York City and Philadelphia." *Housing Policy Debate* 7, issue 2. A good discussion of the homeless issue.

Downs, Anthony. 1973. *Opening Up the Suburbs: An Urban Strategy for America*. New Haven, CT: Yale University Press. A still relevant classic by one of the great critical thinkers about our metropolitan areas. It addresses the need for action by local governments to provide an increased variety of housing opportunities in suburban communities.

————. 1994. *New Visions for Metropolitan America.* Washington, DC: Brookings Institution; and Cambridge, MA: Lincoln Institute for Land Policy. A much more recent work examining the policies that have created our sprawling metropolitan areas and considering alternative policies and patterns of growth.

Haar, Charles M., and Jerold S. Kayden, eds. 1989. *Zoning and the American Dream.* Chicago: Planners Press. A broad examination of the effects of local regulation on the housing market.

Hancock, John. 1988. "The New Deal and American Planning: 1930s," in *Two Centuries of American Planning,* Daniel Schaffer, ed. Baltimore: Johns Hopkins University Press.

Kelly, Eric Damian. 1996. "Fair Housing, Good Housing or Expensive Housing? Are Building Codes Part of the Problem or Part of the Solution?" *John Marshall Law Review* 29, no. 2: 349–368. An examination of the effect of building codes and other regulations on innovation in housing.

Keyes, Langley C., Alex Schwartz, Avis C. Vidal, and Rachel G. Bratt. 1996. "Networks and Nonprofits: Opportunities and Challenges in an Era of Federal Devolution." *Housing Policy Debate* 7, issue 2. A discussion of the shifting roles in providing for housing needs.

REFERENCES

Daniels, Rhonda L. 1994. *Fair Housing Compliance Guide,* 2nd edition. Washington, DC: Home Builder Press. A useful, user-friendly guide to the Fair Housing Act.

Department of Housing and Urban Affairs. 1998. *Building Public-Private Partnerships to Develop Affordable Housing.* Washington, DC: U.S. Government Printing Office. A good guide to CHAS and other federal programs.

Lieder, Constance. 1988. "Planning for housing," in *The Practice of Local Government Planning,* 2nd edition, Frank S. So and Judith Getzels, eds. Washington, DC: International City Management Association. A very practical, how-to reference.

Mallach, Alan. 1984. *Inclusionary Housing Programs: Policies and Practices.* New Brunswick, NJ: Rutgers University, Center for Urban Policy Research. A good discussion of inclusionary housing programs.

NOTES

1. Timothy S. Grall, *Our Nation's Housing in 1993,* U.S. Bureau of the Census, Report No. H121/95-2, Superintendent of Documents (1995).
2. U.S. Bureau of the Census, vol. 1, *Characteristics of the Population,* part 7, table 10, Superintendent of Documents (1992).
3. U.S. Bureau of the Census, Report No. ST96-21, table 2, United States Summary.
4. See http://www.census.gov.
5. Grall, note 1, pp. 11 and 14.
6. See discussion in Langley Keyes et al., "Networks and Nonprofits: Opportunities

and Challenges in an Era of Federal Devolution," *Housing Policy Debate* 7, no. 2: 201–230 (1996).

7. New Jersey Stat. Ann., chapter 52:27D; for a general policy discussion that remains relevant, see Franklin, Falk, and Levin, *In-Zoning: A Guide for Policy-Makers on Inclusionary Land Use Programs,* Washington, DC: The Potomac Institute (1974).

8. Discussed in Nohad Touhan, "Housing as a State Planning Goal," in Carl Abbott, Deborah Howe, and Sy Adler, eds., *Planning the Oregon Way: A Twenty-Year Evaluation,* Corvallis: Oregon State University Press (1994).

9. See Sanjay Jeer et al., *Nonpoint Source Pollution: A Handbook for Local Government,* Planning Advisory Service Report No. 476, Chicago: American Planning Association (1997).

10. 42 U.S.C. § 3601 et seq. Discussed in White, "The National Affordable Housing Act and Comprehensive Planning: An Overview and Analysis," *1992 Institute on Planning, Zoning & Eminent Domain,* 4-1, New York: Matthew Bender, Southwestern Legal Foundation (1993).

11. P.L. No. 101-336, 104 Stat. 327 (codified as 42 U.S.C. § 12101 et seq.).

Chapter 19

Planning for Jobs

In most community planning efforts, "economic development" is high on the list of goals. The bottom line of economic development is jobs—This chapter talks about the relationships among comprehensive planning, economic development, and jobs.

Principles of Economic Development

To some people, "economic development" simply means growth. Those people assume that if the community is growing, it must be healthy, and, conversely, if it is not growing, it must need help. Such assumptions vastly oversimplify the issue.

Most true economic development efforts focus on the "economic base" of the community. The economic base is that part of the local economy that brings in money from outside the community. Every community in the United States sends some money outside the community—to buy automobiles from manufacturers in this country or abroad (even if sold through a local dealer, most of the money goes out of the community), to buy electronics equipment from manufacturers in this country or abroad, to buy clothing from a variety of firms, and, in many cases, to buy products as basic as food. There are no self-sufficient communities in the United States, and few that come close. The only way that a community can afford to continue to send money out of the community to buy such necessary goods is to bring money from other sources into the community. The economic base is the part of the community that brings money into it from outside.

The most typical example of economic base industry is manufacturing. Steel was the mainstay of the economic base of Pittsburgh, Pennsylvania; Gary,

Because manufacturers ship automobiles all over the world, auto assembly and auto parts manufacturing plants are always considered part of the economic base.

Indiana; Birmingham, Alabama; and Pueblo, Colorado. Automobiles supported Detroit, Michigan. Auto parts plants supported many other communities in Michigan, Ohio, and Indiana. Cereal makers drove the economy of Battle Creek, Michigan, and Boeing continues to provide a large part of the economic base in Seattle, Washington. All of those companies make products that serve the nation or the world, and the revenue from them brings new money into the community.

Large-scale agriculture is usually an economic-base industry. Pork from Iowa and North Carolina, wheat from Kansas, oranges from Florida, and corn from Nebraska are shipped to many parts of the country. Although the farmer may sell the commodity to a local or regional packer or elevator, the ultimate sale is to a processor and then to a wholesaler, with the money eventually coming from consumers in other parts of the country. In contrast, truck and dairy farming are often local-service agricultural industries that bring in little or no outside money.

Understanding the economic base has become more complex at the end of the twentieth century. Hospitals were once local-service institutions, but many small, local hospitals have closed, leaving major hospitals to serve regional trade areas and, as a result, to bring in money from outside the community. Although Main Street businesses were always considered a part of the local economy and not the economic base, some regional-scale superstores and malls now draw people from multiple counties, as well as locally, thus making some contribution to the economic base but pulling people away from small-town Main Streets. Microsoft is an information company that has contributed

Grain elevators like these are common landmarks across the Midwest and in other agricultural areas, illustrating dramatically the volume of agricultural products shipped elsewhere via adjacent railroads.

significantly to the economic base in Seattle, but many telemarketing companies serve the entire nation from a few local hubs, thus bringing outside money to those hubs. Airline and hotel reservation centers similarly serve large areas, often from places like Omaha, Nebraska, and Cary, North Carolina—communities that are not particularly famous and that may have no direct service at all from some companies that take reservations in their towns. All of those businesses, like traditional manufacturers, bring new money into the community.

Although the computation of the economic base is complex, understanding it in principle is not. The basic question is, Where are the ultimate customers for the product? For Boeing, Microsoft, General Motors, and Kellogg, they are all over the world. For the new Big X Discount Store, they are probably mostly in the community. Any business that brings in dollars from consumers outside the community (even if the dollars arrive indirectly, through dealers or retailers to wholesalers and back to the manufacturer in your community) is an economic-base industry. Any business that simply recycles local money is not part of the economic-base. A new "big-box" discount store may employ one hundred or more people, but those are not base jobs unless the store serves a large region. On the other hand, a warehouse serving a discount chain's stores in six states does bring in outside money. Sometimes public officials support a new big-box store that is unpopular with neighbors, "because

Table 19.1. Employment Projections for Ames and Story County, Iowa, 1990–2030.

| | | CITY OF AMES | |
| | | 2030 | |
	1990	Low	High
Government	9,980	10,500	10,800
Services	5,480	8,900	9,200
Retail	5,180	7,200	7,400
Manufacturing	1,401	2,400	2,500
Finance/R.E.	978	1,800	1,900
Construction	850	1,100	1,200
Transpo/Utilities	778	1,100	1,200
Agriculture	782	100	115
Wholesale Trade	399	600	700
Mining	50	0	35
Total	25,698	33,700	35,050

| | | STORY COUNTY | |
| | | 2030 | |
	1990	Low	High
Government	11,843	12,600	12,900
Services	8,432	14,200	14,600
Retail	8,621	13,100	13,400
Manufacturing	2,821	5,400	5,600
Finance/R.E.	1,089	2,200	2,300
Construction	490	700	750
Transpo/Utilities	703	900	950
Agriculture	115	100	115
Wholesale Trade	1,032	1,600	1,650
Mining	54	0	35
Total	35,200	50,800	52,300

Source: City of Ames and RM Plan Group, Nashville (1996).

it means jobs for our community." That may be based on a misunderstanding or lack of understanding of the difference between economic-base jobs and other jobs. The big-box store may simply divert sales, and the jobs that support them, from existing businesses in the community. Table 19.1 shows employment projections by sector of the economy for Ames, Iowa.

The economic base is essential to the future of the community, because it brings in the money that the community must send back out to buy a variety of goods. It is, more directly, the driving engine of the local economy. The worker at the auto plant who collects a paycheck spends some of that at the local grocery store; the grocer spends some of that money with local farmers and some of it on local employees, and some of it is sent away. One dollar of revenue in the economic base is likely to turn into four or five dollars in the local economy—that is how many times that dollar changes hands (statistically) before it leaves town.[1] Thus, every economic-base job helps to create several other jobs in the community, largely in local business and service industries.

The Context for Economic Development

All rational planning for economic development focuses on expanding the economic base. Community planners rarely have the primary responsibility for planning for economic development, however. Usually, the local chamber of commerce or economic development agency has that responsibility. Some local governments have a separate office of economic development. Because the revenues of utility companies fluctuate with the economic base, such companies sometimes provide significant support to economic development efforts—including planning.

The principles of planning for economic development are similar to the principles of planning for the community (see chapters 1 and 2). The economic development plan must include a set of goals or a vision, but it also involves data gathering and analysis, assessment of strengths and weaknesses and opportunities and constraints, and, finally, after the goal setting, implementation. In one sense the goal is obvious: to maintain or expand the economic base. But the issue is more complex than that statement suggests, and the community must address other questions, beginning with the question of whether it wants its economic base to expand or remain stable.

Other questions typically evolve from the planning process. A strengths–weaknesses and opportunities–threats analysis is very helpful in economic-base planning. What parts of the economic base are strong? Where are the weaknesses? What are the growth opportunities? What are the threats? Obviously, growing, stable industries provide both strengths and opportunities. Large, strong industries nearing obsolescence can be strengths that are limited by threats. The North American Free Trade Agreement has led some companies to move some parts of their manufacturing operations out of the United States, particularly to Mexico. Such a move, or the potential for such a move, is a threat to the suppliers and service businesses that do business with the manufacturer that moves, as well as to the U.S. employees of the manufacturer. Most economic development professionals would agree that overdependence on one industry is a weakness. At one point in the 1970s, when Boeing was having hard times, someone erected a billboard in Seattle reading, "Will the last one leaving Seattle please turn out the lights?"

From economic-base analysis, most communities will see some obvious weaknesses, which many will view as opportunities. "Diversify the economic base" is a common goal for old manufacturing communities, many of which are overly dependent on one industry. Sometimes goals address threats. If a community has air- or water-quality problems that discourage new industry from relocating there, that community can address those through a plan. A sewer or water plant nearing its capacity is a threat that can be fixed with money. Opportunities also provide goals. A rapidly growing local industry may be acquiring many of its raw materials or parts from suppliers outside the community; meeting some of that demand locally can create a real opportunity by attracting suppliers of such manufacturing inputs to the community.

Understanding the local labor force is also an important part of economic development planning. A midwestern town that has grown up with the auto parts industry is likely to be more successful in attracting a company that makes cases for computers than in luring one that makes the components for computers. The former auto workers can probably build the cases, but they may lack the background to make the components. Some communities address weaknesses in the labor force with job-training programs.

The availability of land and buildings is a key issue in assessing opportunities and constraints for economic development. An old industrial community

A modern but vacant industrial plant can be a community strength in economic development, allowing the community to provide a prompt response to industrial expansion needs.

in North Carolina that desperately wanted and needed to diversify its economic base faced a severe constraint to accomplishing that goal: it had no remaining tracts of land of one hundred acres or more with good access either to rail or to the interstate system. Another community that suffered several plant closures in a row discovered that industries from around the country immediately began making inquiries about the availability of the space represented by the vacant plants—particularly one with some unique and very heavy-duty cranes in it.

As these examples suggest, land is useful for traditional industrial development only if it has good access to transportation. That inverted "L" formed by the Erie Canal and the Hudson River attracted lots of industry when barges were a principal form of transportation. Later the railroad and then the New York State Thruway followed that same route, creating additional and continuing opportunities. At mid-century, railroad access was considered a primary strength for heavy industry. Today, so many goods move by truck that good and direct access to the interstate highway system is a strength. Trucking today is so important that many economic developers would view the lack of direct interstate access as a major local weakness.

The concept of access is not as simple as it sounds, however. If the only route from the community to the nearest interstate highway involves two or three turns, several traffic lights, and a couple of discount stores along the way, those will be weaknesses. The turns along the route, as well as the autos likely to be turning into and pulling out of the discount store parking lots, will impede the travel of trucks and increase the risk of an accident; accidents are a particular concern for freight haulers if the cargo involved is fragile or hazardous.

In the information age, access to communications facilities can be more critical than access to transportation. Omaha has attracted a number of telemarketing and reservations centers because it is located along some major fiber-optic cable lines that provide excellent connections to the rest of the United States. Some cities are far better situated than others for sending and receiving signals to and from satellites. The reliability and stability of the power supply can be an important factor for some high-tech industries.

The issue comes full circle in many ways, however. Increasingly, companies locating new plants are concerned with the quality of life in a community—which comes right back to the issues that a community must address with a comprehensive plan. Good schools, affordable housing (with a reasonable vacancy rate—see chapter 18), a variety of recreational opportunities, and a healthy environment are all important community factors to a responsible employer locating a new plant. Most employers today recognize that healthy, happy employees are far better long-term employees than those who live in communities that they dislike, where there are few things to do besides work, or where the costs of living are so high that they create constant stress.

An Economic Development Plan

Preparation of an economic development plan involves the same sorts of planning steps as those described in chapters 1 and 2. With economic development planning, the process may be truly continuous, with the chamber of commerce or economic development organization providing updates regularly.

Some of the kinds of data that are useful in developing an economic development strategy include: the education and skills of the work force; unemployment rates (higher unemployment means more workers available for new industry); availability of natural resource inputs to some industries; availability of energy and water resources necessary to some industrial processes; accessibility to different types of transportation; availability of existing buildings and their relative suitability to particular industries; and availability of land suitable for industrial use.

The data gathered often require little analysis to create a summary of existing conditions. Analysis of the data consists largely of trying to match the community's assets with needs of particular industries.

Many communities also have overarching visions or goals for economic development. In the 1990s, many communities wanted to become regional high-tech or computer centers, but Chattanooga, Tennessee, focused on building a "sustainable" industrial base using some of the techniques suggested later in this chapter. As with comprehensive planning, it is important to achieve some balance between the strengths and weaknesses of the community and its economic development goals.

Some economic development plans simply target employers of particular sizes and lay out the strengths and opportunities of the community for such industries. Some focus on filling particular needs—replacing jobs from recent plant closures with jobs using similar skills and, hopefully, providing similar wage and benefit scales (although the latter is often an unrealistic expectation).

Strategies for economic development in some communities are truly opportunity driven, simply laying out the industrial facilities, work force, and other assets of the community and leaving fairly open the range of industries that might be attracted to take advantage of those opportunities. Plans focused on reuse of closed military bases are often of that sort, in part because the range of facilities is so great that it makes more sense to use a shotgun marketing strategy than a focused one.

A more sophisticated form of economic development planning involves a tool called a *targeted industry study*. As the name suggests, the purpose of such a study is to identify particular industries that the community ought to target in its economic development strategy. Industries that a community might want to target could include:

• industries that can use local raw materials or natural resources;

- industries that need a labor force similar to the local one;
- industries that can use existing industrial facilities in the community;
- industries with other needs that can be uniquely satisfied by the community, such as access to an unusual transportation or communications facility;
- industries that supply parts for local assembly plants that now buy those parts from elsewhere;
- industries that can use the waste products from local industries to make other products (for example, particle board and some kinds of insulation used in the building industry today are made from waste from other processes);
- industries that can use waste energy from local industries (the heat available from the cooling systems for a power plant can be used for a greenhouse or even to create an environment to breed certain warm-water fish);
- industries with any other close affinity with existing local industries.

A targeted industries study lays the base for a very focused marketing strategy. A community that simply touts its general resources and advantages will probably advertise in economic development publications and make presentations at trade shows. A community working from a targeted industry study can do direct mail to selected companies and can even justify sending out teams to make cold calls on industries meeting the target profile.

Implementation Strategies

Implementation is a critical step in an economic development plan, as it is for any other plan. Implementation of an economic development plan is closely related to comprehensive planning in a number of ways, discussed in the next section. In addition to coordinating it with the comprehensive plan, communities use a variety of strategies to implement an economic development plan. Some of those relate directly to comprehensive planning; other implementation strategies include:

- *Marketing strategies.* All economic development strategies involve marketing. Some communities use direct mail, some advertise in publications likely to reach their target market, many maintain Web sites and printed publications about opportunities in the community, and most regularly scan business publications to identify industries considering relocation or expansion.
- *Technical studies.* A targeted industry study or other local economic development study often provides useful technical information about the opportunities in a particular industry. Information that might be useful to certain new industries includes facts about little-known local natural resources, the availability of electrical power or gas, and even the availability of waste or secondary products from other local industries.

- *Property tax breaks.* Many states allow communities to use enterprise zones, tax increment financing, and other strategies to give direct tax breaks to new industry or to ensure that a designated portion of the taxes paid by a new business directly benefits the area around it.
- *Free land.* A number of communities use free land in a publicly owned industrial park as an incentive to attract new industries.
- *Development assistance.* It is common for local governments to help pay for roads, sewer and water extensions, and other facilities necessary to support a new manufacturing plant. In other circumstances, local governments today expect land developers and other private parties to pay for those facilities (see chapter 11).
- *Shell buildings.* Economic development groups in some communities maintain one or two "shell" industrial buildings—consisting of little more than a concrete floor, industrial walls, and basic plumbing, heating, and electrical service—available for immediate occupancy by potential industries. Typically, the new industry is able to lease or buy the facility at a discounted price if it meets specified conditions.
- *Job training.* Most major economic development packages today include a job-training package, using state or federal funds to prepare workers for jobs with the new industry. Local community colleges are often partners in these job-training programs; some offer a package of regular courses on a special schedule, and others develop custom training programs for a particular industry.
- *Major financial incentives.* The competition for major industries today is significant; relocations like that of the Toyota plants in southern Indiana and the Mercedes plant in Alabama have involved major packages of financial incentives, typically requiring special action by the state legislature as well as local governments.
- *Conditions.* Most financial incentive packages for new industry include conditions requiring that the industry meet certain hiring targets by specified deadlines or forfeit some of the financial benefits.
- *Cultivation of existing industry.* Some local economic development organizations have created programs to cultivate current industry, offering assistance in addressing problems or finding additional space or employees. In some states and communities, the same financial incentives available to new industry are also available to expansions of existing industries.
- *Small business support.* A large percentage of new jobs created in the United States each year are in small businesses. An increasing number of communities offer special services to help small businesses. Those often include: development centers offering counseling and technical support for growing small businesses; "incubators" offering an office facility (often with shared secretarial, computer, phone, and copying services) for start-up businesses, usually packaged with counseling and technical support; and seed capital funds,

pools of local money available for high-risk venture capital investments in start-up businesses.

Many of these strategies and much of the planning for them take place in economic development organizations or chambers of commerce with little participation by traditional planners. There is, however, a critical link between economic development planning and comprehensive planning—a link described in the next section.

Economic Development and Comprehensive Planning

The critical link between economic development and comprehensive planning is land. A community must have appropriate sites to be successful in promoting economic development. Sometimes economic developers are able to place a new industry in an existing building, but new sites are a critical commodity to offer in seeking new industry.

The best plans for new sites for new industry will be based on a targeted industry study or some other detailed economic development plan. Before designating future industrial sites, a community needs to know whether it is likely to attract industry that needs large sites or industry that needs small ones, industry that needs rail access or industry that uses trucks. An auto or truck assembly plant needs a very large site, while many electronic component plants are quite small. Many steel products still ship by rail, but electronics typically ship by truck and some high-value items ship primarily by overnight air service. A brewery or soft drink bottling plant needs access to a significant water supply, while other industries need direct access to heavy-duty natural gas or electrical service. In many communities today, much of the land planned for industry is along rail lines, but much of the demand is for land with good access for trucks.

The issue is even more complicated, however. Both because of state and federal environmental laws and because of potential liability, many industries today seek sites located well away from residential uses. Unfortunately, thirty or forty years ago, many communities allowed the construction of residences in all zoning districts, including industrial zones, and much land planned for industry is unacceptable to industry today because of scattered residences in the area. Further, just having direct access to a major road is not enough for a company heavily dependent on trucks. Most operators prefer direct access to a major road that leads directly to the interstate highway system. A community where the only remaining industrial sites share access roads with strip shopping centers and big-box discount stores may have difficulty attracting users for the industrial land.

A half century ago, when people thought of "industry," they thought of heavy industry: steel works, auto assembly plants, and other large and noisy operations. The typical industrial park was designed to meet the needs of those operations. Today, economic-base employers include as industry many other types of land uses, as described previously: reservations and telemarketing centers, "back-office" processing centers for credit card companies, electronics and other light-assembly plants, and software developers. Such industries do not need large sites in old-style industrial parks, and today they typically do not want to be in such locations. Industrial employers often provide office-like working environments for their employees and want an appropriate setting for the buildings. Some of these operations can actually locate in office parks or in urbanized areas of the city zoned for office uses. Others, however, receive and ship goods by truck; such businesses often want sites with an office-park front door for the offices and an industrial-park back door for the warehouse—separating auto and truck traffic into separate circulation systems. Many office parks and mixed-use business parks today provide amenities such as jogging trails, restaurants, and even health clubs.

In communities where economic development is a priority, planners preparing a comprehensive plan must address the land needs of present and future industry. Land planning for new industry and other economic-base business must address issues like parcel size; land access to roads and railroads, service from high-capacity electrical and gas lines, public sewer and water service, well-rated public fire protection, and, in many cases, good access to other amenities such as facilities for lunchtime walks or runs, shopping, and eating. If a community has locations that satisfy a variety of those needs, its comprehensive plan ought to protect them; if a community lacks such locations, the plan must include strategies for creating them.

Sustainable Economic Development

As the discussion of existing conditions in chapter 3 suggested, concepts of sustainability apply to economic development. Sustainable economic development suggests more than "clean" industry. It suggests a strategy that focuses on optimizing the use of many kinds of resources. Some basic principles of sustainable industrial development include:

- *Using local natural resources.* Economic development strategies have long included this element, and most resource-dependent industries seek to locate near sources of major resource inputs. This strategy is thus likely to occur without much prompting from planners, but it too, represents a strategy of environmental, as well as economic, sustainability.
- *Meeting local manufacturing input needs.* If local manufacturers import many of the parts or assemblies used in their products from other communities, or even from other states or nations, one sustainable economic development

strategy is to seek opportunities to satisfy need locally. If the local lawn-mower manufacturer buys its blades from a company in another state, for example, is it possible to find an existing or new machine shop that can sat-isfy that input locally?

- *Adding value to local manufacturing output.* Another strategy is to try to find manufacturers that use as input existing manufacturing output. Maybe it is the blade manufacturer that is located in the community, and local eco-nomic developers need to seek a lawnmower maker to make the finished products there, also.

- *Adding value to local agricultural products.* Where do agricultural products from the region go? How are they used? Can some of those uses occur locally? Are there new uses that might be made? Are there substitute, higher-value crops that might be grown and used locally in a value-adding industry.

- *Using waste from existing industry.* If there is a major water-cooled power plant in the community, economic developers might seek an industry that can use the heated water in some other process, perhaps in raising plants or fish. Many products that represent waste to one industry represent resources to another; a good economic development strategy is to identify the waste out-puts from local industry and seek manufacturers that can use them.

- *Using other waste.* Ames, Iowa, burns much of its waste in a local power plant that in turn helps to support local industry. Under federal pressure to decrease the amount of waste being buried in landfills, more and more com-munities are seeking ways to recycle or otherwise recover waste products; finding local production uses for those recovered goods can be a good eco-nomic strategy with ecological benefits for the community.

Local economic developers may not relate easily to the term *sustainability,* but they will understand concepts of industrial inputs and outputs and effi-cient use of resources. One strategy of planners trying to create sustainable communities is to educate the local chamber of commerce and economic development officials about such common-sense strategies for sustainable eco-nomic development.

Conclusion

Implementation makes a plan both meaningful and useful. That is true for eco-nomic development plans, just as it is for other plans. Implementing economic development plans, however, is more challenging than implementing most other local plans because economic development is market-driven. A commu-nity could adopt every one of the implementation techniques suggested above and still fail in its economic development efforts. "Build it and they will come" is a positive credo, but it does not always work. In contrast, when a commu-nity decides to build a new park, once it finds the money, it can simply build the park. Planning for economic development is a lot like planning for land use (chapter 6); the community can plan for the future, but it is much more able to prevent certain things from happening than to ensure that other things will happen. Despite the challenges and complexity in implementing an economic development plan, however, one thing is certain. To paraphrase baseball great Yogi Berra, "If you don't know where you are going, you can be pretty sure you will never get there." An economic development plan, or economic development component of a comprehensive plan, reminds the community where it wants to go and even tells it how to get there.

The Role of the Professional Planner

Economic development specialists and, sometimes, community development specialists are often the technical experts involved in the preparation of an economic development plan. In some communities, loaned executives or leaders of the chamber of commerce prepare the economic development plan. Some communities use consultants to prepare the background analysis for the plan, while others use the existing staff of the chamber of commerce or the local planning agency.

In very small communities, one person may do most of the planning for everything—land use, transportation, economic development, and even some utilities. In larger communities, however, the community planner is likely to have a limited role in planning for economic development. There are strong connections between economic development and the comprehensive planning process: a significant overlap in the data needed for planning; a common interest in setting goals; the use of the comprehensive plan to address land needs for economic development; and a common interest in setting implementation priorities and strategies. Thus, the professional community planner must work closely with economic development professionals in planning for economic development. The success of both the comprehensive plan and the community's economic development strategies depend on such cooperation.

The Role of the Individual Citizen

The role of the individual citizen in planning for economic development is often very limited. Many communities keep key aspects of their economic development strategies secret, afraid that competing communities will gain an advantage if they learn of them. Negotiations with prospective industries are almost always kept quiet, at least up to the final stages.

Nevertheless, economic development succeeds only if it is a community priority. A community can effectively establish priorities only with the involvement of its citizens. Individual citizens should be involved in that sort of priority setting both through the comprehensive planning process and, sometimes, through separate community discussions of economic development policy.

Sometimes a comprehensive planning process will suggest that economic development ought to be a major community goal and a higher priority than it currently is. In such cases, individual citizens and the professional planners involved in the process should work together to deliver that message to the community at large and to the elected representatives who set its operating policies. Development and implementation of economic development strategies may have their roots in the comprehensive planning process, but they ultimately require support and resources that go well beyond typical local planning efforts.

EXERCISES

1. What are some of the economic-base industries in your community? Check with the chamber of commerce or economic development agency for a list of the largest employers. Are they all economic-base employers? The local school system may be on that list. Is it part of the economic base?

2. Find out what three employers in your community have most recently added one hundred or more employees or have built new plants with one hundred or more employees. What types of industries are they? Are these economic-base industries?

3. Get out your copy of the community's comprehensive plan. What locations are planned for future industry? Drive (or bicycle) by some of these locations. Do they appear to have good rail access? Highway access? Do they look like good locations for heavy-manufacturing, light-assembly, or service industries? Is there a good variety of land available? Is the land that is available suitable for the types of industry that you identified in response to exercise number 2?

4. Find out if your community has an economic development plan. Get a copy of it. Does it seem like a workable plan? An exciting plan? Is it generally consistent with the comprehensive plan? Does it address any issues of sustainability?

DISCUSSION QUESTIONS

1. What is the general nature of the economic base in your community now? Is it in heavy industry, agriculture, service industry, or something else?

2. What kinds of industries should your community target for economic development? Why? What is there about your community that should make it attractive to those industries?

FURTHER READING

Bingham, Richard D., and Robert Mier, eds. 1997. *Dilemmas of Urban Economic Development: Issues in Theory and Practice.* Thousand Oaks, CA: Sage Publications. A composite of articles based on theories that affect planning practice; relates theory and practice well.

Caves, Roger W. 1994. *Exploring Urban America: An Introductory Reader.* Thousand Oaks, CA: Sage Publications. Basic text has well-developed section of four chapters on the new issues in economic development.

Dalai-Clayton, Barry. 1996. *Getting to Grips with Green Plans: National-Level Experience in Industrial Countries.* Washington, DC: Earthscan. An examination of national approaches to sustainable industry policies.

Kleinberg, Benjamin. 1995. *Urban America in Transformation: Perspectives on Urban Policy and Development.* Thousand Oaks, CA: Sage Publications. Basic review and critique of public policies over the past fifty years—how they have driven urban development—focusing primarily on economic theory and development.

Lyons, Thomas S., and Roger E. Hamlin. 1991. *Creating an Economic Development Action Plan.* Westport, CT: Praeger Publishers. A detailed guide to creating an economic development plan

McLean, Mary L., and Keeneth P. Voytek, with others. 1992. *Understanding Your Economy: Using Analysis to Guide Local Strategic Planning,* 2nd edition. Chicago: Planners Press. An accessible, practical guide to this complex topic; ideal for the generalist planner who needs some knowledge of the field and its techniques.

Roome, Nigel J., ed. 1998. *Sustainability Strategies for Industry.* Washington, DC: Island Press. This book focuses on sustainability at the level of the individual industry, but it provides a good starting point for considering strategies for sustainable economic development.

REFERENCES

Bendavid-Val, Avrom. 1991. *Regional and Local Economic Analysis for Planners,* 4th edition. Westport, CT: Praeger Publishers. A classic text on this subject.

Blair, John P. 1995. *Local Economic Development: Analysis and Practice.* Newbury Park, CA: Sage Publications. A primer on basic techniques of analysis for economic development; also a handy reference.

Gerrard, Michael B. 1998. *Brownfields Law and Practice: The Cleanup and Redevelopment of Contaminated Land.* New York: Matthew Bender. A complex but thorough treatment of government policies and law concerning brownfield sites.

Mills, Edwin S. 1986. *Handbook of Regional and Urban Economics: Vol. 2.* New York: Elsevier Science Publishing. Basic survey of economic development theories and models.

Mills, Edwin S., and John F. McDonald, eds. 1992. *Sources of Metropolitan Growth.* New Brunswick, NJ: Rutgers University, Center for Urban Policy Research. Excellent description of metropolitan economies, providing a good basis for understanding the economic base.

NOTE

1. U.S. Department of Commerce, Bureau of Economic Analysis, *Regional Multipliers: A User Handbook for the Regional Input–Output Modeling System, Washington, DC: Superintendent of Documents (1986).*

Part V

The Planning Profession

Planning is a relatively young profession that probably best traces its roots to the first National Planning Conference, held in 1909. The program at that conference included landscape architects, engineers, lawyers, and some architects, and the evolution of the field reflects the influence of all of those professions.[1] Other landmarks cited in the creation of the profession include:

- the City Beautiful Movement;[2]
- the Columbian Exposition in Chicago in 1893, a landmark revitalization project built on principles of the City Beautiful Movement;[3]
- the formation in 1917 of the American City Planning Institute, the predecessor of the American Institute of Planners, which became the American Institute of Certified Planners in 1978;[4]
- publication in 1926–28 of the two model laws that became the basis for most planning laws in the country;[5] and
- the creation of the first degree program in city planning at Harvard in 1929.[6]

This part of the book deals with the profession today, leaving the history to others. The material in chapter 20 addresses planning as a career, describing where planners work, what they do—and what they are paid for doing it.

This part continues with an examination of ethical issues in planning (chapter 21) and puts those issues in the context of codes and statements of ethics adopted by the American Planning Association and the American Institute of Certified Planners.

The last chapter, chapter 22, examines briefly the professional credentials necessary for planners.

NOTES

1. The conference proceedings were published as *Proceedings of the First National Conference on City Planning,* Washington, D.C., May 21–22, 1909; that document is available in major university libraries. A more accessible source on this early history is Mel Scott's *American City Planning since 1890,* Berkeley: University of California Press (1969). That first conference is described in Scott's book on pp. 95–100.

2. Scott, ibid., chapter 2, pp. 47–109.

3. Scott, ibid., pp. 31–37, 44; see, also, Thomas S. Hines, *Burnham of Chicago: Architect and Planner,* Chicago: University of Chicago Press (1979).

4. Scott, ibid., pp. 163–164.

5. Advisory Committee on Zoning, *A Standard Zoning Enabling Act,* Washington, DC: U.S. Department of Commerce, 1922 (mimeo ed.), 1926 (rev. ed.); Advisory Committee on Planning and Zoning, A Standard City Planning Enabling Act, Washington: U.S. Dept. of Commerce, 1927, 1928 (rev. ed.); for a good history of these acts, see Stuart Meck, "Model Planning and Zoning Enabling Legislation: A Short History," in *Modernizing State Planning Statutes: The Growing Smart Working Papers,* vol. 1, Planning Advisory Service Reports No. 462–463, Chicago: American Planning Association (1996), pp. 1–19.

6. David A. Johnson, "Regional Planning for the Great American Metropolis: New York between the World Wars," in Daniel Schaffer, ed., *Two Centuries of American Planning,* Baltimore: Johns Hopkins University Press (1987), p. 187.

Chapter 20

....

Where Planners Work and What They Do

For many people, planning is an attractive profession because it offers a variety of areas of interest and focus. Planners work on a wide variety of projects and in a wide variety of situations. Most planners work for public agencies, but some work in private firms, often with architects, landscape architects, and engineers; in planning consulting firms; or with private businesses such as utilities or development companies. There are also a number of planners who work for nonprofit corporations and foundations. Whether in the public or private sector, planning projects alone or as part of a team of other professionals from other fields, most planners are involved in helping communities and others prepare for the future and manage the change that comes with it.

Often planners come to the profession through very personal experiences such as planning activities at the neighborhood level or working with a special interest group on a particular community issue. Others see it as a profession with opportunities to make a difference in the world or in an individual community. Whatever the initial reasons for their career choice, planners soon realize there is a wide range of jobs to be done. An understanding of the career possibilities can help the future planner to prepare appropriately.

The Profession of Planning: AICP Definition

The American Institute of Certified Planners (AICP) uses the following criteria to define professional planning.[1]

A. *Influencing public decision making in the public interest.* Recommending specific actions or choices to elected/appointed officials, private sector rep-

Richard Hedman on the value of planners. Copyright by Richard Hedman. Used with permission.

resentatives, or others regarding public decisions concerned with social, economic, or physical change in the public interest.

B. *Employing an appropriately comprehensive point of view.* Appropriate comprehensiveness requires: (1) looking at the consequences (e.g., physical/environmental, social, economic/financial, governmental) of making a proposed decision; (2) conforming a proposed decision to the larger context in which it will occur; and (3) treating multiple policies, actions, or systems simultaneously when interlinkages are too great to treat separately. It does not require looking at everything at once if the above three criteria are met with a proposal, plan, or program of narrower scope.

C. *Applying a planning process appropriate to the situation.* This means a process which is appropriate to its place and situation in: (1) the number and order of its steps—e.g., problem/opportunity definition, goal setting, generating alternate strategies, strategy choice, implementation, evaluation; (2) its orientation to the future, to value change, and to resource constraints; (3) its quality of research and analysis; and (4) its format of policy, program, or plan proposal.

D. *Involving a professional level of responsibility and resourcefulness.* This means initiative, judgment, substantial involvement, and personal accountability for defining and preparing significant substantive elements of planning activities.

Where Planners Work

In 1996, based on 1995 survey data, the American Planning Association reported that urban and regional planners held over 29,000 jobs.[2] According to the survey, some 72.5 percent of those responding worked in the public sector, an increase from 61.9 percent a decade before.[3] Table 20.1 shows the employment of planners responding to the survey.

In contrast, a 1987 study by the Association of Collegiate Schools of Planning (ACSP) found only 52.7 percent of respondents working in the public sector,[4] a significantly lower figure than that found by the APA study conducted at about the same time. There was a difference in methodologies between the two studies, however. APA surveyed its members; the authors of the 1987 study surveyed graduates of planning programs. Not all APA members are graduates of planning programs. Not all graduates of planning programs go into planning careers, and those who do may not join APA. The ACSP study surveyed recent graduate-school graduates,[5] while those respond-

Table 20.1. Employment of Planners, Percentage by Type of Agency

Employer	Percentage
PUBLIC AGENCIES	72.5
City Planning	36.6
County Planning	14.5
Joint City/County	2.6
Metro or Regional	6.8
Other Public	6.0
State or Provincial	3.2
Federal	1.5
Economic Development	1.3
NONPUBLIC AGENCIES	26.5
Private Consultant	16.9
Nonprofit Organization	2.0
Educational Institution	3.3
Law Firm	0.7
Development Firm	1.2
Other Private Agency	2.4

Source: Adapted from table 3 in Marya Morris,
1995 Planners' Salaries and Employment Trends,
Planning Advisory Service Report No. 464.
Chicago: American Planning Association (1996).

ing to the APA survey had an average age of about forty-one.[6] Informal institutional evidence suggests that many planners do not join APA in the early
stages of their career; the average age of the respondents to the APA survey is
consistent with that evidence.

The ACSP survey found that 7.7 percent of the graduates of planning programs went to work in other fields. What is interesting about the ACSP study,
however, is that 37.6 percent of respondents went into "nontraditional" planning careers that were not academic.[7] The authors used a negative definition
of *nontraditional:*

> individuals in fields other than land use planning, current land use
> planning, regional planning, comprehensive planning, environmen-
> tal planning, physical planning, social planning, transportation plan-
> ning, housing, human services planning, redevelopment, and general
> planning.[8]

Unfortunately, the report on the research does not indicate in what nontraditional planning fields these people were engaged or how their employment
differed from that of those who worked in fields other than planning.

What does this mean? It means, very simply, that some people who get a
planning education choose to use it for careers focused on activities other than
those described in this book. Fortunately, a planning education includes broad
principles, described in chapter 1, that are applicable to many fields, including
business, education, industrial production, and a variety of related design fields.

There are planning jobs in communities of all sizes. Of those responding
to the 1995 APA survey, 24.4 percent worked in jurisdictions with populations
of 250,000 or more; 35.9 percent in jurisdictions with populations between
50,000 and 249,999; and 39.2 percent in jurisdictions with populations of less
than 50,000.[9]

The statistics on private employment are somewhat misleading. While
consulting firms employed nearly 17 percent of the planners reporting, many
of those firms consulted partly or primarily to local governments. For larger
communities, those firms typically provided specialized services, such as updating comprehensive plans or preparing traffic studies or impact fee ordinances.
Some smaller jurisdictions have continuing service agreements with consulting firms, using those firms instead of in-house planning staff. Thus, the total
percentage of employment that focuses on planning in the public sector
approaches and may exceed 80 percent.

This pattern of employment is perfectly logical in the context of planning
today, as described in the first four parts of this book. Most comprehensive
planning and implementation take place at the level of local government; con-
sequently, most planners work for local governments. Cities and counties of all
sizes need to plan, so there are jobs in communities of many different sizes.

There is not much regional planning in this country, and there are equally few planning jobs with regional agencies.

What Planners Do

What attracts many people to the profession of planning is the opportunity to fulfill a number of roles. Some planners are focused on the research side of planning, often acting as technical analysts. Others develop programs within specific areas of concern, such as land use or urban design, while still others may focus on social changes. Many planners find themselves, at some point in their careers, in the role of manager or educator. A significant proportion of planners will work in both the public and the private sectors. Almost all professional planners will fill a number of these roles in different stages of their careers.

Land Use and Zoning

Planners, especially those who create comprehensive or strategic plans, review site plans, work at the front desk of planning departments, or work with developers in urban design, are involved in land-use and zoning issues; almost all planning decisions ultimately affect the use of land. In addressing these issues, planners try to implement the comprehensive plan through the administration of such tools as zoning and subdivision regulations.

The most obvious ways that planners conduct land-use planning is through the development of plans for land-use patterns, including separation of land use into districts to meet housing needs, create parks and recreation opportunities, furnish highways and transportation systems, create public facilities such as schools and hospitals, and seek means of development while protecting the built and natural environments. This means that land-use planners deal with both developed and undeveloped land.

While land use is affected by daily decisions through the permitting process, those decisions are based on previous long-range planning efforts that looked at the potential uses of land. In the comprehensive planning process, planners use their technical knowledge, including the analysis of existing and potential problems, to influence policies that will affect the physical needs of the community. This sometimes places planners in the function of mediators since land-use decisions often bring out conflicting community interests.

While land-use planning is identified as a specialization in the interdisciplinary profession of planning, it touches on all issues involving planning. Land-use planners are found at all levels of government, including the national government, where agencies such as the National Park Service must plan for the use of land in their jurisdiction. Land-use planners also abound in the private sector, often working in teams with other professionals such as engineers, landscape architects, and architects. On this subject, see especially chapters 2 through 7, 10, and 11.

Housing and Community Development

At one point, planners looked solely at analyzing housing needs and developing strategies to deal with those needs. More recently, planners involved in housing are looking at social issues beyond housing. Other problems, such as commuting distance to work or job training, lack of child care facilities, and inadequate access to transportation, add to problems in meeting housing needs. More and more often, plans for meeting low-income housing needs include broader community development plans. The purpose of such plans is to improve the standard of living and provide opportunities for those citizens who lack resources and opportunities.

Planners in housing and community development may work on programs that develop housing opportunities for the homeless, provide low-interest loans for mortgages, or establish job training centers or design programs for the elderly. While most communities have planners devoted to housing and social planning, often planners interested in this type of planning are found in nonprofit corporations and foundations. Even the federal government plays a significant role in housing, and many housing planners are found throughout the public sector. Whether in the public or the private sector, these planners focus on issues inherent in our modern society that touch on the quality of life for all residents in the United States today. Chapter 18 discusses the role of planning and government in addressing housing issues.

Health and Human Services

Like planners working in housing and community development, planners in health and human services are involved in creating strategies for residents lacking resources and opportunities. These planners create health and social services programs focused on upgrading the standard of living for residents. They are involved in establishing programs that address such issues as drug treatment and child abuse. While they are often focused on low-income groups, these health and human services planners often deal with issues found throughout the community.

These issues are not limited to our most urban centers. Health and human services planning is also vital in rural areas; many rural communities lack health facilities and important social services. Planners often look at means of attracting the facilities and professionals to rural areas, as well as finding ways to deal with local issues. For example, a mounting problem for many rural areas is the lack of public transportation available to citizens such as the elderly who do not have the ability or the means to provide their own transportation to such services as local clinics.

Health and human services is tied to physical planning but also goes well beyond the most obvious planning needs. These planners are typically found in the public sector at all levels of government from the local human services planner to individuals within such federal departments as Housing and Urban Development. Health and human services planners are also part of a growing number of planners in the nonprofit sector. This subject generally falls within the scope of social planning, a topic that is discussed in the introduction to this book, as well as in Chapters 17 and 18.

Transportation Planning

Transportation planners are involved in planning for the movement of people and goods. Their efforts affect land use, economic development, social opportunities, and the quality of life and the environment. Since transportation, like land-use planning, directly affects all activities, it involves technical and social understanding. In the past, transportation planners have focused on the efficient movement of goods and people, but it has become increasingly apparent that transportation influences urban design, the environment, and economic and social opportunities.

While roadways are the most obvious area of transportation planning, the field also involves airports, trains, rapid transit, buses, bike lanes, and pedestrian ways. Often transportation planning involves concurrently planning for many different modes while ensuring equitable access to these different modes. Social issues such as accommodating the physically challenged and the elderly on public transit are a significant part of transportation planning. This combination of technical and social expertise makes transportation one of the more challenging fields of planning today. Transportation planners are found at all levels of government, as well as in the private sector. Transportation is one of the infrastructure issues covered in chapter 7.

Economic Development Planning

Economic development planning focuses on increasing employment and income opportunities. This involves attracting business, retaining existing business and industry, and assisting small and beginning businesses. The focus is on creating a healthy economy that provides employment opportunities and builds and sustains a strong tax base. These planners are directly involved in community development through the use of human, physical, natural, and financial resources.

These planners work for all levels of government, including the federal and state levels where they work for such agencies and departments as the Department of Labor and the Small Business Administration. Even the Department of Housing and Urban Development is involved in economic development planning through its Community Development Block Grants and other competitive funds. States also assist local communities in economic development efforts through grants, loans, bonds, and tax incentives. One area of assistance often overlooked is that of state grants and loans given to communities for infrastructure development, making it possible for local communities to attract business and industry by meeting such infrastructure needs as adequate roads and airports. Economic development planners are also employed in the non-profit sector by such entities as chambers of commerce, often establishing pub-lic-private partnerships for attracting and retaining businesses and industries in a community.

Economic development planning requires technical expertise in assessing economic-base and growth trends, analyzing businesses and industries, and developing feasibility projections and financing mechanisms. Thus, these plan-ners bring technical, marketing, and financial expertise to their jobs. At the local level, economic development planners often provide marketing and pro-motion assistance in efforts to attract business. They also participate in negoti-ations for final business development. The impacts of economic development are dealt with by other areas of planning but are not ignored by economic development planners, since how these issues are met determines the envi-ronment that will attract or deter new businesses. Planning for economic development is the topic of chapter 19.

Environmental Planning

Environmental planners focus on prevention of pollution and other degrada-tion of the natural environment as well as preservation of resources. These planners are found at all levels of government and in the private and nonprofit sectors working on a range of issues. Many environmental planners deal with environmental impact assessments and environmental land-use plans and reg-ulations. The range of roles goes from the local level and such tasks as creating floodplain ordinances and assessing the environmental impact of a federal con-struction project, to the federal level and such tasks as assessing the impact of tourism on national parks and supervising mitigation of hazardous waste sites. With increasing environmental regulations from the federal government down to the local level and mounting stress on the environment from increasing growth, often in environmentally sensitive areas, the demands on environ-mental planners are growing.

Environmental problems often require extensive intergovernmental and public and private cooperation; special interest groups are becoming increas-ingly active in environmental issues, as well. Thus, the range of environmental planning employment goes through all levels of government as well as the pri-vate and nonprofit sectors. The role of planners in dealing with environmen-tal issues is discussed in chapters 3, 6, 8, and 15.

Urban Design

Urban design planners combine physical design with urban policy making. Their work focuses on creating unified physical plans for subdivisions, downtown revitalization plans, and plans for shopping malls and corridors. While urban design planners are involved in issues of land use, they differ from other planners, who typically work on a larger scale creating policies and programs.

Urban design planning has changed over the years, with the increasing importance placed on the psychological and sociological effects of the physical environment on the quality of life of citizens. In response to this recognition of the importance of the physical setting on human activities and behavior, urban design planners are having to find ways to involve the public in their proposals and designs. Today urban design planners are more involved than ever before in development controls such as zoning and in the different ways of financing projects such as public-private partnerships. For example, these planners have been leading the way in finding ways to create sustainable communities through design and changes in development codes and regulations.

There are many good examples of publicly sponsored urban design in the United States, although there are few if any examples of whole communities that reflect a unified design theme. Some examples of the influence of urban design include the Inner Harbor area of Baltimore, the River Walk in San Antonio, Chicago's Lakeshore Drive and Michigan Avenue, and the monumental core of Washington, D.C. The choices made in the physical design of these areas clearly has had a significant impact on the public perception as well as the functional organization of these cities. Another area in which urban design planners play a significant role is that of historic districts. The desire to maintain and enhance areas of historic and design significance has become increasingly strong in the last few decades, and urban designers have played an important role in leading these efforts, particularly in districts that have new development. Most recently, urban design planners have been leading the way in addressing ways of creating sustainable communities.

While there are urban design planners in all levels of government, they are predominantly found at the local level, particularly in departments that deal with zoning and review of site and subdivision plans. They are also involved in the private sector, especially as consultants to development, engineering, and real estate companies. As public concern over the quality and sustainability of their environment continues to grow, the role of urban design planners will continue to expand. Urban design issues typically arise in the context of planning for special areas, such as historic districts, downtowns, and important corridors. All of those are discussed in chapter 16.

International Development Planning

As we increasingly become a global society, the role of planners in international settings continues to evolve. International development planners are involved in creating strategies for regional and national development in international settings. With the recognition of dwindling nonrenewable resources, the need to evaluate strategies for rational growth and development in many developing countries is growing.

International development planners work primarily in the public sector in national governments in less developed countries and in international agencies such as those under the United Nations. While there are some international development planners at the federal and state levels such as the U.S. Department of Commerce, as yet they are not found at the local level of government. There are an increasing number of private consulting firms and engineering and architecture firms that employ international development planners.

Entry-Level Positions

Many entry-level positions place individuals as the generalist planner—that professional whose work touches on many areas of planning. One of the most important things a new planner does early in her or his career is to work "at the counter." This is where planners most often meet the public. As long-time planning director Bruce McClendon has pointed out, the treatment of "customers" at the counter in the planning office has immense influence on the public's perception of local government.[10] Any function that brings planners into contact with the public is important in determining the success of all planning efforts and in citizens' perceptions of planning. Customer service, regardless of who the customer is, is a key to good planning. For those planners beginning in nonprofit or private-sector positions, this is also a valuable lesson. While it is easy for planners to feel that they have the answers, since that is their training, it is important that the person being served be treated as the real authority.

Planning Salaries

The median salaries for planners have risen consistently over the last two decades.[11] The median salary in the 1995 APA survey was $45,300, with median salaries in local government ranging from $29,200 for those with less than five years' experience to $51,900 for those with more than ten years' experience.[12] The highest salaries appear to be with the federal government, law firms, and with development firms. Like other professions, there is a considerable difference between starting salaries and the median salaries of planners who have ten or more years of experience in the profession. While the top-level salaries have risen significantly over the past decade, entry-level salaries have remained fairly stagnant.

Salaries are also dependent on where planners work. It is not surprising to find that the highest median salaries are also in states that have a higher cost of living than others.[13] It is difficult to find other patterns from which one can draw reasonable conclusions. Clearly, the combination of seniority and education makes a big difference, and managers at a high level are generally paid better than those who work for them.

Besides location and experience, other factors contribute to an individual's earning power, including education, level of responsibility, and employer. Some planners choose to remain in a particular location, even when it means remaining in the same job at a lower salary. Others work in the public sector for a period of time, then move into more lucrative employment in the private sector because of the expertise they have gained on the job in the public sector, while others remain in the public sector and rise to higher positions.

A significant factor in planning salaries in education. Advanced degrees are preferred by employers, although master's degrees in related fields such as geography, engineering, and architecture or equivalent work experience are sometimes acceptable. Often someone with a bachelor's degree from planning and related programs can gain an entry-level job, but it is usually necessary for such an employee to acquire an advanced degree to open better employment opportunities in the profession.

There are numerous books and Internet job listings to assist planners in finding employment and educational opportunities. Some, such as *Jobs in Government*,[14] are very specific in their information, while others, such as *Job Mart*,[15] focus on a range of planning opportunities. Information is available, but an important source of employment information is the networking that planners do, particularly at the annual national conference. Belonging to the local, state, and national chapters of the American Planning Association can help in forming a network to assist in finding that entry-level job and in finding support once a part of the planning profession.

Note that the salary data given in this section are somewhat out of date. Anyone considering entering the field should check current job listings and obtain the latest copy of the APA salary report, which is typically updated every four years.[16]

Working Conditions

Many planning commissions and governing bodies meet at night. Planners who facilitate citizen participation—and most do at some point in their careers—will have other night meetings for that purpose. Night meetings are simply part of a planning career.

In other respects, however, a planning career has significant advantages over careers in many other professions. Most local government office buildings are locked on weekends, leaving planners free to pursue their lives, while their colleagues in architecture, engineering, and law may be working at their respective offices. Local government generally provides more predictable employment, with civil service protection, than private professional firms. Benefit packages are typically attractive.

Working for government can be both satisfying and frustrating. Presumably, those who work for the government are seeking to create better communities (or states or nations). Citizens, however, are sometimes cynical about the motivations of government employees. Government officials are often the bearers of bad news-such as Mr. Jones's new house is too close to the side lot line; there is nothing the city can do to stop the construction of the cellular phone tower across from the nature center; or the new waste disposal site has to go *someplace*—and people rarely greet the messenger who brings bad news with open arms.

On the other hand, planners who believe in working with citizens, who believe that government can provide "customer service" of the sort that the best private enterprises offer, and who truly want to work for the public interest can have a very satisfying career.

Related Fields

Planners work with professionals from several related fields: engineering, landscape architecture, architecture, and law. The nature of those fields defines some boundaries of planning, as well as suggesting the nature of the activities in which planners engage.

Landscape Architecture

Landscape architects deal with the land and the natural systems on it. The field evolved from landscape designers who created the grounds for estates. Today, landscape architects deal with the land at many levels. Some still design elaborate grounds and gardens for public facilities and even some private residences. Others design golf courses, parks, and recreation areas. Landscape architects also deal with planning issues from an ecological perspective, a topic discussed in chapter 2.

Landscape architects are licensed or registered in most states, but not all. Some states require registration or a license to engage in certain types of professional practice, while others limit the use of the title "landscape architect" to those who are registered.

Landscape architects and planners often work together. Many large planning agencies include landscape architects on their staffs, and a number of consulting firms include both planners and landscape architects, often working in the same group. The professional society for landscape architects is the American Society of Landscape Architects, and its members often use its initials after their name to indicate that affiliation.

Civil Engineering

There are many branches of engineering, but the one with which planners interact the most is civil engineering. It is civil engineering professionals who typically design roads and airports, sewer plants, and water distribution systems. Engineers sometimes prepare comprehensive plans, usually with an emphasis on functional values—ensuring that the community is designed so that the road, sewer, water, and other infrastructure systems all work well.

Civil engineers are licensed in all states. A professional engineer typically uses the initials "P.E." after her or his name. The professional society that represents the field is the American Society of Civil Engineers (ASCE). Some engineering firms include planners and landscape architects. Because of concerns about supervision of work requiring licensure, it is unusual for an engineer to work under a planner or a firm managed by a planner.

Architecture

Architects design buildings. Some design other things, but the emphasis of architectural practice is on the design of enclosed spaces for human uses. Many architects practice in firms consisting entirely of architects and support staff, or architects, interior designers, and support staff. Others are part of architectural and engineering firms, often called A&E for short. Architects and planners are sometimes found in the same firm; such firms usually also include engineers and landscape architects.

State laws require registration of architects in every state, and there is a national registration exam that is widely accepted among the states. The professional society for architects is the American Institute of Architects (AIA), and its members also typically use its initials after their names.

Law

Many of the implementation techniques for plans are ordinances and other forms of local laws. Thus, planners have a good deal of contact with lawyers. Although most people probably think of lawyers in court, many lawyers represent their clients in obtaining approvals from government agencies—including approvals for land development projects.

Lawyers are licensed in every state. Their national professional association is the American Bar Association. Planners working for government agencies will work regularly with staff or outside lawyers for those agencies. Historically, the legal profession's own code of ethics has limited lawyers' ability to participate in multidisciplinary firms, but that is changing. Today, a handful of law firms include planners, and several advertise regularly in the "Consultant Calling Card" section of *Planning* magazine.

Urban Design

Urban design is a field of practice, not a defined profession. It is important here, however, because it is the substantive area of practice in which planners, landscape architects, architects, and engineers all interact. Urban design deals with the streetscapes in which buildings exist, bringing together planners and architects; engineers are concerned with the same streetscapes from the perspective of traffic movement. Urban design also addresses public spaces, involving landscape architects as well as planners and architects. And urban design exists in the context of zoning and other codes administered by planners, but many of the actual designs come from architects and landscape architects.

Relationship of Other Professions to Planning

Planners cannot practice law, or architecture, or landscape architecture, or engineering because they are not licensed to do so. On the other hand, in forty-eight states,[17] planning is not a licensed field, and lawyers, architects, landscape architects, and engineers can all essentially engage in planning practice.

The professional advantage that planners have over professionals from these other fields is the emphasis on comprehensiveness. Each of the other fields contains within it a set of values that is a good deal narrower than those represented by a good comprehensive plan. With its comprehensive approach, good planning can include and bring together the expertise of all of those other fields—and it is only planners are specifically educated to do that.

Conclusion

Planning is—first, second, and last—about people. The future is an abstract concept. The role of the planner is to help people collectively define a future for their community. Roads and parks, farmlands and wetlands, land-use plans and GIS systems are simply tools—tools for planners and tools for communities. Ultimately, what matters is how they serve the community and the people who live there.

EXERCISES

1. Check the classified section of the Sunday edition of the nearest big-city newspaper and look for ads for planners. What kinds of jobs are available for entry-level planners? What salaries do they advertise?
2. Invite a local planner with three to five years of experience to come to class and talk about her or his career to date. Alternatively, assign small groups in the class to contact several alumni of your school who have been in practice as planners for three to five years and prepare professional biographies of them to share with the class.
3. Write a position description for what you would consider to be the perfect first job.
4. If you were hiring a new planner, what traits or characteristics would you seek? How might those differ from traits or characteristics you would seek if hiring an architect, a lawyer, an accountant, or a nurse?

Discussion Questions

1. How have planners made a difference in your community? Can you tell by looking at it or by living there? How might better planning, or more planning, in the past have made your community an even better place today?
2. Invite an engineer and a landscape architect to class to talk about the work of planners. You may or may not wish to include a planner as moderator.

References

JobMart. Published multiple times per year. The jobs newsletter of the American Planning Association, available by subscription to its members.

Morris, Marya. 1996. *1995 Planners' Salaries and Employment Trends.* Planning Advisory Service Report No. 464. Chicago: American Planning Association. This work, or a later edition that replaces it, provides more data on planning careers than any other single source.

Planning Magazine. Published monthly by the American Planning Association, Chicago. Contains current news of the planning field. Sent free to members (including student members) of APA and, by subscription, to many libraries.

Notes

1. These criteria are used by the American Institute of Certified Planners to determine what experience is creditable as "professional planning experience" required for AICP membership. Although developed for that more narrow purpose, it provides a good working definition of professional planning practice. Reproduced with permission of the American Institute of Certified Planners.
2. Jeffrey Gruenert, *Occupational Outlook Handbook,* Washington, DC: Bureau of Labor Statistics (1998).
3. Marya Morris, *1995 Planners' Salaries and Employment Trends,* Planning Advisory Service Report No. 464, Chicago: American Planning Association (1996).
4. Amy Glasmeier and Terry Kahn, "Planners in the 80s: Who We Are, Where We Work," *Journal of Planning Education and Research* 9, no. 1: 5–17 (fall 1989), table 6, p. 11; data were gathered in 1987.
5. Ibid. 1982–86 graduates; see discussion of methodology on pp. 6–8.
6. Morris, note 3, p. 6.
7. Ibid., table 4.
8. Ibid., p. 9.
9. See table 4 in Morris, note 3.
10. Bruce W. McClendon, *Customer Service in Local Government,* Chicago: Planners Press (1992).
11. Morris, note 3, p. 7.
12. Ibid., table 7.
13. Ibid., tables 16 and 17.

14. Daniel Lauber. River Forest, IL: Planning Communications (1994).
15. A newsletter available to members of the American Planning Association by sub-scription.
16. The 1996 version is the Morris work cited in note 3.
17. All but Michigan and New Jersey.

Chapter 21

....

Planning Ethics and Values

Ethics and values deal with how people make decisions. The field of ethics attempts to evaluate the rightness or wrongness of a decision based on stated philosophical principles. Values, however, represent fundamental beliefs and underlie decisions that people make. The two subjects are related but different. Because both affect some of the same kinds of decisions that planners make in their daily professional lives, this chapter addresses both topics.

Ethics

Although commonly used as a general term that includes all of the subjects discussed in this chapter, *ethics* technically applies only to issues involved in evaluating the rightness or wrongness of an action. This section discusses ethics, both theoretical and applied.

A Brief Introduction

There are two basic philosophical approaches to ethics:

- *Deontological* principles (principles derived from belief in a deity) evaluate an action based on the rightness or wrongness of the action itself, typically evaluated in the context of well-accepted principles of human behavior like the Golden Rule and the Ten Commandments.
- *Teleological* thought (principles derived from intellectual analysis) considers the results of the action in determining its rightness or wrongness.

How do these two differ? A simple example deals with telling the truth. A deontologist would argue that it is always wrong to tell a lie. A teleologist would respond that it is acceptable to tell a lie to protect the feelings of another person. Similarly, a dedicated deontologist would be likely to argue that killing another human being is always wrong; in contrast, a teleologist would urge that it may be acceptable to kill in self defense, in defense of one's family, or in defense of the nation.

How do these seemingly abstract principles apply to planning practice? Consider a simple example. Suppose that a historic preservation planner, whose values (see that section of this chapter) revolve around preservation of important landmarks, has clandestinely obtained damaging and nonpublic information about a developer proposing a project that would involve demolition of a landmark. Assume further that disclosing the information would lead to disapproval of the project and, at least temporarily, protection of the landmark. A teleologist might support the planner in releasing that information, no matter how it was obtained, because it would lead to a desirable result. A deontologist would be more likely to argue that the planner has no right to release that information and that any use of it would be wrong, no matter what the result.

Which view is "correct" in planning? Neither is necessarily correct. Planners who view themselves as advocates on particular issues—historic preservation, environmental protection, housing opportunities—will often be teleologists, evaluating their actions against the results achieved. Staff planners, who serve as general advisors to local governments without advocating anything other than the public interest, can more easily be deontologists. What is important is that a planner develop a philosophy of professional life based on one principle or the other and follow a consistent set of principles in evaluating ethical actions.

Ethical Guidelines for Planners

There are two sets of ethical guidelines for planners, both reproduced in appendices to this book, because there are two professional organizations in planning. Although the two organizations are described in somewhat more detail in chapter 22, it is useful here to present a brief description of them both:

- The *American Planning Association* (APA) is an umbrella organization that includes professional planners, planning commissioners, and other people interested in planning. Anyone who is interested in planning can join the organization simply by paying dues.
- The *American Institute of Certified Planners* (AICP) is, as its name suggests, an organization that grants professional credentials to planners who complete a required combination of education and experience and pass a test documenting basic knowledge of the profession. Although legally operated as a component of APA, AICP has its own commission and adopts its own policies.

The ethical documents of these related organizations are similar. One is the AICP/APA statement "Ethical Principles in Planning," adopted by the governing bodies of both organizations in May 1992. The other is the AICP "Code of Ethics and Professional Conduct," adopted by AICP in October 1978, the year that it was founded, and amended in October 1991. Although officially only AICP members need be concerned with the AICP code, it is useful to refer to them both.

Applied Ethics

When using the term *ethics* in referring to someone who works in government, as most planners do, most people probably intend to refer to very practical notions of applied ethics, not to abstract or theoretical concepts. Examples of behavior that people might call unethical in a public servant could include accepting a bribe to influence a vote (for a member of a public body) or the content of a staff report (for a staff member); misrepresenting important information to a public body or to the public; or cheating on a time sheet or expense account.

Accepting a bribe or cheating on a time sheet or expense account would violate criminal laws in most states and thus would be illegal, as well as unethical. Accepting a bribe would be wrong under almost any set of ethical principles, because it involves a fundamental breach of loyalty and trust to a body that the person has agreed to serve. Misrepresenting information and cheating on time sheets and expense accounts all represent forms of lying. Deontologists would argue that all are wrong. Cheating on a time sheet or expense account results in personal gain, whereas misrepresenting important information may result in no personal gain, and a teleologist would consider that fact in evaluating the extent of the wrong committed. Note, however, that the AICP/APA statement of ethical principles, discussed immediately below, specifically prohibits misrepresenting information, and any serious teleologist would agree. Where the teleologists and the deontologists would part company on planning issues involves the release of information and, more particularly, the selective release of information. That topic is discussed in more detail below.

The joint AICP/APA statement of principles includes three basic principles, the second of which squarely focuses on ethics, as narrowly defined. It starts:

> Planning process participants continuously strive to achieve high standards of integrity and proficiency so that public respect for the planning process will be maintained.

The first paragraph of that section elaborates, explaining that:

> Planning process participants should: 1. Exercise fair, honest and independent judgment in their roles as decision-makers and advisors.

Set out in full in appendix A, the rest of the section goes on to address such basic ethical issues as: abstaining from matters in which the planner has a direct or indirect conflict of interest; disclosing all personal interests in any matters of public interest; not seeking "gifts or favors" that might affect objectivity; not using confidential information for personal gain; and not misrepresenting facts or distorting information.

The basic concept of "fair, honest and independent judgment" underlies all ethical principles in planning and in other government service. Most of the other provisions fall nicely under that general heading. Accepting gifts or favors clearly makes one's judgment less independent. Failing to disclose a conflict of interest, or acting in a case with a conflict of interest, also undermines the concept of independence and fairness, and both suggest some elements of dishonesty. Misrepresenting information is neither fair nor honest, and it would typically suggest a lack of independence.

The third section of the AICP/APA statement on ethical principles deals primarily with individual activities, such as participating in continuing education, obtaining appropriate credentials, representing those credentials accurately, and generally acting like a professional.

Where the two statements on ethics create a potential for conflict is in the first section of both. In the AICP/APA statement, that principle states:

> The planning process must continuously pursue and faithfully serve the public interest.

Six of the seven paragraphs in that section set out principles with which most planners and public officials would agree, recognizing that planners should encourage citizen participation in decisions; provide them with full, accurate, and accessible information; assist in the "clarification" of community goals; make public information public; and recognize "long-range consequences" of present actions. But paragraph 6 creates the potential for ethical conflict by setting out particular values that the statement defines as being within the public interest:

> [Planning process participants should] strive to protect the integrity of the natural environment and the heritage of the built environment.

The AICP code labels its first section "The Planner's Responsibility to the Public." Its listing of responsibilities is similar to that in the first section of the joint statement, and its last two items read as follows:

6. A planner must strive to protect the integrity of the natural environment

7. A planner must strive for excellence of environmental design and endeavor to conserve the heritage of the built environment.

In both statements, the quoted lines represent values. They are values with which the authors agree, but they are values nonetheless. No common ethical principles hold that it is "right" to protect the natural environment and the "heritage" (presumably historic buildings and monuments) of the human-built environment. Those are widely adopted and accepted public policies, presumably representing the values of many citizens, but they are not ethical principles. In response to those who would argue that taking care of the natural environment is the only course of action, others might respond by quoting the Book of Genesis, in which God is said to have given humans dominion over the earth and all that is on it.

When does such a distinction become important? Suppose that a planner works for a dying small community in which the largest local employer, a grain elevator, closed three years earlier. An outside company has now proposed to build a plant that would turn crops that could be locally grown into synthetic materials that would replace lumber in certain building applications. The plant, however, would require a good deal of water to cool equipment used in the process. No matter how well the plant is designed, it seems likely to disrupt the habitat of a small fish that is plentiful in surrounding counties but lives in only one local stream. People in the community need jobs. The community needs the tax revenues from the plant to support its schools. In short, this is a project of considerable merit. Should it be approved? Not necessarily. What is important to the topic of this chapter, however, is that it would be unreasonable to argue that a planner who recommended approval of such a project was acting unethically by failing to "strive to protect the integrity of the natural environment." That is where values come into play.

In a broader sense, the entire concept of Section A of the AICP/APA statement creates potential for conflict for a planner. Who is to define this "public interest" that the planner is to serve? What if the planner believes that the public interest is different from what the local government where the planner is working is doing? Will "public respect for the planning process . . be maintained," as in section B, if the planner publicly dissents from the official position of the decision makers for whom she or he works, after the fact? Certainly, if those decision makers are engaged in unethical or unlawful behavior, the planner has no choice. But what if the planner simply disagrees with a decision and believes that the "public interest" requires a different result. The AICP/APA joint statement does not address it, and the AICP code essentially leaves the planner to resolve the issue:

> A planner must accept the decisions of a client or employer concerning the objectives and nature of the professional services to be performed unless the course of action to be pursued involves conduct which is illegal or inconsistent with the planner's primary obligation to the public interest.

Again, this issue goes back to the notion of values.

Planning professor Richard Bolan has examined this question from a different perspective, considering the issue of "obligation" and "responsibility" to our communities. He then examines the range of communities of which we are a part, ranging from family and friends, to the nation state and past and future generations, with the local community falling near the middle of the continuum.[1] In systems terms, many of the communities on the continuum define much of the environment for the communities below them on the continuum; thus, the controllable variables change with the system level, and the planner's responsibility may change accordingly. For example, at a community level, a planner may have to accept the fact that the municipal water supply is contaminated by chemical runoff from farm fields and plan treatment systems accordingly; at a state level, it becomes possible to change the policies applicable to agriculture, thus potentially shifting the treatment burden to the farmer (who is the originating agent of the pollution) and away from the community. Again, this relates more to values than to ethics narrowly defined.

The three principal contexts in which planners regularly engage questions of applied ethics involve issues of the handling of information, the disclosure and action on potential conflicts of interest, and the acceptance of gifts and favors. The following subsections discuss those three topics.

Handling Information

Information is power. Investors can go to jail for basing investment decisions on "inside" information not available to the general public. Planners similarly possess a great deal of valuable information, as in the following examples:

- In creating future land-use plans, planners give and take away value from land. Land planned for future shopping centers, office buildings, and apartment complexes is likely to increase in value, while land designated for long-term agricultural or rural use may essentially have its value frozen.
- Planners typically know the probable routes of new highways and other infrastructure before draft plans are made public; land along those routes may become more valuable when the information becomes public.
- Planners often know about proposed new developments before the information becomes public; again, land needed for the developments may rise in value, or at least in price, when information about the development becomes public.
- Developers typically present to the public the most positive possible information about their proposals; planners often know "the rest of the story," including environmental hazards, infrastructure problems, and other challenges that may affect the success of a project.
- Careful planners typically understand the "downside" risks of a project, some of which are inherent in even the best of projects.

Using such information for personal gain is a topic of the next section. The rest of this section addresses the question of how the planner handles such information when there is no potential personal gain.

The AICP/APA statement is very helpful on this topic. It includes the following provisions in sections A and B:

Planning process participants should:

[A2] strive to give citizens (including those who lack formal organization or influence) full, clear and accurate information on planning issues and the opportunity to have a meaningful role in the development of plans and programs;

[A5] ensure that reports, records and any other non-confidential information which is, or will be, available to decision makers is made available to the public in a convenient format and sufficiently in advance of any decision;

[B10] not disclose confidential information acquired in the course of their duties except when required by law, to prevent a clear violation of law or to prevent substantial injury to third persons;

[B11] not misrepresent facts or distort information for the purpose of achieving a desired outcome.

The AICP code contains language that is essentially identical to that of the joint statement on the first two points and similar in effect on the last two.[2]

The principles cited above seem abundantly clear, but their application in practice is apparently troublesome. In a landmark study, Howe and Kaufman outlined fifteen short scenarios involving planners; they asked each respondent to evaluate the behavior of the planner in each scenario as "ethical" or "unethical."[3]

On five of the fifteen scenarios, one-third or more of those polled reached a conclusion opposite that of the majority. Most of those issues related to handling information. The one on which there was the most disagreement (47 percent found it ethical, 43 percent unethical) was the release of a draft report on a project to the developer of the project, one of three separate scenarios asking about the ethical considerations involved in releasing a draft report when there was "no agency policy on releasing such information." Some 65 percent thought it would be ethical to release a report to an environmental group under similar circumstances, and 54 percent thought it would be ethical to release a report to a homeowners' group under similar circumstances; in the latter case, it was stipulated that the group was "white" and the information related to the location of new public housing. Clearly, there were some teleologists responding, reaching different conclusions depending on what group might benefit. Was this behavior ethical or unethical when measured against the (subsequently adopted) statement cited above? It is not clear. If the information was "confidential" (and some would argue that a "draft" is always an in-house working document and thus confidential), the behavior in each case was unethical. If the information was public, then the obligation of the planner involved was to make it accessible to all interested parties; such a requirement does not necessarily preclude giving a copy to someone who requests it a day or even a few days before it goes out in the mail to other parties.

Where it was clear that a planner was "leaking" information against agency policy, most planners in the survey found the behavior unethical: 55 percent found it unethical for a planner to leak information on a proposed slum clearance project to a low-income neighborhood group (but 33 percent thought it ethical); 59 percent thought it was unethical to leak to an environmental group information on a project that would affect wetlands; and 75 percent thought it would be unethical to leak to the chamber of commerce information about proposed changes in downtown parking policies. Although at least 55 percent found all of these information leaks unethical, the 20 percent variation in responses between the leak to the low-income group and the leak to the business group suggests that at least one-fifth of the respondents were teleologists, evaluating the rightness of the action in the context of its apparent beneficiaries. As presented, it would appear that the planners in all of the scenarios were violating paragraph B.10 of the AICP/APA statement by disclosing confidential information obtained in the course of work.

In separate questions involving the distortion of information, the majorities rating the behavior unethical were much larger—but many planners still shared the minority view. Some 13 percent thought it would be ethical to develop a new study on ridership and revenues to counter a regional planning study showing that a mass transit system would not be feasible, and 17 percent thought it would be ethical to ignore an earlier ridership study in preparing a new one; some 22 percent thought it was ethical to represent in a somewhat public forum that "many" neighborhood groups supported a proposal when a "majority" actually opposed it.

Interestingly, the scenario that produced the closest split of opinion was one in which the planner changed a recommendation based on "technical grounds" after pressure from the agency director; while 39 percent of respondents thought it was unethical to change the recommendation, 42 percent thought it was ethical, and 18 percent were not sure. The statement of principles does not directly address such behavior, unless it can be considered "distorting information," although independence of judgment seems to be fairly implied in the notions of "integrity and proficiency" in pursuit of the public interest (AICP/APA statement, section B).

In an advisory ruling on the AICP code, AICP has provided a succinct summary of the responsibilities of a planner in dealing with information:

There is also a positive duty on behalf of ethical treatment of information. In reporting the results of studies, planners must follow the scholar's rule of making it possible for others to follow in our footsteps and check our work. Document the sources of data. Report the statistical procedures used, what was done to bring the raw data into the form that is reported. What assumptions were made at different stages in the study?

Public decision makers must often leap beyond the cautions and reservations of a careful study to achieve political solutions. Planners must take pains that our studies and recommendations are not wrongly interpreted, and that a clear distinction is made between factual findings and policy decisions.[4]

Conflicts of Interest

In section B.3, the AICP code provides succinctly:

A planner shall not perform work if there is an actual, apparent, or reasonably foreseeable conflict of interest, direct or indirect, or an appearance of impropriety, without full written disclosure concerning work for current or past clients and subsequent written consent by the current client or employer. A planner shall remove himself or herself from a project if there is any direct personal or financial gain, including gains to family members. A planner shall not disclose information gained in the course of public activity for a private benefit unless the information would be offered impartially to any person.

The code contains other provisions that address related issues:

[B4] A planner who has previously worked for a public planning body should not represent a private client for one year after the planner's last date of employment with the planning body, in connection with any matter before that body that the planner may have influenced before leaving public employment.

[B5] A planner must not solicit prospective clients or employment through use of false or misleading claims, harassment or duress.

[B7] A planner must not use the power of any office to seek or obtain a special advantage that is not in the public interest nor any special advantage that is not a matter of public knowledge.

The AICP/APA joint statement of ethical principles contains similarly strong language, requiring that its adherents:

[B2]   make public disclosure of any "personal interests" that they may have . . . ;

[B3]   define "personal interest" broadly to include any actual or potential benefits or advantages that they, a spouse, family member or person living in their household might directly or indirectly obtain from a planning decision;

[B4]   abstain completely from direct or indirect participation as an advisor or decision maker in any matter in which they have a personal interest, and leave any chamber in which such a matter is under deliberation, unless their personal interest has been made a matter of public record; their employer, if any, has given approval; and the public official, public agency or court with jurisdiction to rule on ethics matters has expressly authorized their participation.

AICP Advisory Ruling No. 2 elaborates on the situation in which a planner participates in development in a community where that planner also serves as a public employee. It addresses, and rejects, alternative proposals to put the development investment in a spouse's name or to avoid participation in any review of the proposed project. Such a situation clearly involves an "appearance of impropriety" that ought to be avoided. Planners can become developers, but it is better to be either a public-sector planner or a developer, not both at once. For the public-sector planner determined to participate in the development game, the best procedure is to invest in another community, where the planner has no official position and no "inside" information.

Investing in a development in a community where the planner holds a position of public trust is an obvious sort of conflict that most people try to avoid. It is the more subtle conflicts that are troublesome. Here are some examples:

Richard Hedman on conflicts of interest. Copyright by Richard Hedman. Used with permission.

- The community is seeking a consultant to prepare a new comprehensive plan; a local firm, which does work for many local developers, wants to submit a proposal, asserting (probably correctly) that it "knows the community better than anyone else."
- The staff planner's spouse is an associate in the accounting office that handles all the work for the developer proposing a big project; the case can be worse if the planner learns from her or his spouse that the developer's financial survival may depend on this project and that the developer is such a big client that the firm may have to lay off some associates if it loses that work.
- In a small community, the lawyer representing the developer before the planning commission is also the personal lawyer for one or more members of the planning commission, on totally unrelated matters.
- A planning commission member is a trust officer or branch manager at a bank and, although he or she does no real estate lending, is aware that the bank has made a risky loan to a developer now appearing before the commission and that the best hope of getting the loan paid back is for the project to be approved by the planning commission.
- A staff planner, or a member of the planning commission, is a member of an environmental group that has actively and publicly opposed a project now pending before the commission.

The first case, involving the preparation of a comprehensive plan, seems to involve an obvious conflict of interest, which Advisory Ruling No. 2 notes:

> Conflicts of interest are reasonably foreseeable when a planner attempts to serve a real estate development client while also serving a public agency that may have a role in reviewing or approving projects of that client.[5]

The others are far less clear. In none of them is it clear that the planner or a relative will enjoy personal gain (or avoid personal loss) by taking a particular action. On the other hand, there is a real risk that the financial interests in each case may impair the independence of the planner's judgment—particularly in the cases involving the accountant and the banker, where the indirect effect of the planning decision could adversely (or positively) affect the employer, with possible further effects on the individual's job.

The situation with the lawyer is common and perhaps unavoidable in small communities, but it is troublesome—and ought to trouble the lawyer under her or his own code of ethics. Although there may be no direct or even indirect conflict, there is certainly the appearance of impropriety, the kind of situation that results in citizens who are frustrated with the decision saying things like, "He knew somebody—that's how he got that project approved," or "That lawyer had everything worked out beforehand; I saw him having lunch with one of the commissioners just last week."

Environmental advocates may argue that planners can and should be active in environmental groups. Certainly, planners are entitled to pay their dues and receive publications from any organization they choose, just as they are free to join political parties and vote. When an environmental (or other activist) group regularly takes positions regarding proposed developments in a community, however, there is again a potential appearance of impropriety if the planner is actively involved with the group. Further, if the planner is deeply involved with the group or publicly dedicated to its cause, that association may, in cases on which the group takes a position, deprive the planner of the independent judgment required by section B.1 of the AICP code.

What is the solution? At a bare minimum there must be full disclosure, on the record, at the meeting, with approval from the commission or person in charge for the planner to continue to participate. It is far better to have a group saying, "Why did she waste our time by disclosing something that probably happens all the time?" than to have the newspaper or some public official wondering out loud, "Now, why wasn't this little conflict of interest disclosed?"

Gifts and Favors

Probably the clearest form of conflict of interest, at least as far as most people are concerned, involves bribery—or, in the terms of the AICP/APA statement, the seeking of "gifts and favors" to influence public decisions. Both the AICP/APA statement and the AICP code directly prohibit both the acceptance and the solicitation of gifts and favors:

> [Planning process participants should] seek no gifts or favors, nor offer any, under circumstances in which it might reasonably be inferred that the gifts or favors were intended or expected to influence a participant's objectivity as an advisor or decision maker in the planning process.[6]

> A planner must not sell or offer to sell services by stating or implying an ability to influence decisions by improper means.[7]

> A planner must not use the power of any office to seek or obtain a special advantage that is not in the public interest, nor any special advantage that is not a matter of public knowledge.[8]

The concept of bribery may seem so simple and straight forward that it requires no explanation or discussion, but the concept of gifts and favors goes a good bit beyond the image of money changing hands in a dark alley or under the table. Members of Congress are sometimes criticized for accepting free trips for themselves and their families, ostensibly to inspect some business or government operation of interest to the member or his or her district. Although it is rare for a planner to be offered a junket to a far-off land, it is not uncommon for those with interests before a planning agency to provide free lunches, holiday gifts, invitations to elaborate (or simple) parties, or other gifts or favors.

A six-year survey of newspapers in the United States identified 372 cases of apparent corruption involving local officials, of which 83, or a little more than 20 percent, involved land-use matters.[9] That is not a large number of documented cases of corruption, considering the thousands of local governments that engage in land-use and building regulation and the dozens, or even hundreds, of decisions that each one makes each year. On the other hand, it is a measurable number and thus a matter of concern.

Planners who are offered a bribe have one choice and no others: turn it down, document it, and report it. Most situations are far more subtle, however: the free lunch, the free drink at a reception, the free reception, the free tickets to the new theater just opened in the developer's project. Some state laws define the level at which a gift to a public official creates a breach of the public trust. In Iowa, the limit is three dollars;[10] although that limit is surprisingly low and limits free lunches to fast-food establishments, it is indicative of the level of public concern with the issue. Some local governments and individual agencies have adopted policies that define which gifts and "perks" are acceptable and which are not.

In part, however, the issue goes back to the appearance of impropriety. If a public planner regularly socializes with professionals in the community and they occasionally buy one another lunch or drinks, that is not likely to be considered a conflict. On the other hand, if a local engineer or planning consultant with a project pending before the commission suddenly offers to buy the planner lunch at an expensive restaurant, the community may interpret the situation quite differently. Codes of ethics are not intended to cause planners or other public officials to be rude or antisocial, but they are intended to make them aware of both the appearance and the substance of their actions as they relate to the public interest. Note also that laws and policies aimed at bribery typically apply only to those people who have, or are reasonably likely to have, business before the agency with which the public servant is involved. Thus, a planner with a public agency can generally accept free lunches from car dealers and bankers who are not engaged in the development business. On the other hand, environmental and neighborhood groups may have the type of interests before an agency that bar the acceptance of free lunches or other gifts or favors from such organizations.

At a minimum, every planner working in the public sector should know the state law and local government and agency policies regarding the acceptance of gifts and favors from outside the agency. Planners representing private interests before public agencies should similarly be aware of those laws and policies. Within the parameters established by applicable law and policy, every planner should have some set of principles that he or she regularly follows: "I will go to lunch with you if I pay my own way," or "You can pay for lunch today, but it is important to me that we take turns doing so," or "I simply do not socialize with people who have business pending before our agency. Once your case is resolved, give me a call and I would enjoy visiting with you over lunch."

Other Ethical Principles

Both the AICP/APA joint statement of principles and the AICP code contain other requirements characteristic of ethical principles of professions: participating in continuing education; giving pro bono professional time to needy groups and individuals; contributing to the development of planning knowledge; contributing time to assist students and interns; treating others fairly; and representing accurately one's own credentials and the credentials of other professionals.[11]

There is no effective enforcement for these last groups of standards, which might better be called "guidelines for professional conduct" than "ethical" requirements or principles. However desirable it may be to assist students and needy groups, for example, it is difficult to find a generally accepted ethical principle that requires it. On the other hand, any profession can, if it chooses, impose standards for such conduct and adopt reporting requirements to attempt to measure it. Many professions adopt and enforce continuing education requirements with measurable benchmarks for each reporting period; there is so far no such requirement for planners.

Values

In *Urban Planning and Politics,* William Johnson defines a value in the context of city planning as "[a] good that people seek, a quality in an object or situation that makes it valuable. In the context of urban development, a value is a benefit that can be drawn from the built environment and the activities it supports." He goes on to note that: "Because urban areas contain so much social and cultural diversity, planners and developers who think on the largest scale must also be sensitive to the personal values that people hold about the locations in which they live, work, shop, and play."[12]

Similarly, planners must be sensitive to their own values, which help to shape their views of the world—and the communities for which they plan. Johnson's work (pp. 19–24) lists a series of values likely to influence urban planning:

- asthetic values, which relate to the visual character of the community;
- functional values, which focus on the optimal use of land and the operation of efficient transportation and utility systems;[13]
- social values, which address human needs, with a particular emphasis on those who have the fewest choices;[14]

- ecological values, which deal with the natural environment and the effects of the built environment on it.[15]

There are certainly other values that influence public decisions today:

- the desire for more and better jobs for a community, to enhance the economy and provide more opportunities for residents;[16]
- a concern for individual safety, which is a basic human need;[17]
- suspicion of government programs and the desire by many to accomplish more things with less government intervention.

The documents on ethics included in appendices A and B both emphasize the obligation of the planner to work for "the public interest." It is in defining the public interest that values come into play. Suppose that a community is considering a proposal for a new industry that will bring in two hundred high-paying jobs but will affect five acres of wetlands. A planner whose work and values focus on economic development is likely to view that project differently from a planner whose personal philosophy revolves around ecological values. One may recommend approval of the project as being in the public interest, and the other may suggest that it be disapproved because it is *not* in the public interest. Which one would be right? In a pure sense, neither is right. In a relative sense, considered in the context of their individual values, both are right. What should the public officials who must vote on the project do? Presumably, their decision will reflect the values of the community.

How do public officials know what the values of the community are? The best record of the values of the community related to physical changes is a comprehensive plan. See chapters 2, 8, and, especially, 5, which describes methods of determining community goals—which are focused statements of community values.

One of the great complications of making decisions in a democracy is that we share the decision-making process with people who have different values—and we all get to participate. That is both the strength and the weakness of democracy. Values are like ethics in that they influence how people think about planning and how they make decisions. They are quite different, however, because we accept and truly expect a diversity of values in any public process. We hope, however, that we all share a basic set of ethical principles and that we all rely on that set of principles in our decision-making processes.

Walk the Walk

It is important that the individual planner consider and act on professional ethics at a personal level, as well as a professional level, because it is the individual who upholds and strives to meet the standards. It is the individual who continues to seek new and innovative ways of solving problems and who must always carry out his or her work with integrity.

Both ethics documents recognize the importance of individual behavior and individual decisions to professional ethics. While section C of the AICP/APA joint statement addresses both individual development and contributions to the profession, the AICP code separates those topics into two sections, section C addressing individual contributions to the profession and section D focusing on issues of "professional integrity." Paragraph 2 in section D prohibits planners from engaging in "deliberately wrongful acts," while paragraph 3 emphasizes respect for the rights of others.

Planners must walk the walk of planning and community values. Although an individual planner may believe that economic values are the most important values to the community, that planner must respect other community values and demonstrate that in her or his daily life. Taking public transportation or a bicycle to a meeting, allowing the front lawn to go brown when there is a water shortage, recycling everything practicable, and treating people of all backgrounds with respect are simple behaviors through which planners can demonstrate their commitment to the types of values typically represented in planning. Just talking the talk of planning is not enough; effective planners walk the walk, and the citizens with whom they work are very likely to know the difference.

Conclusion

Some planners believe that their duties begin and end with accurate data that are thoroughly analyzed and impartially presented so that all facts are known and understood. In essence, such a planner would serve only as a technocrat, removed from value-laden decisions by the rational use and interpretation of data. Others argue that a value-free approach is not possible, even with scientific methodology. Values are reflected in the selection of data and data analysis used and in the interpretation of the data. While the process itself may be totally rational, subjective decisions are made by planners throughout the process. Recognizing that the planning process involves community and individual values helps in upholding professional ethics.

All planners come to the profession with a set of values and ethics. Their professional responsibility is to make those personal ethics and values clear, particularly when there is a potential for conflict. While the ethics described in the AICP "Code of Ethics" seem straightforward, ethical issues are not always so clear-cut. Often, obligations to clients conflict with obligations to the public, and professional integrity appears to be in direct conflict with democratic decision making. It is easy for the guidance from the code of ethics to be hazy. The dilemma starts with the most basic point of planners' concern for protecting the public interest: What is the public interest? It is neither easily determined nor always possible to protect. In general terms it means that resources are used to accomplish public purposes; and, because resources are limited, they must be utilized as efficiently and effectively as possible in achieving the goal. That implies making choices, and when choices are made, they often benefit some while sacrificing the interests of others.

Complicating issues of ethics is the difficulty of readily identifying the actual impacts of alternatives on a community. While there are models that can show the economic impacts of certain decisions, there are no models that can tell us what the social or cultural impacts might be. Professional ethics charge planners with the responsibility of protecting and projecting into the future the values of today without affecting the existing social and cultural environment. However, it is impossible and not even desirable to have that effect. While the system is imperfect, it does not mean that professional ethics should be discarded. Only by being ethical in the planning process can there be hope that the intended results of plans create the changes envisioned.

EXERCISES

1. What basic ethical principles guide your life? The Golden Rule? The Ten Commandments? What is the source of those ethical principles? Is it religious or civil? Do you and most of your classmates share some basic ethical beliefs, regardless of your backgrounds? Are there some ethical principles on which you disagree?

2. What values that you hold are likely to influence you in a planning career? Are you strongly committed to environmental values, or to creating opportunities for people who are disadvantaged, or to creating opportunities for those who are aggressive and entrepreneurial to succeed? How do your values differ from those of other people in the class? How might they influence your approach to planning issues in your community?

3. Contact your municipal or county clerk or another public official and find out what level of gift amounts to a "bribe" or unlawful gift in your state or community. What would that amount of money buy? Do you think that is a large enough amount to influence someone's vote on an important public issue?

4. Find out the policy of your local planning department on releasing staff reports on proposed developments to the developer, to the public and to the planning commission. Who gets it first? Is there a mailing list of interested groups that get advance copies (or at least notice) of such reports? Is this a reasonable process?

DISCUSSION QUESTION

Assume that you live in an agricultural community in the Midwest. You know from growing up there that many of the farms in your state were once swamps and that the only reason the land can be farmed today is that farm families have installed and maintained drain tiles in the fields for more than one hundred years. You have now learned that the federal government is buying up some farmland to turn it back to wetlands, in part to help alleviate downstream flooding. Is this program in the "public interest"? Why or why not? How do your values influence your answer to this question?

FURTHER READING

American Planning Association, ed. 1994. *Planning and Community Equity: A Component of APA's Agenda for America's Communities Program.* Chicago: Planners Press. This book is a collection of articles concerning specific issues of social equity, a subject more reflective of values than ethics in the narrow sense. These articles serve to connect different areas of physical planning to social consequences.

Frankena, William K. 1973. *Ethics,* 2nd edition. Englewood Cliffs, NJ: Prentice-Hall. An excellent and very readable introduction to the general topic of ethics.

Howe, Elizabeth. 1994. *Acting on Ethics in City Planning.* New Brunswick, NJ: Rutgers University, Center for Urban Policy Research. This is a study on how planners define ethical issues and choices. Case studies use real people making difficult ethical decisions.

Johnson, William C. 1997. *Urban Planning and Politics.* Chicago: Planners Press. Includes a good discussion of values and the influence of values on planning.

Wachs, Martin, ed. 1985. *Ethics in Planning.* New Brunswick, NJ: Rutgers University, Center for Urban Policy Research. This collection of articles from diverse individuals looks at planning ethics in general, ethics in making policy and fighting corruption, and environmental ethics. With authors from several different fields, the points of view vary, but the issues they address are challenging.

NOTES

1. Richard Bolan, "The Structure of Ethical Choice in Planning Practice," *Journal of Planning Education and Research* 3: 23–24 (1983); reprinted as chapter 4 in Martin Wachs, ed., *Ethics in Planning,* New Brunswick, NJ: Rutgers University, Center for Urban Policy Research (1985).
2. AICP code, sections. A.1–A.5, B.9.
3. Elizabeth Howe and Jerome Kaufman, "The Ethics of Contemporary American Planners," *Journal of the American Planning Association* 45, no.3 (July 1979), pp. 243–255, reprinted as chapter 2 in Wachs, note 1.
4. AICP Advisory Ruling No. 4: "Honesty in the Use of Information," March 1991, reproduced in appendix C.
5. AICP Advisory Ruling No. 2: "Conflicts of Interest When a Public Planner has a Stake in Private Development," May 1988, reproduced in appendix C.
6. AICP/APA statement of principles, section B.5.
7. AICP code, section B.6.
8. Ibid., section B.7.

9. John Gardiner, "Corruption and Reform in Land-Use and Building Regulation: Incentives and Disincentives," included as chapter 6 in Wachs, note 1.

10. Iowa Code §68B.22(4)(i) (1997).

11. In the AICP/APA statement (Appendix A), see section C; in the AICP code (Appendix B), see sections C and D.

12. Ibid.

13. This relates closely to the subject of chapter 7.

14. See discussions of issues of "social equity" in chapter 17.

15. See discussions of the natural environment in chapter 3 and of issues of sustainability throughout the text.

16. Discussed in chapter 19.

17. See, for example, Oscar Newman's discussion of the design implications of this issue in *Creating Defensible Space,* Washington, DC: Department of Housing and Urban Development (1996).

Chapter 22

Entering the Profession

This chapter examines briefly the considerations—and the steps—involved in entering the planning profession.

What Makes a Good Planner

An initial question for anyone considering any career field is whether the career fits the individual's interests, skills, and personality. Anyone who has read this far in this book should have some sense of whether planning as a field will fit her or his interests.

Among skills, so-called people skills are the ones most essential to anyone entering this field. Planning does not offer the kinds of jobs that allow professionals to work behind a drafting table or a computer terminal all day. Much of every day is likely to involve a combination of formal meetings, scheduled appointments, and informal responses to questions and requests for information.

Bruce McClendon, a planner with experience in running a large public agency, and Anthony Catanese, a planner who became a university president, collected essays from twenty-one planners containing "real-life lessons on what works, what doesn't, and why."[1] Several themes emerge repeatedly in the essays, and they are described in the sections below.

Basic Skills

Two skills dominate the discussions: written communication and oral communication. Planners must communicate their ideas effectively. That requires the ability to write concise but clear reports and to present the same material orally, before a neighborhood group or before a packed house for a public meeting.

Close behind those two skills in frequency of appearance are listening skills. Much of planning focuses on learning—about community needs and desires, about existing opportunities and constraints, and learning clearly requires effective listening.

Several of the contributors to that book discuss the importance of organizational skills. The variety of work in which planners engage, and the constant interruptions for meetings and citizen queries, create practical obstacles to completing tasks; as in most fields, completing tasks is important, and that requires organization.

Clearly, technical skills are important. Those range from narrow technical skills, such as the ability to analyze population data, to the ability to use computers and modern information systems. Most planners work in teams, however, and it is typically not necessary that every member of the team possess every technical skill needed at the time—one member may map natural resources while another manipulates census data. There are successful planners who hate math and talented planners who cannot draw a straight line, although both mathematical and graphic skills are useful in planning.

Leadership and Educational Ability

Planners must have the leadership skills to help make community goals and objectives reality. A particular kind of leadership skill is required to accomplish that when others hold the important titles, such as mayor, planning commission chair, city manager, and president of the chamber of commerce.

Planners must be able to educate both public officials and the general public about the value of planning and the importance of the ideas included in an adopted plan. That requires a combination of public relations and traditional education—sometimes topped off by some good, old-fashioned, sales skills.

Planners often must facilitate meetings, finding ways to include everyone who wants to participate while keeping the meeting focused and on schedule. Managing groups of people and leading meetings require specialized leadership skills.

Political Savvy

Planning is always political, though usually not partisan. Tip O'Neill, long time speaker of the U.S. House of Representatives, is reputed to have said, "All politics is local," suggesting to his colleagues the importance of remaining in touch with their constituents back home. His comment is relevant to planners because nothing is more local than planning, and it is highly political.

The role of politics is simple. The planner exists in a political environment. Many planning directors serve at the pleasure of a city manager or mayor. Even planners who have the protection of civil service employment depend on a political system to adopt and implement their plans. The planner's personal political savvy will have a significant impact on his or her ability to get things done.

At a different level, the very discussion of community values, goals, and objectives is a political discussion. It is a process that goes to the heart of democracy—trying to bring a group of people to consensus on a course of action.

Personal Characteristics and Values

Trust is a word that appears repeatedly in the essays in the McClendon and Catanese book. Planners must build trust with public officials and citizens alike—and then maintain that trust.

Effective planners believe in a participatory, democratic process. Although some may succeed by imposing a vision on a community, that is not the norm and not a model for success. Good planners make citizen participation work, because they believe in the process.

Planners must continue to learn. It is more than an ethical requirement, discussed in chapter 20—according to the planners who wrote the essays, it is a practical necessity.

Finally, as former Orlando planning director Richard Bernhardt notes, "To be effective, planners must be committed."[2] *Commitment* is another term that appears repeatedly in the essays.

Planning Education

The Planning Accreditation Board (PAB) accredits planning degree programs. There are sixty accredited graduate programs in planning and nine accredited undergraduate degree programs. That number has remained relatively constant in recent years. There are programs in all parts of the country and in most states.

Through the accreditation process, the PAB sends teams of "site visitors" to each program at least once every five years. Those site visitors prepare a report to the board in which they describe how well the program meets current accreditation criteria. That process provides an objective, outside evaluation of how well a program performs.

Anyone intending to enter planning as a profession should seriously consider an accredited program. A current list is always available from the PAB.[3]

Some planners enter the profession with other degrees, however. There are professionals with degrees in the related fields of engineering, landscape architecture, law, and architecture who essentially practice planning. There are also practicing planners who hold degrees in nonprofessional fields like geography and urban studies. Anyone choosing between a nonprofessional degree program that includes some planning courses and a professional planning program ought to compare the course requirements of the two carefully to see what may be missing from the nonprofessional program.

The predominant professional degree in planning is the master's degree. Graduates of accredited undergraduate programs are well accepted in the job market where the programs are prominent or where there are many graduates in the workforce. Those areas include the Midwest, where there are four programs, parts of the Carolinas, and parts of California. In other parts of the country, graduates may need to explain to employers that they are accredited by the same criteria as the more numerous master's programs.

Professional Associations

The American Planning Association is a service organization that offers membership to anyone who is interested in planning and who is willing to pay the dues.[4] Its members receive a subscription to the monthly magazine *Planning,* as well as automatic membership in a state chapter, which includes a periodic newsletter subscription. APA members can attend state and regional conferences as well as the annual national planning conference. The organization also offers other periodical subscriptions and operates a bookstore.

The American Institute of Certified Planners provides credentials that attest to the professionalism of planners who meet its standards.[5] Membership requires a combination of education and experience, with professional experience requirements ranging from two years for those with professional master's degrees to four years for those with unrelated degrees. Those who meet the education and experience requirements must pass a test to become members.

Ads for advanced jobs, including directorships in the field, often require AICP membership. We encourage students to seek AICP membership early in their careers, typically before seeking a second or third professional position.

In 1998, the AICP created a College of Fellows. Membership is by nomination and review by a national panel. Nominees must have at least fifteen years of professional experience as members of AICP. Nominations must be submitted by state chapters of the American Planning Association or cosigned by ten different AICP members. Categories in which prospective members can be nominated include professional practice; teaching and mentoring; research; public/community service and leadership; and communication. There are required findings for each category, all of which include a requirement of "exceptional accomplishment over an extended period of time."[6] In April 1999, the College of Fellows inducted its first forty-six members, each of whom can now use the "FAICP" designation after her or his name.

Practical Considerations

"You can't go home again" is practically a fact of life for planners. If a planner's hometown of fifty thousand people has a staff of eight planners, it is statistically unlikely that one of those planners will decide to leave at just the time that the new planner wants a job there. Even if someone does leave, it is unlikely that there will be a match between the needs of the job now vacant and the skills of the incoming planner.

For similar reasons, it is often necessary to move on to move up. Bruce McClendon started his career in Oklahoma, developed it in Texas, and left a major position in Fort Worth to head the agency in Orange County, Florida, which surrounds Orlando. Norman Whitaker, one of the chapter authors in the McClendon-Catanese book, who worked under McClendon in a small city in Texas, left that state to become planning director in Portsmouth, Virginia, from which place he moved to Knoxville, Tennessee. One of the authors is a native of Colorado now living in Indiana. Another is a Texas native who took her current position in Arizona after a stint in Missouri.

The planning job market has been very good for many years, but there may not be an opening in a particular community at a particular time. That has implications not only for planners but for their spouses and significant others in these days of two-career couples. If one spouse aspires to be a high school band director and the other a planning director, the best hope is to locate in a major metropolitan area, where jobs in both fields may open—that is unlikely to occur in a small community. In a limited field like planning, it is helpful to have a spouse or companion whose field is more portable.

Conclusion

Like most careers, planning provides great opportunities for the right people. The last two chapters and some of the resources cited here and in chapter 20 may help a student or other user of this book to determine whether she or he is likely to be a good—and happy—planner, or, worded differently, whether planning is the right career choice.

EXERCISES

1. Contact your career services office and ask to take an interest inventory or other test used to identify logical career choices for individuals. Planning may not be one of the careers listed on the test, but there should be similarities between some of those fields and planning.

2. Make a list of the attributes that you have liked best about your summer and part-time jobs. Group and organize them. Compare them to what you know about planning. Now do the same thing with the attributes you have liked least about your summer and part-time jobs. Do you think planning will be a good career choice for you?

3. Invite a group of two or three planners to class and ask them to talk with you about what makes a good planner.

4. Obtain one of the recent guides to planning schools and study the information on those schools. Identify two or three that are of particular interest to you.

Discussion Question

How would your class, collectively, identify people who would make good planners? Are there certain types of people whom you would encourage not to enter the field?

Notes

1. Bruce W. McClendon and Anthony James Catanese, *Planners on Planning: Leading Planners Offer Real-Life Lessons on What Works, What Doesn't, and Why.* San Francisco: Jossey-Bass (1996).
2. Ibid. p. 42.
3. Planning Accreditation Board, Merle Hay Tower, Suite 302, 3800 Merle Hay Road, Des Moines, IA 50310; (515) 252-0729.
4. For membership information, write APA at 122 South Michigan Avenue, Suite 1600, Chicago, IL 60603, or go to the Web site at http://www.planning.org.
5. For membership information, write AICP, 1776 Massachusetts Avenue, NW, Washington, DC 20036, or go to the APA Web site (see note 4) and click on "AICP."
6. Fellow of AICP, Year 2000 Nomination Materials, American Institute of Certified Planners, Washington, D.C., 1999.

Appendix A
....

AICP/APA Statement of Ethical Principles in Planning

This statement is a guide to ethical conduct for all who participate in the process of planning as advisors, advocates, and decision makers. It presents a set of principles to be held in common by certified planners, other practicing planners, appointed and elected officials, and others who participate in the process of planning.

The planning process exists to serve the public interest. While the public interest is a question of continuous debate, both in its general principles and in its case-by-case applications, it requires a conscientiously held view of the policies and actions that best serve the entire community. Section A presents what we hold to be necessary elements in such a view.

Planning issues commonly involve a conflict of values and, often, there are large private interests at stake. These accentuate the necessity for the highest standards of fairness and honesty among all participants. Section B presents specific standards.

Those who practice planning need to adhere to a special set of ethical requirements that must guide all who aspire to professionalism. These are presented in Section C.

Section D is the translation of the principles above into the AICP Code of Ethics and Professional Conduct. The Code is formally subscribed to by each certified planner. It includes an enforcement procedure that is administered by AICP. The Code, however, provides for more than the minimum threshold of enforceable acceptability. It also sets aspirational standards that require conscious striving to attain.

The ethical principles derive both from the general values of society and from the planner's special responsibility to serve the public interest. As the basic values of society are often in competition with each other, so do these principles sometimes compete. For example, the need to provide full public information may compete with the need to respect confidences. Plans and programs often result from a balancing among divergent interests. An ethical judgment often also requires a conscientious balancing, based on the facts and context of a particular situation and on the entire set of ethical principles.

This statement also aims to inform the public generally. It is also the basis for continuing systematic discussion of the application of its principles that is itself essential behavior to give them daily meaning.

A. The planning process must continuously pursue and faithfully serve the public interest.

Planning Process Participants should:

1. recognize the rights of citizens to participate in planning decisions;
2. strive to give citizens (including those who lack formal organization or influence) full, clear and accurate information on planning issues and the opportunity to have a meaningful role in the development of plans and programs;
3. strive to expand choice and opportunity for all persons, recognizing a special responsibility to plan for the needs of disadvantaged groups and persons;
4. assist in the clarification of community goals, objectives and policies in planmaking;
5. ensure that reports, records and any other nonconfidential information which is, or will be, available to decision makers is made available to the public in a convenient format and sufficiently in advance of any decision;
6. strive to protect the integrity of the natural environment and the heritage of the built environment;
7. pay special attention to the interrelatedness of decisions and the long-range consequences of present actions.

B. Planning process participants continuously strive to achieve high standards of integrity and proficiency so that public respect for the planning process will be maintained.

Planning Process Participants should:

1. exercise fair, honest and independent judgment in their roles as decision makers and advisors;
2. make public disclosure of all "personal interests" they may have regarding any decision to be made in the planning process in which they serve, or are requested to serve, as advisor or decision maker (see also Advisory Ruling Number 2, "Conflicts of Interest When a Public Planner Has a Stake in Private Development" [in appendix C]);

3. define "personal interest" broadly to include any actual or potential benefits or advantages that they, a spouse, family member or person living in their house might directly or indirectly obtain from a planning decision;

4. abstain completely from direct or indirect participation as an advisor or decision maker in any matter in which they have a personal interest, and leave any chamber in which such a matter is under deliberation, unless their personal interest has been made a matter of public record; their employer, if any, has given approval; and the public official, public agency or court with jurisdiction to rule on ethics matters has expressly authorized their participation;

5. seek no gifts or favors, nor offer any, under circumstances in which it might reasonably be inferred that the gifts or favors were intended or expected to influence a participant's objectivity as an advisor or decision maker in the planning process;

6. not participate as an advisor or decision maker on any plan or project in which they have previously participated as an advocate;

7. serve as advocates only when the client's objectives are legal and consistent with the public interest.

8. not participate as an advocate on any aspect of a plan or program on which they have previously served as advisor or decision maker unless their role as advocate is authorized by applicable law, agency regulation, or ruling of an ethics officer or agency; such participation as an advocate should be allowed only after prior disclosure to, and approval by, their affected client or employer; under no circumstance should such participation commence earlier than one year following termination of the role as advisor or decision maker;

9. not use confidential information acquired in the course of their duties to further a personal interest;

10. not disclose confidential information acquired in the course of their duties except when required by law, to prevent a clear violation of law or to prevent substantial injury to third persons; provided that disclosure in the latter two situations may not be made until after verification of the facts and issues involved and consultation with other planning process participants to obtain their separate opinions;

11. not misrepresent facts or distort information for the purpose of achieving a desired outcome (see also Advisory Ruling Number 4, "Honesty in the Use of Information" [in appendix C];

12. not participate in any matter unless adequately prepared and sufficiently capacitated to render thorough and diligent service;

13. respect the rights of all persons and not improperly discriminate against or harass others based on characteristics which are protected under civil rights laws and regulations (see also Advisory Ruling Number 1, "Sexual Harassment" [in appendix C]).

C. APA members who are practicing planners continuously pursue improvement in their planning competence as well as in the development of peers and aspiring planners. They recognize that enhancement of planning as a profession leads to greater public respect for the planning process and thus serves the public interest.

APA Members who are practicing planners:

1. strive to achieve high standards of professionalism, including certification, integrity, knowledge, and professional development consistent with the AICP Code of Ethics;
2. do not commit a deliberately wrongful act which reflects adversely on planning as a profession or seek business by stating or implying that they are prepared, willing or able to influence decisions by improper means;
3. participate in continuing professional education;
4. contribute time and effort to groups lacking adequate planning resources and to voluntary professional activities;
5. accurately represent their qualifications to practice planning as well as their education and affiliations;
6. accurately represent the qualifications, views, and findings of colleagues;
7. treat fairly and comment responsibly on the professional views of colleagues and members of other professions;
8. share the results of experience and research which contribute to the body of planning knowledge;
9. examine the applicability of planning theories, methods and standards to the facts and analysis of each particular situation and do not accept the applicability of a customary solution without first establishing its appropriateness to the situation;
10. contribute time and information to the development of students, interns, beginning practitioners and other colleagues;
11. strive to increase the opportunities for women and members of recognized minorities to become professional planners;
12. systematically and critically analyze ethical issues in the practice of planning (see also Advisory Ruling Number 3, "Outside Employment or Moonlighting" [in appendix C]).

Appendix B

....

AICP Code of Ethics and Professional Conduct

This Code is a guide to the ethical conduct required of members of the American Institute of Certified Planners. The Code also aims at informing the public of the principles to which professional planners are committed. Systematic discussion of the application of these principles, among planners and with the public, is itself essential behavior to bring the Code into daily use.

The Code's standards of behavior provide a basis for adjudicating any charge that a member has acted unethically. However, the Code also provides more than the minimum threshold of enforceable acceptability. It sets aspirational standards that require conscious striving to attain.

The principles of the Code derive both from the general values of society and from the planning profession's special responsibility to serve the public interest. As the basic values of society are often in competition with each other, so also do the principles of this Code sometimes compete. For example, the need to provide full public information may compete with the need to respect confidences. Plans and programs often result from a balancing among divergent interests. An ethical judgment often also requires a conscientious balancing, based on the facts and context of a particular situation and on the precepts of the entire Code. Formal procedures for filing of complaints, investigation and resolution of alleged violations and the issuance of advisory rulings are part of the Code.

The Planner's Responsibility to the Public

A. A planner's primary obligation is to serve the public interest. While the definition of the public interest is formulated through

continuous debate, a planner owes allegiance to a conscientiously attained concept of the public interest, which requires these special obligations:

1. A planner must have special concern for the long-range consequences of present actions.
2. A planner must pay special attention to the interrelatedness of decisions.
3. A planner must strive to provide full, clear and accurate information on planning issues to citizens and governmental decision makers.
4. A planner must strive to give citizens the opportunity to have a meaningful impact on the development of plans and programs. Participation should be broad enough to include people who lack formal organization or influence.
5. A planner must strive to expand choice and opportunity for all persons, recognizing a special responsibility to plan for the needs of disadvantaged groups and persons, and must urge the alteration of policies, institutions and decisions which oppose such needs.
6. A planner must strive to protect the integrity of the natural environment.
7. A planner must strive for excellence of environmental design and endeavor to conserve the heritage of the built environment.

The Planner's Responsibility to Clients and Employers

B. A planner owes diligent, creative, independent and competent performance of work in pursuit of the client's or employer's interest. Such performance should be consistent with the planner's faithful service to the public interest.

1. A planner must exercise independent professional judgment on behalf of clients and employers.
2. A planner must accept the decisions of a client or employer concerning the objectives and nature of the professional services to be performed unless the course of action to be pursued involves conduct which is illegal or inconsistent with the planner's primary obligation to the public interest.
3. A planner shall not perform work if there is an actual, apparent, or reasonably foreseeable conflict of interest, direct or indirect, or an appearance of impropriety, without full written disclosure concerning work for current or past clients and subsequent written consent by the current client or employer. A planner shall remove himself or herself from a project if there is any direct personal or financial gain, including gains to family members. A planner shall not disclose information gained in the course of public activity for a private benefit unless the information would be offered impartially to any person.

4. A planner who has previously worked for a public planning body should not represent a private client for one year after the planner's last date of employment with the planning body, in connection with any matter before that body that the planner may have influenced before leaving public employment.

5. A planner must not solicit prospective clients or employment through use of false or misleading claims, harassment or duress.

6. A planner must not sell or offer to sell services by stating or implying an ability to influence decisions by improper means.

7. A planner must not use the power of any office to seek or obtain a special advantage that is not in the public interest, nor any special advantage that is not a matter of public knowledge.

8. A planner must not accept or continue to perform work beyond the planner's professional competence or accept work which cannot be performed with the promptness required by the prospective client or employer, or which is required by the circumstances of the assignment.

9. A planner must not reveal information gained in a professional relationship which the client or employer has requested to be held inviolate. Exceptions to this requirement of nondisclosure may be made only when (a) required by process of law, or (b) required to prevent a clear violation of law, or (c) required to prevent a substantial injury to the public. Disclosure pursuant to (b) and (c) must not be made until after the planner has verified the facts and issues involved and, when practicable, has exhausted efforts to obtain reconsiderations of the matter and has sought separate opinions on the issue from other qualified professionals employed by the client or employer.

The Planner's Responsibility to the Profession and to Colleagues

C. A planner should contribute to the development of the profession by improving knowledge and techniques, making work relevant to solutions of community problems, and increasing public understanding of planning activities. A planner should treat fairly the professional views of qualified colleagues and members of other professions.

1. A planner must protect and enhance the integrity of the profession and must be responsible in criticism of the profession.

2. A planner must accurately represent the qualifications, views and findings of colleagues.

3. A planner who reviews the work of other professionals must do so in a fair, considerate, professional and equitable manner.

4. A planner must share the results of experience and research which contribute to the body of planning knowledge.

5. A planner must examine the applicability of planning theories, methods and standards to the facts and analysis of each particular situation and must not accept the applicability of a customary solution without first establishing its appropriateness to the situation.

6. A planner must contribute time and information to the professional development of students, interns, beginning professionals and other colleagues.

7. A planner must strive to increase the opportunities for women and members of recognized minorities to become professional planners.

8. A planner shall not commit an act of sexual harassment.

The Planner's Self-Responsibility

D. A planner should strive for high standards of professional integrity, proficiency and knowledge.

1. A planner must not commit a deliberately wrongful act which reflects adversely on the planner's professional fitness.

2. A planner must respect the rights of others and, in particular, must not improperly discriminate against persons.

3. A planner must strive to continue professional education.

4. A planner must accurately represent professional qualifications, education and affiliations.

5. A planner must systematically and critically analyze ethical issues in the practice of planning.

6. A planner must strive to contribute time and effort to groups lacking in adequate planning resources and to voluntary professional activities.

Appendix C

AICP Advisory Rulings

The AICP Code of Ethics and Professional Conduct provides for advice by the executive director on specific problems and questions concerning ethical behavior by members. The AICP Ethics Committee asked that such advice be codified as advisory rulings specified by the code.

Advisory Ruling No. 1: Sexual Harassment

Sexual harassment is unethical under the AICP Code of Ethics and Professional Conduct. Sexual harassment is also subject to penalty under law. The U.S. Equal Employment Opportunity Commission defines sexual harassment as follows: "Unwelcome sexual advances, requests for sexual favors, and other verbal or physical conduct of a sexual nature constitute sexual harassment when: (1) Submission to such conduct is made either explicitly or implicitly a term or condition of an individual's employment; (2) Submission to or rejection of such conduct by an individual is used as the basis for employment decisions affecting such individual; or (3) Such conduct has the purpose or effect of unreasonably interfering with an individual's work performance or creating an intimidating, hostile, or offensive working environment."

Two of the general principles in the Code are applicable to specific instances of harassment: Principle D.1 of the Code says that a planner must not commit a deliberately wrongful act which reflects adversely on the planner's professional fitness; and Principle D.2 of the Code says that a planner must respect the rights of others and, in particular, must not improperly discriminate against persons. Unlawful sexual harassment as defined by the EEOC is a deliberately wrongful act.

Respecting the rights of others, under the Code, requires a standard of behavior higher than that defined as coercive or intimidating by EEOC. Conduct that may not have illegal effect may nevertheless be harassment. Joking or bantering about sexual subjects, comments suggesting sexual attractiveness, and comments disparaging women or men or their abilities generally may constitute petty harassment. If any such behavior is found offensive, offended persons should so say. The offensive behavior becomes harassment if continued after the offender is notified.

Negligence or omission on the part of an employer who is dismissive of a complaint of sexual harassment and encourages the complainant to be tolerant of the offense is itself a form of harassment. So is a deliberately false accusation of sexual harassment.

Harassment is decidedly distinct from behavior occasioned when a genuinely mutual affection springs up between coworkers. [Adopted May 1988.]

Advisory Ruling No. 2: Conflicts of Interest When a Public Planner Has a Stake in Private Development

The Code of Ethics and Professional Conduct addresses conflicts of interest in Principle B.3: "A planner must not, without the consent of the client or employer, and only after full disclosure, accept or continue to perform work if there is an actual, apparent, or reasonably foreseeable conflict between the interests of the client or employer and the personal or financial interest of the planner or of another past or present client or employer of the planner."

Conflicts of interest are reasonably foreseeable when a planner attempts to serve a real estate development client while also serving a public agency that may have a role in reviewing or approving projects of that client.

Inquiries from planners who contemplate combining activity in real estate business with public planning work have fallen into a pattern, as have the responses:

Real estate is a popular investment, and planners, knowing a lot about it, are attracted to it.

"I have an opportunity to invest in a small development, but the proposal will come before my agency for approval. What do you advise?" Don't do it. There are other investment opportunities.

"What if it's put in my wife's name?" Your wife's financial interest is your financial interest and yours is hers.

"But, when it comes before us, I will exclude myself from the decision, and only other staff members will recommend on the proposal. I won't take part at all." Your colleagues work with you, know that your interests are involved, and can't eliminate the influence of your relationship with them, even if unexpressed.

"My influence really can be a positive one on the developer. I know what would be good for the public and can work for a good design." That's what your agency is there for, and that's why it has the power to review and approve.

"But what if I disclose everything to the director, and he gives his consent?" He shouldn't. I certainly would advise him not to.

"I will work for a broker in a neighboring jurisdiction across the state line. He doesn't have a license in that state." No, but some of his colleagues do. And some of the decisions affecting the broker's business are regional decisions involving both jurisdictions.

A code of ethics should not be a what-can-I-get-away-with code. It should not be tortured into loopholes and technicalities that would allow a person to be formally correct while ethically wrong. The AICP Code looks for "more than the minimum threshold of enforceable acceptability. It sets aspirational standards that require conscious striving to attain."

Developers can benefit from professional planning services and are just as entitled to fully conscientious advocacy of their interests as a public planning agency. A conflict of interest is inherent, however, in any assumption of both roles simultaneously.

There may also be a conflict when the roles overlap. A planner may move from employment by a public agency to employment by a private client. A conflict arises as soon as discussion is initiated for such a move. The public employer must, therefore, be notified promptly that such discussion has taken place whether or not it matures in a change of employment. This is decidedly earlier notice than is normal for a job change and it is notice of a change that may not take place. It is necessary, however, to guard against the substantial conflicts that would occur if a planner is in a position to influence the resolution of certain issues in public employ that will later affect the interests of a new, private employer.

Private planners and consultants who undertake work for a public agency, or change employment from private to public, must disclose any conflicts or potential conflicts to the public agency employer. [Adopted May 1988.]

Advisory Ruling No. 3: Outside Employment or Moonlighting

A planner's responsibility to an employer places significant restraints on accepting work for employers outside of the fulltime commitments to the primary employer. A fulltime member of a planning agency staff owes loyalty, energy and powers of mind primarily to its service.

The Principles in the Code that concern conflict of interest [B.3] and using an office to seek special advantage [B.7] must especially be applied.

A planning staff member must take no employment outside of official duties unless such employment creates no conflict with those duties either in the interests to be served or in competition for time and energy. If the planner decides that there will be no such conflicts, then outside employment must, in addition, receive the explicit approval of the employer.

No outside employment must be undertaken if its performance will reduce the quality or dispatch with which the staff member executes primary responsibilities. The number of hours and the scheduled times devoted to outside employment must not interrupt or interfere with the time that the primary responsibilities demand.

Outside employment must never deal with any matter that may require an action or recommendation by the primary employing agency. Neither must employment be taken with any person or organization that does business with any agency of the primary employer.

Public property must not be used for any private purpose including work that is performed for other employers.

Principle B.8 says that "A planner must not accept . . . work beyond the planner's professional competence or accept work which cannot be performed with the promptness required . . . " Since the schedules, deadlines, priorities and unanticipated time demands of the primary employer must always take precedence, the volume of outside work must necessarily be small and an outside employer must be informed that prompt execution will not necessarily be satisfied.

Both the planner requesting, and the authority giving, approval for outside employment should consider the main justification for approval is a demand for whatever special professional knowledge and experience the planner has that is not otherwise readily available. Service as a teacher or instructor is outside employment that is most justifiable and an unspecialized, general consulting practice least justifiable. [Adopted May 1988.]

Advisory Ruling No. 4: Honesty in the Use of Information

As professional givers of advice—advice that may affect the wellbeing of communities and individuals for many years—we have a special obligation to cherish honesty in the information that supports our advice.

Yet many daily pressures do battle against honesty. We are pressed to be effective advocates for a community, a private client, an elected administration or a cause. A political agenda is often formed before dispassionate study; those who have campaigned for it then look with passion for studies to support. Decision makers may demand a greater degree of certainty, or impose more rigorous criteria for decision, than the capability of analysis or sufficiency of data can satisfy.

The Code of Ethics and Professional Conduct is filled with prescriptions for honesty:

A.3) "provide full, clear and accurate information on planning issues to citizens and governmental decision makers."

B.3) "only after full disclosure (on conflicts of interest)."

B.5) "must not ... through use of false or misleading claims."

B.8) "must not accept ... work beyond the planner's professional competence."

C.1) "must protect and enhance the integrity of the profession."

C.2) "must accurately represent the qualifications, views and findings of colleagues."

D.4) "must accurately represent professional qualifications, education and affiliations."

In some situations, planners must not provide full information. Planners frequently have the role of negotiators whose effectiveness depends on not disclosing final positions that are acceptable. And, as the Code points out, "the need to provide full public information may compete with the need to respect confidences." Information that is disclosed in such circumstances must, however, be honest and accurate.

It is part of professional conduct to communicate our ethical standards to clients, employers and the public. Communicating them early, before they need to be applied to a specific controversy, may erase pressures to abuse them.

There should be no need to explain what the code requires as full, clear and accurate information. Halftruths, deceptions and undocumented assertions don't pass. A halftruth is a whole lie. Don't cook the numbers.

There is also a positive duty on behalf of ethical treatment of information. In reporting the results of studies, planners must follow the scholar's rule of making it possible for others to follow in our footsteps and check our work. Document the sources of data. Report the statistical procedures used, what was done to bring the raw data into the form that is reported. What assumptions were made at different stages in the study?

Public decision makers must often leap beyond the cautions and reservations of a careful study to achieve political solutions. Planners must take pains that our studies and recommendations are not wrongly interpreted, and that a clear distinction is made between factual findings and policy decisions. [Adopted March 1991.]

Comprehensive Bibliography

Books and Technical Reports

Ackoff, Russell. 1968. *A Concept of Corporate Planning*. New York: Wiley-Interscience.

———. 1978. *The Art of Problem Solving: Accompanied by Ackoff's Fables*. New York: John Wiley.

Alexander, Ernest R. 1986. *Approaches to Planning: Introducing Current Planning Theories, Concepts and Issues*. New York: Gordon and Breach Science Publishers.

American Planning Association, ed. 1994. *Planning and Community Equity: A Component of APA's Agenda for America's Communities Program*. Chicago: Planners Press.

Arendt, Randall. 1994. *Rural by Design: Maintaining Small Town Character*. Chicago: Planners Press.

———. 1996. *Conservation Design for Subdivisions: A Practical Guide to Creating Open Space Networks*. Washington, DC: Island Press.

Asher, Herbert. 1995. *Polling and the Public: What Every Citizen Should Know*. Washington, DC: CQ Press.

Babcock, Richard F. 1966. *The Zoning Game: Municipal Practices and Policies*. Madison: University of Wisconsin Press.

Babcock, Richard F., and Charles L. Siemon. 1985. *The Zoning Game Revisited*. Cambridge, MA: Lincoln Institute for Land Policy.

Bartik, Timothy J. 1991. *Who Benefits from State and Regional Economic Development Policies?* Kalamazoo, MI: W.E. Upjohn Institute.

Baskin, Yvonne, ed. 1997. *The Work of Nature: How the Diversity of Life Sustains Us*. Washington, DC: Island Press.

Beatley, Timothy. 1994. *Ethical Land Use: Principles of Policy and Planning*. Baltimore: Johns Hopkins University Press.

Bendavid-Val, Avrom. 1991. *Regional and Local Economic Analysis for Planners*, 4th edition Westport, CT: Praeger Publishers.

Bingham, Richard D., and Robert Mier, eds. 1997. *Dilemmas of Urban Economic Development: Issues in Theory and Practice*. Thousand Oaks, CA: Sage Publications.

Bishop, Kirk R. 1989. *Designing Urban Corridors*. Planning Advisory Service Report No. 418. Chicago: American Planning Association.

Blair, John P. 1995. *Local Economic Development: Analysis and Practice.* Newbury Park, CA: Sage Publications.

Bowyer, Robert A. 1993. *Capital Improvements Programs Linking Budgeting and Planning.* Chicago: American Planning Association. Planning Advisory Service Report No. 442.

Branch, Melville C. 1985. *Comprehensive City Planning: Introduction and Explanation.* Chicago: Planners Press.

———. 1988. *Regional Planning: Introduction and Explanation.* Westport, CT: Praeger Publishers.

Braybrooke, David, and Charles E. Lindblom. 1970. *A Strategy of Decision: Policy Evaluation as a Social Process.* New York: The Free Press.

Brevard, Joseph H. 1985. *Capital Facilities Planning.* Chicago: Planners Press.

Buchsbaum, Peter A., and Larry J. Smith. 1993. *State & Regional Comprehensive Planning: Implementing New Methods for Growth Management.* Chicago: American Bar Association, Section of Urban, State & Local Government Law.

Buck, Susan J. 1996. *Understanding Environmental Administration and Law.* Washington, DC: Island Press.

Byrum, Oliver E. 1992. *Old Problems in New Times: Urban Strategies for the 1990s.* Chicago: Planners Press.

Calthorpe, Peter. 1993. *The Next American Metropolis: Ecology, Community, and the American Dream.* Princeton, NJ: Princeton Architectural Press.

Carlson, Daniel, with Lisa Wormser and Cy Ulberg. 1995. *At Road's End: Transportation and Land Use Choices for Communities.* Washington, DC: Island Press, Surface Transportation Policy Project.

Caves, Roger W. 1994. *Exploring Urban America: An Introductory Reader.* Thousand Oaks, CA: Sage Publications.

Churchman, G. West. 1968. *The Systems Approach.* New York: Delacorte Press.

Dalai-Clayton, Barry. 1996. *Getting to Grips with Green Plans: National-Level Experience in Industrial Countries.* Washington, DC: Earthscan.

Dandekar, Hemalata C., ed. 1988. *The Planner's Use of Information.* Chicago: Planners Press.

Daniels, Rhonda L. 1994. *Fair Housing Compliance Guide,* 2nd edition. Washington, DC: Home Builder Press.

DeGrove, John M. 1992. *Planning & Growth Management in the States.* Cambridge, MA: Lincoln Institute of Land Policy.

Department of Housing and Urban Affairs. 1998. *Building Public-Private Partnerships to Develop Affordable Housing.* Washington, DC: U.S. Government Printing Office.

Diehl, Janet, and Thomas H. Barrett. 1988. *The Conservation Easement Handbook: Managing Land Conservation and Historic Easement Programs.* Washington, DC: Trust for Public Land and Land Trust Exchange.

Downs, Anthony. 1973. *Opening Up the Suburbs: An Urban Strategy for America.* New Haven, CT: Yale University Press.

————. 1994. *New Visions for Metropolitan America.* Washington, DC: Brookings Institution; and Cambridge: Lincoln Institute for Land Policy.

Dramstad, Wence E., James D. Olson, and Richard T.T. 1996. *Landscape Ecology Principles in Landscape Architecture and Land-Use Planning.* Washington, DC: Island Press.

Endicott, Eve, ed. (Lincoln Institute of Land Policy). 1993. *Land Conservation through Public/Private Partnerships.* Washington, DC: Island Press.

Ewing, Reid. 1997. *Transportation & Land Use Innovations: When You Can't Pave Your Way out of Congestion.* Chicago: American Planning Association.

Faludi, Andreas. 1973 (reprinted multiple times). *A Reader in Planning Theory.* Oxford, U.K.: Pergamon Press.

Fisher, Peter S., and Alan H. Peters. 1998. *Industrial Incentives: Competition Among American States and Cities.* Kalamazoo, MI: W.E. Upjohn Institute.

Forester, John. 1989. *Planning in the Face of Power.* Berkeley: University of California Press.

Frank, James E., and Robert M. Rhodes, eds. 1987. *Development Exactions.* Chicago: Planners Press.

Frankena, William K. 1973. *Ethics,* 2nd edition. Englewood Cliffs, NJ: Prentice-Hall.

Freilich, Robert H., and Michael Shultz. 1995. *Model Subdivision Regulations: Planning and Law,* 2nd edition. Chicago: American Planning Association.

Friedmann, John. 1987. *Planning in the Public Domain: From Knowledge to Action.* Princeton, NJ: Princeton University Press.

Gallup, George. 1944. *A Guide to Public Opinion Polls.* Princeton, NJ: Princeton University Press.

Garvin, Alexander, Gayle Berens, and others. 1997. *Urban Parks and Open Space.* Washington, DC: Urban Land Institute and Trust for Public Land.

Gerrard, Michael B. 1998. *Brownfields Law and Practice: The Cleanup and Redevelopment of Contaminated Land.* New York: Matthew Bender.

Haar, Charles M., and Jerold S. Kayden, eds. 1989. *Zoning and the American Dream.* Chicago: Planners Press.

Howe, Elizabeth. 1994. *Acting on Ethics in City Planning.* New Brunswick, NJ: Rutgers University, Center for Urban Policy Research.

Institute of Transportation Engineers. 1997. *Trip Generation Manual,* 7th edition. Washington, DC: Institute of Transportation Engineers.

Insurance Services' Office. 1992. *The Fire Suppression Rating Schedule.* New York: ISO Commercial Risk Services.

Jacobs, Jane. 1961. *The Death and Life of Great American Cities.* New York: Random House.

Jeer, Sanjay. 1997. *Online Resources for Planners.* Planning Advisory Service Report No. 474/475. Chicago: Planners Press.

Johnson, William C. 1997. *Urban Planning and Politics.* Chicago: Planners Press.

Kaiser, Edward J., David R. Godschalk, and F. Stuart Chapin, Jr. 1995. *Urban Land Use Planning,* 4th edition. Urbana: University of Illinois Press.

Kellert, Stephen R. 1996. *The Value of Life: Biological Diversity and Human Society.* Washington, DC: Island Press and Shearwater Books.

Kelly, Eric Damian. 1993. *Managing Community Growth: Policies, Techniques and Impacts.* Westport, CT: Praeger Publishers.

————. 1993. *Planning, Growth and Public Facilities: A Primer for Public Officials.* Planning Advisory Service Report No. 447. Chicago: American Planning Association.

————. 1993. *Selecting and Retaining a Planning Consultant: RFQs, RFPs, Contracts and Project Management.* Planning Advisory Service Report No. 443. Chicago: American Planning Association.

————. ed. 1998. *Zoning and Land Use Controls.* New York: Matthew Bender. Original author is Patrick Rohan.

Kent, T.J., Jr. 1990. *The Urban General Plan.* Chicago: Planners Press. Originally published in 1964.

Kleinberg, Benjamin. 1995. *Urban America in Transformation: Perspectives on Urban Policy and Development.* Thousand Oaks, CA: Sage Publications.

Krumholz, Norman, and Pierre Clavel. 1994. *Reinventing Cities: Equity Planners Tell Their Stories.* Philadelphia, PA: Temple University Press.

Krumholz, Norman, and John Froester. 1990. *Making Equity Planning Work: Leadership in the Public Sector.* Philadelphia, PA: Temple University Press.

Land Trust Alliance. 1990. *Starting a Land Trust: A Guide to Forming a Land Conservation Organization in Your Community.* Alexandria, VA: Land Trust Alliance.

Lerable, Charles A. 1995. *Preparing a Conventional Zoning Ordinance.* Planning Advisory Service Report No. 460. Chicago: American Planning Association.

Listokin, David, and Carole Walker. 1989. *The Subdivision and Site Plan Handbook.* New Brunswick, NJ: Rutgers University, Center for Urban Policy Research.

Lyons, Thomas S., and Roger E. Hamlin. 1991. *Creating an Economic Development Action Plan.* Westport, CT: Praeger Publishers.

Makower, Joel, ed. 1990. *The Map Catalog,* 2nd edition. New York: Vintage Books.

Mallach, Alan. 1984. *Inclusionary Housing Programs: Policies and Practices.* New Brunswick, NJ: Rutgers University, Center for Urban Policy Research.

Mandelker, Daniel R. 1971. *The Zoning Dilemma: a Legal Strategy for Urban Change.* New York: Bobbs-Merrill.

McBee, Susanna, with Ralph J. Basile, Robert T. Dunphy, John M. Keeling, Ben C. Lin, David C. Petersen, Patrick L. Phillips, and Richard D. Wagner. 1992. *Downtown Development Handbook,* 2nd edition. Washington, DC: Urban Land Institute.

McClendon, Bruce W., and Ray Quay. 1988. *Mastering Change: Winning Strategies for Effective City Planning.* Chicago: Planners Press.

McHarg, Ian. 1992. *Design with Nature, 25th Anniversary Edition.* New York: John Wiley.

Original publication 1969, Garden City, NY: Natural History Press for the American Museum of Natural History.

McLean, Mary L., and Kenneth P. Voytek, with others. 1992. *Understanding Your Economy: Using Analysis to Guide Local Strategic Planning,* 2nd edition. Chicago: Planners Press.

Mertes, James D., and James R. Hall. 1996. *Park, Recreation, Open Space and Greenway Guidelines.* Alexandria, VA: National Recreation and Park Association and American Academy for Park and Recreation Administration.

Miles, Mike E., Emil E. Malizi, Marc A. Weiss, Gayle L. Berens, and Ginger Travis. 1991. *Real Estate Development: Principles and Process.* Washington, DC: Urban Land Institute.

Miller, Ross. 1996. *Here's the Deal: The Buying and Selling of a Great American City.* New York: Alfred A. Knopf.

Miller, Thomas I., and Michelle A. Miller. 1991. *Citizen Surveys: How to Do Them, How to Use Them, What They Mean.* Washington, DC: International City Management Association.

Mills, Edwin S. 1986. *Handbook of Regional and Urban Economics: Vol. 2.* New York: Elsevier Science Publishing.

Mills, Edwin S., and John F. McDonald, eds. 1992. *Sources of Metropolitan Growth.* New Brunswick, NJ: Rutgers University, Center for Urban Policy Research.

Moore, C. Nicholas. 1995. *Participation Tools for Better Land-Use Planning.* Washington, DC: Center for Livable Communities.

Morris, Marya. 1996. *1995 Planners' Salaries and Employment Trends.* Planning Advisory Service Report No. 464. Chicago: American Planning Association.

———. 1997. *Subdivision Design in Flood Hazard Areas.* Planning Advisory Service Report No. 473. Chicago: American Planning Association.

Myers, Dowell. 1992. *Analysis with Local Census Data.* Boston: Academic Press.

Nelessen, Anton C. 1994. *Visions for a New American Dream.* Chicago: Planners Press.

Nelson, Arthur C., and James B. Duncan. 1995. *Growth Management: Principles and Practices.* Chicago: American Planning Association.

Newman, Oscar E. 1996. *Creating Defensible Space.* Washington, DC: U.S. Department of Housing and Urban Development.

Patterson, William T. 1979. *Land Use Planning Techniques of Implementation.* Dallas, TX: Van Nostrand Reinhold.

Petersen, John E., and Dennis R. Strachota, eds. 1991. *Local Government Finance: Concepts and Practices.* Chicago: Government Finance Officers Association.

Porter, Douglas R. 1997. *Managing Growth in America's Communities.* Washington, DC: Island Press.

Porter, Douglas R., Patrick L. Phillips, and Terry J. Lassar. 1988. *Flexible Zoning and How it Works.* Washington, DC: Urban Land Institute.

Porter, Douglas R., and David A. Salvesen, eds. 1995. *Collaborative Planning for Wetlands and Wildlife: Issues and Examples.* Washington, DC: Island Press.

Reid, David. 1995. *Sustainable Development: An Introductory Guide.* London: Earthscan.

Reps, John. 1980. *Town Planning in Frontier America.* Columbia: University of Missouri Press. Originally published by Princeton University Press, 1965 and 1969.

Robinson, Susan G., ed. 1990. *Financing Growth: Who Benefits? Who Pays? And How Much?* Chicago: Government Finance Officers Association.

Robinson, Susan G., John E. Petersen, Thomas Muller, and Isaac F. Megbolugbe. 1990. *Building Together: Investing in Community Infrastructure.* Washington, DC: National Association of Counties and National Association of Home Builders.

Rodgers, Joseph Lee, Jr. 1977. *Citizen Committees: A Guide to Their Use in Local Government.* Cambridge, MA: Ballinger Publishing.

Roome, Nigel J., ed. 1998. *Sustainability Strategies for Industry.* Washington, DC: Island Press.

Rothblatt, Donald N., and Andrew Sancton, eds. 1993. *Metropolitan Governance Perspectives: American/Canadian Intergovernmental Perspectives.* Berkeley: University of California Press.

Rusk, David. 1993. *Cities without Suburbs.* Baltimore: Woodrow Wilson Center/Johns Hopkins University Press.

Scott, Mel. 1971. *American City Planning.* Los Angeles: University of California Press.

Smith, Herbert H. 1979. *The Citizen's Guide to Planning.* Chicago: Planners Press.

So, Frank S., and Judith Getzels, eds. 1988. *The Practice of Local Government Planning,* 2nd edition. Washington, DC: International City Management Association.

Solnit, Albert. 1987. *The Job of the Planning Commissioner,* 3rd edition. Chicago: Planners Press.

Stein, Jay M. 1995. *Classic Readings in Urban Planning.* New York: McGraw-Hill.

Strong, Ann L. 1973. *Private Property and the Public Interest: The Brandywine Experience.* Baltimore: Johns Hopkins University Press.

Thompson, George F., and Frederick R. Steiner, eds. 1997. *Ecological Design and Planning.* New York: John Wiley.

Transportation Research Board. 1985. *Highway Capacity Manual.* Washington, DC: Transportation Research Board, National Research Council.

Urban Land Institute. 1975. *Residential Storm Water Management: Objectives, Principles & Design Considerations.* Washington, DC: Urban Land Institute, American Society of Civil Engineers, and National Association of Home Builders.

van Houten, Therese, and Harry P. Hatry. 1987. *How to Conduct a Citizen Survey.* Planning Advisory Service Report No. 404. Chicago: American Planning Association.

Wachs, Martin, ed. 1985. *Ethics in Planning.* New Brunswick, NJ: Rutgers University, Center for Urban Policy Research.

Wackernagel, Mark, and William Rees. 1996. *Our Ecological Footprint.* New York: New Society Publishers.

Walsh, Mary L. 1997. *Building City Involvement.* Washington, DC: International City Management Association.

Weiss, Marc A. 1987. *The Rise of the Community Builders: The American Real Estate Industry and American Land Planning.* New York: Columbia University Press.

Whyte, William H. 1959. *Securing Open Space for Urban America: Conservation Easements.* Technical Bulletin 36. Washington, DC: Urban Land Institute.

Articles

Camon, Naomi. 1997. "Neighborhood Regeneration: The State of the Art." *Journal of Planning Education and Research* 17, no. 2: 131–144.

Chen, Donald D.T. 1998. "If You Build It, They Will Come . . . " *Progress* 8, no. 1 (March).

Culhane, Dennis P., Chang-Moo Lee, and Susan M. Wachter. 1996. "Where the Homeless Come From: A Study of the Prior Address Distribution of Families Admitted to Public Shelters in New York City and Philadelphia." *Housing Policy Debate* 7, issue 2.

Davidoff, Paul. 1965. "Advocacy and Pluralism in Planning." *Journal of the American Institute of Planners* 31, no. 6:331–337.

Kelly, Eric Damian. 1986. "Planning vs. Democracy." *Land Use Law & Zoning Digest* 38, no. 7 (July).

———. 1996. "Fair Housing, Good Housing or Expensive Housing? Are Building Codes Part of the Problem or Part of the Solution?" *John Marshall Law Review* 29, no. 2, 349–368.

Keyes, Langley C., Alex Schwartz, Avis C. Vidal, and Rachel G. Bratt. 1996. "Networks and Nonprofits: Opportunities and Challenges in an Era of Federal Devolution." *Housing Policy Debate* 7, issue 2.

Chapters in Books

Gil, Efraim, and Enid Lucchesi. 1988. "Citizen participation in planning," in *The Practice of Local Government Planning,* 2nd edition, Frank S. So and Judith Getzels, eds.

Hammack, David C. 1988. "Comprehensive Planning before the Comprehensive Plan: A New Look at the Nineteenth Century American City," in *Two Centuries of American Planning,* Daniel Schaffer, ed. Baltimore: Johns Hopkins University Press.

Hancock, John. 1988. "The New Deal and American Planning: 1930s," in *Two Centuries of American Planning,* Daniel Schaffer, ed. Baltimore: Johns Hopkins University Press.

Hollander, Elizabeth L., Leslie S. Pollock, Jeffry D. Reckinger, and Frank Beal. 1988. "General Development Plans," in *The Practice of Local Government Planning,* 2nd edition, Frank S. So and Judith Getzels, eds. Baltimore: Johns Hopkins University Press.

Kelly, Eric Damian. 1988. "Zoning," in *The Practice of Local Government Planning,* 2nd edition, Frank S. So and Judith Getzels, eds., Washington, DC: International City Management Association.

Lieder, Constance. 1988. "Planning for Housing," in *The Practice of Local Government Planning,* 2nd edition, Frank S. So and Judith Getzels, eds. Washington, DC: International City Management Association.

McGuire, Chester C. 1979. "Maintenance and Renewal of Central Cities," in *The Practice of Local Government Planning*, Frank S. So, Isreal Stollman, Frank Beal, and David S. Arnold, eds. Washington, DC: International City Management Association.

Rosenbloom, Sandra. 1988. "Transportation Planning," in *The Practice of Local Government Planning*, 2nd edition, Frank S. So and Judith Getzels, eds. Washington, DC: International City Management Association.

Sedway, Paul H. 1988. "District Planning." in *The Practice of Local Government Planning*, 2nd edition, Frank S. So and Judith Getzels, eds. Washington, DC: International City Management Association.

Wachs, Martin. 1985. "Ethical Dilemmas in Forecasting for Public Policy," in *Ethics in Planning*, Martin Wachs, ed. New Brunswick, NJ: Rutgers University, Center for Urban Policy Research.

Local Plans

Ames (Iowa), City of. 1996. "Land Use Policy Plan." Prepared by RM Plan Group, Nashville.

Lake County (Waukegan, Illinois). 1994. "Framework Plan." Prepared by Lake County Department of Planning, Zoning & Environmental Quality.

Muncie-Delaware County (Indiana). 1998 (working draft). "Muncie-Delaware County Comprehensive Plan." Prepared by HNTB Corp., Indianapolis and Kansas City; in association with Duncan Associates, Austin and Chicago; and Hammer, Siler George Associates, Silver Spring and Denver.

Norman (Oklahoma), City of. 1996. "Development Capacity Technical Memorandum." Prepared by the Burnham Group, Cincinnati, Little Rock, Birmingham.

———. 1996. "Land Demand Technical Memorandum." Prepared by the Burnham Group, Cincinnati, Little Rock, Birmingham.

———. 1996. "Land Use Plan Implementation Techniques Technical Memorandum." Prepared by the Burnham Group, Cincinnati, Little Rock, Birmingham.

———. 1997. "Norman 2020 Land Use and Transportation Plan." Prepared by the Burnham Group, Cincinnati, Little Rock, Birmingham.

Orange County (Florida). 1998 (poster version). "Development Framework: A Guide to Growth Management." Prepared by Orange County Planning Department.

Stillwater, Oklahoma. 1998 (working draft). "Comprehensive Community Development Plan." Prepared by RM Plan Group, Nashville.

———. 1998. "Comprehensive Community Development Plan: Technical Memoranda 1 through 7. Prepared by RM Plan Group, Nashville.

Wichita-Sedgwick County (Kansas). 1993. "Preparing for Change: The Wichita-Sedgwick County Comprehensive Plan." Prepared by Metropolitan Area Planning Department.

———. 1996. "Parks and Pathways: Park and Open Space Master Plan." Prepared by Metropolitan Area Planning Department and Wichita Park and Recreation Department.

Index